The Elusive Mr. Wesley

Richard P. Heitzenrater

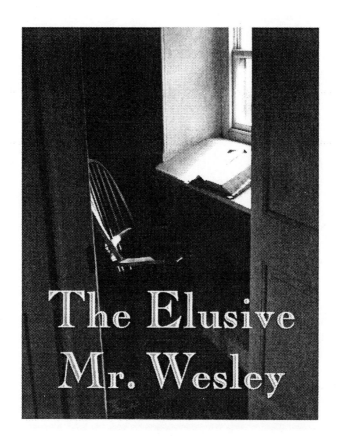

The Elusive Mr. Wesley

Second Edition

Abingdon Press
Nashville

THE ELUSIVE MR. WESLEY

Second Revised Edition © 2003 by Richard P. Heitzenrater
Revised Edition © 1993 by Richard P. Heitzenrater
Original Volumes 1 and 2 © 1984 by Abingdon Press assigned to Richard P. Heitzenrater

This book is printed on recycled, acid-free, elmental-chlorine–free paper.

Library of Congress Cataloging-in-Publication Data

Heitzenrater, Richard P., 1939-
  The elusive Mr. Wesley / Richard P. Heitzenrater.—2nd rev. ed.
    p. cm.
Includes bibliographical references and index.
  ISBN 0-687-07461-4 (pbk.)
  1. Wesley, John, 1703-1791. 2. Methodist
  Church—England—Clergy—Biography. I. Title.

BX8495.W5H43 2003
287'.092—dc21

                            2003004482

Figure 3 appears courtesy of Frank Baker.

Figure 4 is reproduced by courtesy of the Directors and Librarian of the John Rylands University of Manchester and the Archives and History Committee of the Methodist Church.

Figure 6 appears by courtesy of the National Portrait Gallery, London.

Figure 8 appears courtesy of the Divinity School Library, Duke University.

Figures 11 and 13 appear by permission of Duke University Rare Book, Manuscript, and Special Collections Library.

Figure 15 appears courtesy of John Wesley's House and The Museum of Methodism, London.

The Works of John Wesley. vol. 1, 1984, Abingdon Press.

The Works of John Wesley. vol. 7, 1983, Abingdon Press.

The Works of John Wesley. vol. 9, 1989, Abingdon Press.

The Works of John Wesley. vol. 18, 1988, Abingdon Press.

The Works of John Wesley. vol. 19, 1990, Abingdon Press.

The Works of John Wesley. vol. 20, 1991, Abingdon Press.

The Works of John Wesley. vol. 25, 1980, Clarendon Press.

The Works of John Wesley. vol. 26, 1982, Clarendon Press.

03 04 05 06 07 08 09 10 11 12 – 10 9 8 7 6 5 4 3 2

MANUFACTURED IN THE UNITED STATES OF AMERICA

To my family

for their encouragement

and support of my continuing pursuit

of the elusive Mr. Wesley

Contents

LIST OF ILLUSTRATIONS 13

PREFACE 15

NOTE ON THE SECOND EDITION 19

INTRODUCTION: THE ELUSIVE MR. WESLEY 21

The Quest of the "Real" John Wesley 22
Considerations in the Quest for Historical Accuracy 26
Twice-Told Tales: Two Centuries of Wesley Studies 36

Part I—Wesley, His Own Biographer

CHAPTER 1. A SON OF EPWORTH 41

A Brand Plucked Out of the Burning 42
A Child of Destiny 44
A Collector of Ghostlore 46

CHAPTER 2. THE OXFORD DON 52

The Careful Diarist 53

"Primitive Christianity" 57
The Compulsive Pietist 59

CHAPTER 3. THE OXFORD METHODIST 63

Apologist for the Oxford Methodists 63
The Settled and Unsettled Tutor 71

CHAPTER 4. THE COLONIAL MISSIONARY 74

The Hard-pressed Pastor 75
The Rejected Suitor 77
The Wrongfully Accused Defendant 82
The Ostracized Reporter 87

CHAPTER 5. THEOLOGICAL AND SPIRITUAL PILGRIM 90

One Tossed About 91
The Assured Conqueror 94
The Humbled Doubter 99

CHAPTER 6. THE EXTRA-PAROCHIAL PREACHER 101

The Field Preacher 102
The Itinerant Preacher 109

CHAPTER 7. APOLOGIST AND PROPAGANDIST 112

Purposeful Journalist 112
Public Defendant 115

CHAPTER 8. THE PERSECUTED PREACHER 120

Providentially Protected Person 120
Unjustly Treated Citizen 125

CHAPTER 9. THE MEDICAL PRACTITIONER 129

Dispenser of Medicine 130
Prescriber of Remedies 131

CHAPTER 10. PRACTICAL THEOLOGIAN 140

The Proclaimer of Plain Truth 140
The Aspiring Perfect Christian 145
The Prison Evangelist 149

CHAPTER 11. PRACTICING POET 153

Collector of Poetry 154
Writer of Poetry 157
Translator of Poetry 161
Editor of Poetry 163

CHAPTER 12. THE WOULD-BE HUSBAND 166

The Jilted Fiancé 166
The New Husband 176
The Rejected Husband 178

CHAPTER 13. THE ANXIOUS EARTHEN VESSEL 186

The Modest Epitaph Writer 186
An Honest Heathen 188

CHAPTER 14. THE CATHOLIC AND ANTI-CATHOLIC
SPIRIT 191

The Irenic Theologian 192
Protestant Patriot 198

CHAPTER 15. THE CAREFUL PLANNER 202

The Center of Union 202
The Perpetual Image 204
The Philanthropic Testator 206

Part II—Wesley as Seen By His Contemporaries

CHAPTER 16. THE FAMILY PERSPECTIVE 213

Son to Susanna 213

Son to Samuel 219
Brother John 222

CHAPTER 17. THE METHODIST FELLOW 225

Attack on the Sons of Sorrow 226
The Oxford Methodists Defended 229

CHAPTER 18. THE UNASSUMING SPIRITUAL TUTOR:
JOHN GAMBOLD'S DESCRIPTION 233

CHAPTER 19. WESLEY IN GEORGIA 242

The Christian Exemplar 242
The Partisan Priest 246
The Bail-Jumping Deserter 251
The Improper Pastor 255

CHAPTER 20. BEFORE AND AFTER ALDERSGATE 258

A Brother's Faith 258
A Wild Enthusiast 261
An Open Enemy of Christ 264

CHAPTER 21. THE RABBLE-ROUSER RECONSIDERED 266

A Soldier of Christ 266
The Author of Confusion 269
That Good Man 272

CHAPTER 22. WESLEY AS PREACHER 276

A Rigid Zealot 278
The Personification of Piety 280

CHAPTER 23. RADICAL PROTESTANT OR PERNICIOUS
PAPIST? 282

A Moravian Sympathizer 284

A Jesuit in Disguise 288

CHAPTER 24. THE FANATIC SAINT DISPLAYED:
PROFANE POLEMICAL POETRY 294

CHAPTER 25. THE OLD FOX UNMASKED 304

The Plagiarist Politician 304
The Arminian Fox 310
The Patriotic Politician Vindicated 313

CHAPTER 26. THE PRETENDING PHYSICIAN:
WILLIAM HAWES'S CRITIQUE 316

CHAPTER 27. THE PITIABLE DESPOT: FORGED
LETTER ON METHODIST DIVISIONS 326

CHAPTER 28. THE DYING PATRIARCH 329

The Revered Father in God 329
A Most Extraordinary Character 335
The Venerable John Wesley 341

Part III—Wesley in Restropect

CHAPTER 29. THAT VENERABLE MAN OF GOD:
THE WESLEY OF THE EULOGIES 345

CHAPTER 30. IMAGES OF POWER: THE
CONTROVERSIAL EARLY BIOGRAPHIES 350

CHAPTER 31. TESTING THE MEMORY: EARLY
NINETEENTH-CENTURY BIOGRAPHIES 356

CHAPTER 32. POLISHING THE IMAGE: TOWARD
A "STANDARD" VIEW OF WESLEY 362

CHAPTER 33. REFINING THE SOURCES: TOWARD
THE "STANDARD" WORKS OF WESLEY 370

CHAPTER 34. WESLEY AND THE SPECIALISTS:
BROADENING THE TRADITIONAL IMAGE 376

CHAPTER 35. SEEING WESLEY WHOLE: TOWARD
A NEW SYNTHESIS 387

SELECTED BIBLIOGRAPHY OF BIBLIOGRAPHIES 395

INDEX 397

List of Illustrations

1. John Wesley, engraved by Bodlidge in *The Arminian Magazine,* 1778

2. John Wesley, in *The Arminian Magazine,* 1779

3. John Wesley, engraved by Vertue, 1742, with vignette of Epworth rectory fire

4. Page from Wesley's Oxford Diary, March 17, 1734

5. John Wesley, painted by Hone, engraved by Bland, in *Explanatory Notes,* 1755

6. John Wesley, painted by Hamilton in National Portrait Gallery, London

7. John Wesley, in *The Arminian Magazine,* 1783

8. Wesley's Death Mask, replica at Duke University, 1791

9. John Wesley, engraved by Wm. Bromley in *The European Magazine,* 1791

10. John Wesley, engraved by W. Greatback in Isaac Taylor's *Wesley and Methodism,* 1851

11. Wesley as Reynard the Fox frontispiece to *Fanatical Conversion,* 1779

12. John Wesley, bust by Enoch Wood, 1781 or 1784

13. The Apotheosis of John Wesley "Carried by Angels into Abraham's Bosom," 1791

14. John Wesley, engraved by T. A. Dean, painted by John Jackson, 1827

15. John Wesley painted by Frank O. Salisbury, 1927

Preface

Every generation discovers the past for itself. The process can be as simple as repeating long-held traditions or as complicated as tracing centuries-old genealogies. The historian's task is to help disentangle fact from fantasy in our various rehearsals of past events. In a sense, this book is intended to encourage the reader to participate in the historian's craft by exhibiting some of the problems confronted, the methods used, the conclusions reached, and the loose ends left dangling when one tries to uncover the past "as it really happened."

The focus of our study is John Wesley, the "founder" of Methodism. Our quest is a part of the current interest in discovering "roots"—in this case, the roots of a particular religious heritage. My introduction to this adventure came some fifteen years ago when I accepted the challenge of decoding Wesley's previously unpublished personal diaries. Struggling through the ciphers, shorthands, and symbols of these fascinating private documents, I became increasingly aware that the emerging image of the young man Wesley was quite different in many ways from the typical portrayals in most biographies of the man. To add to the confusion, Wesley's own later recollections at times differed in significant ways from some of these early daily records of his activities.

As my efforts to reconstruct an accurate portrait of the young Wesley broadened into a study of the whole of his life and thought, I discovered further problems. The confusion evident among contemporary observers of Wesley was only compounded by the variety of sometimes conflicting images given to the public over the subsequent two centuries by artists, biographers, historians, and iconographers. Over three hundred studies of Wesley have been written, many of them more confusing than helpful in the process of trying to recapture a historically accurate basis upon which to build a fully adequate picture of the man. The consternation caused by such a lack of consensus has given rise to my fascination with what might be called "the search for the real John Wesley."

The biographer's endeavor is similar in many ways to the task of the portrait painter; both try to help us see beyond the obvious to the essential. But every such interpretive attempt, to be adequately edifying, should be based on full and accurate information. During the last two decades, an increasing number of critical studies of Wesley have provided helpful information in this regard, though not always noticed by the biographers. Future studies will also benefit from the completion of the new critical edition of Wesley's works now in progress. In the meantime, however, we can try to work our way toward a better understanding of Wesley by recognizing that our currently popular portraits of Wesley are shaped in large part by nineteenth- and early twentieth-century stereotypes that were constructed with a specific apologetic purpose in mind. We need also to keep in mind that some parts of the well-rehearsed Wesley story are based on little or no hard evidence and have become part of the time-honored tradition simply through repetition—the succession of twice-told tales soon taking on the appearance of historical fact.

This work attempts to help the reader discover Wesley anew by displaying a unique combination of material, some of it quite familiar, some readily accessible but generally unfamiliar and waiting rediscovery, and some only recently discovered and never before published. Samuel Johnson once remarked, in *The Idler No. 84,* that although autobiographical reflection is subject to the temptation of disguising the truth, one might expect at least as much impartiality from the writer of his own life as from a biographer. Such a note of expectation has an overtone of caution: both the autobiographical writer and the biographer are faced with difficult tasks of assessment.

The first half of such a cautionary proposition is tested in the first portion of our present study. The Introduction lays out the dimensions of the task of discovering the "real" John Wesley. Part I then illustrates the possibilities and pitfalls of such an endeavor both by displaying selections of Wesley's own writings that reflect his developing self-image and by showing how some aspects of the Wesley "legend" began to develop.

Part II focuses on accounts written by his contemporaries. These selections contribute additional details to the picture of Wesley and provide different points of view from which to perceive his image. Besides illustrating the wide variety of reactions to Wesley by friend and foe, these writings to some degree provide a helpful corrective to Wesley's own self-portrait.

Part III traces the history of Wesley studies, showing how he has fared in the eyes of historians and biographers through successive generations of interpretation. This summary of Wesleyan historiography provides a critical guide through the maze of material that has been written about Wesley during the last two centuries.

Having thus surveyed many of the ways in which Wesley saw himself, looked at the variety of descriptions of him by his contemporaries, and examined the manner in which he has been treated by a host of writers down through the years, the reader will have begun to grasp the major events and issues of Wesley's life and thought, as well as to have discovered that the possibility of recapturing the "real" John Wesley is an elusive ideal that has never been (and perhaps never can be) totally comprehended by any single book, at any given time, in any one place. Though many good books on Wesley have been written, this study will, I hope, demonstrate why it is difficult to suggest any one book that will satisfactorily "explain" the whole Wesley, and will also act as a critical guide through the maze of published material available on Wesley. At the same time, I hope that this effort will also introduce many people to the excitement of discovering the elusive Mr. Wesley for themselves.

I wish to thank the many people who have aided and encouraged me in this work, especially Professor Albert C. Outler, whose expertise provided many suggestions that helped shape and refine the manuscript; Professor Frank Baker, whose mastery of detail has continued to help me discover John Wesley; Professor John Walsh, whose insight and advice helped me shape the project; my assistant Wanda Willard Smith, whose proficiency in the topic made the deadlines manageable; and my wife, Karen, whose editorial skills preserved me from many infelicities of style.

R. P. H.

Southern Methodist University

1983

Note on the Second Edition

This edition, besides being in one volume, as the work was originally intended by the author, has been revised to extend the history of Wesley scholarship in Part III into the new century. The Wesley texts in this revision are based upon the Bicentennial Edition of his *Works* when possible (as noted). The choice of selections remains the same as in the original edition of this work, which many people found to be useful.

R. P. H.

Duke University

September 2002

The Elusive Mr. Wesley

His history, if well written," concludes the writer of Wesley's lengthy obituary in the *Gentleman's Magazine,* "will certainly be important, for in every respect, as the founder of the most numerous sect in the kingdom, as a man, and as a writer, he must be considered as one of the most extraordinary characters this or any age ever produced." This piece of effusive eloquence is perhaps only slightly exaggerated. John Wesley has come to be known as one of the major figures of the eighteenth century, his impact being felt both in Great Britain and in America. He played a major role as one of the leaders of the evangelical revival that swept much of the Protestant world in his day. His literary production was prolific, and writings such as his *Journal* are still seen as models of eighteenth-century style.

But Wesley's importance goes beyond the realm of literature and religion. Concerned with such issues as education, prison conditions, and poverty, he played an important role in the development of early social reforms in an increasingly industrialized society. Trained at Christ Church, Oxford, he was intrigued by the current trends of science and medicine, and he published many popular treatises on diverse subjects ranging from experiments in electricity to home remedies for the gout. He produced a flood of pamphlets on a wide assortment of topics ranging from linguistics to music. As a recognized leader among the people, he entered into the political swirl surrounding the revolutionary movements of his day, offering his services to the king to raise a regiment of troops to fight the French, and giving his advice to the colonial secretary on the explosive matter of the American revolt.

Wesley sensed the spirit of the English people perhaps as well as any person in his day. The true nature of his own mind and spirit, however, appears somewhat more elusive. His own breast felt the heartbeat of a staunchly loyal Tory; yet he could feel well the pulse of a nation that stirred with the rumblings of revolution. He was able to remain an Anglican clergyman to his dying breath and at the same time harness the energies of revival into a new form that was to become a major force in Protestant Christianity as Methodism.

From the very beginning of his public activities, Wesley was a controversial figure. Persons of differing religious and political persuasions did not hesitate to attack him in print as well as in person. His fledgling movement was already being decried in the newspapers in 1732, and his character was publicly slandered and attacked in court as early as 1737. Through all the controversies he was not without supporters; every spirited attack elicited a zealous defense that tended to bolster the developing Wesley legend. At his death, friend and foe alike rushed to produce biographical portraits of the Wesley they knew. From the beginning, the descriptions of Wesley presented to the public have caused no small amount of confusion, as well as controversy, as successive generations have tried to sift through the various accounts of this complex and rather elusive man, looking for the "real" John Wesley.

The Quest of the "Real" John Wesley

The problems confronting persons looking for the "real" John Wesley are typified in the attempt to find an "accurate" pictorial representation of the man. Dismissing for the moment the problems faced by nineteenth- and twentieth-century artists who tried to depict Wesley long after his death, we would expect to find some standard, recognizable visage among the eighteenth-century portraits of Wesley. The wide variety of images that confront us, even among portraits done by the best artists of the day (many of whom were looking directly at the man as they painted), is confusing and serves to symbolize and illustrate the larger problem of trying to catch the essence of his life and thought. There is no consensus in either case, visual or interpretive, and the variety of representations can be disconcerting.

In the search for the elusive John Wesley, the question of physical appearance is more than just the passing fancy of an antiquarian historian. It is, among other things, one indication of the limits of factual information that might be retrieved from a given period. For example, we might ask the simple question, What color was Wesley's hair when he was a young man? One eyewitness, who lived under the same roof with him in Georgia in 1737, referred to his "Adonis locks of *auburn* hair, which he took infinite pains to have in the most exact order." Just a few years later (1744) another eyewitness, describing Wesley's appearance in the pulpit of St. Mary's, Oxford, mentioned in particular his "*black* hair quite smooth, parted very exactly." The contradiction of these two literary descriptions is further confused by a third impression, portrayed on canvas by John William at about the same time (1741). The painting does exhibit the neatness of Wesley's hair, as mentioned by the other observers, but shows the color to be black in general, with a brownish tint where the light reflects off the curls and waves. On the basis of the contemporary sources of evidence, we are left with no definitive answer to the question.

The problem of hair color is difficult in one sense because few descriptions (literary or graphic) were drawn up of Wesley as a young man. The portraits proliferate as he grew older and more famous. The problem of hair color disappears, since his hair turned gray and then white. But another, even more surprising problem arises. Among the dozens of paintings, drawings, busts, and other representations, there is little or no consensus as to Wesley's facial features. The most one can say is that he apparently had a rather prominent, pointed nose. This, combined with the usual portrayal of his hair as long with curls on the end, and the almost universal presence of Geneva bands around his neck, gives a note of uniformity and recognition to a vast array of portraits that otherwise do not much resemble one another. In some cases, on these grounds alone, portraits have occasionally been identified as "possibly" representing John Wesley, even though the general impression would otherwise cause the viewer to be skeptical. The problem was somewhat upsetting to some nineteenth-century British Methodists who, in the face of such confusing evidence, commissioned an artist to create a "standard" portrait of Wesley in the 1820s, a generation after his death. The resulting "synthetic" portrait (see fig. 14) was conceded by most to be notably unconvincing as a replica of Wesley's visage and was unable to garner lasting support as a standard portrait.

Our inability to specify with any assurance the color of Wesley's hair or the exact nature of his visage is, perhaps, a minor point. Nevertheless, it does suggest the sense of caution with which we should approach our attempt to discover the "facts" on other, perhaps more significant, questions even when we are using firsthand, eyewitness accounts (about or even by, Wesley). A simple illustration can be seen in the question of Wesley's name (see page 41). Contemporary evidence, usually very illuminating and valuable, can also at times be skimpy, inaccurate, misleading, contradictory, and confusing. Although often the best source of information, primary source material must be used critically and carefully.

In trying to sort through the contemporary accounts of Wesley's activities, character, and significance, one must do more than merely differentiate those views that attack him from those that defend him. In some cases, the most virulent attack or vicious satire may, in fact, be built upon some grain of truth that might be overlooked in a more favorable description of the man. Most biographers have either disregarded Wesley's detractors as a source of information, or seen their attacks as simply spurious fabrications, and have been willing to rely almost entirely on the defenders of Wesley for their view of the situation. But what judge would ever assume that the defense, no matter how pious, was by nature or necessity the only reliable source of believable or factual information?

To make the matter more complicated, both Wesley's enemies and friends were attracted to him not only by who or what he *actually* was (if that could in fact ever be known for sure), but by what they (and he) *thought* he was. Observations of contemporaries can, of course, be analyzed on the basis of their known prejudices and purposes. But these same guidelines must also be applied to Wesley's own descriptions of himself; his autobiographical comments need always to be tested against other available evidence.

In some cases, Wesley makes statements that either can be easily misinterpreted or simply exhibit a bad memory. For instance, he mentions in his *Journal* that in 1771 he visited South Leigh, adding that "here it was that I preached my first sermon, six and forty years ago." Based on this reference, biographers have assumed that Wesley must have preached there the first Sunday after his ordination in 1725. A brass plaque on the pulpit of that church still proclaims this to be the case. However, Wesley's own handwritten copy of his first sermon (with his note on the cover, "The first sermon I ever wrote") tells another story. It lists on the back the places and occasions of preaching, with South Leigh listed as the *ninth* occasion, in 1727. This does in a sense confirm that Wesley "preached his first sermon" in South Leigh, but it was not his first occasion for preaching, nor his first preaching of that first sermon!

Biographers have often repeated many such inaccuracies and half-truths and have magnified many of the legends that sprang up in Wesley's own day; then they have often recast all these to fit their own purposes. Many an account of Wesley is but an editorial gloss on the man, an attempt on the part of an author to prove some point about either Wesley's thought or, more likely and less obviously, the author's own. By careful selection and editing, an author can make Wesley appear in a number of guises. Our task is to recognize as many of the guises as possible, then to ferret out the disguises in which he has been placed, and thereby to discover as accurately as possible the full range of thought and activity that characterize this remarkable man.

One of our primary tasks, then, in trying to discover the elusive John Wesley is to recognize that all the information that comes to us must be examined critically, no matter whether it was written by Wesley himself, recounted by an eyewitness (friendly or otherwise), or compiled years after the events. No single type of source, in and of itself, is necessarily a sufficient resource for our quest. Firsthand accounts are in many ways, of course, the best, but are not without problems of bias and shortsightedness in that they are in some cases too close to the events they describe. Secondary accounts, while suffering from the problems of historical distance, might at the same time benefit from the more inclusive objectivity that such hindsight makes possible. Taken as a whole, these materials provide a vast amount of information that must be sifted carefully by the observer with an eye toward discovering a full and accurate basis upon which to develop a credible and edifying picture of the man and his times.

Having recognized the problems of personal bias in the sources we are using, we must also then realize that the same problem will exist in the mind of the person examining the materials. We all come at historical data with certain prejudices, sometimes anticipating the results of our investigation, while at other times actually molding the material to fit our own preconceptions. Recognizing these tendencies, and consciously resisting the temptation to impose our own biases onto the historical material, we must realize the result of our quest might not be what we expect or even desire. Especially when looking at primary documents for the first time, we must expect surprises. Such expectations of the unexpected make the historical enterprise both exciting and rewarding.

Considerations in the Quest for Historical Accuracy

The success of any exploratory journey depends not only on the selection of a potentially fruitful direction of inquiry, but also on careful preparation. Wesley's recognized significance as a historical figure and the wide variety of sources available for our study almost guarantee the value of our venture for the person interested in discovering John Wesley. But the confusing variety of images of Wesley portrayed in his own day as well as over the past two centuries gives us some pause as we start on this journey. Part of our preparation must include the anticipation of problems that will confront us in our quest of the elusive John Wesley.

There are several reasons why Wesley was and is a rather elusive figure, as a person, as a leader, and as a writer. Some of these are normal considerations that confront almost any attempt to reconstruct the life and thought of a historic person. Other situations are more particular to Wesley's own situation. In every case, a recognition of these considerations will make the search for an accurate and full basis for the portrayal of Wesley, though perhaps no easier, more fruitful.

(1) *Wesley was a legend in his own day.* He had a heroic public image based on a lifestyle that approached epic proportions. The traditional rehearsal of the statistics of his life speaks for itself: 250,000 miles traveled on horseback, over 40,000 sermons preached during a span of sixty-six years, more than 400 publications on nearly every conceivable topic, all of this activity continuing almost to his dying day in his eighty-eighth year. These are the marks of a man certain to appear larger than life-size, in spite of his small physical stature (five feet three inches, 126 pounds). Never mind that some of those miles in later life were actually covered in a finely appointed chaise or that many of those publications were extracts from other authors or quite brief tracts. These statistics still represent a monumental production for one lifetime, and many of the people of his day, though perhaps not familiar with the precise statistics, were aware of Wesley's reputation as a notoriously busy, seemingly tireless person who was always on the move.

To say that Wesley's reputation may have outstripped his "real" capabilities (an element of any legendary status) is not to say that we must disregard or throw aside any resource that tends toward hyperbole. What people (as well as Wesley) believed to be true about him is an important consideration in his own autobiographical development, in the flow of historical events around him, and in our attempt to understand the whole story. One of the most ticklish tasks that confronts the historian in reconstructing the past is to sort through various perceptions of reality as expressed by contemporary participants and observers, for each of whom, we should remember, reality was based upon whatever they believed to be true.

Wesley himself seems to have adopted a self-perception that was based upon, or at least contributed to, a heroic image. His writings often contain autobiographical recollections that reflect a somewhat magnified, or perhaps idealized, view of his character or personality. This tendency resulted in part from the necessity of defending himself in the forum of public opinion. Part of his apologetic method was quite naturally to put forth his best side whenever possible, even if his editorial management of the truth might result in some distortion of the historical facts.

In spite of his good intentions, Wesley's accounts of himself are occasionally marked by discrepancies and contradictions that at times tend to inflate his good image. A simple example of this can be seen in Wesley's sermon, "Redeeming the Time," in which he promotes the virtues of rising early in the morning. He cites his own experience at Oxford as an example of one practical way to discover just how much (or little) sleep a person needs each night. His solution to the problem of spending more time in bed than was necessary (indicated in part by persistent insomnia) was to procure an alarm that woke him an hour earlier each morning for four or five days until he settled on an hour of rising that suited both his physical and spiritual needs—4:00 A.M. A good story to illustrate a good point. As for the historical facts of the matter, Wesley in his diary had recorded the process of working back toward the 4:00 A.M. rising time as a gradual development that took place over several months. In the sermon illustration, he simply telescoped several months into four days, making a much better story, but at the same time giving a picture of himself that is perhaps more remarkable than the facts warrant. The main point being made in the sermon is no less true, but the illustrative story should not be taken either as a historical episode in its details or as an accurate indication of Wesley's capacity for effecting instant solutions. That the people (and perhaps even Wesley himself) came to believe these stories to be accurate representations of his character is, however, a fact that must be considered in our attempt to recover the perceptions of the eighteenth century.

Wesley's heroic image was built in part upon his own inclination toward seeing himself as a martyr. This self-impression is not often explicit in his own writings. He did, however, often express the opinion that persecution was a necessary mark of a true Christian, and his *Journal* is in one sense a lengthy rehearsal of events that display in great detail the confirmation of that truth in his own life.

The underlying tone of these accounts is perhaps as revealing as the actual content. For example, his narrative of the riots at Wednesbury (see page 121) concludes with a comment that indicates Wesley was not at all ruffled by the violent physical struggles that had just occurred. He then goes on to analyze the various ways in which God's providence might be perceived as evident in those events. His brother's journal for that period records an even more telling reflection; Charles indicates that his brother John understood how the early Christian martyrs could stand in the persecutors' flames and not feel any pain. Wesley's self-perceptions of this sort could not help finding their way into the consciousness of the public, and the biblical allusions and martyr-like experiences were certainly not lost on them.

(2) *Wesley's public image can be distinguished from his private image.* This rather commonplace observation could be made about almost any famous person and is mentioned here simply because it is often overlooked in many studies of Wesley. His own writings display this point rather nicely. The "public" documents, such as his sermons and journal, at times give quite a different picture from that contained in his private documents, such as his letters and diaries. To say this is not to imply any devious intent on Wesley's part. Rather, the distinction between the two images is based upon the difference in design and intent of these two types of material. Sermons designed for the propagation of practical divinity, whether preached or published, have quite different perimeters of self-revelation from letters written to one's brother in the depths of despair. To read each with an eye toward discerning the "actual" situation being described, we must have an analytical sensitivity to the circumstances out of which the writing was generated. Such is also the case when we look at the writings of contemporary observers who claim to be able to describe the private, as distinguished from the public, image of a person.

Wesley's public image, nearly legendary in scope and proportion, certainly fed the tendency toward hero worship on the part of many of his followers. But at the same time, the exaggerated picture of piety and perfection inherent in such a perception of the man served to fuel the antagonism expressed by many of his detractors. Many critics inflamed the imagination of the public by contrasting this public, almost unreal image, with a demonic portrait of the "real" nature and intentions of the private person that lurked behind that public image. These attacks, often dismissed by Wesleyan adherents as the work of twisted minds, we should not simply discard out of hand without first recognizing that the sale and popularity of such writings, scurrilous as they may seem, depended upon their having a degree of credibility in the public eye. Just as there was a public image of Wesley that approached sainthood and was undergirded by a repertoire of appropriate anecdotes, there was also a public view of him that resembled a dangerous, ranting enthusiast and could believe the vilest of epithets. Both were flawed interpretations, yet both gained that degree of credibility because they contained a kernel of truth. The task of the careful historian is to try to discern just what the kernel of truth might be in specific instances that would allow seemingly obvious scurrility (or exaggerated virtue) to pass for a believable representation.

One might note in passing that many of the persons who were quite ready to attack Wesley in the public eye and to do almost anything in their power to bring ridicule upon him and his movement found it difficult if not impossible to attack him privately as a person. This may, in part, reflect Wesley's own method of disputation, focusing on principles rather than personalities, but also may demonstrate a recognition of Wesley's personal integrity even by most of his enemies. This tendency to distinguish between the private and the public Mr. Wesley, for better or worse, is only one part of the larger picture of his controversial involvements, which have even wider repercussions in the attempt to discover the elusive John Wesley.

(3) *Wesley was a controversial figure.* This consideration, like the last two points, is by no means a new observation on the life of John Wesley. But likewise, it carries with it certain implications that are often overlooked by persons trying to recapture an accurate picture of the man.

Wesley faced opposition from many quarters on a variety of issues. From the very beginning, the attacks came from both inside and outside the movement. The Oxford Methodists were not "of one mind," in spite of Wesley's oft-repeated comment to that effect; his own diary shows that some members who were "piqued" at him bolted from his group and even, in one case, wrote a theme "against the Methodists." As the movement grew and developed, some of Wesley's preachers challenged his ideas and leadership, especially in the 1750s and 1760s. His brother Charles often disagreed with him on important matters of policy and procedure. The continuing reaction to many of Wesley's controversial actions and ideas during his lifetime set the stage for many of the disputes within the movement after his death.

The external attacks came from several directions, including opposite ends of the theological, political, and social spectra.

Different opponents portrayed Wesley in a mind-boggling variety of garbs; he was seen as a Quaker by some, a Papist by others, a ranting enthusiast by many, and an upper-crust snob by others. To discover the real Wesley simply on the basis of these attacks is of course impossible, even though they might unwittingly tell us something useful about the public's perception of him, as we have seen.

The writings generated by these controversies, however, should not be overlooked as a valuable source of information in our quest. Although they present a confusing picture in many ways, a careful look at this material will tell us quite a bit about the inner character of Wesley's life and thought, and particularly about his intellectual methodology. The writings include not only the attacks by Wesley's opponents and the defense by Wesley, but also the observations of many third parties, some quite obviously friendly to Wesley's cause but others less certain about their affiliation. The problem facing us is not to decide who is friend or foe, or to figure out who is right or wrong. Rather, we must decide what the attacks and the friendly defenses can tell us about Wesley, and what we can discern about Wesley from his writings in his own defense.

Wesley's own writings have caused the most problems for some recent authors who have been quick to point out that his controversial works (which represent a significant proportion) do not seem to maintain or develop any sort of consistent or systematic treatment of the major themes in Christian doctrine. It is difficult at best for a person to find anything approaching a well-developed system of thought, easily defined as "Wesleyan," in the whole of his works. Therefore many conclude that Wesley was not a major thinker of any significance. In the writings that arise from his many controversies, Wesley does appear from time to time to have made statements that even seem to be quite contradictory, in tone or emphasis at least, if not in substance. Some scholars, therefore, treat Wesley as a self-contradicting, confusing intellectual "lightweight," and dismiss him with comments such as that of Ronald Knox, who said that Wesley "is not a good advertisement for reading on horse-back."

We should not be too quick, however, to pass judgment on Wesley based only on someone's evaluation of the "rightness" or "wrongness" of his positions or the consistency or inconsistency of his writings. Wesley was neither a "Mr. Facing-both-ways" in the Bunyan tradition, nor an indifferent (much less, superficial) theologian. At

31

the same time, he had neither the luxury of time nor the inclination of mind to spend time in his study developing a thoroughly consistent theological system. He faced issues as they arose, in the midst of an active ministry to the poor. His theology was hammered out on the anvil of controversy. He was, you might say, a man fighting in the trenches, waging his battle for truth (as he saw it) with the enemy wherever it raised its head, countering attacks from left and right as they came. In that context, he often found it necessary to change his stance to face an opponent more effectively, not unlike a swordsman changing his direction and shifting his footing while holding his ground. When defending himself against the left, he appears to be coming from the right; when facing right, he seems to be defending the left. This is an important consideration when we are trying to discover a basic "Wesleyan" theological position; and, when we look at Wesley's controversial writings in this light, we are likely to discover that he was more consistent than many persons have acknowledged. In fact, he was in most cases trying to hold a middle ground, a stance that is characteristic of his theological method.

(4) *Wesley embodied ideals and qualities not always easily held together or reconciled.* Part of the enigma of Wesley is characterized by the frequent portrayal of him in such guises as a "radical conservative," a "romantic realist," or a "quiet revolutionary." While these designations seem to be inherently inconsistent, they do speak to the tension and balance that is a basic element of Wesley's life and thought.

Wesley was an educated upper-class Oxford don who spent most of his life working among the poor and disadvantaged. This paradoxical lifestyle left its mark on the character of many of his activities. He was a champion of the poor, yet a defender of the political establishment that had caused many of their problems. He was a master of expression in several languages, yet strove to express "plain truth for plain people." In his outlook and activities, he attempted to unite, in his brother Charles's words, "the pair so long disjoined, knowledge and vital piety." He combined in his ministry the preaching of the revivalist and the concerns of the social worker. His religious perspective was at the same time evangelical and sacramental. If we fail to keep in mind this tendency to hold seeming opposites together in unity (though not without some internal tension), we will miss one of the significant keys to understanding his life and thought.

The eclectic methodology that underlies much of Wesley's work, both as a controversial writer and as a mediating theologian in the Anglican tradition, entails the holding together of ideas or emphases that appear to come from opposing sides of the religious spectrum. In a given controversy, Wesley at times found himself having to defend or emphasize one side of such a tandem set, often at the apparent expense of the other side. This combination of eclectic and polemical methodologies on Wesley's part has often confused many observers (past and present), especially if they have seen a particular selection from his writings, containing only one side of Wesley's view, without the larger context of the whole of his life and writings. So we can find, for example, quotations from Wesley that appear to sound a note of advanced liberalism and to play down the importance of theological differences among professed Christians (e.g., "if your heart is as my heart, give me your hand"), and yet in close proximity we find a call for firmness on fundamental doctrines. If one side of this balance is lost, or one side is overemphasized, the wholeness of the basic Wesleyan position is destroyed (even though Wesley can be cited to support either side in an argument). All this is to say that, in trying to recapture the whole John Wesley, we should look at the context in which his writings were produced. We should pay attention to the nature of controversies that gave rise to certain writings as well as remember that his writings can be best understood when viewed in the light of both the variety of sources that provide the tapestry upon which his developing thought was woven, and in the rather massive body of his own works, written over a long lifetime. This observation leads us to a final consideration.

(5) *Wesley's life and thought are marked by growth and change.* The story is told of a professor who once lectured on Wesley to a group of inquisitive youngsters. At the conclusion of his presentation, one of the questions from his young audience was "How old was Wesley?" The professor thought for a moment before replying, "Well, you see, he was different ages at different times." A silly comment, perhaps, but it points to a truism that is frequently overlooked—Wesley grew and changed and developed. We like to define Wesley's life and thought in categorical and simplistic statements that overlook the obvious fact that Wesley was at one time young, that he matured, and that he grew old. His life spanned nearly the whole of the

eighteenth century. It is quite natural that he developed and changed in many ways (as did the environment around him). His activities, his outlooks, his habits, and his thoughts do certainly exhibit some continuity throughout his life, but historians and biographers have had a tendency to see more continuity than is warranted in some areas while overlooking it in others. Wesley's sermons, especially the forty-four "standard" ones, are often treated as a unified body of doctrine, as though they can somehow define the whole of his thought from beginning to end. They are treated, moreover, as though they can stand apart from any historical context or any other sermons he may have written earlier or later. The underlying assumption seems to be that he had all his worthwhile thoughts between the ages of thirty-five and sixty, and that everything before and after was either consistent with those views or otherwise inconsequential. We must be careful to recognize that Wesley developed many of his lifelong habits and ideas as a young man, and also that many of his finest and most mature reflections are exhibited in his writings from the three decades of his life after age sixty.

The problem of analyzing Wesley's development is not simply confined to distinguishing areas of change that are often overlooked. Another tendency to be guarded against is that of seeing changes themselves as being more pervasive and definitive than they might in fact have been. In the most radical of changes there are usually significant threads of continuity. In Wesley's case, the traditional division of his life into two time periods—before and after "Aldersgate"—distorts the picture of his spiritual development and in some ways clouds the actual significance of that crucial event in his life. There has been a tendency in some circles to view the early Wesley as being less than fully Christian and not worth studying, while assuming that the transformation of his evangelical experience of 1738 resulted in a totally new person who was thenceforth consistently persuasive and successful in both his proclamation and experience of the gospel (and therefore more important and worthy of study, if not emulation).

We must recognize, then, that there is more *continuity* between the young Wesley and the mature Wesley than is generally recognized. At the same time we must realize that there is also more *difference* between the mature Wesley and the elderly Wesley than has usually been noticed. The early Wesley, often portrayed as "unenlightened" and "unconverted," exhibits a mind and spirit that provided the foundation and framework for many of his later thoughts and activities. A simple indication of this is the fact that many of the works quoted in his later sermons come from his reading list as a student and tutor at Oxford. On the other hand, some of Wesley's best reflective writing came after his sixtieth birthday, after the last of the "standard" sermons had been written. When he finally published a collected edition of his works in the 1770s, he incorporated nine of these later sermons into the earlier group (bringing the total to fifty-three). Some of these new sermons modified or extended the ideas expressed in the earlier writings. A decade later, he produced yet another edition of his sermons, more than doubling the number of his published sermons by including dozens written after his seventy-fifth birthday. These and other writings from Wesley's later years deserve more attention than they usually receive.

One pitfall that must be avoided in the attempt to discern the nature and character of Wesley's development is, again, the temptation to generalize on the basis of Wesley's own comments, taken out of context. He does occasionally express a view of his own growth and development that he himself later challenges. This is most noticeable in his *Journal* comments regarding the state of his soul in the 1730s. These comments were first published in the 1740s, and then later qualified in the 1770s. We must assume that what he believed about himself at any given time is true for him at that time. Later reflections upon his earlier conditions must be accepted for what they are, an indication of his self-awareness at a later time. That is to say, neither one is "right" or "wrong" absolutely, but simply must be understood in the historical context of his own developing self-consciousness. Thus in 1725, he thought he was a Christian; for awhile after 1738, he thought he had not truly been a Christian in 1725; by the 1770s, he was willing to admit that perhaps his middle views were wrong, and that he could understand himself as having been in some real sense a Christian in 1725.

Each of these five considerations listed above, then, emphasizes the necessity to view Wesley in the light of the *whole* of his life and thought. The private man must be considered along with the public; his defense must be placed alongside the attack; his apparent leanings in any given direction must be measured against his penchant for a mediating balance; his views from any given period must stand the test of his own changing mind. We must look for the elusive John Wesley in the context of the many events and controversies that shaped his mind and spirit from beginning to end. And we must look at the sources with a critical eye, noting whether they are early or late, friendly or antagonistic, public or private, exaggerated or simplistic, firsthand or secondary accounts. As a result of this approach, the object of our quest, John Wesley, though still elusive, will in the end be more understandable and believable as a human being.

Twice-Told Tales: Two Centuries of Wesley Studies

Many biographies of Wesley are still repeating favorite, timeworn images of the man that are as inadequate (if not inaccurate) today as they were two hundred years ago. A handful of stock answers have developed over the years to respond to a short list of standard questions that seem to fascinate most authors who join the attempt to portray Wesley for their generation. The questions are usually phrased something like this:

Was Wesley's Aldersgate experience a "conversion"?
Did his influence prevent a revolution in eighteenth-
    century England?
Did a mother-fixation cause problems in his developing
    relationships with other women?
Did he intend to start a new denomination?
Was he fascinated more by organizational schemes than by
    theological consistency?

These questions cry for a yes or no answer, and traditional arguments abound to support both sides. If the truth were known, in most cases *both* answers would likely be possible, and *neither* by itself would be fully appropriate.

Part of the problem is that in many cases the wrong questions are being asked, and therefore the answers often do not focus on the most significant issues. It has been said that historians have an uncanny penchant for answering questions that nobody is asking. Many Wesley biographies demonstrate a slight variant of this tendency, answering questions that are being asked, to be sure, but that are off the mark or poorly phrased. As an example, the first question above (about Aldersgate) certainly can be answered yes if one is to believe Wesley's own testimony in the weeks and months immediately following the event. It can also be answered no if one is to believe Wesley's own later alteration of his earlier opinion. A question that would serve us better in trying to understand the significance of this event in Wesley's life would be: What part did Wesley's Aldersgate experience have in his own developing self-perception (at the time and later) and in his lifelong theological and spiritual development? Asking the question this way begins to point us toward areas of investigation that demand no less interpretation, but are less prone to invite an immediate division into polemical parties or opposing sides, which in the end would have only limited usefulness in moving us toward a more adequate view of Wesley. It is of little value to continue to ask these same questions and then to pick one or another of the old (or even new) stereotypes that argue a poor answer to a bad question.

One reason that traditional questions about Wesley have been the focus of concern over the last two centuries is that most of the major studies of Wesley have been written by persons who would claim to be in the Wesleyan tradition (though not necessarily with a "Methodist" affiliation). Not that the followers of Wesley are somehow inherently incapable of producing good work—fortunately there are many good books and articles around that disprove such an assumption. There has been a tendency, however, for Wesleyans (including Methodists) of various persuasions to "use" Wesley to prove their own point of view or to substantiate the perspective of their own particular branch of the developing, increasingly fragmented heritage. Anyone of several brands of "Wesleyanism" can be identified by their use of a predictable litany of certain answers to the timeworn list of standard questions.

A similar tendency toward interpretive categorization can be seen in writings that come out of other, transdenominatonal groupings. "Evangelicals" have portrayed a Wesley who looks much like a frontier revivalist; the "social gospel" folk like to see Wesley the philanthropist and social worker; the "holiness" faction stresses the centrality of his doctrine of sanctification; the "ecumenical" types emphasize his catholic spirit; the "fundamentalists" build upon a defined package of his essential doctrines—each of these, and others besides, editing Wesley carefully so as to fit into a mold that is, not surprisingly, identical to their own. Most of these interpretive positions tell us something important about Wesley, but fall short of seeing the larger scope of his life and thought.

In the face of all this, many Methodists began to disregard Wesley some time ago, and most non-Methodists have seen little reason to change their long-standing tendency to ignore him. The hagiographical tinfoil that the hero cults put around Wesley's image certainly was not designed to attract serious scholars, and the variety of sectarian claims for a "true Wesleyan" position often discouraged nearly all but the partisans of one side or another. The interpretive writings of specialists provided help only within limited areas of interest.

Writings focused on Wesley by non-Methodists generally decreased in number over the years until very recently. The polemical attacks died out early in the nineteenth century, and subsequent less polemical works were more often than not politely ignored by the majority of readers (for the large part, Methodists) or even treated with a hint of disdain (to think that an "outsider" would presume to understand "their" man!). This trend began to change early in this century as the ecumenical movement began to gain momentum, and the interest in Wesley by non-Methodists has been sustained and promoted by the move toward more interdisciplinary studies in the last twenty years. Students and scholars in many fields are increasingly attracted to the richness and variety of motifs wrapped together in this one fascinating eighteenth-century person.

Unfortunately, in the face of this renewed interest in Wesley's life and thought both from inside and outside the Methodist traditions, we stand in dire need of basic resources such as a fully adequate biographical study and a critical, annotated edition of his works. While not a biography, and certainly short of definitive, this study is intended to introduce the reader to the problems of and procedures for discovering John Wesley—to introduce the novice to, and to remind the expert of, the many possibilities as well as the pitfalls that await persons trying to understand John Wesley. Through looking at a variety of selections of writings by Wesley himself, and by his contemporaries and by successive generations of historians and biographers, we will be able to see the origin of many of the timeworn stereotypes and legends, as well as the places where some revisions need to be made. And through it all we will recognize and be reminded that Wesley is a fascinatingly complex and elusive (though not incomprehensible) eighteenth-century personality.

Part I

Wesley,
His Own Biographer

CHAPTER 1

A Son of Epworth

Strange as it may seem, Samuel Wesley, rector of Epworth and ex officio keeper of the parish records, had trouble keeping track of how many children had been born of Susanna, his wife. John Wesley was either the thirteenth or fourteenth; no one is quite sure. We do know that John was, up to the point of his birth on June 17, 1703, only the seventh child in the household to survive the first year of life. At least one baby girl, Susanna, and five boys had already died in infancy. Their names were sometimes used again; the next girl born after Susanna was given the same name.

John was the third boy to be christened with that name. The first John had died shortly after birth in 1699 along with a twin, Benjamin. The second, also a twin (with Anne), had been named John Benjamin, but died at seven months of age, less than eighteen months before the birth of our John (called "Jacky") in 1703.

As the years passed, the parents seem to have confused the circumstances surrounding the naming of these children, giving rise to a family tradition that it was the surviving John who had a middle name. Later in the century, one of John Wesley's preachers heard him repeat this tradition and recorded it in an early published history of Methodism: "I have heard him say, that he was baptized by the name of John Benjamin; that his mother had buried two sons, one called John, and the other Benjamin, and that she united their names in him." The author, Jonathan Crowther, went on to say, "But he never made use of the second name."

The tradition of Wesley's middle name is manifestly false and can be so proved from copies of baptismal records preserved in Samuel Wesley's own hand. That John himself perpetuated such a tradition is perhaps simply an indication of his tendency toward credulity in such matters. But that this and many other such traditions still persist and are repeated in many of the most recent biographies of Wesley is an early warning of the problems that, at every turn, confront the person interested in trying to discover the elusive John Wesley.

We rely on very slim evidence for information about the early life of John Wesley. Two events, however, did etch themselves on his mind—a fire that devastated his home when he was only five years old, and the appearances of a poltergeist that haunted the rectory for a time while John was away at grammar school. These are both well documented in the writings of the Wesley family and seem to have been firmly fastened in John's self-consciousness.

A Brand Plucked Out of the Burning

Young John was rescued from the rectory fire "by almost a miracle," as his father reported in a letter at the time. His mother's account was slightly less exuberant in many respects, and Wesley later published it, highly edited and abridged, along with some other letters in the first issue of his monthly Arminian Magazine *in 1778. He prefaced the collection of letters with a note saying that he hoped "what has been of use to ourselves, may be of use to others also." The letter that Susanna had written describing the rectory fire to a neighboring clergyman, Joseph Hoole, was introduced by John to his readers as "an account of a very remarkable Providence," adding: "But it is imperfect with regard to me. That part none but I myself can supply."*

In this published version, John made some alterations in Susanna's account and paraphrased or abridged much of the story.

On Wednesday night, February the ninth [1709], between the hours of eleven and twelve, some sparks fell from the roof of our house, upon one of the children's (Hetty's) feet. She immediately ran to our chamber and called us. Mr. Wesley, hearing a cry of "Fire" in the street, started up (as I was very ill, he lay in a separate room from me), and opening his door, found the fire was in his own house. He immediately came to my room and bid me and my two eldest daughters rise quickly and shift for ourselves. Then he ran and burst open the nursery door and called to the maid to bring out the children. The two little ones lay in the bed with her; the three others, in another bed. She snatched up the youngest and bid the rest follow, which the three elder did. When we were got into the hall and were surrounded with flames, Mr. Wesley found he had left the keys of the door above stairs. He ran up and recovered them, a minute before the staircase took fire. When we opened the street door, the strong northeast wind drove the flames in with such violence that none could stand against them. But some of our children got out through the windows, the rest through a little door into the garden. I was not in a condition to climb up to the windows; neither could I get to the garden door. I endeavoured three times to force my passage through the street door, but was as often beat back by the fury of the flames. In this distress, I besought our blessed Saviour for help and then waded through the fire, naked as I was, which did me no farther harm than a little scorching my hands and my face.

When Mr. Wesley had seen the other children safe, he heard the child in the nursery cry. He attempted to go up the stairs, but they were all on fire and would not bear his weight. Finding it impossible to give any help, he kneeled down in the hall and recommended the soul of the child to God.

[At this point, Wesley broke off his mother's account and continued with his own description of the manner by which he was rescued:]

I believe it was just at that time I waked, for I did not cry, as they imagined, unless it was afterwards. I remember all the circumstances as distinctly as though it were but yesterday. Seeing the room was very light, I called to the maid to take me up. But none answering, I put my head out of the [bed] curtains and saw streaks of fire on the top of the room. I got up and ran to the door but could get no farther, all the floor beyond it being in a blue. I then climbed up on a chest which stood near the window. One in the yard saw me and proposed running to fetch a ladder. Another answered, "There will not be time; but I have thought of another expedient. Here I will fix myself against the wall; lift a light man and set him on my shoulders." They did so, and he took me out of the window. Just then the whole roof fell, but it fell inward, or we had all been crushed at once. When they brought me into the house where my father was, he cried out, "Come, neighbours! Let us kneel down! Let us give thanks to God! He has given me all eight children; let the house go, I am rich enough!"

A Child of Destiny

Both narratives of the fire, by John and Susanna, emphasize the provi-dential deliverance of all the children. At some point, however, the focus of the remembered story began to center on John who, by at least 1737, adopted for himself the phrase from the Old Testament prophets, "a brand plucked out of the burning" [cf. Amos 4:11, Zech. 3:2]. This image he later included in a self-composed epitaph, written in 1753 when he thought death was immi-nent. It also formed the caption to a small vignette of the rectory fire placed at the bottom of an early portrait of Wesley circulated at midcentury. This biblical image, taken out of its context, became part of the Wesley legend, not only as an indication of his providential delivery from the fire but also as a divine designation of some extraordinary destiny for him (as with Moses, Jesus, Luther, et al.). After Wesley's death, his biographers made this connec-tion quite readily, using a comment from a prayer in Susanna's meditational journal of 1711 as a key element of their interpretation ("I do intend to be more particularly careful of the soul of this child, that thou hast so mercifully provided for, than ever I have been").

This part of the Wesley legend, however, was firmly fixed in the popular imagination long before the biographers made any artificial connection by such proof-texting. Even Wesley's own denials of any special self-consciousness on his part (much less his mother's) did little to squelch an image that had already been implicitly nurtured by the tone as well as the content of some of his own writings, such as his Journal. *His own denials may even have helped perpetu-ate and strengthen the image. One particularly firm and pointed disclaimer was published by Wesley in response to a brief review by Samuel Badcock, in the* Gentleman's Magazine *of 1784, of John Nichols's* Bibliotheca Topographica Britannica *(XX), which contained a short notice of Wesley. Badcock commented particularly on the rectory fire and its implications:*

This extraordinary incident explains a certain device in some of the earlier prints of John Wesley, viz., *a house in flames,* with this motto from the prophet, "Is he not a brand plucked out of the burning?" Many have supposed this device to be merely *emblematical* of his spiritual deliverance. But from this circumstance you must be convinced that it hath a *primary* as well as a *secondary* meaning. It is real as well as *allusive*—this fire happened when John was about six years old. . . . He had early a very strong impression (like Count Zinzendorf) of his designation to some extraordinary work. This impression received additional force from some domestic incidents, all which his active fancy turned to his own account. His wonderful preservation, already noticed, naturally tended to cherish the idea of his being designed by Providence to accomplish some purpose or other that was out of the ordinary course of human events.

Wesley's reply, published in the next volume of the Gentleman's Magazine *(and reprinted for his own readers in* The Arminian Magazine)*, attempts to clear up some points on which he says Badcock and the public had been "misinformed." In two paragraphs, Wesley gives an outline of his early life in an attempt to discount any claims to a self-conscious special destiny:*

I was born in June 1703 and was between six and seven years old *[sic]* when I was left alone in my father's house, being then all in flames, till I was taken out of the nursery window by a man strangely standing on the shoulders of another. Those words in the picture, "Is not this a brand plucked out of the burning?" chiefly allude to this.

"He had early a very strong impression of his designation to some extraordinary work [quoting Badcock]." Indeed not I; I never said so. I am guiltless in this matter. The strongest impression I had till I was three or four and twenty was, *Inter sylvas Academi quaerere verum* [to seek for truth in the groves of Academe], and afterwards (while I was my father's curate), to save my own soul and those that heard me. When I returned to Oxford [in 1729], it was my full resolve to live and die there, the reasons for which I gave in a long letter to my father, since printed in one of my Journals. In this purpose I continued till Dr. Burton, one of the trustees for Georgia, pressed me to go over with General Oglethorpe (who is still alive and well knows the whole transaction) in order to preach to the Indians. With great difficulty I was prevailed upon to go and spent upwards of two years abroad. At my return, I was more than ever determined to lay my bones at Oxford. But I was insensibly led, without any previous plan or design, to preach first in many of the churches in London, then in more public places; afterwards in Bristol, Kingswood, Newcastle, and throughout Great Britain and Ireland. Therefore all that Mr. Badcock adds, of the incidents that "gave additional force" to an impression that never existed, is very ingenious, yet is in truth a castle in the air.

Such "castles in the air," however, capture the imagination and are the stuff of which legends are made, legends that survive long after the history is forgotten.

A Collector of Ghostlore

A second "domestic incident" mentioned by Badcock as "giving additional force" to Wesley's self-consciousness was the appearance of strange noises that disrupted the Epworth rectory in 1716–17:

There were some strange *phaenomena* perceived at the parsonage at Epworth and some uncommon noises heard there from time to time, which he was very curious in examining into and very particular in relating. I have little doubt but that he considered himself as the chief object of this *wonderful* visitation. Indeed, Samuel Wesley's credulity was in some degree affected by it; since he collected all the evidences that tended to confirm the story and arranged them with scrupulous exactness in a MS consisting of several sheets, and which is still in being. I know not what became of the Ghost of Epworth, unless, considered as a prelude to the noise Mr. John Wesley made on a more ample stage, it ceased to speak when he began to act.

Wesley's reply to Badcock completely ignored this reference to the ghost of Epworth, no doubt in large part because of its nasty conclusion, but also perhaps because Wesley could not honestly deny his long-standing and lively interest in supernatural phenomena. In August 1726, John had in fact transcribed his father's collected account of the "disturbances" of 1716–17. During the following fortnight he also collected further evidence for himself in the form of recollections from other family members and friends who had heard "Old Jeffrey" (as sister Emily had named the ghost). It is perhaps no strange coincidence that during the very period he was gathering these stories,

John himself experienced two similarly strange happenings in the rectory,
which he recorded in his diary:

Tuesday morning, September 13 [1726], I waked a little before
two o'clock and could not go to sleep again. About a quarter after
two, the chamber door opened and clapped to again twice, loud and
distinctly. Tory [the dog], who was in bed, growled and barked all
the time. On Wednesday, as my brother and I were trying to catch a
chicken in the same room about twelve o'clock, I stayed at the door
to catch it, if it came that way. While I was standing about a yard from
it, and looking at it, the door which made wide open moved slowly
to. I opened it and looked, but no one beside us two was above stairs.

Wesley's fascination with haunted houses, witches, and other objects of
local folklore was firmly grounded in his early experiences in the rural hin-
terlands of Epworth, isolated as it was on the Isle of Axholme. His firsthand
acquaintance with country superstitions may indeed have played a major
role in helping him bridge the "culture gap" between his Oxford-educated out-
look and the rather primitive worldview of many of the folk throughout the
kingdom to whom he later ministered.

Perhaps it was this point of contact that he was cultivating when he pub-
lished in the 1784 Arminian Magazine *"An Account of the Disturbances*
in My Father's House." As early as 1730, he had broadcast his father's
account of the noises, reading it to the prisoners in the Oxford Castle. But for
his readers fifty years later, he put together his own version of the story.
Although based on the testimonies he had taken earlier, the sequence of events
he outlined is far from accurate, specific incidents being sometimes combined
or altered to make the story flow better. The narrative, however, does provide
the essential elements of the story, as remolded by Wesley's memory and edito-
rial pen, while also presenting an interesting glimpse into the daily routine
of the Epworth household, as the following selections show.

When I was very young, I heard several letters read, wrote to my
elder brother by my father, giving an account of strange disturbances, which were in his house, at Epworth, in Lincolnshire.

1. When I went down thither, in the year [1726], I carefully
enquired into the particulars. I spoke to each of the persons who
were then in the house, and took down what each could testify of his
or her own knowledge. The sum of which was this.

2. On December 2, 1716, while Robert Brown, my father's servant, was sitting with one of the maids a little before ten at night, in the dining-room which opened into the garden, they both heard one knocking at the door. Robert rose and opened it, but could see nobody. Quickly it knocked again and groaned. "It is Mr. Turpin," said Robert, "he had the stone and used to groan so." He opened the door again twice or thrice, the knocking being twice or thrice repeated. But still seeing nothing, and being a little startled, they rose and went up to bed. . . .

When he was in bed, he heard as it were the gobbling of a turkey-cock, close to the bedside, and soon after, the sound of one stumbling over his shoes and boots. But there were none there; he had left them below.

3. The next day, he and the maid related these things to the other maid, who laughed heartily, and said, "What a couple of fools are *you*? I defy anything to fright me." After churning in the evening, she put the butter in the tray, and had no sooner carried it into the dairy, than she heard a knocking on the shelf where pancheons of milk stood, first above the shelf, then below. She took the candle and searched both above and below; but being able to find nothing, threw down butter, tray and all, and ran away for life.

4. The next evening between five and six o'clock my sister Molly, then about twenty years of age, sitting in the dining-room, reading, heard as if it were the door that led into the hall open, and a person walking in, that seemed to have on a silk nightgown, rustling and trailing along. It seemed to walk round her, then to the door, then round again; but she could see nothing. She thought, "It signifies nothing to run away, for whatever it is, it can run faster than me." So she rose, put her book under her arm, and walked slowly away.

5. After supper, she was sitting with my sister Suky (about a year older than her) in one of the chambers, and telling her what had happened, she quite made light of it, telling her, "I wonder you are so easily frighted; I would fain see what would fright *me*." Presently a knocking began under the table. She took the candle and looked, but could find nothing. Then the iron casement began to clatter, and the lid of a warming-pan. Next the latch of the door moved up and down without ceasing. She started up, leaped into the bed without undressing, pulled the bedclothes over her head, and never ventured to look up till next morning. . . .

8. The next morning my sister telling my mother what had happened, she said, "If I hear anything myself, I shall know how to judge." Soon after, [Emily] begged her [mother] to come into the nursery. She did, and heard in the corner of the room, as it were the violent rocking of a cradle; but no cradle had been there for some years. She was convinced it was preternatural, and earnestly prayed it might not disturb her in her own chamber at the hours of retirement. And it never did.

She now thought it was proper to tell my father. But he was extremely angry, and said, "Suky, I am ashamed of you. These boys and girls fright one another; but you are a woman of sense, and should know better. Let me hear of it no more."

At six in the evening, he had family prayers as usual. When he began the prayer for the king, a knocking began all round the room, and a thundering knock attended the *Amen*. The same was heard from this time every morning and evening while the prayer for the king was repeated.

As both my father and mother are now at rest, and incapable of being pained thereby, I think it my duty to furnish the serious reader with a key to this circumstance. The year before King William died, my father observed my mother did not say "Amen" to the Prayer for the king. She said she could not, for she did not believe the Prince of Orange was king. He vowed he would never cohabit with her till she did. He then took his horse and rode away, nor did she hear anything of him for a twelvemonth. He then came back and lived with her as before. But I fear his vow was not forgotten before God.

9. Being informed that Mr. Hoole, the Vicar of Haxey (an eminently pious and sensible man) could give me some farther information, I walked over to him. He said, "Robert Brown came over to me, and told me, your father desired my company. When I came he gave me an account of all that had happened, particularly the knocking during family prayer. But that evening (to my great satisfaction) we had no knocking at all. But between nine and ten, a servant came in and said, Old Jeffries is coming (that was the name of one that died in the house) for I hear the signal. This they informed me was heard every night about a quarter before ten. It was toward the top of the house on the outside, at the northeast corner, resembling a loud creaking of a saw, or rather that of a windmill when the body of it is turned about in order to shift the sails to the wind. We

then heard a knocking over our heads, and Mr. Wesley catching up a candle, said, Come, Sir, now you shall hear for yourself. We went upstairs; he with much hope and I (to say the truth) with much fear. When we came into the nursery, it was knocking in the next room; when we were there, it was knocking in the nursery. And there it continued to knock, though we came in, particularly at the head of the bed (which was of wood) in which Miss Hetty and two of her younger sisters lay. Mr. Wesley observing that they were much affected though asleep, sweating and trembling exceedingly, was very angry, and pulling out a pistol, was going to fire at the place from whence the sound came. But I catched him by the arm and said, Sir, you are convinced this is something preternatural. If so, you cannot hurt it, but you give it power to hurt you. He then went close to the place and said sternly, 'Thou deaf and dumb devil, why dost thou fright these children that cannot answer for themselves? Come to *me* in my study, that am a man?' Instantly it knocked *his* knock (the particular knock which he always used at the gate [1–23456–7]) as if it would shiver the board in pieces, and we heard nothing more that night."

10. Till this time, my father had never heard the least disturbance in his study. But the next evening, as he attempted to go into his study (of which none had any key but himself) when he opened the door, it was thrust back with such violence as had like to have thrown him down. However, he thrust the door open and went in. Presently there was knocking first on one side, then on the other; and after a time, in the next room, wherein my sister Nancy was. He went into that room, and (the noise continuing) adjured it to speak, but in vain. He then said, "These spirits love darkness; put out the candle and perhaps it will speak." She did so, and he repeated his adjuration, but still there was only knocking and no articulate sound. Upon this he said, "Nancy, two Christians are an over-match for the devil. Go all of you downstairs; it may be, when I am alone, he will have courage to speak." When she was gone, a thought came in and he said, "If thou art the spirit of my son Samuel, I pray, knock three knocks and no more." Immediately all was silence, and there was no more knocking at all that night. . . .

13. A few nights after, my father and mother were just gone to bed and the candle was not taken away, when they heard three blows, and a second, and a third three, as it were with a large oaken staff

struck upon a chest which stood by the bedside. My father immediately arose, put on his nightgown, and hearing great noises below, took the candle and went down. My mother walked by his side. As they went down the broad stairs, they heard as if a vessel full of silver was poured upon my mother's breast and ran jingling down to her feet. Quickly after there was a sound as if a large iron ball was thrown among many bottles under the stairs. But nothing was hurt. Soon after our large mastiff dog came and ran to shelter himself between them. While the disturbances continued, he used to bark and leap, and snap on one side and the other, and that frequently, before any person in the room heard any noise at all. But after two or three days, he used to tremble and creep away before the noise began. And by this, the family knew it was at hand; nor did the observation ever fail....

14. Several gentlemen and clergymen now earnestly advised my father to quit the house. But he constantly answered, "No; let the devil flee from *me;* I will never flee from the devil." But he wrote to my eldest brother at London, to come down. He was preparing so to do, when another letter came, informing him the disturbances were over, after they had continued (the latter part of the time, day and night) from the second of December to the end of January.

CHAPTER 2

The Oxford Don

Wesley finished his preliminary schooling at Charterhouse in London in 1720 and went up to Christ Church, Oxford, to do his collegiate studies. He graduated as a bachelor of arts in 1724 and remained at Oxford to continue studies for a master of arts degree. His desire to pursue the scholarly life as a fellow and tutor at the University led him to seek ordination, a prerequisite for such a position. His father reassured him that there was "no harm" in such a rationale for entering into Orders, but suggested that "a desire and intention to lead a stricter life" was a better reason. His mother concurred, pleased by the "alteration of [his] temper," and sent him a few lines of advice in February 1725: "Dear Jacky, I heartily wish you would now enter upon a serious examination of yourself, that you may know whether you have a reasonable hope of salvation. . . . I approve the disposition of your mind; I think this season of Lent the most proper for your preparation for Orders."

Within days of receiving the encouragement from his parents, John began listing rules and resolutions in a small notebook that would become his daily diary. His reading that Lenten season set him on a course of self-examination that was designed to promote "holy living." His progress was to be both encouraged and measured by the strict "care of time" entailed in keeping a diary. Wesley continued to keep a private daily diary for the rest of his life. The first few volumes, covering ten years (as yet unpublished), provide an unmatched resource for discovering details about Wesley's life at Oxford.

The following selections, chosen from his private writings (diaries and letters), illustrate a small portion of the variety of Wesley's personal concerns and interests during the decade that saw "the first rise of Methodism" at Oxford. The grand theme of holy living had begun to set the direction of his life, even though the specific agenda of activities and his theological underpinnings would continue to experience some shifts though the coming years. He was increasingly obsessed with a desire for some clear sense of assurance that his approach and method of Christian living would provide adequate grounds for his hope of salvation.

The Careful Diarist

Wesley's diary entries (even the developing format) show an increasingly introspective manner, which is perhaps best characterized as "meditative piety." The temptations that beset him are transparent, not only in his explicit comments but also implicitly in his lists of resolutions and rules, beginning with the very first in 1725:

[Good] Friday, March 26, 1725. I found a great many unclean thoughts arising in Chapel, and discovered these temptations to it:
   a. Too much addicting myself to light behaviour at all times;
   b. Listening too much to idle talk, and reading vain plays and books;
   c. Idleness; and lastly
[d.] Want of due consideration in whose presence I am.
From which I perceive it is necessary:
   a. To labour for a grave and modest carriage;
   b. To avoid vain and light company; and
   c. To entertain awful apprehensions of the presence of God;
   d. To avoid idleness, freedom with women, and high-seasoned meats;
   e. To resist the very beginnings of lust, not by arguing with, but by thinking no more of it or by immediately going into company; and lastly,
[f.] To use frequent and fervent prayer.

Wesley's early diary reveals him participating in activities and exercises typical of the Oxford curriculum: reading basic texts, writing themes (geneses), discussing philosophical, political, and religious questions. The pattern of his study can be seen in a schedule drawn up in the diary just a year after his ordination as a deacon and a few months before standing for his master's degree; the rationale for such can be seen outlined in a subsequent letter to his mother.

Sunday morning: read Divinity, collect, compose.
      Afternoon: read Divinity, collect.
Monday (Greek and Latin Classics)
  Morning: read Greek poets, Homer; historians, Xenophon.
  Afternoon: read Latin poets, Terence; historians, Sallust;
                Oratory, Tully.
Tuesday (Greek and Latin Classics)
  Morning: Terence and Sallust or Tully. Afternoon: Homer
                and Xenophon.
Wednesday (Sciences)
  Morning: Logic—Aldrich, Wallis, Sanderson.
  Afternoon: Ethics—Langbain, More, Eustachius.
Thursday (Languages)
  Morning: Hebrew Grammar, Psalter.
  Afternoon: Arabic grammar.
Friday (Sciences)
  Morning: Metaphysicks—LeClerc, Locke, Clark, Jackson.
  Afternoon: Physics—Bartholine, Rohoult (per Clark),
                Robinson's Collection.
Saturday (Oratory and Poetry)
  Morning: write sermons and letters or verses.
  Afternoon: letters or sermons or verses.
                    September 24, 1726

[To Susanna, his mother, January 24, 1727; see Works, 25:208]

I am shortly to take my Master's degree. As I shall from that time be less interrupted by business not of my own choosing, I have drawn up for myself a scheme of studies from which I do not intend, for some years at least, to vary. I am perfectly come over to your opinion that there are many truths it is not worthwhile to know. Curiosity indeed might be a sufficient plea for our laying out some time upon them, if we had half a dozen centuries of life to come, but methinks it is great ill-husbandry to spend a considerable part of the small pittance now allowed us in what makes us neither a quick nor a sure return.

The daily entries of Wesley's diary for the first few years are punctuated by weekly periods of self-examination listing his sins and shortcomings. Anger, lying, lack of devotion, immoderate play or sleep—these and many other failings are noted fairly regularly (with "idleness" the most common) as indicators that all the virtues are not yet firmly implanted in his soul. Holidays provided something of a change of pace in all this, and the diary records many visits with friends in the Cotswold Hills, especially the Kirkhams of Stanton, whose daughters Betty ("Athenais") and Sally ("Varanese") were attracted to Wesley. The selections below display some of the wide range of interests that Wesley had developed at this time as well as the emotional ties that seemed to distract him at times from his professed religious aspirations. The first selection is a marginal note that reveals the motions for gracious entry to a room, apparently learned from a dancing-master who Susanna had brought into the Rectory to teach her children a genteel style in their social graces (see his letter of October 1, 1773).

A Step and a Sink with the other foot
First, Let the Sink be twice as long as the Step;
Secondly, Rise very slow;
Thirdly, Walk slowly into a room until your bow;
Fourthly, Let your hind foot never move; your hindmost
    always bends;
Fifth, Walk a little faster for a lady; first salute her, then bow
    and hand her to a chair.

....

Saturday, October 8, 1726. Rode to Stanton.... Walked with Nancy to Buckland. Supped there. A fine Aurora Borealis, first in the north, then northwest and northeast, then all round, etc; all the rays terminating near the zenith, rather northwards; appearing by turns of all colours, chiefly red or brick colour; at the height at 8 but very visible at 12; lighted home by it.

Friday, October 14. ... Walked to Varanese and Betty's; sat with them on the hill an hour. "My sister and I were reflecting as we came hither whether, if we were to die immediately, the action we were upon would give us any pain; and we both agreed that in such a circumstance this design would give us much more pleasure than uneasiness." —Varanese. "You make me less complaisant than I was before, for methinks 'tis almost a sin to prostitute those expressions of tenderness to others which I have at any time applied to you. I can't think it expedient, nor indeed lawful, to break off that acquaintance which is one of the strongest incentives I have to Virtue." —Varanese.

Sunday, October 16. Read prayers twice and preached at Stanton. . . . Walked to Horrel [Hill], sat down an hour with Varanese and Betty. I told them, in spite of the wise maxims of our sex, I was not ashamed to say I loved them sincerely. Varanese replied they were not behindhand with me and that she loved me more than all mankind except her father and her husband, and believed Betty did so too, though a maid must not say too much. At night Betty sat with me again. I told her I desired just the same freedom with her as with my sisters. She told me I had it; goodnight brother at eleven.

Monday, October 17. . . . Varanese and Betty said they would walk with me; walked near two hours.... "I would certainly acquit you if my husband should ever resent our freedom, which I am satisfied he never will. Such an accident as this would make it necessary to restrain in some measure the appearance of the esteem I have for you; but the esteem itself, as it is grounded on reason and virtue, and entirely agreeable to both, no circumstance of life shall ever make me alter." —Varanese.... Sat with Varanese and Betty till eleven. Leaned on Varanese' breast and kept both her hands within mine. She said very many obliging things. Betty looked tenderly. Thank God; long-suffering.

Friday, December 23. At Stanton; rose at nine; thought what I should talk of; with Betty and Varanese; ... talk of reason in brutes; how flies and fishes respire; of Miss Tooker, she was noted for good humour ever since she was two years old. At "Take care of thyself, Gentle Yahoo," Betty burst out a-crying; ... till five with Betty in the kitchen; grave, then merry; wished she had been a man for my sake.

Monday, December 26. . . . Played at cards, lost; much company; talk of sheep and price of corn; read the rest of *Ambitious Stepmother* to Miss Tooker. She commends Mr. Hutchins much for telling her her faults. . . .

Thursday, December 29. Read Henry N;...discussed with Mrs. Chapone [Varanese] of the use of astronomy, particularly of comets; why physicians [are] commonly atheists, inured to sickness and death; played at Pope Joan till twelve, won; talk with Varanese till one; of the use of languages, particularly Arabic—how should that be so elegant when the speakers of it for the most part have been so unpolished.

Friday, December 30. Rose at eight, read part of *Way of the World;* ...played at Ombre till nine; went into kitchen for Athenais, burst into tears at my saying, "how prettily shall we reflect on our past lives thirty or forty years hence?" Said she would tell me then why she would never marry. I told her what [her brother] said of it! She was a little piqued; said I used artifice to get a secret out of her.

Monday, January 9. With Varanese in little parlour; said she always thought she had a vast many things to say to me when I was away, but still forgot them when I came.... "The greatest pleasures of my life, I freely own, have been owing to friendship; and in the number of my friends there is no one I see, and always shall, in a stronger view than you."—Varanese.

"Primitive Christianity"

Wesley continued these close friendships for several years, accepting the name "Cyrus" from classical literature as part of the social style among this small literary circle (Charles being "Araspes," a friend of Cyrus the Great; Ann Granville, "Selima"; Mary Granville Pendarves, "Aspasia"; Betty Kirkham, "Athenais"; and Sally Kirkham Chapone, "Varanese"). Wesley's correspondence with Aspasia and Selima, as well as with members of his family, provides not only a picture of events at Oxford but also an expression, at a very pure and untarnished level, of Wesley's concept of his ideal, the true Christian. The personal discipline that such an ideal evoked in the Oxford don's lifestyle, implicit in the following selections, caused his lady friends occasionally to apply another nickname to Wesley—"Primitive Christianity."

[To Aspasia, February 11, 1731; see Works, *25:270]*

Who can be a fitter person than one that knows it by experience to tell me the full force of that glorious rule, "Set your affections on things above, and not on things of the earth"? Is it equivalent to,

"Thou shalt love the Lord thy God with all thy heart, soul, and strength"? But what is it to love God? Is not to love anything the same as habitually to delight in it? Is not then the purport of both these injunctions this, that we delight in the Creator more than his creatures? That we take more pleasure in him than in anything he has made? And rejoice in nothing so much as in serving him? That (to take Mr. Pascal's expression) while the generality of men use God and enjoy the world, we on the contrary only use the world while we enjoy God.

[To Susanna, his mother, June 11, 1731; see Works, *25:283]*

The point debated was, What is the meaning of being "righteous overmuch," or by the more common phrase, of being too strict in religion? And what danger there was of any of us falling into that extreme.

All the ways of being too righteous or too strict which we could think of were these: either the carrying some one particular virtue to so great a height as to make it clash with some others; or the laying too much stress on the instituted means of grace, to the neglect of the weightier matters of the law; or the multiplying prudential means upon ourselves so far, and binding ourselves to the observance of them so strictly, as to obstruct the end we aimed at by them, either by hindering our advance in heavenly affections in general, or by retarding our progress in some particular virtue. Our opponents seemed to think my brother and I in some danger of being too strict in this last sense, of laying burdens on ourselves too heavy to be borne, and consequently too heavy to be of any use to us.

...This is a subject which we would understand with as much accuracy as possible, it being hard to say which is of the worse consequence: the being too strict, the really carrying things too far, the wearying ourselves and spending our strength in burdens that are unnecessary; or the being frightened by those terrible words from what, if not directly necessary, would at least be useful.

[To Aspasia, July 19, 1731; see Works, *25:293-94]*

I was made to be happy; to be happy I must love God; in proportion to my love of whom my happiness must increase. To love God I must be like him, holy as he is holy; which implies both the being pure from vicious and foolish passions and the being confirmed in those virtues and rational affections which God comprises in the word "charity." In order to root those out of my soul and plant these in their stead I must use (1) such means as are ordered by God, (2) such as are recommended by experience and reason.

[To Selima, Aug. 14, 1731; see Works, *25:306]*

I have indeed spent many thoughts on the necessity of method to a considerable progress either in knowledge or virtue, and am still persuaded that they who have but a day to live are not wise if they waste a moment, and are therefore concerned to take the shortest way to every point they desire to arrive at.

The method of, or shortest way to, knowledge, seems to be this: (1) to consider what knowledge you desire to attain to; (2) to read no book which does not some way tend to the attainment of that knowledge; (3) to read no book which does tend to the attainment of it unless it be the best in its kind; (4) "to finish one before you begin another," and lastly, to read them all in such an order that every subsequent book may illustrate and confirm the preceding.

The Compulsive Pietist

Wesley's own rigorous style of life during this period can be discovered quite readily by looking at his developing diary, which by 1733 had become an exacting instrument for taking his spiritual pulse.

Part of Wesley's "method" of holy living was to test himself daily (and eventually hourly) by various sets of questions. The primary concerns of these periods of self-examination can be seen in a list of "General Questions" which he began developing in 1730, enlarging and altering the list as he transcribed it into successive notebook diaries. These concerns provided the framework within which he reflected hourly upon his activities, as seen in a sample daily entry, which records not only his activities every hour (conversations, readings, and so forth) but also the resolutions he had either broken or kept, and his temper of devotion, rated on a scale of 1 to 9. Few major personalities in history have left us quite such an exhaustive record of their activities and attitudes.

General Questions
1. Have I prayed with fervor, by myself and at Chapel?
2. Have I used the Collects at 9, 12, and 3? Grace [at meals]?

3. Have I used the Ejaculations seriously, deliberately, and fervently once an hour?
4. Have I at ingress and egress prayed...for the virtue of the day?
5. Have I done or said anything without a present or previous perception of its direct or remote tendency to the glory of God?
6. Have I after every pleasure immediately given thanks?
7. Did I in the morning plan the business of the day?
8. Did I in every action consider the duty of the day? Have I been simple and recollect in everything? The signs?
9. Have I been zealous in undertaking and active in doing what good I could?
10. Have I, before I visited or was visited, prepared and considered what end, what means?
11. Has good will been and appeared the spring of all my actions toward others?
12. Have I conversed with Charles as Aspasia with Selima? Negative, positive?
13. Have I been or seemed angry?
14. Have I thought or spoken unkindly of or to anyone?
15. Have I felt or entertained or seemed to approve any proud, vain, or unchaste thought?
16. Have I been particularly recollect, temperate, and thankful in eating or drinking?

Sunday, March 17, 1734

6 thirteen times, 7 five times.*

		Temper of Devotion	Resolutions Broken	Kept
4 e	Dressed. 4.15 Necessary business. 4.30 Called; writ diary; private prayer.	6	8	4/2
5 e	Questions; private prayer. 5.45 Fire [lighted].	6		1
6 e	Called; began Clemens			

60

	Romanus; Ingham, religious talk. 6.45 Robson, tea.	6	8	5/2
7 e	Religious talk of diaries. 7.45 Dressed; Grove.	6	6	
8 e	Clemens. 8.30 Morning Prayers [each part listed separately].	7		1
9 e	Morning Prayers [continued]. 9.20 Writ diary. 9.30 Castle, Morning Prayers.	7		1
10 e	Morning Prayers [continued].	7		1
11 e	Sermon, spoke to laughers in faith, looked; Sacrament; resolved not try with Morgan.	7	15	
12 e	Bible, Hall's, private prayer; Robson and Salmon, dinner, religious talk.	6	6	16
1 e	Pupil; writ diary. 1.50 Laughed at.	6	3/10	
2 e	Sermon; ended Reasonable Communicant.	6		
3 e	Grove, meditated.			
4 e	Questions. 4.10 Evening Prayers. 4.50 Examined.	7	5	1
5 e	Private prayer. 5.30 Eagle's, he not [home], religious talk.	6		
6 e	Salmon's, Horn, etc; examined, tea.	6	5/5	16
7 e	Morgan, Nowell, Walker, began St. Clemens.	6		
8 e	Clemens. 8.15 Religious talk, overbore Morgan.	6		
9 e	Writ diary; private prayer; undressed. 9.30.	6	8	

[Notes to diary page]

* *Summary of hourly ratings on "temper of devotion" on a scale of 1 to 9 (higher is better).*

"e" stands for ejaculatory prayer at the beginning of each hour, a short sentence prayer of praise; the symbol over it (and many other entries, see fig. 4) indicates the "degree of attention" ranging from dead or cold, to fervent or zealous.

The "resolutions broken or kept" are keyed to various lists by number: the whole numbers (1, 5, 6, 15, 16) refer to the list of "General Questions" (see page 59); the numbers that look like fractions (4/2, 5/2, etc.) refer to a list of "Particular Questions" arranged according to the virtues:

> *4/2—mortification and self-denial, question 2: "Have I submitted my will to the will of everyone that opposed it?"*
>
> *5/2—Resignation and meekness, question 2: "Have I endeavoured to thank Him for whatever has been mine without my choosing?"*
>
> *5/5—Resignation and meekness, question 5: "Have I been cheerful (without levity), mild and courteous in all I said?"*
>
> *3/10—Humility, question 10: "Have I omitted justifying myself? Submitted to be thought in the wrong?"*

CHAPTER 3

The Oxford Methodist

By mid-1732, Wesley had gathered around him a group of five or six friends who shared his commitment to disciplined Christian living. Toward the end of that year, a seething undercurrent of criticism aimed at Wesley and his small group of seemingly fanatical religious friends came to the surface. Word spread around the university that William Morgan, one of the original members of their group, had died as a result of extreme ascetic practices encouraged by Wesley. The furor that followed, swept on by rumor and the printed word, pushed Wesley into the public eye not only in Oxford and Dublin (Morgan's hometown), but also in London and throughout the British Isles. The attacks put Wesley into a defensive posture that forced him both to explain his ideas and activities to the public, and to satisfy himself about the validity of his vocation as well as his state of salvation.

Apologist for the Oxford Methodists

Two writings by Wesley at that time contain his personal defense and proclaim his theological program. First, a letter to Morgan's father explains the *background and rationale of their little society. Second, a sermon preached before the university ("Circumcision of the Heart") proclaims the central thrust of the doctrine that would be the keystone of his theology, Christian perfection. The second writing appears in every collection of Wesley's "standard" sermons. The first, the "Morgan letter," however, became the first instrument of Wesley's defense before officials of the university—he read this letter to the vice-chancellor, the provost of Queen's, the rector of Lincoln, and anyone else who raised questions about the Methodists' activities. During the following months, several copies of the letter were made by Wesley and his friends; the surviving manuscript is in Charles Wesley's handwriting.*

The Morgan letter, used by Wesley as the standard defense of Oxford Methodism in 1732, has also become the standard account of its rise and design, even though it does not describe the fullest state of its organization, which emerged only after 1732. The letter's wide circulation, as well as the popularization of the term "Methodist" (apparently first used in 1732), was due in part to an anonymous author who included it nearly verbatim in the first published pamphlet describing Wesley and his group, The Oxford Methodists *(1733), a not wholly favorable answer to the charges made against the group in a letter to the editor of a London newspaper (see page 230). No one, including Wesley, has ever discovered the author of that pamphlet (Wesley retraced his steps with the Morgan letter trying in vain to uncover the "leak"). To set the record straight, Wesley included an unexpurgated copy of the "Morgan letter" as an introductory section to his first published journal extract in 1740, a prominent position it has occupied in nearly every edition since that time. As a result, the descriptions in this letter, somewhat oversimplified as they are, have become etched in the minds of succeeding generations and have provided the basis for many of the stereotypes of the early Wesley and Oxford Methodism. See* Works, *18:123-33.*

Oct. [19], 1732
Oxon,

Sir,

The occasion of my giving you this trouble is of a very extraordinary nature. On Sunday last I was informed (as no doubt you will be ere long) that my brother and I had killed your son; that the rigorous fasting which he had imposed upon himself, by our advice, had increased his illness and hastened his death. Now though, considering it in itself, "it is a very small thing with me to be judged by man's judgment," yet as the being thought guilty of so mischievous an imprudence might make me the less able to do the work I came into the world for, I am obliged to clear myself of it by observing to you, as I have done to others, that your son left off fasting about a year and a half since, and that it is not yet half a year since I began to practice it.

I must not let this opportunity slip of doing my part toward giving you a juster notion of some other particulars relating both to him and myself, which have been industriously misrepresented to you....

In November 1729, at which time I came to reside at Oxford, your son, my brother, myself, and one more, agreed to spend three or four evenings in a week together. Our design was to read over the classics, which we had before read in private, on common nights and on Sunday some book in divinity. In the summer following, Mr. Morgan told me he had called at the jail to see a man who was condemned for killing his wife, and that, from the talk he had with one of the debtors, he verily believed it would do much good if anyone would be at the pains of now and then speaking with them. This he so frequently repeated that on the 24th of August, 1730, my brother and I walked with him to the Castle. We were so well satisfied with our conversation there that we agreed to go thither once or twice a week, which we had not done long, before he desired me, Aug. 31, to go with him to see a poor woman in the town who was sick. In this employment too, when we came to reflect upon it, we believed it would be worthwhile to spend an hour or two in a week, provided the minister of the parish in which any such person was, were not against it. But that we might not depend wholly on our own judgments, I wrote an account to my father of our whole design, withal begging that he, who had lived seventy years in the world and seen as much of it as most private men have ever done, should advise us whether we had yet gone too far and whether we should now stand still or go forward.

Part of his answer, dated Sept. 28, 1730, was this:

> And now, as to your own designs and employments, what can I say less of them than, *Valde probo* [I greatly approve], and that I have the highest reason to bless God that he has given me two sons together at Oxford to whom he has given grace and courage to turn the war against the world and the devil, which is the best way to conquer them. They have but one more enemy to combat with, the flesh; which if they take care to subdue by fasting and prayer,

there will be no more for them to do but to proceed steadily in the same course and expect the crown which fadeth not away. You have reason to bless God, as I do, that you have so fast a friend as Mr. Morgan, who, I see, in the most difficult service, is ready to break the ice for you.... Go on then in God's name in the path to which your Saviour has directed you and that track wherein your father has gone before you. For when I was an undergraduate at Oxford, I visited those in the Castle there and reflect on it with great satisfaction to this day. Walk as prudently as you can, though not fearfully, and my heart and prayers are with you....

Your most affectionate and joyful father.

In pursuance of these directions, I immediately went to Mr. Gerard, the Bishop of Oxford's chaplain, who was likewise the person that took care of the prisoners when any were condemned to die (at other times they were left to their own care). I proposed to him our design of serving them as far as we could, and my own intention to preach there once a month, if the Bishop approved of it. He much commended our design and said he would answer for the Bishop's approbation, to whom he would take the first opportunity of mentioning it. It was not long before he informed me he had done so, and that his lordship not only gave his permission, but was greatly pleased with the undertaking and hoped it would have the desired success.

Soon after, a gentleman of Merton College, who was one of our little company, which now consisted of five persons, acquainted us that he had been much rallied the day before for being a member of "The Holy Club," and that it was become a common topic of mirth at his college, where they had found out several of our customs, to which we were ourselves utter strangers.... We still continued to meet together as usual, and to confirm one another as well as we could in our resolutions, to communicate as often as we had opportunity (which is here once a week), and do what service we could do our acquaintance, the prisoners, and two or three poor families in the town. But the outcry daily increasing, that we might show what ground there was for it, we proposed to our friends, or opponents, as we had opportunity, these or the like questions:

I. Whether it does not concern all men of all conditions to imitate Him as much as they can "who went about doing good"?...

II. Whether, upon these considerations, we may not try to do good to our acquaintance? Particularly, whether we may not try to convince them of the necessity of being Christians?...

III. Whether, upon the considerations above-mentioned, we may not try to do good to those that are hungry, naked, or sick? In particular, whether, if we know any necessitous family, we may not give them a little food, clothes, or physic, as they want?...

IV. Lastly, whether, upon the consideration above mentioned, we may not try to do good to those that are in prison? In particular, whether we may not release such well-disposed persons as remain in prison for small sums?

I do not remember that we met with any person who answered any of these questions in the negative, or who even doubted whether it were not lawful to apply to this use that time and money which we should else have spent in other diversions. But several we met with who increased our little stock of money for the prisoners and the poor by subscribing something quarterly to it, so that the more persons we proposed our designs to, the more we were confirmed in the belief of their innocency and the more determined to pursue them in spite of the ridicule, which increased fast upon us during the winter. However, in the spring I thought it could not be improper to desire farther instructions from those who were wiser and better than ourselves, and accordingly (on May 18th, 1731), I wrote a particular account of all our proceedings to a clergyman of known wisdom and integrity. After having informed him of all the branches of our design as clearly and simply as I could, I next acquainted him with the success it had met with, in the following words:

> Almost as soon as we had made our first attempts this way, some of the men of wit in Christ Church entered the list[s] against us and, between mirth and anger, made a pretty many reflections upon the Sacramentarians, as they were pleased to call us. Soon after, their allies at Merton changed our title and did us the honour of styling us "The Holy Club." But most of them being persons of well-known characters, they had not the good fortune to gain any proselytes from the *Sacrament* till a gentleman, eminent for learning and well esteemed for piety, joining them, told his nephew that if he dared to go to the weekly communion any longer, he would immediately turn him out of doors. That argument indeed had no success: the young gentleman communicated

next week; upon which his uncle, having again tried to convince him that he was in the wrong way, by shaking him by the throat to no purpose, changed his method, and by mildness prevailed upon him to absent from it the Sunday following, as he has done five Sundays in six ever since. This much delighted our gay opponents, who increased their number apace; especially when, shortly after, one of the seniors of the college having been with the Doctor, upon his return from him sent for two young gentlemen severally who had communicated weekly for some time, and was so successful in his exhortations that for the future they promised to do it only three times in a year. About this time there was a meeting (as one who was present at it informed your son) of several of the officers and seniors of the college, wherein it was consulted what would be the speediest way to stop the progress of enthusiasm in it. The result we know not, only it was soon publicly reported that Dr. Terry and the censors were going to blow up "The Godly Club." This was now our common title, though we were sometimes dignified with that of "The Enthusiasts," or "The Reforming Club...."

Your son was now at Holt; however, we continued to meet at our usual times, though our little affairs went on but heavily without him. But at our return from Lincolnshire in September last we had the pleasure of seeing him again, when, though he could not be so active with us as formerly, yet we were exceedingly glad to spend what time we could in talking and reading with him.

It was a little before this time my brother and I were at London when, going into a bookseller's shop (Mr. Rivington's in St. Paul's Churchyard), after some other conversation, he asked us whether we lived in town, and upon our answering, "No, at Oxford": "Then, gentlemen," said he, "let me earnestly recommend to your acquaintance a friend I have there, Mr. Clayton, of Brasenose." Of this, having small leisure for contracting new acquaintance, we took no notice for the present. But in the spring following (April 20 [1732]), Mr. Clayton meeting me in the street and giving Mr. Rivington's service, I desired his company to my room, and then commenced our acquaintance. At the first opportunity I acquainted him with our whole design, which he immediately and heartily closed with. And not long after, Mr. Morgan having then left Oxford, we fixed two evenings in a week to meet on, partly to talk upon that subject and partly to read something in practical divinity.

The two points whereunto, by the blessing of God and your son's help, we had before attained, we endeavoured to hold fast: I mean, the doing what good we can, and, in order thereto, communicating as often as we have opportunity. To these, by the advice of Mr. Clayton, we have added a third—the observing the fasts of the Church, the general neglect of which we can by no means apprehend to be a lawful excuse for neglecting them. And in the resolution to adhere to these and all things else which we are convinced God requires at our hands, we trust we shall persevere till he calls us to give an account of our stewardship. As for the names of "Methodists," "Supererogation Men," and so on, with which some of our neighbours are pleased to compliment us, we do not conceive ourselves to be under any obligation to regard them, much less to take them for arguments. "To the law and to the testimony" we appeal, whereby we ought to be judged. If by these it can be proved we are in an error, we will immediately and gladly retract it; if not, we "have not so learned Christ" as to renounce any part of his service, though men should "say all manner of evil against us" with [no] more judgment and as little truth as hitherto. We do, indeed, use all the lawful means we know to prevent "the good which is in us" from being "evil spoken of." But if the neglect of known duties be the one condition of securing our reputation, why, fare it well. We know whom we have believed, and what we thus lay out he will pay us again....

I have now largely and plainly laid before you the real bound of all the strange outcry you have heard, and am not without hope that by this fairer representation of it than you probably ever received before, both you and the clergyman you formerly mentioned may have a more favourable opinion of a good cause, though under an ill name. Whether you have or no, I shall ever acknowledge my best services to be due to yourself and your family, both for the generous assistance you have given my father and for the invaluable advantages your son has (under God) bestowed on,

> Sir,
>
> > your ever obliged,
> > and most obedient servant.

Wesley's letter explaining the nature and design of Methodism at Oxford so successfully convinced Richard Morgan, Sr., of the harmlessness of the Oxford Methodists' practices (and in fact of their value) that the elder

Morgan sent his second son and namesake to Oxford under Wesley's care.
Richard, Jr., was quickly repelled by Wesley's methods and informed his father
of his feelings in no uncertain terms. The father wrote to Wesley. The follow-
ing excerpt is from Wesley's reply to the father's plea for moderation in deal-
ing with this, his recalcitrant son. Their developing dispute hinges on the
question of the nature of religion and the expectations one might impose upon
others. The second selection, written by Wesley to his mother, illustrates
Wesley's positions and methods with regard to the implicit matter of indoctri-
nation.

[To Richard Morgan, Sr., January 15, 1734; see Works, *25:369]*

Why, you say, I am to incite [your son] to "live a sober, virtuous,
and religious life." Nay, but first let us agree what religion is. I take
religion to be, not the bare saying over so many prayers morning
and evening, in public or in private; not anything superadded now
and then to a careless or worldly life; but a constant ruling habit of
soul; a renewal of our minds in the image of God; a recovery of the
divine likeness; a still-increasing conformity of heart and life to the
pattern of our most holy Redeemer. But if this be religion, if this be
that way to life which our Blessed Lord hath marked out for us, how
can anyone, while he keeps close to this way, be charged with running into extremes?

[To Susanna, his mother, August 17, 1733; see Works, *25:354-55]*

I cannot say whether I "rigorously impose any observances on others" till I know what that phrase means. What I do is this. When I am
entrusted with a person who is first to understand and practice, and
then to teach the law of Christ, I endeavour by an intermixture of
reading and conversation to show him what that law is; that is, to
renounce all insubordinate love of the world, and to love and obey
God with all his strength. When he appears seriously sensible of this
I propose to him the means God hath commanded him to use in
order to that end; and a week or a month or a year after, as the state
of his soul seems to require it, the several prudential means recommended by wise and good men. As to the times, order, measure, and
manner wherein these are to be proposed, I depend upon the Holy
Spirit to direct me, in and by my own experience and reflection,
joined to the advices of my religious friends here and elsewhere.
Only two rules it is my principle to observe in all cases: first, to

begin, continue, and end all my advices in the spirit of meekness, as knowing that "the wrath" or severity "of man worketh not the righteousness of God"; and secondly, to add to meekness, long-suffering, in pursuance of a rule which I fixed long since—"never to give up anyone till I have tried him at least ten years. How long hath God had pity on thee!"

The Settled and Unsettled Tutor

Wesley's view of religion, its requirements and its restrictions, was certainly a minority position at Oxford. Consequently, he was the brunt of a great deal of criticism, even from his friends and family. Under this pressure, Wesley was continually looking for some sense of assurance, some sign that he was truly a Christian. Two traditional positions he adopted, though not fully satisfying, seemed to assuage his uneasiness: that hope of salvation rested on one's sincerity, and that persecution was a necessary mark of a Christian.

Wesley used the latter argument as part of his rationale for staying at Oxford in spite of his father's request that John succeed him as rector of Epworth. In a lengthy letter written to Samuel Wesley, Sr., whose health was weakening in his old age, John outlined in some detail the nature of his vocation and his reasons for desiring to stay at Oxford even though many despised him there. Although he saw his position in a new light six months later after his father had died, he clearly shows his sense of determination at the time in these selections from the letter.

[To Samuel Wesley, Sr., December 10, 1734; see Works, *25:397-409; 19:39-45]*

1. The authority of a parent and the call of providence are things of so sacred a nature that a question in which these are any way concerned deserves the most serious consideration....

2. I entirely agree that "the glory of God and the different degrees of promoting it are to be our sole consideration and direction in the choice of any course of life."...

4. That course of life tends most to the glory of God wherein we can most promote holiness in ourselves and others....

6. By holiness I mean, not fasting, or bodily austerity, or any other external means of improvement, but that inward temper to which all these are subservient, a renewal of soul in the image of God....

16. From all this I conclude that where I was most holy myself,

there I could most promote holiness in others; and consequently that I could more promote it here than in any place under heaven....

20. Notwithstanding, therefore, their present prejudice in my favour, I cannot quit my first conclusion, that I am not likely to do that good anywhere, not even at Epworth, which I may do at Oxford....

22. With regard to contempt, then ... my first position, in defiance of worldly wisdom, is this: "Every true Christian is contemned wherever he lives by all who are not so, and who know him to be such; that is, in effect, by all with whom he converses, since it is impossible for light not to shine."...

23. My next position is this: "Till he be thus contemned, no man is in a state of salvation."...

25. And hence ... I infer one position more, that the being despised is absolutely necessary to our doing good in the world....

26. These are a part of my reasons for choosing to abide (till I am better informed) in the station wherein God has placed me.

Wesley was increasingly frustrated in his desire for self-conscious assurance that his persistently practiced methods at Oxford were in fact promoting holiness of heart and mind in his life. By the beginning of 1735, a growing concern for the "liberty" of the gospel (partly derived from the mystic writers) led him to begin testing his scheme of living; he began to question some of his practices. He began to cast lots to see if, in specific circumstances, providential determination would confirm his long-held practices of early rising or fasting. In the midst of these tensions, he disclosed both his theological quandary and his operating principles in a list of questions and answers. These he copied onto an extra page in the front of his last Oxford diary sometime during the fall or winter of 1734–35.

Q. How examine—daily, weekly, monthly?
A. Hourly only, revising in the morning.
Q. How steer between scrupulosity, as to particular instances of self-denial, and self-indulgence?
A. *Fac quod in te est, et Deo aderit bonae tuae voluntati* [Do what lies in your power, and God will assist your good will].
Q. How steer between impatience and want of zeal for improvement? Between niceness in marking my progress and carelessness in it?
A. Think not at all of anything either past or future any farther than is necessary for improving the present hour.

Although his motivation for religious activity ("doing the best you can") relied heavily on "sincerity" in typical eighteenth-century fashion, the result was not, as many have claimed, simply works-righteousness. The main factor in the equation was still the grace of God. "Resume all your externals," he advised George Whitefield early in 1735, "but do not depend on them in the least." That same insight was at the heart of Wesley's comment to John Burton later that year as Wesley waited to sail for Georgia: "Nor indeed till he does all he can for God, will any man feel that he can himself do nothing."

CHAPTER 4

The Colonial Missionary

Wesley set sail for Georgia in the fall of 1735 with a grand vision of his role as missionary to the Indians. His parting letter to a friend, John Burton, explained that he not only had "hope of doing more" among the "heathens" in America than in England; he also hoped to "learn the true sense of the gospel of Christ" through his ministry to those unspoiled "Gentiles" and thus be able to attain a higher degree of holiness himself. Two years later, his mission was in a shambles—not only had he been yet unable to "go among the Indians," but his basic morality (not to say his holiness) was being questioned in a court of law.

Wesley's strict high-church perspective was not well received by many of the rougher settlers in the newly established colony. His single-mindedness occasionally nettled the leadership (including James Oglethorpe). His ineptness in romance resulted in a lost love, and his spiteful reaction to his loss brought a warrant for his arrest. The strange intertwining of these problems resulted in a series of grand jury indictments that led to his hasty departure from the colony.

In the midst of these trials, emotional, pastoral, and legal, Wesley wrote several different accounts describing his situation. At least five manuscript narratives have survived in addition to his daily diary. A slightly different picture emerges from each of these journals, depending upon the time it was written and the readers for whom it was intended.

The first selection below was written after only half a year in the colony and focuses on his pastoral duties. The second was compiled after a full year, just after the woman he loved had married another man. The third was drawn up five months later in the midst of his legal problems with a grand jury. The fourth selection is from an account that was written last; it became the basis for his published version. But throughout them all is the picture of a young man trying to stamp his identity upon his surroundings during a period when his own self-understanding was being severely tested.

The Hard-pressed Pastor

Before Wesley's ship had landed at Savannah, the Georgia Trustees in London had appointed him minister of the parish. Wesley probably anticipated this assignment, though he certainly hoped it would not interfere with his primary goal, to preach to the Indians. Increasingly frustrated in his attempts to go among the Indians, however, he began to turn his attention to his congregation at Savannah. He performed his ministerial functions in a zealous, if somewhat rigid, fashion. A relatively small but faithful following responded positively. From among these he even formed a small extracurricular society that met frequently in his home after the daily service of Evening Prayer. This event he later called "the second rise of Methodism" (after Oxford).

However, Wesley's method of exercising his ministerial office brought him many trials and a great deal of criticism. The following selection from his journal, drawn up in September 1736, is part of a copy that he seems to have sent as a report back to England, either to the Trustees or to friends. This narrative reflects his own understanding that he was simply doing his duty as a good Church of England priest, operating under difficult circumstances. He calls out for assistance, presumably to his friends back in England, where his brother Charles had just returned. These comments are not found in any other of the extant journal extracts that he wrote or published (see Works, *18:411-21).*

Saturday, August 21 [1736], I spent an hour with Mr. Horton and laboured to convince him I was not his enemy. But it was labour in vain; he had heard stories which he would not repeat, and was consequently immovable as a rock. Many things indeed he mentioned in general, as, that I was always prying into other people's concerns in order to set them together by the ears; that I had betrayed every one who had trusted me; that I had revealed the confessions of dying men; that I had belied every one I had conversed with: himself, in particular, to whom I was determined to do all the mischief I could. But whenever I pressed him to come to particulars, he absolutely refused it. I asked him what motive he thought I had to proceed thus? He said he believed it was a pure delight in doing mischief, and added, "I believe in a morning, when you say your prayers, you resolve against it. But by the time you have been abroad two hours, all your resolutions are vanished and you can't be easy till you are at it again."

Here Mrs. Welch coming up, asked with a curse what I meant by saying she was an adulteress, and entertained me and a pretty many other auditors with such a mixture of scurrility and profaneness as I had not heard before. God deliver thee from the gall of bitterness and the bond of iniquity! . . .

On Friday [September 10, 1736], we began our Morning Prayers at quarter past five, an hour we hope to adhere to all the winter. Between fifteen and twenty persons constantly attend them, besides the children and the rest of our own family.

I had often observed that I scarce ever visited any persons, in health or sickness, but they attended Public Prayers for some time after. This increased my desire of seeing not only those who were sick, but all my parishioners as soon as possible at their own houses. Accordingly, I had long since begun to visit them in order from house to house. But I could not go on two days, the sick increasing so fast as to require all the time I have to spare (which is from one in the afternoon till five). Nor is even that enough to see them all (as I would do) daily. So that even in this town (not to mention Frederica and all the smaller settlements) there are above five hundred sheep that are (almost) without a shepherd. He that is unjust must be unjust still; here is none to search out and lay hold on the *mollia tempora fandi* [favorable opportunities for talk] and to persuade him to save his soul alive. He that is a babe in Christ may be so still; here is none to attend the workings of grace upon his spirit, to feed him by degrees with food convenient for him, and gently lead him till he can follow the Lamb wherever he goeth. Does any err from the right way? Here is none to recall him; he may go on to seek death in the error of his life. Is any wavering? Here is none to confirm him. Is any falling? There is none to lift him up. What a single man can do is not seen or felt. Where are ye who are very zealous for the Lord of Hosts? Who will rise up with me against the wicked? Who will take God's part against the evildoers? Whose spirit is moved within him to prepare himself for publishing glad tidings to those on whom the Sun of Righteousness never yet arose, by labouring first for these his countrymen who are else without hope as well as without God in the world? Do you ask, What you shall have? Why, all you desire. Food to eat, raiment to put on, a place where to lay your head (such as your Lord had not) and a crown of life that fadeth not away! Do you seek means of building up yourselves in the knowledge and love of God? I call the God whom we serve to witness, I know of no place under heaven where there are more, or perhaps so many, as in this place. Does your heart burn within you to turn many others to righteousness? Behold, the whole land, thousands of thousands are before you! I will resign to any of you, all or any part of my charge. Choose what seemeth good in your own eyes.

The Rejected Suitor

Wesley's role as pastor in Savannah resulted in some tensions with his flock, to be sure, but it also provided the circumstances for him to cultivate a relationship with Sophia Christiana Hopkey, niece of the Chief Magistrate of the colony, Thomas Causton. They were quickly attracted to each other though she was fifteen years younger than Wesley.

Wesley's ideal of celibacy as "the more excellent way" was severely tested during the days and weeks after Wesley met Sophy. They spent many hours together in the mornings and evenings after Public Prayers. Sophy seems to have been more interested than John in a permanent relationship, although his heart was certainly not absolutely disinclined in that direction.

Through a series of misunderstandings, this amorous relationship suddenly ended in frustration and spite one year after their first meeting. Sophy married William Williamson on three days' notice—without the proper publishing of the banns, an omission that further irritated an already irate

Wesley. John's subsequent discovery of Sophy's "dissimulation" (i.e., deceitful two-timing) came several weeks after she had married Williamson. In the meantime, he wrote a narrative account of their acquaintance which tended always to give her the benefit of the doubt.

This particular journal extract, like the one in the section above, was never published in Wesley's lifetime—it was intended only for private use and was probably sent to his close friends or perhaps his family; it sounds very much like something he would have written for his mother. The story ends with Miss Sophy's marriage in March 1737 and was written two weeks later, although the extant manuscript copy was not transcribed until one year later (see Works, *18:365-488).*

1. At my first coming to Savannah, in the beginning of March 1736, I was determined to have no intimacy with any woman in America. Notwithstanding which, by the advice of my friends and in pursuance of my resolution to speak once a week at least to every communicant apart from the congregation, on March the 13th, I spoke to Miss Sophy Hopkey, who had communicated the Sunday before, and endeavoured to explain to her the nature and necessity of inward holiness. On the same subject I continued to speak to her once a week, but generally in the open air, and never alone.

2. I had a good hope that herein I acted with a single eye to the glory of God and the good of her soul. . . .

6. My friends believed it was now my duty to see her more frequently than before; in compliance with whose advice I accordingly talked with her once in two or three days. In all those conversations I was careful to speak only on things pertaining to God. But on July [23?], after I had talked with her for some time, I took her by the hand, and, before we parted, kissed her. And from this time, I fear there was a mixture in my intention, though I was not soon sensible of it. . . .

13. After giving her in writing, as she desired, a few advices relating to the presence of God, I left Frederica, September 2, not doubting but he who had begun a good work in her would establish her heart unblameable in holiness unto the day of the Lord Jesus. I then found I had not only a high esteem but a tender affection for her; but it was as for a sister and this I thought strictly due both to her piety and her friendship. . . .

18. In the evening we landed on an uninhabited island, made a

fire, supped, went to Prayers together, and then spread our sail over us on four stakes to keep off the night dews....

19. I can never be sensible enough of the exceeding goodness of God, both this night and the four following, all which we spent together, while none but the All-Seeing Eye observed us. I know that in me there was no strength; God knoweth if there were more in her. To him alone be the praise, that we were both withheld from anything which the world counts evil. Yet am I not thereby justified, but must justify God for whatever temporal evils may befall me on her account....

27. Monday, November 1, she was eighteen years old. And from the beginning of our intimate acquaintance till this day, I verily believe she used no guile. [At this point, Wesley fills five pages describing Sophy, the portrait perhaps revealing Wesley's idea of the virtuous person as much as (or more than) Sophy's actual qualities.] ...She was all life: active, diligent, indefatigable...; nor did she at all favour herself...; she was patient of labour, of cold, heat, wet, of badness or want of food, and of pain to an eminent degree...; though always neat, she was always plain...; she had a large share of common sense, and particularly of prudence;...she was so teachable in things either of a practical or speculative nature, so readily convinced of any error in her judgment or oversight in her behaviour...; as her humility was, so was her meekness; she seemed to have been born without anger...; she was a friend to humankind; to whoever was distressed, she was all sympathy, tenderness, compassion...; the utmost anguish never wrung from her a murmuring word: she saw the hand of God and was still...

34. Such was the woman, according to my closest observation, of whom I now began to be much afraid. My desire and design still was to live single. But how long it would continue, I knew not. I therefore consulted my friends whether it was not best to break off all intercourse with her immediately. Three months after, they told me, "It would have been best." But at this time they expressed themselves so ambiguously that I understood them to mean the direct contrary, viz., that I ought not to break it off. And accordingly she came to me (as had been agreed) every morning and evening....

36. This I began with a single eye. But it was not long before I found it a task too hard for me, to preserve the same intention with which I began, in such intimacy of conversation as ours was. My greatest

difficulty was, while I was teaching her French, when being obliged (as having but one book) to sit close to her, unless I prayed without ceasing, I could not avoid using some familiarity or other which was not needful. Sometimes I put my arm round her waist, sometimes took her by the hand, and sometimes kissed her. To put a short stop to this, on November 10, I ... told her, ... "I desire to converse, not as a lover, but a friend. And so I have often told you. But some parts of my behaviour might make you question my sincerity. Those I dislike, and have therefore resolved never to touch you more." She appeared surprised and deeply serious, but said not one word.

37. ...When [Phoebe Hird] asked her, "What if Mr. Wesley would have her," she smiled, looked down, and said nothing. I told Mr. Delamotte when we were alone that now I perceived myself to be in real danger since it was probable, even from that little circumstance, that the marriage stopped, not at her, but at me....

46. I was now more clear in my judgment every day. Beside that I believed her resolved never to marry, I was convinced it was not expedient for me.... And on Monday [February] 14, about seven in the morning, I told her in my own garden, "I am resolved, Miss Sophy, if I marry at all, not to do it till I have been among the Indians."...

51. Saturday, [February] 26. Calling at Mr. Causton's, she was there alone. And this was indeed an hour of trial. Her words, her eyes, her air, her every motion and gesture, were full of such a softness and sweetness! I know not what might have been the consequence, had I then but touched her hand. And how I avoided it, I know not. Surely God is over all!

52. ...I was so utterly disarmed, that this hour I should have engaged myself for life, had it not been for the full persuasion I had of her entire sincerity, in consequence of which I doubted not but she was resolved (as she had said) "Never to marry while she lived."

53. ...I told [Mr. Delamotte] I had no intention to marry her. He said I did not know my own heart; but he saw clearly it would come to that very soon unless I broke off all intercourse with her. I told him this was a point of great importance and therefore not to be determined suddenly. He said I ought to determine as soon as possible, for I was losing ground daily. I felt what he said to be true and therefore easily consented to set aside the next day for that purpose. ... At length we agreed to appeal to the Searcher of Hearts.

I accordingly made three lots. In one was writ, "Marry"; in the second, "Think not of it this year." After we had prayed to God to "give us a perfect lot," Mr. Delamotte drew the third, in which were these words: "Think of it no more." Instead of the agony I had reason to expect, I was enabled to say cheerfully, "Thy will be done." . . .

55. On Monday the 7th [of March, Miss Sophy said,] "Well, I find what you have often said is true. There is no trusting any but a Christian. And for my part I am resolved never to trust anyone again who is not so." I looked upon her, and should have said too much had we had a moment longer. But in the instant, Mrs. Causton called us in. So I was once more "snatched as a brand out of the fire."

56. Tuesday, March 8. Miss Sophy breakfasting with me, . . . I said, "I hear Mr. Williamson pays his addresses to you. Is it true?" She said, after a little pause, "If it were not, I would have told you so. . . . I have no inclination for him." I said, "Miss Sophy, if you deceive me, I shall scarce ever believe anyone again." She looked up at me and answered with a smile, "You will never have that reason for distrusting anyone. I shall never deceive you." When she was going away, she turned back and said, "Of one thing, sir, be assured, I will never take any step in anything of importance without first consulting you." . . .

59. The next morning, Wednesday, March 9, about ten, I called on Mrs. Causton. She said, "[Sophy] desires you would publish the Banns of Marriage between her and Mr. Williamson on Sunday. . . . But if you have any objection to it, pray speak. Speak to her . . . ; she will be very glad to hear anything Mr. Wesley has to say. . . .

60. I doubted whether all this were not artifice, merely designed to quicken me. But though I was uneasy at the very thought of her marrying one who I believed would make her very unhappy, yet I could not resolve to save her from him by marrying her myself. Besides, I reasoned thus: "Either she is engaged or not. If she is, I would not have her if I might; if not, there is nothing in this show which ought to alter my preceding resolution."

61. Thus was I saved purely by my ignorance; for though I did doubt, I would not believe. . . .

68. . . . The next morning she set out for Purrysburg, and on Saturday, March 12, 1737, was married there, this being the day which completed the year from my first speaking to her!

[Wesley's diary entry for Wednesday, March 9, 1737, the day he discovered Miss Sophy was to marry Mr. Williamson:]

4 Private prayer; prayers; diary. 4.45 Private prayer. 5 Meditated; Public Prayers. 6 Coffee, religious talk. 6.30 Clement. 7 Necessary talk (religious) with Mrs. Andrews. 7.45 With Mrs. Bush, necessary talk (religious). 8.30 Clement. 9.45 Logic. 10 Mrs. Causton's, necessary talk with her; Miss Sophy to be married! 11 Amazed, in pain, prayed, meditated. 12 At the lot, necessary talk (religious) with her; I quite distressed! 1 Necessary talk (religious); confounded! 2 Took leave of her. 2.30 At home, could not pray! 3 Tried to pray, lost, sunk! 4 Bread; religious talk with Delamotte; little better. 5 Mr. Causton came, necessary talk, tea. 6 Kempis; Germans; easier! 7 Public Prayers. 8 Miss Sophy, etc. 8.30 Necessary talk (religious) with her. 8.45 With Delamotte, prayers.

No such day since I first saw the sun!
O deal tenderly with thy servant!
Let me not see such another!

The Wrongfully Accused Defendant

When Wesley discovered in April that Sophy had in fact been "two-timing" him for some weeks before her "sudden" turnabout marriage, he exercised his prerogative as parish priest. He warned her that such sinful behavior as she had exhibited (including also her frequent absence from Holy Communion) would force him to exclude her from the Sacrament unless she confessed her sin. His action was a proper, though blatantly spiteful application of the directions in the Prayer Book. The inevitable confrontation at the altar occurred. Wesley publicly repelled Miss Sophy from the Table, and thereby unleashed a floodtide of events that quite literally swept him out of the colony and back to England before the legal implications of many of his controversial actions as a pastor, priest, and suitor could be fully resolved in the colonial court.

Sophy's husband, Mr. Williamson, brought charges against Wesley to a grand jury that returned ten "true bills of indictment" against Wesley. As the jury deliberations were taking place in August 1737, Wesley drew up a legal brief to use as a part of his defense in the expected trial. The manuscript of his "Case," as he called it in his diary, sketches in detail the development of his relationship with Miss Sophy, drawn in such a fashion as to portray his actions and intentions as the completely innocent acts of a diligent priest, good pastor, and trusting friend.

The outline of his defense was (1) that he, Wesley, had had no designs on Miss Sophy other than to preserve her soul from various influences in the colony and to protect her happiness in whatever ways he could; (2) that Sophy had been deceitful and misleading in many of her words and actions toward Wesley; and (3) that Mr. Causton (who was Sophy's legal guardian and who also presided over the grand jury) was not only a silent party with the prosecution, but in fact had been, with his wife, the primary instigator of false charges against Wesley and, through his "artful disingenuity," had been just as deceitful as his niece in the whole affair, since Causton had allowed his household to become a sounding board for many of the charges trumped up against Wesley.

From the opening sentence, Wesley's "Case," intended to be read in the courtroom, constructs the picture of a long-suffering, ill-used servant of God (and friend of the Trustees) who has been misled by the wiles of a beautiful young woman, confused by the matchmaking of her two-faced aunt, and wrongfully treated by the maliciousness of the political powers in the colony. Wesley claimed the proceedings against him were illegal since most of the charges were of an ecclesiastical nature and should not be tried in a civil court (see the list of indictments on page 117). Wesley also wanted to make it clear, on record in the courtroom, that it was Mr. Causton's distrust of the Trustees' supposedly "dilatory manner" that made the magistrate unwilling to submit the case to the proper authorities. See Works, *18:365-543.*

1. It was not my desire, but the desire of the Trustees, disappointed of another minister, which induced me to take charge of Savannah, till I could pursue my first design. And [the] very day I entered on this charge I told you that offences would come; indeed I expected greater, long before this day.

2. In March 1736, observing Miss Sophy Hopkey to be a constant communicant, I thought it my duty to speak to her apart from the congregation; I did so from that time once a week....

3. ...In June following, [Mrs. Causton] told me, "Sir, you want a woman to take care of your house." I said, "But women, madam, are scarce in Georgia. Where shall I get one?" She answered, "I have two here. Take either of them.... Take Phily [Sophy], she is serious enough." I said, "You are not in earnest, madam!" She said, "Indeed, sir, I am; take her to you and do what you will with her."...

5. Friday, August 13. I came to Frederica, where Mr. Oglethorpe gave me a large account of Miss Sophy and desired me to be with her as much as I could, "Because she was in deep distress."

6. The time I was with her was spent chiefly in reading. The books I now read and explained to her were first, *A Collection of Prayers,* next *Tracts on the Presence of God,* and then Dr. Cave's *Primitive Christianity....*

9. Tuesday, October 12, about five in the evening, being to set out for Frederica the next day, I asked Mr. Causton what commands he had to Miss Sophy? Some of his words were as follows: "The girl will never be easy till she is married."...I asked, "Sir, what directions do you give me with regard to her?" He said, "I give her up to you. Do what you will with her. Take her into your own hands. Promise her what you will; I will make it good."

18. The time she spent at my house was spent thus: immediately after breakfast we all joined in prayer. She was then alone till eight. I taught her French between eight and nine, and at nine we joined in prayer again. She then either read or wrote French till ten. In the evening I read to her and some others, several parts of Ephrem Syrus, and afterwards Dean Young's and Mr. Reeves' Sermons. We always concluded our reading with a psalm.

20. ...On Thursday, February 3,...I hinted at a desire to marry her, but made no direct proposal. For indeed it was only a sudden thought which had not the consent of my own mind. Yet I verily believe had she closed with me at that time, my judgment would have been overruled. But she said she thought it was best for clergymen not to be incumbered with worldly cares; and that it was best for her too, and she was resolved never to marry while she lived. I made no reply, nor used any argument to induce her to alter her resolution....

22. If it be asked, why I did not propose it, though I had so great a regard for her, I answer, for three reasons chiefly: (1) Because I did not think myself strong enough to bear the temptations of a married state; (2) because I feared it would have obstructed the design on which I came, the going among the Indians; and (3) because I thought her resolved not to marry....

30. [On March 9, 1737,] about ten, I called on Mrs. Causton. She said, "Sir, Mr. Causton and I are exceedingly obliged to you for all the pains you have taken about Sophy. And so is Sophy too; and she desires you would publish the banns of marriage between her and

Mr. Williamson on Sunday." She added, "Sir, you don't seem well-pleased. Have you any objections to it?" I answered, "Madam, I don't seem to be awake. Surely I am in a dream." She said, "They agreed on it between themselves last night, and later Mr. Williamson asked Mr. Causton's and my consent, which we gave him. But if you have any objection to it, pray speak. Speak to her. She is at the lot. Go to her. She will be very glad to hear anything Mr. Wesley has to say...."

31. If I may speak what was then the inmost thought of my heart, it was that all this was mere artifice, purely designed to quicken me; and that as much engaged as she was, had I only said, "I am willing to marry her myself," that engagement would have vanished away. But though I was very uneasy at the very mention of her marrying Mr. Williamson, who I believed would make her thoroughly miserable, yet I could not resolve to save her from him by marrying her myself. This was the only price I could not pay, and which therefore I never so much as hinted at in any of those following conversations wherein I so earnestly endeavoured to prevent that unhappy union....

[On July 5] I sent the following note to Mrs. Williamson, which I wrote in the most mild and friendly manner I could, both in pursuance of my resolution to proceed with all mildness, and because (Mrs. Causton told me) she was so much grieved already.

> If the sincerity of friendship is best to be known from the painful offices, then there could not be a stronger proof of mine than that I gave you on Sunday, except this which I am going to give you now and which you may perhaps equally misinterpret....
>
> In your present behaviour I dislike, (1) your neglect of half the Public Service ... (2) your neglect of fasting ... (3) your neglect of almost half the opportunities of communicating which you have lately had.
>
> But these things are small in comparison of what I dislike in your past behaviour. For (1) you told me over and over you had entirely conquered your inclination for Mr. Mellichamp. Yet at the very time you spoke, you had not conquered it. (2) You told me frequently you had no design to marry Mr. Williamson. Yet at the very time you spoke, you had that design. (3) In order to conceal both these things from me, you went though a course of deliberate dissimulation. O how fallen! How changed! Surely there was a time when in Miss Sophy's lips there was no guile....

58. On Sunday evening [August 7], Mrs. Williamson, in conversation with Mrs. Burnside, expressed much anger at my repelling her from the Holy Communion. Mrs. Burnside told her, "You was much to blame after receiving that letter from Mr. Wesley, to offer yourself at the Table before you had cleared yourself to him. But you may easily put an end to this by going to Mr. Wesley now and clearing yourself of what you are charged with." She replied, "No, I will not show such a meanness of spirit as to speak to him about it myself, but somebody else shall."

59. The next day, August 8, the following warrant was issued out by Mr. Recorder:

> To all constables, tithingmen, and others whom these may concern:
>
> You, and each of you, are hereby required, to take the body of John Westly [*sic*], Clerk, and bring him before one of the bailiffs of the said town to answer the complaint of William Williamson and Sophia his wife, for defaming the said Sophia and refusing to administer to her the Sacrament of the Lord's Supper in a public congregation without cause; by which the said William Williamson is damaged one thousand pounds sterling.

65. I was now the constant subject of conversation at Mr. Causton's, where the account given of me to all company was, that I "was a sly hypocrite, a seducer, a betrayer of my trust, an egregious liar and dissembler, an endeavourer to alienate the affections of married women from their husbands, a drunkard, the keeper of a bawdy-house, an admitter of whores, whore-mongers, drunkards, ay and of murderers and spillers of blood to the Lord's Table, a repeller of others out of mere spite and malice, a refuser of Christian burial to Christians, a murderer of poor infants by plunging them into cold water, a Papist, if not a Jesuit, or rather, an introducer of a new religion which as nobody ever heard of, a proud priest whose view it was to be a bishop, a spiritual tyrant, an arbitrary usurper of illegal power, a false teacher enjoining others under peril of damnation to do what I would omit myself to serve a turn, a denier of the king's supremacy, an enemy to the colony, a sower of sedition, a public incendiary, a disturber of the peace of families, a raiser of uproars, a ringleader of mutiny"; in a word, such a monster, "that the people would rather die than suffer him to go on thus."

66. Coming home in the evening, I found Mr. Causton with Mr. Parker and Mr. Jones at my house. He broke out, "Wesley, I am ashamed of this. I could not have believed it of thee. Why is all this uproar?...I have been insulted in the streets; I have been called Judas to my face. And why must one of my family be the first to be repelled from the Holy Communion?" He added many reproaches and upbraidings. The sum of my answer was, "I am sorry if there has been any disturbance and will do all that in me lies to preserve peace and the respect due to all Magistrates, whom I reverence as the ministers of God."...

68. After he went, I writ the following note, the second and last proposal of accommodation I have made:

> To Mrs. Sophia Williamson: At Mr. Causton's request I write once more. The rules whereby I proceed are these: "So many as intend to be partakers of the Holy Communion shall signify their names to the curate at least some time the day before." This you did not do....
>
> If you offer yourself at the Lord's Table on Sunday, I will advertise you (as I have done more than once) wherein you "have done wrong"; and when you have "openly declared yourself to have truly repented," I will administer to you the mysteries of God....

Mrs. Williamson insisted she had done nothing amiss. Mr. Causton said, "I am the person that am injured, I am ill used; the affront is offered to me, and I will espouse the cause of my niece. It will be the worse thing Mr. Wesley ever did in his life, to fix upon my family....I am injured, and I will have satisfaction, if it is to be had in the world." "And I," said Mr. Williamson, "will never leave him to my life's end."

The Ostracized Reporter

Wesley explains his hasty retreat from Georgia in another pair of manuscript journals that are less selective in content. This version of his story provided the basis for the published "extract" of his Georgia journal in 1740 (see page 113). The published version differs somewhat from both the manuscripts. The portion in brackets was omitted from the published version. The portion in parentheses is in the published version but not in the manuscripts. See Works, 18:566-69.

Friday, October 7. I consulted my friends whether God did not call me to (return to) England [not on my own account, but for the sake of the poor people]. (The reason for which I left it had now no force, there being no possibility, as yet, of instructing the Indians; neither had I, as yet, found or heard of any Indians on the continent of America who had the least desire of being instructed. And as to Savannah, having never engaged myself, either by word or letter, to stay there a day longer than I should judge convenient, nor ever taken charge of the people any otherwise than as in my passage to the heathen, I looked upon myself to be fully discharged therefrom by the vacating of that design. Besides, there was a probability of doing more service to that unhappy people in England than I could do in Georgia, by representing, without fear or favour to the Trustees, the real state the colony was in....I laid the thoughts of it aside for the present, being persuaded that when the time was come, God would "make the way plain before my face."...)

Tuesday, November 22. (...I again consulted my friends, who agreed with me that the time we looked for was now come....)

Friday, December 2. I proposed to set out for [Port Royal] (Carolina) about noon, the tide then serving. But about ten the magistrates sent for me and told me I must not go out of the province [till I had entered into recognizance to appear at the Court] for I had not answered the allegations laid against me. I replied, "I have appeared at [four] (six or seven) Courts successively in order to answer them. But I was not suffered so to do, when I desired it time after time." [But as they had now referred them to the Trustees, to the Trustees I desired to go.] Then they said, however, I must not go, unless I would give security to answer those allegations at their Court....I then told them plainly, "Sir [all this is mere trifling], you use me very ill, and so you do the Trustees. I will give neither any bond nor any bail at all. You know your business, and I know mine."

In the afternoon the magistrates published an order requiring all the officers and sentinels to prevent my going out of the province, and forbidding any person to assist me so to do. Being now only a prisoner at large in a place where I knew by experience every day would give fresh opportunity to procure evidence of words I never spoke and actions I never did, I saw clearly the hour was come for [me to fly for my life,] leaving this place; and as soon as evening prayers were over, about eight o'clock, the tide then serving, I shook off the dust of my feet and left Georgia, after having preached the gospel there [with much weakness indeed and many infirmities] (not as I ought, but as I was able), one year and nearly nine months.

CHAPTER 5

Theological and Spiritual Pilgrim

The year 1738 was another crucial period in Wesley's life. He began the year in the mid-Atlantic, on board the ship Samuel returning from his frustrating mission to Georgia. During the subsequent spring and summer, he came to know and feel the "assurance of faith in its 'true' sense" (according to his Moravian friends). During the autumn he became acquainted with the work of the Holy Spirit in the Great Awakening in New England through the writings of Jonathan Edwards. Shortly thereafter, he rediscovered in the Homilies of the Church of England an understanding of faith and salvation nearly identical to what he had been putting together for himself for the past decade or more.

Three times during this period Wesley paused to analyze his spiritual condition and evaluate his spiritual progress. In early June, he wrote an account of his "Aldersgate experience, familiar to many readers of Wesley's journal. It represents his outlook almost immediately after his 'heart was strangely warmed.'" Just five months earlier in the mid-Atlantic, he had written an autobiographical summary that similarly reviewed his spiritual progress. After the year was over, he again reflected on his spiritual condition in a summary later published in his Journal. The reflections in these three accounts help us measure and put in perspective the significance of the events of this important year in Wesley's continuing spiritual and theological development.

One Tossed About:
Theological Autobiography, January 1738

Wesley's experience in Georgia tested his self-understanding in several ways, not least of which was theological. His contacts with the German Pietists among the colonists (Moravians and Salzburgers) had made him very much aware that his own religious faith was inadequate in times of stress. At this point in his life, he still tended to treat the question of salvation as primarily an intellectual, theological problem. His Oxford years had instilled in him the value of tracing through a problem logically, in written form. Thus, as Wesley's ship approached the shores of England on his return from Georgia, he penned what amounts to a scholastic exercise, a genesis problematica, *summarizing his plight in a survey of his doctrinal development up to that time.*

Wesley's main question was that of the rich young ruler, "What must I do to be saved?" At this time, Wesley saw the problem as twofold: what is the proper understanding and relationship of faith and works, and upon what authority should a correct theological answer be based? He was still working on the assumption that his assurance of salvation (knowing he was a Christian) was a sort of intellectual confidence that depended upon holding a correct set of beliefs, grounded upon the appropriately ranked authorities (Scripture, tradition, reason) and resulting in a proper set of actions. His hope for salvation was still placed in a trust that his own sincerity would suffice, that he was in fact "doing the best he could," as Kempis had instructed in the Imitatio Christi *("Fac quod in te est," I.vii.2). He had only recently been introduced to the idea that faith and hope might rest on a more personal appropriation of the atoning work of Christ, experienced through the Holy Spirit. But there is not yet even a hint of that perspective in this shipboard survey of his condition. See* Works, *18:212-13.*

Μὴ κλυδωνιζόμενοι παντὶ ἀνέμῳ τῆς διδαχῆς
["Not tossed to and fro by every wind of doctrine"; cf. Eph. 4:14]

91

Different views of Christianity are given (1) by the Scripture, (2) the Papists, (3) the Lutherans and Calvinists, (4) the English Divines, (5) the Essentialist Nonjurors, (6) the Mystics.

January 25, 1738

1. For many years have I been tossed about by various winds of doctrine. I asked long ago, What must I do to be saved? The Scripture answered, "Keep the Commandments. Believe, hope, love. Follow after these tempers till thou hast fully attained, that is, till death, by all those outward works and means which God hath appointed, by walking as Christ walked."

2. I was early warned against laying, as the Papists do, too much stress either on outward works or on a faith without works, which, as it does not include, so it will never lead to, true hope or charity. Nor am I sensible that to this hour I have laid too much stress on either, having from the very beginning valued both faith, the means of grace, and good works, not on their own account, but as believing God, who had appointed them, would by them bring me in due time to the mind that was in Christ.

3. But before God's time was come, I fell among some Lutheran and Calvinist authors, whose confused and indigested accounts magnified faith to such an amazing size that it quite hid all the rest of the commandments. I did not then see that this was the natural effect of their overgrown fear of [or zeal against] Popery; being so terrified with the cry of "merit and good works" that they plunged at once into the other extreme. In this labyrinth I was utterly lost, not being able to find out what the error was, nor yet to reconcile this uncouth hypothesis either with Scripture or common sense.

4. The English writers, such as Bishop Beveridge, Bishop Taylor, and Mr. Nelson, a little relieved me from these well-meaning, wrong-headed Germans. Their accounts of Christianity I could easily see to be, in the main, consistent both with reason and Scripture. Only, when they interpreted Scripture in different ways, I was often much at a loss. And again, there was one thing much insisted on in Scripture, the unity of the Church, which none of them I thought clearly explained or strongly inculcated.

5. But it was not long before Providence brought me to those who showed me a sure rule for interpreting Scripture, viz., *Consensus veterum:* "Quod ab omnibus, quod ubique, quod semper creditum"

[The consensus of antiquity: "What is believed by everyone, everywhere, and always"]. At the same time they sufficiently insisted upon a due regard to the One Church at all times and in all places. Nor was it long before I bent the bow too far the other way, (1) by making antiquity a coordinate (rather than subordinate) rule with Scripture; (2) by admitting several doubtful writings as undoubted evidences of antiquity; (3) by extending antiquity too far, even to the middle or end of the fourth century; (4) by believing more practices to have been universal in the ancient Church than ever were so; (5) by not considering that the decrees of one provincial synod could bind only that province, and the decrees of a general synod only those provinces whose representatives met therein; (6) by not considering that most of those decrees were adapted to particular times and occasions, and consequently when those occasions ceased, must cease to bind even those provinces.

6. These considerations insensibly stole upon me as I grew acquainted with the mystic writers, whose noble descriptions of union with God and internal religion made everything else appear mean, flat, and insipid. But in truth, they made good works appear so too, yea, and faith itself, and what not? These gave me an entire new view of religion, nothing like any I had had before. But alas! It was nothing like that religion which Christ and his Apostles lived and taught. I had a plenary dispensation from all the commands of God. The form ran thus, "Love is all; all the commands beside are only means of love. You must choose those which you feel are means to you and use them as long as they are so." Thus were all the bands burst at once. And though I could never fully come into this, nor contentedly omit what God enjoined, yet I know not how, I fluctuated between obedience and disobedience. I had no heart, no vigour, no zeal in obeying; continually doubting, whether I was right or wrong, and never out of perplexities and entanglements. Nor can I at this hour give a distinct account, how or when I came a little back toward the right way. Only, my present sense is this, All the other enemies of Christianity are triflers; the mystics are the most dangerous of all its enemies. They stab it in the vitals and its most serious professors are most likely to fall by them. May I praise Him who hath snatched me out of this fire likewise, by warning all others, that it is set on fire of hell.

The Assured Conqueror:
Spiritual Autobiography, May 1738

Wesley's desire to experience "assurance" of his salvation was fulfilled in May 1738, three days after his brother Charles had felt "a strange palpitation of heart" on Pentecost Sunday (see page 259). Within just a few numbered days, John wrote an account of these events, recounting in eighteen numbered paragraphs the important steps in his life that had led up to this experience, and describing his "new" state of self-knowledge. He read this narrative to his mother when he visited her in early June (see page 109). Wesley was able now to conceive of himself as having truly met the criteria necessary for calling oneself a "Christian," as defined by his Moravian friends. He began to proclaim their doctrine as his own, namely that one is not a Christian until he or she has experienced assurance, a doctrine that marked his preaching for several years to come, but that he later altered.

That Wesley felt this experience was pivotal in his spiritual development at this time is obvious in the document itself. That he continued to think so, in some qualified sense, for at least some months is also evident from his own writings (see his letter to brother Samuel, April 4, 1739). That he eventually abandoned his hard line on the necessity of assurance as a prerequisite for salvation comes through very clearly in the minutes of conference as early as 1744 and in letters to his brother Charles (e.g., July 31, 1747). That he later began to qualify some of his own self-analysis from this earlier period is very clear from subsequent alterations he made in the published text of the Journal *itself (viz., the* errata *sheet in 1775). That his seasoned view could see the whole train of events with a sense of humorous self-criticism is evident in a comment to a friend, Melville Horne, in his old age: "When fifty years ago my brother Charles and I, in [the] simplicity of our hearts, told the good people of England that unless they knew their sins were forgiven they were under the wrath and curse of God, I marvel, Melville, they did not stone us!" (Southey, 1:295). See* Works, *18:242-50.*

What occurred on Wednesday the 24th [of May 1738], I think best to relate at large, after premising what may make it the better understood. Let him that cannot receive it ask of the Father of lights that He would give more light to him and me.

1. I believe, till I was about ten years old I had not sinned away that "washing of the Holy Ghost" which was given me in baptism; having been strictly educated and carefully taught that I could only be saved

by universal obedience, by keeping all the commandments of God; in the meaning of which I was diligently instructed. And those instructions, so far as they respected outward duties and sins, I gladly received and often thought of. But all that was said to me of inward obedience or holiness I neither understood nor remembered. So that I was indeed as ignorant of the true meaning of the law as I was of the gospel of Christ.

2. The next six or seven years were spent at school, where, outward restraints being removed, I was much more negligent than before, even of outward duties, and almost continually guilty of outward sins, which I knew to be such, though they were not scandalous in the eye of the world. However, I still read the Scriptures, and said my prayers morning and evening. And what I now hoped to be saved by, was (1) *not being so bad as other people;* (2) *having still a kindness for religion;* and (3) *reading the Bible, going to church, and saying my prayers.*

3. Being removed to the University for five years, I still said my prayers both in public and in private, and read, with the Scriptures, several other books of religion, especially comments on the New Testament. Yet I had not all this while so much as a notion of inward holiness; nay, went on habitually, and (for the most part) very contentedly, in some or other known sin....I cannot well tell what I hoped to be saved by now, when I was continually sinning against the little light I had, unless by those transient fits of what many divines taught me to call repentance.

4. When I was about twenty-two, my father pressed me to enter into holy orders. At the same time, the providence of God directing me to Kempis' *Christian Pattern,* I began to see that true religion was seated in the heart and that God's law extended to all our thoughts as well as words and actions.... I began to alter the whole form of my conversation and to set in earnest upon *a new life....* I began to aim at and pray for inward holiness. So that now, *doing so much, and living so good a life,* I doubted not but I was a good Christian.

5. Removing soon after to another College, I executed a resolution which I was before convinced was of the utmost importance, shaking off at once all my trifling acquaintance. I began to see more and more the value of time. I applied myself closer to study. I watched more carefully against actual sins; I advised others to be religious, according to that scheme of religion by which I modelled my own life. But meeting now with Mr. Law's *Christian Perfection* and

Serious Call (although I was much offended at many parts of both, yet) they convinced me more than ever of the exceeding height and breadth and depth of the law of God. The light flowed in so mightily upon my soul that everything appeared in a new view. I cried to God for help and resolved not to prolong the time of obeying Him as I had never done before. And by my continued *endeavour to keep His whole law,* inward and outward, *to the utmost of my power,* I was persuaded that I should be accepted of him, and that I was even then in a state of salvation.

6. In 1730, I began visiting the prisons, assisting the poor and sick in town, and doing what other good I could by my presence or my little fortune to the bodies and souls of all men. To this end I abridged myself of all superfluities, and many that are called necessaries of life. I soon became a by-word for so doing....I diligently strove against all sin....I carefully used, both in public and in private, all the means of grace at all opportunities. I omitted no occasion of doing good....Yet when, after continuing some years in this course, I apprehended myself to be near death, I could not find that all this gave me any comfort or any assurance of acceptance with God....

7. Soon after, a contemplative man convinced me still more than I was convinced before, that outward works are nothing, being alone; and in several conversations instructed me how to pursue inward holiness, or a union of the soul with God. But even of his instructions (though I then received them as the words of God) I cannot but now observe...these were, in truth, as much *my own works* as visiting the sick or clothing the naked; and the "union with God" thus pursued was as really *my own righteousness* as any I had before pursued under another name.

In this *refined* way of trusting to my own works and my own righteousness (so zealously inculcated by the Mystic writers) I dragged on heavily, finding no comfort or help therein till the time of my leaving England. On shipboard, however, I was again active in outward works; where it pleased God of His free mercy to give me twenty-six of the Moravian brethren for companions, who endeavoured to show me "a more excellent way." But I understood it not at first. I was too learned and too wise....

9. All the time I was at Savannah I was thus "beating the air." Being ignorant of the righteousness of Christ, which, by a living faith in

Him, bringeth salvation "to every one that believeth," I sought to establish my own righteousness, and so laboured in the fire all my days. I was now properly "under the law.". . .

10. In this vile, abject state of bondage to sin, I was indeed fighting continually, but not conquering. . . . During this whole struggle between nature and grace (which had now continued above ten years) I had many remarkable returns to prayer, especially when I was in trouble; I had many sensible comforts, which are indeed no other than short anticipations of the life of faith. But I was still "under the law," not "under grace" (the state most who are called Christians are content to live and die in); for I was only "striving with," not "freed from sin." Neither had I "the witness of the Spirit with my spirit," and indeed could not; for I "sought it not by faith, but as it were by the works of the law."

11. In my return to England, January 1738, being in imminent danger of death, and very uneasy on that account, I was strongly convinced that the cause of that uneasiness was unbelief, and that the gaining a true, living faith was the "one thing needful" for me. But still I fixed not this faith on its right object: I meant only faith in God, not faith in or through Christ. Again, I knew not that I was *wholly void of this faith;* but only thought *I had not enough* of it. So that when Peter Böhler, whom God prepared for me as soon as I came to London, affirmed of true faith in Christ (which is but one) that it had those two fruits inseparably attending it, "dominion over sin and constant peace from a sense of forgiveness," I was quite amazed and looked upon it as a new gospel. If this was so, it was clear I had not faith. But I was not willing to be convinced of this. Therefore I disputed with all my might, and laboured to prove that faith might be where these were not; . . . I well saw no one could (in the nature of things) have such a sense of forgiveness and not *feel* it. But I felt it not. If, then, there was no faith without this, all my pretensions to faith dropped at once.

12. When I met Peter Böhler again, he consented to put the dispute upon the issue which I desired, viz., Scripture and experience. I first consulted the Scripture. But when I set aside the glosses of men and simply considered the words of God, comparing them together and endeavouring to illustrate the obscure by the plainer passages, I found they all made against me, and was forced to retreat to my last hold, "that experience would never agree with the *literal interpretation*

of those Scriptures. Nor could I therefore allow it to be true till I found some living witnesses of it." He replied he could show me such at any time; if I desired it, the next day. And accordingly the next day he came again with three others, all of whom testified of their own personal experience that a true, living faith in Christ is inseparable from a sense of pardon for all past, and freedom from all present sins. They added with one mouth that this faith was the gift, the free gift of God, and that He would surely bestow it upon every soul who earnestly and perseveringly sought it. I was now thoroughly convinced. And, by the grace of God, I resolved to seek it unto the end, (1) by absolutely renouncing all dependence in whole or in part upon *my own* works or righteousness, on which I had really grounded my hope of salvation, though I knew it not, from my youth up; (2) by adding to "the constant use of all the *other* means of grace," continual prayer for this very thing: justifying, saving faith, a full reliance on the blood of Christ shed for *me;* a trust in him as *my* Christ, as *my* sole justification, sanctification, and redemption.

13. I continued thus to seek it (though with strange indifference, dullness, and coldness, and unusually frequent relapses into sin) till Wednesday, May 24. I think it was about five this morning that I opened my Testament on those words, Τὰ μέγιστα ἡμίν καὶ τίμια ἐπαγγέλματα δεδώρηται, ἵνα γένησθε θείας κοινωνοὶ φύσεως ["There are given unto us exceeding great and precious promises, even that ye should be partakers of the divine nature" 2 Peter 1:4]. Just as I went out, I opened it again on those words, "Thou are not far from the kingdom of God." In the afternoon I was asked to go to St. Paul's. The anthem was, "Out of the deep have I called unto Thee, O Lord. Lord, hear my voice. . . . "

14. In the evening I went very unwillingly to a society in Aldersgate Street, where one was reading Luther's Preface to the Epistle to the Romans. About a quarter before nine, while he was describing the change which God works in the heart through faith in Christ, I felt my heart strangely warmed. I felt I did trust in Christ, Christ alone for salvation, and an assurance was given me that He had taken away *my* sins, even *mine,* and saved *me* from the law of sin and death.

15. I began to pray with all my might for those who had in a more especial manner despitefully used me and persecuted me. I then testified openly to all there what I now first felt in my heart. But it was not long before the enemy suggested, "This cannot be faith; for

where is thy joy?" Then was I taught that *peace and victory over sin are essential to faith in the Captain of our salvation, but that, as to the transports of joy* that usually attend the beginning of it, especially in those who have mourned deeply, *God sometimes giveth, sometimes withholdeth them, according to the counsels of His own will.*

16. After my return home, I was much buffeted with temptations; but cried out, and they fled away. They returned again and again. I as often lifted up my eyes, and he "sent me help from his holy place." And herein I found the difference between this and my former state chiefly consisted. I was striving, yea, fighting with all my might under the law as well as under grace. But then I was sometimes, if not often, conquered; now, I was always conqueror.

The Humbled Doubter

Many were surprised at the claims that John began making after his "heart-warming" experience of assurance. Wesley's friend, Mrs. Hutton, wrote to his brother Samuel that very weekend saying that John "seems to be turned a wild enthusiast or fanatic, [telling] the people that five days before he was not a Christian." To this she had responded, "If you was not a Christian ever since I knew you, you was a great hypocrite, for you made us all believe you was one" (see page 261).

The Journal *tells the continuing story of John's quest for lasting peace and joy in his newfound state, a story punctuated by frequently recurring moments of despair: "I waked in peace, but not in joy"; "I felt a kind of soreness in my heart, so that I found my wound was not fully healed" (see page 188).*

As the year 1739 began, John noted in his diary, "writ account of myself." This summary of his spiritual state, written nearly a year after his shipboard self-analysis and seven months after his experience at Aldersgate, lays his spiritual quandary before the public eye, because it soon became part of his published Journal *(see* Works, *19:29-31).*

Thursday, [January] 4. One who had had the form of godliness many years wrote the following reflections:

My friends affirm *I am mad,* because I said "I was not a Christian a year ago." I affirm I am not a Christian now. Indeed, what I might have been I know not, had I been faithful to the grace then given, when, expecting nothing less, I received such a sense of the forgiveness of my sins as till then I never knew. But that I am not a Christian at this day I as assuredly know as that Jesus is the Christ.

For a Christian is one who has the fruits of the Spirit of Christ, which (to mention no more) are love, peace, joy. But these I have not. I have not any love of God. I do not love either the Father or the Son. Do you ask how do I know whether I love God? I answer by another question, How do you know whether you love me? Why, as you know whether you are hot or cold. You *feel* this moment that you do or do not love me. And I *feel* this moment I do not love God; which therefore I *know* because I *feel* it. There is no word more proper, more clear, or more strong.

And I know it also by St. John's plain rule, "If any man love the world, the love of the Father is not in him." For I love the world. I desire the things of the world, some or other of them, and have done all my life. I have always placed some part of my happiness in some or other of the things that are seen. Particularly in meat and drink, and in the company of those I loved. For many years I have been, yea, and still am, hankering after a happiness in loving and being loved by one or another. And in these I have from time to time taken more pleasure than in God. . . .

Again, joy in the Holy Ghost I have not. I have now and then some starts of joy in God. But it is not *that* joy. For it is not abiding. Neither is it greater than I have had on some worldly occasions. So that I can in no wise be said to "rejoice evermore," much less to "rejoice with joy unspeakable and full of glory."

Yet again, I have not "the peace of God"; *that* peace peculiarly so called. The peace I have may be accounted for on natural principles. I have health, strength, friends, a competent fortune, and a composed, cheerful temper. Who would not have a sort of peace in such circumstances? But I have none which can with any propriety be called "a peace which passeth all understanding."

From hence I conclude (and let all the "saints of the world" hear, that whereinsoever they boast they may be found even as I), though I have given, and do give, all my goods to feed the poor, I am not a Christian. Though I have endured hardship, though I have in all things denied myself and taken up my cross, I am not a Christian. My works are nothing, my sufferings are nothing; I have not the fruits of the Spirit of Christ. Though I have constantly used all the means of grace for twenty years, I am not a Christian.

CHAPTER 6

The Extra-Parochial Preacher

The year 1739 is a watershed in Wesley's spiritual and vocational self-understanding. His religious struggles of the previous years had brought him to a point where his personal affirmation of faith was accompanied by a personal assurance of faith. What was lacking in his continuing trial of spirit was any constant sense of confidence in his salvation and any strong public affirmation of the authenticity of his faith. He was now barred from preaching in many of the pulpits he had frequently occupied. The Moravians, who had helped him take some of the crucial steps in his spiritual pilgrimage, spurned him from the Lord's Table while he was visiting them in Germany. To them, he seemed still to be homo perturbatus *(a troubled person), because he did not exhibit that sure sense of confidence and joy they felt was a necessary mark of a valid faith. Even his rediscovery in the fall of 1738 that the Homilies of the Church of England outlined the precise understanding of salvation that he had been formulating for at least a decade was not fully satisfying; the faith described therein—a sure trust and confidence—still seemed in many ways to elude him.*

A crucial turning point seems to have occurred in early April 1739, when he moved from a somewhat personal and parochial sort of ministry to a more public and evangelical sense of vocation. In his Journal *Wesley introduced what he called "this new period of my life" by reprinting a letter he had written to his father in 1734 (see page 71). In it he had explained that his decision to remain at Oxford was based on the principle that whatever life best promoted holiness in himself would not only tend most to the glory of God but would thus also promote holiness in others. He had acknowledged at that time that the obverse might also be true. He was now about to discover that it would indeed become true in his own life and ministry.*

Wesley's pastoral concerns had previously focused almost entirely on the nurturing of fellow Christians within the structure of the church. In this work, his own life of holiness was a basic and almost obsessive concern. This combination of personal and parochial concerns had marked the rise of Methodism during its first decade. Now his public mission would subsume his personal quest and would provide what affirmation was necessary for his personal stance.

The Field Preacher

The following account, later published in the Journal, *describes the events in Bristol that turned Wesley into a public evangelist who proclaimed the grace and love of God to crowds gathered in all sorts of places. The* Journal *account not only describes the rather amazing response of the people to this ministry (in many cases far beyond his own understanding or comfort), but also tries to explain his own rationale for entering into these activities. A letter inserted into the text (probably to John Clayton, an early Methodist at Oxford) presents his classic defense of his adopted method of spreading scriptural holiness: itinerant preaching. Since Wesley's collegiate ordination was not to any single parish, he was not limited by any parish boundaries, but rather he saw "the whole world" as his parish. See* Works, *19:46-69.*

["This new period of my life," 1739.]

Saturday, [March] 31. In the evening I reached Bristol and met Mr. Whitefield there. I could scarce reconcile myself at first to this *strange way* of preaching in the fields, of which he set me an example on Sunday, having been all my life (till very lately) so tenacious of every point relating to decency and order that I should have thought the saving of souls almost a sin if it had not been done in a church.

April 1. In the evening (Mr. Whitefield being gone), I began expounding our Lord's Sermon on the Mount (one pretty remarkable precedent of *field-preaching*, though I suppose *there were churches* at that time also) to a little society which was accustomed to meet once or twice a week in Nicholas Street.

Monday 2. At four in the afternoon, I submitted to "be more vile" and proclaimed in the highways the glad tidings of salvation, speaking from a little eminence in a ground adjoining to the city to about three thousand people. The Scripture on which I spoke was this (is it possible anyone should be ignorant that it is fulfilled in every true minister of Christ?): "The Spirit of the Lord is upon me, because he hath anointed me to preach the gospel to the poor. He hath sent me to heal the broken-hearted, to preach deliverance to the captives and recovery of sight to the blind, to set at liberty them that are bruised, to proclaim the acceptable year of the Lord."

At seven, I began expounding the Acts of the Apostles to a society meeting in Baldwin Street, and the next day the Gospel of St. John in the chapel at Newgate, where I also daily read the Morning Service of the Church.

Wednesday 4. At Baptist Mills (a sort of a suburb or village about half a mile from Bristol), I offered the grace of God to about fifteen hundred persons from these words, "I will heal their backsliding, I will love them freely."

In the evening, three women agreed to meet together weekly with the same intention as those at London, viz., "To confess their faults one to another and pray one for another that they may be healed." At eight, four young men agreed to meet in pursuance of the same design. How dare any man deny this to be (as to the substance of it) a means of grace, ordained by God? Unless he will affirm (with Luther in the fury of his solifidianism) that St. James's Epistle is "an epistle of straw." . . .

Sunday 29. I declared the *free* grace of God to about four thousand people from those words, "He that spared not his own Son, but delivered him up for us all, how shall he not with him also freely give us all things?" At that hour it was, that one who had long continued in sin, from a despair of finding mercy, received a full, clear sense of his pardoning love, and power to sin no more. I then went to Clifton (a mile from Bristol) at the minister's desire, who was dangerously ill, and thence returned to a little plain near Hanham Mount, where about three thousand were present. After dinner I went to Clifton again. The church was quite full at the prayers and sermon, as was the churchyard at the burial which followed. From Clifton we went to Rose Green, where were (by computation) near seven thousand, and thence to Gloucester Lane society. After which was our first love-feast in Baldwin Street. O how had God renewed my strength! who used ten years ago to be so faint and weary with preaching *twice* in *one* day!

Monday 30. We understood that many were offended at the cries of those on whom the power of God came, among whom was a physician who was much afraid there might be fraud or imposture in the case. Today one whom he had known many years was the first (while I was preaching in Newgate) who broke out "into strong cries and tears." He could hardly believe his own eyes and ears. He went and stood close to her and observed every symptom, till great drops of sweat ran down her face and all her bones shook. He then knew not what to think, being clearly convinced it was not fraud, nor yet any natural disorder. But when both her soul and body were healed in a moment, he acknowledged the finger of God....

Monday, [May] 7. I was preparing to set out for Pensford, having now had leave to preach in the church, when I received the following note: "Sir, our minister, having been informed you are beside yourself, does not care you should preach in any of his churches." I went, however, and on Priestdown, about half a mile from Pensford, preached Christ our "wisdom, righteousness, sanctification, and redemption."

Tuesday 8. I went to Bath, but was not suffered to be in the meadow where I was before, which occasioned the offer of a much more convenient place, where I preached Christ to about a thousand souls.

Wednesday 9. We took possession of a piece of ground near St. James's churchyard in the Horse Fair, where it was designed to build a room large enough to contain both the societies of Nicholas and Baldwin Street, and such of their acquaintance as might desire to be present with them at such times as the Scripture was expounded. And on Saturday, 12, the first stone was laid, with the voice of praise and thanksgiving.

I had not at first the least apprehension or design of being personally engaged, either in the expense of this work or in the direction of it, having appointed eleven feoffees on whom I supposed these burdens would fall of course. But I quickly found my mistake; first with regard to the expense. For the whole undertaking must have stood still had not I immediately taken upon myself the payment of all the workmen, so that before I knew where I was, I had contracted a debt of more than a hundred and fifty pounds. And this I was to discharge how I could, the subscriptions of both societies not amounting to one quarter of the sum. And as to the direction of the work, I presently received letters from my friends in London, Mr. Whitefield in particular, backed with a message by one just come from thence, that neither he nor they would have any thing to do with the building, neither contribute anything towards it, unless I would instantly discharge all feoffees and do everything in my own name. Many reasons they gave for this, but one was enough, viz., "that such feoffees always would have it in their power to control me, and if I preached not as they liked, to turn me out of the room I had built." I accordingly yielded to their advice and, calling all the feoffees together, cancelled (no man opposing) the instrument made before, and took the whole management into my own hands. Money, it is true, I had not, nor any human prospect or probability of procuring it; but I knew "the earth is the Lord's and the fullness thereof," and in his name set out, nothing doubting. ...

My ordinary employment in public was now as follows. Every morning I read prayers and preached at Newgate. Every evening I expounded a portion of Scripture at one or more of the societies. On Monday in the afternoon I preached abroad near Bristol; on Tuesday at Bath and Two-Mile Hill alternately; on Wednesday at Baptist Mills; every other Thursday near Pensford; every other Friday in another part of Kingswood; on Saturday in the afternoon, and Sunday morning, in the Bowling Green (which lies near the middle of the city); on Sunday at eleven near Hanham Mount, at two at Clifton, and at five on Rose Green. And hitherto, as my days, so my strength hath been....

During this whole time I was almost continually asked, either by those who purposely came to Bristol to inquire concerning this strange work, or by my old or new correspondents, "How can these things be?" And innumerable cautions were given me (generally grounded on gross misrepresentations of things) not to regard visions or dreams or to fancy people had remission of sins because of their cries, or tears, or bare outward professions. To one who had many times wrote to me on this head, the sum of my answer was as follows:

> The question between us turns chiefly, if not wholly, on matter of fact. You deny that God does *now* work these effects; at least, that he works them in *this* manner. I affirm both, because I have heard these things with my own ears and have seen them with my eyes. I have seen (as far as a thing of this kind can be seen) very many persons changed in a moment from the spirit of fear, horror, despair, to the spirit of love, joy, and peace, and from sinful desire, till then reigning over them, to a pure desire of doing the will of God.... I will show you him that was a lion *till then,* and is now a lamb; him that *was* a drunkard, and *is* now exemplarily sober; the whoremonger that *was,* who now abhors the very "garment spotted by the flesh." These are my living arguments for what I assert, viz., that "God does now, as aforetime, give remission of sins and the gift of the Holy Ghost, even to us and to our children; yea, and that always suddenly; as far as I have known, and often in dreams or in the visions of God." If it be not so, I am found a false witness before God. For these things I *do,* and by his grace *will,* testify.

...Yet many would not believe. They could not indeed *deny* the facts, but they could *explain* them away. Some said, "These were purely *natural* effects; the people fainted away only because of the heat and closeness of the rooms." And others were sure "It was all a cheat: they might help it if they would. Else why were these things only in their private societies? Why were they not done in the face of the sun?" Today, Monday 21, our Lord answered for himself. For while I was enforcing these words, "Be still, and know that I am God," he began to make bare his arm, not in a close room, neither in private, but in the open air and before more than two thousand witnesses. One, and another, and another was struck to the earth, exceedingly trembling at the presence of his power. Others cried with a loud and bitter cry, "What must we do to be saved?" And in less than an hour seven persons, wholly unknown to me till that time, were rejoicing and singing, and with all their might giving thanks to the God of their salvation.... Surely God hath yet a work to do in this place. I have not found such love, no, not in England;

nor so childlike, artless, teachable a temper, as he hath given to this people.

Yet during this whole time, I had many thoughts concerning the *unusual manner* of my ministering among them. But after frequently laying it before the Lord and calmly weighing whatever objections I heard against it, I could not but adhere to what I had some time since wrote to a friend who had freely spoken his sentiments concerning it. An extract of that letter I here subjoin, that the matter may be placed in a clear light.

Dear Sir,

The best return I can make for the kind freedom you use is to use the same to you. O may the God whom we serve sanctify it to us both and teach us the whole truth as it is in Jesus!

You say you cannot reconcile some parts of my behaviour with the character I have long supported. No, nor ever will. Therefore I have disclaimed that character on every possible occasion. I told all in our ship, all at Savannah, all at Frederica, and that over and over, in express terms, "I am not a Christian; I only follow after, if haply I may attain it." When they urged my works and self-denial, I answered short, "Though I give all my goods to feed the poor and my body to be burned, I am nothing." For I have not charity. I do not love God with all my heart. If they added, "Nay, but you could not preach as you do if you was not a Christian," I again confronted them with St. Paul: "Though I speak with the tongues of men and angels, and have not charity, I am nothing." Most earnestly, therefore, both in public and private, did I inculcate this: "Be not ye shaken, however I may fall, for the foundation standeth sure."

If you ask on what principle, then, I acted, it was this: a desire to be a Christian, and a conviction that whatever I judge conducive thereto, that I am bound to do; wherever I judge I can best answer this end, thither it is my duty to go." On this principle I set out for America; on this I visited the Moravian Church; and on the same am I ready now (God being my helper) to go to Abyssinia or China or whithersoever it shall please God by this conviction to call me.

As to your advice that I should settle in College, I have no business there, having now no office and no pupils. And whether the other branch of your proposal be expedient for me, viz., to "accept of a cure of souls," it will be time enough to consider when one is offered to me.

But in the meantime, you think I ought to sit still because otherwise I should invade another's office if I interfered with other people's business and intermeddled with souls that did not belong to me. You accordingly ask, "How is it that I assemble Christians who are none of my charge, to sing psalms, and pray, and hear the Scriptures expounded?" and think it hard to justify doing this in other men's parishes, upon Catholic principles.

Permit me to speak plainly. If by *catholic* principles you mean any other than *scriptural*, they weigh nothing with me: I allow no other rule, whether of faith or practice, than the Holy Scriptures. But on scriptural principles, I do not think it hard to justify whatever I do. God in Scripture commands me, according to my power, to instruct the ignorant, reform the wicked, confirm the virtuous. Man forbids me to do this in another's parish; that is, in effect, to do it at all, seeing I have now no parish of my own nor probably ever shall. Whom then shall I hear? God or man? "If it be just to obey man rather than God, judge you." "A dispensation of the gospel is committed to me, and woe is me if I preach not the gospel." But where shall I preach it, upon the principles you mention? Why, not in Europe, Asia, Africa, or America; not in any of the Christian parts, at least, of the habitable earth. For all these are, after a sort, divided into parishes. If it be said, "Go back, then, to the heathens from whence you came," nay, but neither could I now (on your principles) preach to them, for all the heathens in Georgia belong to the parish either of Savannah or Frederica.

Suffer me now to tell you my principles in this matter. I look upon *all the world* as my parish; thus far I mean, that in whatever part of it I am, I judge it meet, right, and my bounden duty to declare unto all that are willing to hear, the glad tidings of salvation. This is the work which I know God has called me to. And sure I am that his blessing attends it. Great encouragement have I therefore to be faithful in fulfilling the work He hath given me to do. His servant I am and as such am employed according to the plain direction of his word, "As I have opportunity, doing good unto all men." And his providence clearly concurs with his word; which has disengaged me from all things else that I might singly attend on this very thing, "and go about doing good."

If you ask, "How can this be? How can one do good, of whom men say all manner of evil?" I will put you in mind (though you once knew this, yea, and much established me in that great truth), the more evil men say of me for my Lord's sake, the more good will he do by me....Blessed be God, I enjoy the reproach of Christ! O may you also be vile, exceedingly vile for his sake! God forbid that you should ever be other than *generally* scandalous; I had almost said *universally*. If any man tell you there is a new way of following Christ, "he is a liar and the truth is not in him."

I am, etc.

Wednesday, [June] 13. In the morning I came to London, and after receiving the Holy Communion at Islington, I had once more an opportunity of seeing my mother, whom I had not seen since my return from Germany.

I can't but mention an odd circumstance here. I had read her a paper in June last year containing a short account of what had passed in my own soul till within a few days of that time. She greatly approved it and said she heartily blessed God, who had brought me to so just a way of thinking. While I was in Germany, a copy of that paper was sent (without my knowledge) to one of my relations. He sent an account of it to my mother, whom I now found under strange fears concerning me, being convinced by "an account taken from one of my own papers," that I had greatly erred from the faith. I could not conceive what paper that should be; but on inquiry found it was the same I had read her myself. How hard is it to form a true judgment of any person or thing from the account of a prejudiced relater! Yea, though he be ever so honest a man: for he who gave this relation was one of unquestionable veracity. And yet by his *sincere* account of a writing which lay before his eyes was the truth so totally disguised that my mother knew not the paper she had heard from end to end, nor I that I had myself wrote.

The Itinerant Preacher

Though itinerant preaching was not illegal, it was quite irregular within the highly refined parochial system of the Church of England. Consequently, Wesley was invited by the Bishop of Bristol to explain his actions. The interview, which took place on August 16, 1739, brought forth from Wesley a carefully worded explanation. It was not published in his Journal, *but is here transcribed from his own manuscript narrative of the encounter.*

[*Butler*] Mr. Wesley, I will deal plainly with you. I once thought Mr. Whitefield and you well-meaning men. But I can't think so now. For

I have heard more of you—matters of fact, sir. And Mr. Whitefield says in his *Journal,* "There are promises still to be fulfilled in me." Sir, the pretending to extraordinary revelations and gifts of the Holy Ghost is a horrid thing, a very horrid thing.

[Wesley] My Lord, for what Mr. Whitefield says, Mr. Whitefield and not I is accountable. I pretend to no extraordinary revelations or gifts of the Holy Ghost, none but what every Christian may receive and ought to expect and pray for. But I do not wonder your lordship has heard facts asserted which, if true, would prove the contrary. Nor do I wonder that your lordship, believing them true, should alter the opinion you once had of me. A quarter of an hour I spent with your lordship before, and about an hour now. And perhaps you have never conversed one other hour with anyone who spoke in my favour. But how many with those who spoke on the other side? So that your lordship could not but think as you do. But pray, my lord, what are those facts you have heard?

[Butler] I hear you administer the Sacrament in your societies.

[Wesley] My lord, I never did yet, and I believe never shall.

[Butler] I hear, too, many people fall into fits in your societies and that you pray over them.

[Wesley] I do so, my lord. When any show by strong cries and tears that their soul is in deep anguish, I frequently pray to God to deliver them from it, and our prayer is often answered in that hour.

[Butler] Very extraordinary indeed! Well, sir, since you ask my advice, I will give it you very freely. You have no business here. You are not commissioned to preach in this diocese. Therefore I advise you to go hence.

[Wesley] My lord, my business on earth is to do what good I can. Wherever therefore I think I can do most good, there must I stay, so long as I think so. At present I think I can do most good here. Therefore here I stay.

As to my preaching here, a dispensation of the gospel is committed to me, and woe is me if I preach not the gospel wheresoever I am in the habitable world. Your lordship knows, being ordained a priest, by the commission then received, I am a priest of the Church universal. And being ordained as Fellow of a College, I was not limited to any particular cure, but have an indeterminate commission to preach the Word of God to any part of the Church of England.

I do not therefore conceive that in preaching here by this commission, I break any human law. When I am convinced I do, then it will be time to ask, "Shall I obey God or man?" But if I should be convinced in the meanwhile that I could advance the glory of God and the salvation of souls in any other place more than in Bristol and the parts adjoining, in that hour, by God's help, I will go hence, which till then I may not do.

CHAPTER 7

Apologist and Propagandist

John Wesley has often been credited as being the prime instigator of the Evangelical Revival in England. Though his cumulative influence over the whole of the eighteenth century gives some weight to this claim, we should remember that the most noticeable figure during the early years of the Revival was George Whitefield. When pamphlets appeared on the streets of London and Bristol in the 1730s attacking the Methodists, the barbs were usually aimed at Whitefield, not Wesley. Whitefield was the more popular public figure; the crowds who came to hear him preach were enthralled as much by the theatrics of his performance as by the content of his message. He gave life to the image of an "enthusiast."

Wesley began to attract the attention of the opposition only after he had followed in several of the footsteps of Whitefield—first of all, preaching to crowds in the open air, as we saw in the last section, and second, publishing extracts from his journal as a means of both advertisement and apology.

Purposeful Journalist

The occasion for Wesley's decision to publish an account of his activities came in the spring of 1740. Robert Williams, who had served on the grand jury in Savannah that had indicted Wesley, printed a broadside in Bristol, spreading before the public his account of Wesley's legal problems in Georgia, doing his best to discredit the budding new evangelist in the eyes of the public (see page 252). Wesley decided the time had come for him to present the public with an "extract" from his Journal so that his side of the Georgia story might be heard. In the process of preparing the material for the press, he decided also to include an account of the beginnings of Methodism at Oxford. The "Morgan letter" (see page 64) served this purpose.

Two more extracts closely followed the first and brought the story nearly to the end of the year 1739. The prefaces for the first and third extracts explain Wesley's purposes in publishing this material. See Works, 18:212-22, 19:3-4.

An Extract of the Rev. Mr. John Wesley's Journal, from his Embarking for Georgia to his Return to London (1740)

The Preface

1. It was in pursuance of an advice given by Bishop Taylor in his *Rules for Holy Living and Dying* that about fifteen years ago I began to take a more exact account than I had done before of the manner wherein I spent my time, writing down how I had employed every hour. This I continued to do, wherever I was, till the time of my leaving England. The variety of scenes which I then passed through induced me to transcribe from time to time the more material parts of my diary, adding here and there such little reflections as occurred to my mind. Of this journal thus occasionally compiled, the following is a short extract, it not being my design to relate all those particulars which I wrote for my own use only and which would answer no valuable end to others, however important they were to me.

2. Indeed I had no design or desire to trouble the world with any of my little affairs, as can't but appear to every impartial mind from my having been so long "as one that heareth not," notwithstanding the loud and frequent calls I have had to answer for myself. Neither should I have done it now had not Captain Williams' affidavit, *published as soon as he had left England,* laid an obligation upon me to do what in me lies, in obedience to that command of God, "Let not the good which is in you be evil-spoken of." With this view I do at length

"give an answer to every man that asketh me a reason of the hope which is in me," that in all these things "I have a conscience void of offence, towards God and towards man."

3. I have prefixed hereto a letter wrote several years since, containing a plain account of the rise of that little society in Oxford which has been so variously represented. Part of this was published in 1733, but without my consent or knowledge. It now stands as it was wrote, without any addition, diminution, or amendment, it being my only concern herein nakedly to "declare the thing as it is."

4. Perhaps my employments of another kind may not allow me to give any farther answer to them who "say all manner of evil of me falsely" and seem to "think that they do God service." Suffice it that both they and I shall shortly "give an account to him that is ready to judge the quick and the dead."

[Extract III]

The Preface

3. What I design in the following extract is openly to declare to all mankind what it is that the Methodists (so called) have done and are doing now—or rather, what it is that God hath done and is still doing in our land. For it is not the work of man which hath lately appeared. All who calmly observe it must say, "This is the Lord's doing and it is marvelous in our eyes." ...

7. Yet I know even this will by no means satisfy the far greater part of those who are now offended. And for a plain reason—because they "will never read it": they are resolved to hear one side, and one only. I know also that many who *do* read it will be just of the same mind they were before because they have fixed their judgment already and "do not regard anything" which such a fellow can say. Let them see to that. I have done my part. I have delivered mine own soul. Nay, I know that many will be greatly offended at this very account. It must be so from the very nature of things which are therein related. And the best appellation I expect from them is that of a fool, a madman, an enthusiast. All that in me lies is to relate simple truth, in as inoffensive a manner as I can. Let God give it the effect which pleaseth him and which is most for his glory!

Public Defendant

Captain Williams's broadside (see page 252) was reprinted in the summer of 1741 after the first two portions of Wesley's Journal *had been published. Wesley responded by selecting from his first* Journal *twelve pages of material that answered Williams's charges and publishing them separately as a small tract in September 1741. His efforts did not lay the problem to rest, however. The following summer yet another reprint of the Williams broadside appeared, which Wesley answered directly in a letter to Williams in July 1742, specifically refuting the charges in the broadside and repeating (for the third time in print) the minority report of the Savannah Grand Jury, which had defended Wesley. This letter was also published as a broadside (with the addendum that follows below) and circulated among the public. See* Works, *26:83-85.*

*A Letter from the Rev. Mr. John Wesley
to Capt. Robert Williams,
occasioned by an affidavit made some time since
and lately reprinted.*

Sir,

To prove that Robert Williams "traded very largely during the time he was at Savannah," that "he built very considerable buildings both at Savannah and other parts of the colony," that he "greatly improved large tracts of land there, and was esteemed to have one of the chief settlements in the colony," you have not so much as quoted "common fame." So he that will believe it, let him believe it.

But you have quoted "common fame" to support several charges against John Wesley, Clerk; as, that "he seduced the common persons settled there to idleness," that "he used too great familiarities with Mrs. Hopkey and continued so to do till she was married to Mr. William Williamson of Savannah, a gentleman of considerable note there" ('tis much "a gentleman of so considerable note" as Mr. William Williamson would marry her!), that "he sent her several letters and messages after her marriage, desiring her to meet him at divers unseasonable hours and places, many of which" (hours or places?) "were at his, the said Wesley's own closet." "A report was," you say, that "these things were so." Would any man desire better proof?

I am not surprised at all that upon such evidence you should advance such assertions. But I really am, at what you afterwards assert, as upon your own personal knowledge, viz., that "two bills of indictment being preferred against John Wesley and sent to the Grand Jury of Savannah" (bills of indictment *sent* to the Grand Jury! what kind of proceeding is this?) "this deponent and the rest of the Grand Jury did *unanimously* agree to the said bills." How dare you, sir, assert so gross a falsehood? Have you *no* regard either for your reputation or your soul? Do you think there is no God to judge the earth? You know, you *must* know, how large a part of that Grand Jury did absolutely disagree to every bill of the two presentments, and gave those reasons of their disagreement to the Trustees, which neither you nor any man has yet chose to answer. You assert farther that I "was bailed by two freeholders of Savannah for my appearance at the then next sessions." Here I charge you with a second, gross, willful falsehood. You know I never was bailed at all. If I was, name the men (Henry Lloyd is ready to confront you) or produce an attested copy of the record of court. You assert, thirdly, that "a little before the sessions came on" (viz., the next sessions after those bills were found) "I deserted my bail." Here is another gross, willful, palpable untruth. For (1) no bail was ever given, (2) I appeared at seven sessions successively after those bills were found, viz., on Thursday, Sept. 1, on Friday, Sept. 2, at three other sessions held in September and October, on Thursday, November 2, and lastly on Thursday, Nov. 22. (Your smaller falsehood, as that I "quitted the colony about the middle of the night," that "from Purrysburg to Charleston is about two hundred miles" [you should have said about ninety], that "I walked on foot from thence to Charlestown," I pass over as not material.) You lastly assert, "that the justices threatened to prosecute and imprison my bail for such my desertion, who were in the utmost confusion concerning the same. But by the interposition of this deponent and several others on behalf of the said bail, and to prevent destruction to their several families, the justices respited their recognizances during pleasure."

And this is altogether fit to crown the whole. Now, sir, as you know in your own soul that every word of this is pure invention, without one grain of truth from the beginning of it to the end; what amends can you ever make, either to God or to me or to the world? Into what a dreadful dilemma have you here brought yourself? You must either openly retract an open slander or you must wade through thick and thin to support it; till that God, to whom I appeal, shall maintain his own cause and sweep you away from the earth.

I am, sir, your friend,

John Wesley.

N.B. This was written July 16, but I had not leisure to transcribe it before August 3, 1742.

Touching some of the particulars above-mentioned, for the satisfaction of all calm and impartial men, I have added a short extract from the larger account which was published some years ago.

On Monday, August 22, Mr. Causton, then the Chief Magistrate of Savannah (having before told me himself, "I have drawn the sword and will never sheath it till I have satisfaction"), delivered to an extraordinary Grand Jury which he had summoned to meet there, a paper entitled, "A List of Grievances, presented by the Grand Jury for Savannah, this ____ day of August, 1737."

This the majority of the Grand Jury altered in some particulars, and on Thursday, Sept. 1, delivered it again to the Court under the form of two presentments, containing ten bills, which were then read to the people.

Herein they asserted upon oath, "That John Wesley, Clerk, had broken the laws of the realm, contrary to the peace of our Sovereign Lord the King, his Crown and Dignity.

1. By speaking and writing to Mrs. Williamson, against her husband's consent;
2. By repelling her from the Holy Communion;
3. By not declaring his adherence to the Church of England;
4. By dividing the Morning Service on Sundays;
5. By refusing to baptize Mr. Parker's child otherwise than by dipping, except the parents would certify it was weak and not able to bear it;
6. By repelling Mr. Gough from the Holy Communion;
7. By refusing to read the Burial Service over the body of Nathaniel Polhill;
8. By calling himself Ordinary of Savannah;
9. By refusing to receive William Aglionby as a Godfather, only because he was not a communicant;
10. By refusing Jacob Matthews for the same reason, and baptizing an Indian trader's child with only two sponsors" (this I own was

wrong, for I ought at all hazards to have refused baptizing it
'till he had procured a third).

The sense of the minority of the Grand Jurors concerning these
presentments may appear from the following paper, which they
transmitted to the Trustees:

To the Honourable the Trustees for Georgia.

Whereas two presentments have been made for the Town and
County of Savannah in Georgia, against John Wesley, Clerk, we
whose names are underwritten, being members of the said Grand
Jury, do humbly beg leave to signify our dislike of the said presentments, and give the reasons of our dissent from the particular
bills.

With regard to the first bill, we do not apprehend that Mr.
Wesley acted against any law by writing or speaking to Mrs.
Williamson, since it does not appear to us that the said Mr. Wesley
has either spoke in private or wrote to the said Mrs. Williamson
since March [12] (the day of her marriage) except one letter of
July the 5th, which he wrote at the request of her aunt, as a pastor,
to exhort and reprove her.

The second we do not apprehend to be a true bill because we
humbly conceive Mr. Wesley did not assume to himself any authority contrary to law; for we understand, "every person intending to
communicate should signify his name to the Curate at least some
time the day before," which Mrs. Williamson did not do, although
Mr. Wesley had often in full congregation declared he did insist on
a compliance with that rubric and had before repelled divers persons for non-compliance therewith.

The third we do not think a true bill because several of us have
been his hearers when he has declared his adherence to the
Church of England in a stronger manner than by a formal declaration, by explaining and defending the Apostles, the Nicene, and
the Athanasian Creeds, the Thirty-Nine Articles, the whole Book of
Common Prayer, and the Homilies of the said Church; and
because we think a formal declaration is not required but from
those who have received Institution and Induction.

The fact alleged in the fourth bill we cannot apprehend to be
contrary to any law in being.

The fifth we do not think a true bill because we conceive Mr.
Wesley is justified by the rubric, viz., "If they (the Parents) certify
that the child is weak it shall suffice to pour water upon it."

Intimating, as we humbly suppose, it shall not suffice if they do not certify.

The sixth cannot be a true bill because the said William Gough, being one of our members, was surprised to hear himself named, without his knowledge or privity, and did publicly declare, "It was no grievance to him because the said John Wesley had given him reasons with which he was satisfied."

The seventh we do not apprehend to be a true bill, for Mr. Nathaniel Polhill was an Anabaptist and desired in his lifetime that he might not be interred with the office of the Church of England. And farther we have good reason to believe that Mr. Wesley was at Frederica, or on his return thence, when Polhill was buried.

As to the eighth bill we are in doubt, as not well knowing the meaning of the word 'Ordinary.' But for the ninth and tenth we think Mr. Wesley is sufficiently justified by the Canons of the Church, which forbid 'any person to be admitted Godfather or Godmother to any child before the said person has received the Holy Communion,' whereas William Aglionby and Jacob Matthews had never certified Mr. Wesley that they had received it."

This was signed by twelve of the Grand Jurors of whom three were constables and six more tithingmen; who consequently would have made a majority, had the jury consisted, as it ought to have done, of only fifteen members, viz., the four constables and eleven tithing-men.

CHAPTER 8

The Persecuted Preacher

Wesley's early journals give the impression that he spent much of his time and effort coping with the physical as well as the literary attacks being made upon him. His preaching was as likely to bring riots among some people as it was to bring repentance among others. Parsons and parishioners who disliked Wesley's intrusions into their parishes found numerous ways to make his life uncomfortable, such as ringing the church bells to drown out his voice, tossing rocks and eggs at his head, or driving cows through his outdoor congregations.

Wesley's usual public response, as seen in the first selection below, was to go on about his business as much as possible, assuming that the true Christian must expect to face persecution and, therefore, must simply trust in God's providential care (see also page 71). This attitude did not, however, deter him from seeking legal counsel or even from threatening legal action at times to protect his individual liberties as a citizen, as the second selection below illustrates.

Providentially Protected Person

When Wesley visited Wednesbury in October 1743, he discovered that the once friendly vicar, Edward Egginton, had since April been advising the peo-

120

ple to "drive these fellows [Methodists] out of the country." This area, just outside Birmingham, was full of rough and ready folk willing to take justice into their own hands if the justice of the peace would not oblige them. Wesley's account of the rioting on this particular visit is remarkable for its explicit analysis of the manner in which he saw the providence of God demonstrated in these events. The tone as well as the content of the narrative is significant and lends firsthand support to the growing idea that Wesley's ministry had the stamp of divine authority, just as his person had the protection of divine providence. That Wesley saw himself in the same light as the martyrs can be seen in his brother Charles' account of these events (see pages 266-69).

The following account of the Wednesbury riot is taken from Wesley's Journal *(see* Works, *19:343-48). He also published a version of this narrative as part of a tract entitled* Modern Christianity Exemplified at Wednesbury *(1744).*

Thursday, 20 [October]. After preaching to a small, attentive congregation, I rode to Wednesbury. At twelve I preached in a ground near the middle of the town to a far larger congregation than was expected, on "Jesus Christ, the same yesterday, and today, and forever." I believe every one present felt the power of God. And no creature offered to molest us, either going or coming; but "the Lord fought for" us and we "held our peace."

I was writing at Francis Ward's in the afternoon when the cry arose that the mob had beset the house. We prayed that God would disperse them. And it was so: one went this way and another that, so that in half an hour not a man was left. I told our brethren, "Now is the time for us to go." But they pressed me exceedingly to stay. So that I might not offend them, I sat down, though I foresaw what would follow. Before five the mob surrounded the house again in greater numbers than ever. The cry of one and all was, "Bring out the minister; we *will* have the minister." I desired one to take their captain by the hand and bring him into the house. After a few sentences interchanged between us, the lion was become a lamb. I desired him to go and bring one or two more of the most angry of his companions. He brought in two, who were ready to swallow the ground with rage, but in two minutes they were as calm as he. I then bade them make way, that I might go out among the people. As soon as I was in the midst of them I called for a chair and, standing up, asked, "What do any of you want with me?" Some said, "We want you

to go with us to the Justice." I replied, "That I will, with all my heart."
I then spoke a few words, which God applied, so that they cried out
with might and main, "The gentleman is an honest gentleman, and
we will spill our blood in his defense." I asked, "Shall we go to the
Justice tonight, or in the morning?" Most of them cried, "Tonight,
tonight." On which I went before, and two or three hundred followed, the rest returning whence they came.

The night came on before we had walked a mile, together with
heavy rain. However, on we went to Bentley Hall, two miles from
Wednesbury. One or two ran before to tell Mr. Lane they had
brought Mr. Wesley before his worship. Mr. Lane replied, "What
have I to do with Mr. Wesley? Go and carry him back again." By this
time the main body came up and began knocking at the door. A servant told them Mr. Lane was in bed. His son followed and asked
what was the matter. One replied, "Why an't please you, they sing
psalms all day; nay, and make folks rise at five in the morning. And
what would your worship advise us to do?" "To go home," said Mr.
Lane, "and be quiet."

Here they were at a full stop, till one advised to go to Justice
Persehouse at Walsall. All agreed to this, so we hastened on and,
about seven, came to his house. But Mr. Persehouse likewise sent
word that he was in bed. Now they were at a stand again; but at last
they all thought it the wisest course to make the best of their way
home. About fifty of them undertook to convey me. But we had not
gone a hundred yards when the mob of Walsall came, pouring in
like a flood, and bore down all before them. The Darlaston mob
made what defense they could, but they were weary, as well as out-
numbered. So that in a short time, many being knocked down, the
rest ran away and left me in their hands.

To attempt speaking was vain, for the noise on every side was like
the roaring of the sea. So they dragged me along till we came to the
town, where, seeing the door of a large house open, I attempted to
go in. But a man, catching me by the hair, pulled me back into the
middle of the mob. They made no more stop till they had carried
me through the main street, from one end of the town to the other.
I continued speaking all the time to those within hearing, feeling no
pain or weariness. At the west end of the town, seeing a door half
open, I made toward it and would have gone in. But a gentleman in
the shop would not suffer me, saying they would "pull the house

down to the ground." However, I stood at the door and asked, "Are you willing to hear me speak?" Many cried out, "No, no! Knock his brains out; down with him; kill him at once." Others said, "Nay, but we will hear him first." I began asking, "What evil have I done? Which of you all have I wronged in word or deed?" And continued speaking for above a quarter of an hour, till my voice suddenly failed. Then the floods began to lift up their voice again, many crying out, "Bring him away, bring him away!"

In the meantime my strength and my voice returned and I broke out aloud into prayer. And now the man who just before headed the mob turned and said, "Sir, I will spend my life for you. Follow *me*, and not one soul here shall touch a hair of your head." Two or three of his fellows confirmed his words and got close to me immediately. At the same time, the gentleman in the shop cried out, "For shame, for shame, let him go." An honest butcher, who was a little farther off, said it *was* a shame they should do thus, and pulled back four or five, one after another, who were running on the most fiercely. The people then, as if it had been by common consent, fell back to the right and left, while those three or four men took me between them and carried me through them all. But on the bridge the mob rallied again. We therefore went on one side, over the mill-dam, and thence through the meadows, till, a little before ten, God brought me safe to Wednesbury, having lost only one flap of my waistcoat and a little skin from one of my hands.

I never saw such a chain of providences before; so many convincing proofs that the hand of God is on every person and thing, overruling all as it seemeth Him good.

The poor woman of Darlaston who had headed that mob and sworn that none should touch me, when she saw her followers give way, ran into the thickest of the throng and knocked down three or four men, one after another. But many assaulting her at once, she was soon overpowered, and had probably been killed in a few minutes (three men keeping her down and beating her with all their might) had not a man called to one of them, "Hold, Tom, hold!" "Who is there?" said Tom. "What, honest Munchin? Nay, then, let her go." So they held their hand, and let her get up and crawl home as well as she could.

From the beginning to the end I found the same presence of mind as if I had been sitting in my own study. But I took no thought for one moment before another; only once it came into my mind that if they should throw me into the river it would spoil the papers that were in my pocket. For myself, I did not doubt that I should swim across, having but a thin coat and a light pair of boots.

The circumstances which follow, I thought, were particularly remarkable: (1) That many endeavoured to throw me down while we were going downhill on a slippery path to the town, as well judging, that if I was once on the ground, I should hardly rise any more. But I made no stumble at all, nor the least slip till I was entirely out of their hands. (2) That although many strove to lay hold on my collar or clothes to pull me down, they could not fasten at all; only one got fast hold of the flap of my waistcoat, which was soon left in his hand. The other flap, in the pocket of which was a bank-note, was torn but half off. (3) That a lusty man just behind struck at me several times with a large oaken stick, with which, if he had struck me once on the back part of my head, it would have saved him all farther trouble. But every time, the blow was turned aside, I know not how; for I could not move to the right hand or left. (4) That another came rushing through the press and, raising his arm to strike, on a sudden let it drop and only stroked my head, saying, "What soft hair he has!" (5) That I stopped exactly at the mayor's door, as if I had known it (which the mob doubtless thought I did), and found him standing in the shop, which gave the first check to the madness of the people. (6) That the very first men whose hearts were turned were the heroes of the town, the captains of the rabble on all occasions, one of them having been a prize-fighter at the bear-garden. (7) That from first to last, I heard none give a *reviling* word or call me by any *opprobrious* name whatever. But the cry of one and all was, "The preacher! The preacher! The parson! The minister!" (8) That no creature, at least within my hearing, laid anything to my charge, either true or false; having in the hurry quite forgot to provide themselves with an accusation of any kind. And lastly, that they were as utterly at a loss what they should do with me, none proposing any determinate thing, only, "Away with him; kill him at once!"

By how gentle degrees does God prepare us for his will! Two years ago a piece of brick grazed my shoulders. It was a year after that the stone struck me between the eyes. Last month I received one blow, and this evening two: one before we came into the town and one after we were gone out. But both were as nothing, for though one man struck me on the breast with all his might and the other on the mouth with such a force that the blood gushed out immediately, I felt no more pain from either of the blows than if they had touched me with a straw....

When I came back to Francis Ward's I found many of our brethren waiting upon God. Many also whom I never had seen before came to rejoice with us. And the next morning, as I rode through the town on my way to Nottingham, every one I met expressed such a cordial affection that I could scarce believe what I saw and heard.

Unjustly Treated Citizen

Wesley considered the riotous opposition to his preaching to be unprovoked; he did not intentionally bring persecution upon himself. In some cases, he felt his liberties as an Englishman had been blatantly disregarded not only by the mobs but also by the authorities.

In August 1748, Wesley and some friends were attacked at Roughlee in the West Riding of Yorkshire by a mob incited to action by George White, the Anglican minister at the neighboring town of Colne (see page 269). The Rev. Mr. White had gone so far as to issue the following notice to mobilize the anti-Wesleyan forces:

NOTICE is hereby given, that if any men be mindful to enlist into his Majesty's service under the command of the Rev. Mr. George White, commander-in-chief, and John Bannister, lieutenant-general of his Majesty's forces, for the defense of the Church of England and the support of the manufactory in and about Colne, both of which are now in danger, etc., etc., let them now repair to the Drum Head at the Cross, where each man shall have a pint of ale for advance, and other proper encouragements.

The day after the confrontation with the mob, Wesley sent the following letter to the local constable, James Hargrave, describing and protesting the "lawless violence" he had suffered under Hargrave's jurisdiction. Wesley published excerpts from the middle portion of this letter in his Journal *account of the event; he omitted, however, the portions of the letter indicated below within brackets, including the implied threat of legal action at the end (see* Works, *26:324-27).*

Sir,

[When I came last night to Roughlee I found abundance of people, many of whom pressed me to preach there; but I told them, I had given my word I would not preach there that evening. They then desired me to stay with them all night; but this also I refused, staying no longer than till our horses were ready, and till I had given them a short exhortation not to be out late at night, and as much as lay in them to live peaceably with all men.

This is a short account of what I've done. I must now mention a little what you have done. I say you, because all that was done yesterday was in the eye of the law, as much your act and deed as if you had done all with your own hands; seeing (not to touch now upon some other points, evidence of which may be produced in due time) all those actions are imputable to you which you could have prevented and would not.]

Between twelve and one o'clock, when I was speaking to some quiet people, without any noise or tumult, a drunken rabble came with clubs and staves, in a tumultuous and riotous manner, the captain of whom, Richard Bocock by name, said he was a deputy constable, and that he was come to bring me to you. I made no resistance (though he had no warrant to show, and consequently all he did was utterly illegal), but went with him. I had scarce gone ten yards when a man of his company struck me with his fist in the face, with all his might. I told him it was not well, and went on. Quickly after, another threw his stick at my head. I then made a stand, having little encouragement to go forward. But another of the champions, cursing and swearing in the most shocking manner, and flourishing his club over his head, cried out, "Bring him away!" So perceiving there was no remedy, I walked on to Barrowford (where they informed me you was), their drummer going before to draw all the rabble together and encourage them in their work.

[I must just stop to inform you (if you know it not) that the whole action of carrying me along against my will was an assault upon the king's highway, contrary to his peace, crown, and dignity.]

When your deputy had brought me prisoner into the house, he permitted Mr. Grimshaw, the minister of Haworth, Mr. Colbeck of Keighley, and one more, to be with me, promising none should hurt them. Soon after, you and your friends came in and required me to promise I would "come to Roughlee no more." I told you I would "cut off my hand rather than make any such promise." Neither would I promise that none of my friends should come. After abundance of rambling discourse...you seemed a little satisfied with my saying, "I will not preach at Roughlee this time. Nor shall I be here again till August next. Then I will show you the authority by which I preach." You then undertook to quiet the mob, to whom you went and spoke a few words, and their noise immediately ceased, while I walked out with you at the back door.

I should have mentioned that I had desired you to let me go several times before, but could not prevail, and that when I attempted to go with Richard Bocock the mob came immediately to me, cursing and swearing and throwing whatever came to hand. One of them beat me down to the ground, and when I rose again the rest came about me like lions and forced me back into the house.

While you and I went out at one door, Mr. Grimshaw and Mr. Colbeck went out at the other. The mob immediately closed them in and tossed them to and fro with the utmost violence, threw Mr. Grimshaw down, and loaded them both with dirt and mire, not one of your friends offering to assist them or call off the bloodhounds from the pursuit. The other quiet, harmless people, which followed me at a distance to see what the end would be, they treated still worse, not only by your connivance, but by the express order of your deputy. They made them flee for their lives amidst showers of dirt and stones, without any regard to age or sex. Some of them they trampled in the mire and dragged by the hair, particularly a young man who came with me from Newcastle. Many they beat with their clubs without mercy. One they forced to leap down (or they would have cast him headlong) from a rock ten or twelve foot high into the river, and even when he crawled out, wet and bruised, they swore they would throw him in again, and he hardly escaped out of their hands.

At this time, you sat well-pleased close to the scene of action, not attempting in the least to hinder them. And all this time you was talking of justice and law. Alas! Suppose we were dissenters (which I utterly deny, consequently laws against dissenting conventicles are nothing at all to us); suppose we were Turks or Jews; still are we not to have the benefit of the law of our country? Proceed against us by law, if you can or dare, but not by lawless violence—not by making a drunken, cursing, swearing, riotous mob both judge, jury, and executioner. This is flat rebellion both against God and the king.

[But before I take any further step herein I think myself obliged to make you a fair proposal. If you will promise me under your hand to suppress all mobs at Roughlee and the parts adjacent (as your duty both to God and the king require you to do, even at the hazard of your life); if you will promise to proceed only by law against those you apprehend to act contrary to law (which indeed I absolutely deny you to do)—nor can it be supposed that none of the lawyers in Leeds, Newcastle, Bristol, or London, should find it out (if it were so), but only the Solomons in Pendle Forest [*i.e.,* the vicinity of Roughlee]; if I accordingly find a letter from you to this effect when I come to London, directed to the Foundery near Moorfields, I shall be satisfied and proceed no further. If not, I shall try another course.

Only one piece of advice permit me to give. Do not consult herein with some petty attorney (who will certainly say your cause is good), but with some able barrister-at-law. This is the course I take. The counsel to whom I applied on this very Act of Parliament before I left London were Counselor Glanville, a barrister of Gray's Inn, and Sir Dudley Ryder, the King's Attorney-General.

I am your real friend.]

CHAPTER 9

The Medical Practitioner

The year 1739 is a watershed in Wesley's spiritual and vocational self—Wesley never fancied himself a medical doctor, but he did exhibit a lifelong interest in the prevention and cure of disease. The earliest records of his reading at Oxford list books on health; his Georgia diary notes his participation in an autopsy in 1736; his letters contain frequent suggestions to friends regarding their physical well-being; and his Journal displays his continual fascination with cures and remedies.

Wesley's dipping into matters of "physic" was more than the casual preoccupation of a busy but inherently curious mind. He understood himself having a responsibility as a Christian for meeting the needs of his neighbor, whether those needs be the result of sin, poverty, ignorance, or even illness. His interest in medicine arose out of a holistic concern for persons, including their health. The focus of his interest was in prevention as well as cure. He spent little time with the theory of disease, but rather emphasized the practical, experimental approach to prevention and cure.

Two activities best exhibit Wesley's role as a practitioner of the medical arts. He established free medical dispensaries and published a popular collection of cures and remedies.

Dispenser of Medicine

Wesley's work among the poor increasingly confirmed his prejudices against self-serving physicians and apothecaries whom he saw conspiring to take advantage of sick persons for their own selfish gain. His direct, practical solution to the problem was to provide for the sick himself in ways he felt most appropriate to their needs.

One step was to ask members of the Methodist societies to act as "Visitors to the Sick." He assigned this small army of volunteers by pairs to designated areas of town, asking them to follow these simple rules: "(1) Be plain and open in dealing with souls. (2) Be mild, tender, patient. (3) Be cleanly in all you do for the sick. (4) Be not nice [rude]."

Wesley soon became aware of the pressing need for more direct and adequate medical assistance. He then took the rather astonishing step in 1746 of opening a medical clinic on his own in Bristol. Within a short time, he established other free public dispensaries in London and Newcastle as well. These are often said to be the first free clinics in England.

Wesley explained his rationale for these activities in a letter to his friend, the Rev. Vincent Perronet, later published (1749) as section XII of "A Plain Account of the People Called Methodists" (see Works, *9:275-76).*

1. But I was still in pain for many of the poor that were sick: there was so great expense and so little profit. And first I resolved to try whether they might not receive more benefit in the *hospitals.* Upon the trial, we found there was indeed less expense—but no more good done than before. I then asked the advice of several physicians for them; but still it profited not. I saw the poor people pining away, and several families ruined, and that without remedy.

2. At length I thought of a kind of desperate expedient. "I will prepare and give them physic myself." For six or seven and twenty years I had made anatomy and physic the diversion of my leisure hours; though I never properly studied them, unless for a few months when I was going to America, where I imagined I might be of some service to those who had no regular physician among them. I applied to it again. I took into my assistance an apothecary and an experienced surgeon; resolving at the same time not to go out of my depth, but to leave all difficult and complicated cases to such physicians as the patients should choose.

3. I gave notice of this to the Society; telling them that all who

were ill of *chronical* distempers (for I did not care to venture upon *acute*) might, if they pleased, come to me at such a time, and I would give them the best advice I could and the best medicines I had.

4. Many came (and so every Friday since). Among the rest was one William Kirkham, a weaver, near Old Nichol Street. I asked him, "What complaint have you?" "O sir," said he, "a cough, a very sore cough. I can get no rest day nor night."

I asked, "How long have you had it?" He replied, "About three-score years. It began when I was eleven years old." I was nothing glad that this man should come first, fearing our not curing him might discourage others. However, I looked up to God and said, "Take this three or four times a day. If it does you no good, it will do you no harm." He took it two or three days. His cough was cured, and has not returned to this day.

5. Now, let candid men judge, does humility require me to deny a notorious fact? If not, which is *vanity:* to say, I, by my own skill, restored this man to health? or to say, God did it, by his own almighty power? By what figure of speech this is called *boasting* I know not. But I will put no name to such a fact as this. I leave that to the Rev. Dr. Middleton [author of *A Free Inquiry into the Miraculous Powers which are supposed to have subsisted in the Christian Church* (1748)].

6. In five months, medicines were occasionally given to above five hundred persons. Several of these I never saw before; for I did not regard whether they were of the Society or not. In that time seventy-one of these, regularly taking their medicines and following the regimen prescribed (which three in four would not do), were entirely cured of distempers long thought to be incurable. The whole expense of medicines during this time was (nearly) forty pounds. We continued this ever since, and by the blessing of God with more and more success.

Prescriber of Remedies

Wesley's growing notoriety as a medical practitioner became more firmly fixed in the public mind with the publication in 1747 of his Primitive Physick; or An Easy and Natural Method of Curing Most Diseases. *This curious collection of folk remedies, "tried and true," was revised and enlarged several times, going through at least twenty-two editions in England during Wesley's lifetime. Beginning at mid-century, it was frequently republished in Ireland and America and was translated into French and Welsh before the century was out. It was the companion of many a pioneer on the American frontier well into the nineteenth century.*

The popularity of this little book was explained in part by Wesley's comment in the preface—every person who owned it had "a physician always in his house, and one that attends without fee or reward." It also carried the weight of Wesley's authority and experimental imprimatur: those remedies he could vouch for personally, he marked "Tried"; those he felt worked best, he marked with an asterisk; and those which never failed, he claimed as "Infallible," indicated by an "I."

Wesley had no qualms about undercutting part of the medical profession of his day. In the preface, he explains that he is simply reviving the ancient art of healing diseases by using remedies that are known to cure the illnesses. He claims that the medical faculty had in large part lost their effectiveness as well as the trust of the public through an obscurantist fascination with the theory of diseases and a selfish desire to increase their wealth (even if it meant intentionally prolonging the plight of the poor sick). Wesley recommends that in cases of continuing or severe illness, the sick person search out a "physician who fears God." The profession struck back in the writings of William Hawes (see page 316).

The following selections from the 1772 (15th) edition of Primitive Physick *explain Wesley's understanding of his role in providing these prescriptions for health and illustrate a cross section of his suggested recipes. To the present reader, some of these may seem obvious (#117), or ridiculous (#729), or even surprisingly modern (#582).*

Preface

'Tis probable, physic, as well as religion, was in the first ages chiefly traditional; every father delivering down to his sons what he had himself in like manner received concerning the manner of healing both outward hurts, with the diseases incident to each climate, and the medicines which were of the greatest efficacy for the cure of each disorder....Thus ancient men, having a little experience joined with common sense and common humanity, cured both themselves and their neighbours of most of the distempers, to which every nation was subject.

But in the process of time, men of a philosophical turn were not satisfied with this. They began to enquire how they might account for these things?...And hence the whole order of physic, which had obtained to that time came gradually to be inverted. Men of learning began to set experience aside; to build physic upon hypotheses; to form theories of diseases and their cure, and to substitute these in the place of experiments...till at length physic became an abstruse science, quite out of the reach of ordinary men....

Yet there have not been wanting from time to time, some lovers of mankind who have endeavoured (even contrary to their own interest) to reduce physic to its ancient standard: who have laboured to explode out of it all hypotheses and fine spun theories and to make it a plain intelligible thing, as it was in the beginning, having no more mystery in it than this—"Such a medicine removes such a pain." These have demonstrably shown that neither the knowledge of astrology, astronomy, natural philosophy, nor even anatomy itself, is absolutely necessary to the quick and effectual cure of most diseases incident to human bodies; nor yet any chemical, or exotic, or compound medicine, but a single plant or fruit duly applied. So that every man of common sense (unless in some rare cases) may prescribe either to himself or his neighbour, and may be very secure from doing harm, even where he can do no good.

...Without any concern about the obliging or disobliging any man living, a mean hand has made here some little attempt toward a plain and easy way of curing most diseases. I have only consulted herein, experience, common sense, and the common interest of mankind. And supposing they can be cured this easy way, who would desire to use any other? Who would not wish to have a physician always in his house, and one that attends without fee or reward?...Experience shows that one thing will cure most disorders at least as well as twenty put together. Then why do you add the other nineteen? Only to swell the apothecary's bill; nay, possibly on purpose to prolong the distemper, that the doctor and he may divide the spoil....

As to the manner of using the medicines here set down, I should advise, as soon as you know your distemper (which is very easy, unless in a complication of disorders, and then you would do well to apply to a physician that fears God), *first,* use the first of the remedies for that disease which occurs in the ensuing collection (unless some other of them be easier to be had, and then it may do just as well). *Secondly,* after a competent time, if it takes no effect, use the second, the third, and so on. I have purposely set down (in most cases) several remedies for each disorder, not only because all are not equally easy to be procured at all times and in all places, but likewise because the medicine which cures one man will not always cure another of the same distemper. Nor will it cure the same man at all times. Therefore it was necessary to have a variety. However, I have subjoined the letter *(I)* to those medicines which are thought to be *Infallible. Thirdly,* observe all the time the greatest exactness in your regimen or manner of living. Abstain from all mixed, all high-seasoned food. Use plain diet, easy of digestion, and this as sparingly as you can, consistent with ease and strength. Drink only water, if it agrees with your stomach; if not, good, clear, small beer [weak beer]. Use as much exercise daily in the open air as you can without weariness. Sup at six or seven on the lightest food. Go to bed early and rise betimes. To persevere with steadiness in this course is often more than half the cure. Above all, add to the rest (for it is not labour lost) that old unfashionable medicine, prayer. And have faith in God, who "killeth and maketh alive, who bringeth down to the grave and bringeth up." ...

London, June 11, 1747

POSTSCRIPT

... Alterations are still in pursuance of my first design, to set down cheap, safe, and easy medicines, easy to be known, easy to be procured, and easy to be applied by plain, unlettered men.

Bristol, Oct. 16, 1755

... I have now added the word *Tried* to those which I have found to be of the greatest efficacy. I believe many others to be of equal virtue, but it has not lain in my way to make the trial.

London, Nov. 10, 1760

** Most of those medicines which I prefer to the rest are now marked with an asterisk.

Oct. 20, 1772

A COLLECTION OF RECEIPTS

To cure Baldness

76. Rub the part morning and evening, with onions, till it is red; and rub it afterwards with honey.

Or, wash it with a decoction of box-wood.

Or, electrify it daily.

Blisters

104. On the feet, occasioned by walking, are cured by drawing a needle full of worsted through them. Clip it off at both ends, and leave it till the skin peels off.

Hard Breasts

109. Apply turnips roasted till soft, then mashed and mixed with a little oil of roses. Change this twice a day, keeping the breast very warm with flannel.

A Bruise

*111. Immediately apply treacle spread on brown paper: Tried. . . .

114. Or, apply a plaister of chopped parsley mixt with butter.

To prevent Swelling from a Bruise

117. Immediately apply a cloth, five or six times doubled, dipt [*sic*] in cold water, and new dipt when it grows warm: Tried.

To cure a Swelling from a Bruise

118. Foment it half an hour, morning and evening, with cloths dipped in water, as hot as you can bear.

A Cold

*176. Drink a pint of cold water lying down in bed: Tried. . . .

178. Or, to one spoonful of oatmeal, and one spoonful of honey, add a piece of butter, the bigness of a nutmeg; pour on gradually near a pint of boiling water; drink this lying down in bed.

A Cold in the Head

179. Pare very thin the yellow rind of an orange. Roll it up inside out, and thrust a roll into each nostril.

A Cough

253. Make a hole through a lemon and fill it with honey. Roast it and catch the juice. Take a teaspoonful of this frequently: Tried.

A Cut

280. Keep it closed with your thumb a quarter of an hour. Then double a rag five or six times; dip it in cold water and bind it on: Tried.

281. Or, bind on toasted cheese. This will cure a deep cut.

A settled Deafness

295. Take a red onion, pick out the core; fill up the place with oil of roasted almonds. Let it stand a night; then bruise and strain it. Drop three or four drops into the ear, morning and evening, and stop it with black wool.

The Ear-Ache

325. Rub the ear hard a quarter of an hour: Tried.

326. Or, be electrified....

328. Or, put in a roasted fig, or onion, as hot as may be: Tried.

329. Or, blow the smoke of tobacco strongly into it.

Dull Sight

350. Drop in two or three drops of juice of rotten apples often.

The Head-Ache

478. Rub the head for a quarter of an hour: Tried.

479. Or, be electrified: Tried.

480. Or, apply to each temple the thin yellow rind of a lemon, newly pared off....

484. Or, snuff up the nose camphorated spirits of lavender;

486. Or, a little juice of horse-radish.

A Chronical Head-Ache

488. Keep your feet in warm water a quarter of an hour before you go to bed, for two or three weeks: Tried.

489. Or, wear tender hemlock leaves under the feet, changing them daily.

490. Or, order a tea-kettle of cold water to be poured on your head, every morning, in a slender stream.

The Heart-Burning

502. Drink a pint of cold water: Tried....

509. Or, a teaspoonful of crab's eyes, ground to an impalpable powder.

The Hiccup

510. Swallow a mouthful of water, stopping the mouth and ears: Tried.

511. Or, take any thing that makes you sneeze....

514. Or three drops of oil of cinnamon on a lump of sugar: Tried.

The Itch

540. Wash the parts affected with strong rum: Tried....

544. Or, anoint them with black soap.

*545. Or, steep a shirt half an hour in a quart of water, mixed with half an ounce of powdered brimstone. Dry it slowly and wear it five or six days. Sometimes it needs repeating: Tried.

For one seemingly Killed with Lightning, a Damp, or Suffocated

581. Plunge him immediately into cold water.

582. Or, blow strongly with bellows down his throat. This may recover a person seemingly drowned. It is still better if a strong man blows into his mouth.

The Piles (to cure)

652. Apply warm treacle.

653. Or, a tobacco-leaf steeped in water twenty-four hours.

655. Or, a bruised onion skinned or roasted in ashes. It perfectly cures the dry piles.

The Plague (to prevent)

666. Eat marigold flowers daily, as a salad, with oil and vinegar.

The Pleurisy

675. Apply to the side, onions roasted in embers, mixed with cream.

676. Or, take half a dram of soot.

677. Or, take out the core of an apple; fill it with white frankincense; stop it close with the piece you cut out, and roast it in ashes. Mash and eat it. *I.*

A windy Rupture

729. Warm cow-dung well. Spread it thick on leather, strewing some cummin-seeds on it, and apply it hot. When cold, put on a new one. It commonly cures a child (keeping his bed) in two days.

A Sore Throat

780. Take a pint of cold water lying down in bed: Tried.

781. Or, apply a chin-stay of roasted figs.

783. Or, snuff a little honey up the nose.

784. An old sore throat was cured by living wholly upon apples and apple-water.

To clean the Teeth

867. Rub them with ashes of burnt bread.

To prevent the Tooth-Ache

868. Wash the mouth with cold water every morning and rinse them [*sic*] after every meal.

869. Or, rub the teeth often with tobacco ashes.

To cure the Tooth-Ache

870. Be electrified through the teeth: Tried.

871. Or, apply to the aching tooth an artificial magnet....

*878. Or, lay bruised or boiled nettles to the cheek: Tried....

880. Or, hold a slice of apple, slightly boiled, between the teeth: Tried.

Testicles inflamed

892. Boil bean-flour, in three parts water, one part vinegar. Apply it as a Poultice.

The Vertigo, or Swimming in the Head

902. Take a vomit or two....

905. Or, in a May morning about sunrise snuff up daily the dew that is on the mallow leaves.

*906. Or, apply to the top of the head, shaven, a plaister of flour of brimstone, and whites of eggs: Tried.

Warts

968. Rub them daily with a radish.

969. Or, with juice of dandelion.

970. Or, with juice of marigold-flowers: it will hardly fail.

971. Or, water in which sal armoniac is dissolved. . . .

973. Or, apply bruised purslain as a poultice, changing it twice a day. It cures in seven or eight days.

Weakness in the Ankles

974. Hold them in cold water a quarter of an hour morning and evening.

Wounds
(If you have not an honest Surgeon at Hand)

1003. Apply juice or powder of yarrow: *I.*

1004. Or, bind leaves of ground-ivy upon it. . . .

1007. Or keep the part in cold water for an hour, keeping the wound closed with your thumb. Then bind on the thin skin of an egg shell for days or weeks, till it falls off of itself. Regard not, though it prick or shoot for a time.

*** I advise all in or near London, to buy their medicines at Apothecaries Hall. There they are sure to have them good.

CHAPTER 10

Practical Theologian

When Wesley told his Conference that the purpose of God in raising up the Methodist preachers was "to reform the nation (particularly the Church) and to spread scriptural holiness across the land," he was, more than anything else, describing his own vocation. Promoting holiness was the practical goal for his every endeavor, the implicit purpose of his every activity. At the same time, he was both interested and knowledgeable in theology. The list of books he read, beginning with his early days in Oxford, contains a full range of theological works, from the writings of the early church leaders to the latest works of his contemporaries. He was, however, neither a speculative nor a systematic theologian. Theology was for him the "handmaid of piety." The challenge was to put his learning into the employ of his vocation, so that the truths of the gospel might be understood and appropriated by the poor as well as the rich, the tin miner as well as the university student.

The Proclaimer of Plain Truth

Preaching was central to Wesley's vocation; his sermons are an exemplary body of Wesleyan divinity. The image of this Oxford don, dressed in his cler-

ical garb, standing on a miner's cart, preaching to a group of workers at Kingswood, is a fitting reminder that Wesley saw learning not as a ticket to preferment or privilege, but as a tool of his ministry to the poor. His primary congregation was the working class; his most frequent pulpit, the nearest stump or market cross. Observers of Wesley's preaching noticed that he could preach in a learned style in the churches and among great people, but "when he came among simple people, he laid all his greatness aside." The poet William Cowper is said to have described Wesley as "learned without pride." Wesley himself cultivated a "plain style" in his discourse and his writing. His design was not simple display but rather an unfolding of the grace of God.

Wesley's published sermons were for the most part written especially for publication. Of the one hundred thirty-one sermons he published during his lifetime, only fifteen bear any indication of having been preached in that specific form. Eyewitness accounts of his preaching do testify that, in some cases at least, a preached sermon might have the same basic content as a published sermon on the same text. The oral sermons, however, seem to have been longer and more anecdotal. Robert Walpole recalled that Wesley "told stories" in his sermons. Peter Williams described Wesley's preaching as "a string of mystical raptures, richly interlarded with texts of Scripture and childish anecdotes about his own life and conversation." Although the published sermons are in some sense a mosaic of scriptural quotations and allusions, the anecdotal quality is not so prevalent; they probably, therefore, do not represent very well his oral style of delivery.

They do, however, contain the "essential truths of the gospel" as Wesley understood them. The practical purposes and the theological rationale for Wesley's sermons can best be seen in the preface he wrote in 1746 for the first volume of his collected edition of Sermons on Several Occasions *(see* Works, *1:103-7).*

Preface

1. The following sermons contain the substance of what I have been preaching for between eight and nine years last past. During that time I have frequently spoken in public on every subject in the ensuing collection, and I am not conscious, that there is any one point of doctrine on which I am accustomed to speak in public which is not here—incidentally, if not professedly—laid before every Christian reader. Every serious man who peruses these will therefore see in the clearest manner what those doctrines are which I embrace and teach as the essentials of true religion.

2. But I am thoroughly sensible these are not proposed in such a manner as some may expect. Nothing here appears in an elaborate, elegant, or oratorical dress. If it had been my desire or design to write thus, my leisure would not permit. But in truth, I at present designed nothing less; for I now write (as I generally speak) *ad populum*—to the bulk of mankind—to those who neither relish nor understand the art of speaking, but who, notwithstanding, are competent judges of those truths which are necessary to present and future happiness. I mention this, that curious readers may spare themselves the labour of seeking for what they will not find.

3. I design plain truth for plain people: Therefore, of set purpose I abstain from all nice and philosophical speculations, from all perplexed and intricate reasonings, and as far as possible from even the show of learning, unless in sometimes citing the original Scriptures. I labour to avoid all words which are not easy to be understood, all which are not used in common life, and in particular those kinds of technical terms that so frequently occur in bodies of divinity: those modes of speaking which men of reading are intimately acquainted with, but which to common people are an unknown tongue. Yet I am not assured that I do not sometimes slide into them unawares: it is so extremely natural to imagine that a word which is familiar to ourselves is so to all the world.

4. Nay, my design is in some sense to forget all that ever I have read in my life. I mean to speak, in the general, as if I had never read one author, ancient or modern (always excepting the inspired). I am persuaded that, on the one hand, this may be a means of enabling me more clearly to express the sentiments of my heart, while I simply follow the chain of my own thoughts, without entangling myself with those of other men; and that, on the other, I shall come with fewer weights upon my mind, with less of prejudice and prepossession, either to search for myself or to deliver to others the naked truths of the gospel.

5. To candid, reasonable men I am not afraid to lay open what have been the inmost thoughts of my heart. I have thought, I am a creature of a day, passing through life as an arrow through the air. I am a spirit come from God and returning to God; just hovering over the great gulf, till a few moments hence I am no more seen—I drop into an unchangeable eternity! I want to know one thing, the way to heaven—how to land safe on that happy shore. God himself has con-

descended to teach the way: for this very end he came from heaven. He hath written it down in a book. O give me that book! At any price give me the book of God! I have it. Here is knowledge enough for me. Let me be *homo unius libri* [a person of one book]. Here then I am, far from the busy ways of men. I sit down alone: only God is here. In his presence I open, I read his Book; for this end, to find the way to heaven. Is there a doubt concerning the meaning of what I read? Does anything appear dark or intricate? I lift up my heart to the Father of Lights: "Lord, is it not thy word, 'If any man lack wisdom, let him ask of God?' Thou 'givest liberally and upbraidest not.' Thou hast said, 'If any be willing to do thy will, he shall know.' I am willing to do, let me know, thy will." I then search after and consider parallel passages of Scripture, "comparing spiritual things with spiritual." I meditate thereon with all the attention and earnestness of which my mind is capable. If any doubt still remains, I consult those who are experienced in the things of God, and then the writings whereby, being dead, they yet speak. And what I thus learn, that I teach.

6. I have accordingly set down in the following sermons what I find in the Bible concerning the way to heaven, with a view to distinguish this way of God from all those which are the inventions of men. I have endeavoured to describe the true, the scriptural, experimental religion, so as to omit nothing which is a real part thereof, and to add nothing thereto which is not. And herein it is more especially my desire, first, to guard those who are just setting their faces toward heaven (and who, having little acquaintance with the things of God, are the more liable to be turned out of the way) from formality, from mere outside religion, which has almost driven heart-religion out of the world; and, secondly, to warn those who know the religion of the heart, the faith which worketh by love, lest at any time they make void the law through faith, and so fall back into the snare of the devil.

7. By the advice and at the request of some of my friends, I have prefixed to the other sermons contained in this volume three sermons of my own and one of my brother's preached before the University of Oxford. My design required some discourses on those heads. And I preferred these before any others, as being a stronger answer than any which can be drawn up now to those who have frequently asserted that we have changed our doctrine of late and do

not preach now what we did some years ago. Any man of understanding may now judge for himself, when he has compared the latter with the former sermons.

8. But some may say I have mistaken the way myself, although I take upon me to teach it to others. It is probable many will think this, and it is very possible that I have. But I trust, whereinsoever I have mistaken, my mind is open to conviction. I sincerely desire to be better informed. I say to God and man, "What I know not, teach thou me."

9. Are you persuaded you see more clearly than me? It is not unlikely that you may. Then treat me as you would desire to be treated yourself upon a change of circumstances. Point me out a better way than I have yet known. Show me it is so by plain proof of Scripture. And if I linger in the path I have been accustomed to tread and am therefore unwilling to leave it, labour with me a little, take me by the hand, and lead me as I am able to bear. But be not displeased if I entreat you not to beat me down in order to quicken my pace. I can go but feebly and slowly at best—then, I should not be able to go at all. May I not request of you, further, not to give me hard names in order to bring me into the right way? Suppose I were ever so much in the wrong, I doubt this would not set me right. Rather, it would make me run so much the farther from you—and so get more and more out of the way.

10. Nay, perhaps, if you are angry, so shall I be too, and then there will be small hopes of finding the truth. If once anger arise, ἠΰτε καπνός [like smoke] (as Homer somewhere expresses it), this smoke will so dim the eyes of my soul that I shall be able to see nothing clearly. For God's sake, if it be possible to avoid it, let us not provoke one another to wrath. Let us not kindle in each other this fire of hell, much less blow it up into a flame. If we could discern truth by that dreadful light, would it not be loss rather than gain? For how far is love, even with many wrong opinions, to be preferred before truth itself without love! We may die without the knowledge of many truths and yet be carried into Abraham's bosom. But if we die without love, what will knowledge avail? Just as much as it avails the devil and his angels!

The God of love forbid we should ever make the trial! May he prepare us for the knowledge of all truth by filling our hearts with all his love and with all joy and peace in believing.

The Aspiring Perfect Christian

The plan of salvation was the focus of Wesley's preaching—the renewal of the individual in the image of God. "Christian perfection" was the keystone of his theology, the highest expression of the love of God in the soul of man. The goal of the Christian life was to "have the mind of Christ and walk as he walked." To be more explicit, the call to responsible Christian living centered for Wesley upon the Great Commandment, to love God and neighbor.

This theme of holy living, or sanctification, runs as a main thread throughout Wesley's sermons, determining both the shape of his theology and the tone of his preaching. In 1743 he wrote and published a tract which characterized "the perfect Christian," as he later said, basing his portrait on the "true Gnostic" described by Clement of Alexandria in Stromata, *but drawing the character "in a more scriptural manner." His purpose in publishing "The Character of a Methodist" was not only to put flesh on the bones of his doctrine of Christian perfection, but also thereby to remove some prejudice from the minds of candid persons. Wesley was not hesitant to point out that the principles and practices described in this treatise were "the marks of a true Methodist—i.e., a true Christian." The equation was not accidental; within the decade he published another tract entitled "An Account of Genuine Christianity" which was simply a portion of his defense of Methodism against the attacks of Dr. Conyers Middleton.*

"The Character of a Methodist" became a fixture in the list of Methodist publications, both alluring and disarming in the simplicity and directness of its answer to the question, "What are the marks of a Methodist?" This work is not a description of Wesley, but rather an outline of the ideal toward which he was personally striving (see Works, *9:33-40). As his friend Alexander Knox remarked, "to realize in himself the perfect Christian of Clemens Alexandrinus was the object of his heart." That he had not yet (or would never claim to have) reached that goal is attested in the verse prefixed to the work: "Not as though I had already attained" (see Phil. 3:12).*

1. The distinguishing marks of a Methodist are not his *opinions* of any sort. His assenting to this or that scheme of religion, his embracing any particular set of notions, his espousing the judgment of one man or of another, are all quite wide of the point. Whosoever, therefore, imagines that a Methodist is a man of such or such an *opinion* is grossly ignorant of the whole affair; he mistakes the truth totally. We believe, indeed, that "all Scripture is given by the inspiration of

God"; and herein we are distinguished from Jews, Turks, and Infidels. We believe the written word of God to be the *only and the sufficient* rule both of Christian faith and practice; and herein we are fundamentally distinguished from those of the Romish Church. We believe Christ to be the Eternal Supreme God; and herein we are distinguished from the Socinians and Arians. But as to all opinions which do not strike at the root of Christianity, we "think and let think." So that whatsoever they are, whether right or wrong, they are no "distinguishing marks" of a Methodist.

2. Neither are *words* or *phrases* of any sort. We do not place our religion, or any part of it, in being attached to any peculiar mode of speaking, any quaint or uncommon set of expressions. The most obvious, easy, common words wherein our meaning can be conveyed we prefer before others, both on ordinary occasions and when we speak of the things of God. We never therefore willingly or designedly deviate from the most usual way of speaking; unless when we express Scripture truths in Scripture words—which, we presume, no Christian will condemn. Neither do we affect to use any particular expressions of Scripture more frequently than others, unless they are such as are more frequently used by the inspired writers themselves. So that it is as gross an error to place the marks of a Methodist in his *words* as in *opinions* of any sort.

3. Nor do we desire to be distinguished by *actions, customs,* or *usages* of an *indifferent* nature. Our religion does not lie in doing what God has not enjoined, or abstaining from what he hath not forbidden. It does not lie in the form of our apparel, in the posture of our body, or the covering of our heads; nor yet in abstaining from marriage, or from meats and drinks, which are all good if received with thanksgiving. Therefore neither will any man who knows whereof he affirms, fix the mark of a Methodist here—in any actions or customs purely indifferent, undetermined by the word of God.

4. Nor, lastly, is he distinguished by laying the *whole stress* of religion on any *single part* of it. If you say, "Yes, he is; for he thinks 'we are saved by faith alone,' " I answer, "You do not understand the terms." By *salvation* he means holiness of heart and life. And this he affirms to spring from true *faith alone.* Can even a nominal Christian deny it? Is this placing a part of religion for the whole? "Do we then make void the law through faith? God forbid! Yea, we establish the law." We do not place the whole of religion (as too many do, God

knoweth) either in doing no harm, or in doing good, or in using the ordinances of God. No, not in all of them together; wherein we know by experience a man may labour many years and at the end have no religion at all, no more than he had at the beginning. Much less in any one of these; or, it may be in a scrap of one of them—like her who fancies herself a *virtuous* woman only because she is not a prostitute; or him who dreams he is an *honest* man merely because he does not rob or steal. May the Lord God of my fathers preserve me from such a poor, starved religion as this! Were this the mark of a Methodist, I would sooner choose to be a sincere Jew, Turk, or Pagan.

5. "What then is the mark? Who is a Methodist, according to your own account?" I answer: a Methodist is one who has "the love of God shed abroad in his heart by the Holy Ghost given unto him"; one who "loves the Lord his God with all his heart, and with all his soul, and with all his mind, and with all his strength." God is the joy of his heart and the desire of his soul, which is constantly crying out, "Whom have I in heaven but thee? and there is none upon earth that I desire beside thee! My God and my all! Thou art the strength of my heart, and my portion for ever!"...

9. And while he thus always exercises his love to God, by praying without ceasing, rejoicing evermore, and in everything giving thanks, this commandment is written in his heart, "That he who loveth God, loves his brother also." And he accordingly "loves his neighbour as himself": he loves every man as his own soul. His heart is full of love to all mankind, to every child of "the Father of the spirits of all flesh." That a man is not personally known to him, is no bar to his love. No, nor that he is known to be such as he approves not, that he repays hatred for his goodwill. For he "loves his enemies"; yea, and the enemies of God, "the evil and the unthankful." And if it be not in his power to do good to them that hate him, yet he ceases not to pray for them, though they continue to spurn his love and still "despitefully use him and persecute him."

10. For he is "pure in heart." The love of God has purified his heart from all revengeful passions, from envy, malice, and wrath, from every unkind temper or malign affection. It hath cleansed him from pride and haughtiness of spirit, whereof alone cometh contention. And he hath now "put on bowels of mercies, kindness, humbleness of mind, meekness, longsuffering"; so that he "forbears and

forgives, if he had a quarrel against any, even as God in Christ hath forgiven him." And indeed all possible ground for contention, on his part, is utterly cut off....

11. Agreeable to this his one desire is the one design of his life, namely, "not to do his own will, but the will of Him that sent him." His one intention at all times and in all things is, not to please himself, but Him whom his soul loveth. He has a single eye. And because "his eye is single, his whole body is full of light." Indeed, where the loving eye of the soul is continually fixed upon God, there can be no darkness at all, "but the whole is light, as when the bright shining of a candle doth enlighten the house.". . .

12. And the tree is known by its fruits. For as he loves God, so he "keeps his commandments." Not only some, or most of them, but all, from the least to the greatest. He is not content to "keep the whole law, and offend in one point," but has in all points "a conscience void of offence towards God and towards man." Whatever God has forbidden, he avoids; whatever God hath enjoined, he doeth—and that whether it be little or great, hard or easy, joyous or grievous to the flesh. He "runs the way of God's commandments, now he hath set his heart at liberty.". . .

13. All the commandments of God he accordingly keeps, and that with all his might. For his obedience is in proportion to his love, the source from whence it flows. And therefore, loving God with all his heart, he serves him with all his strength. He continually presents his soul and body a living sacrifice, holy, acceptable to God; entirely and without reserve devoting himself, all he has, and all he is, to his glory. All the talents he has received he constantly employs according to his Master's will; every power and faculty of his soul, every member of his body. . . .

14. By consequence, whatsoever he doeth, it is all to the glory of God. In all his employments of every kind, he not only *aims* at this (which is implied in having a single eye) but actually *attains* it. His business and refreshments, as well as his prayers, all serve this great end. Whether he sit in his house or walk by the way, whether he lie down or rise up, he is promoting in all he speaks or does the one business of his life; whether he put on his apparel, or labour, or eat and drink, or divert himself from too wasting labour, it all tends to advance the glory of God, by peace and goodwill among men. His one invariable rule is this: "Whatsoever ye do, in word or deed, do it

all in the name of the Lord Jesus, giving thanks to God and the Father by him."

The Prison Evangelist

Wesley's concern for the poor and the imprisoned began during the early days of Methodism at Oxford and continued throughout his life. Although he gave a great deal of time and money toward the relief of the prisoners' physical and financial problems, his primary focus was the salvation of persons, not a reform of the welfare and prison systems. William Hogarth's portrayal of a Methodist preacher reading Wesley's Sermons *to "The Idle Prentice" being carted off to be hanged at Tyburn is an accurate picture of the Wesleyan concern.*

Wesley could not personally reach every individual in need across the country and began to use the printed word to extend his message into the nooks and crannies of society. He began to publish tracts that were designed to speak to the problems of specific groups of persons, entitling them "A Word to.... " The targets of the tract were a variety of sorts, including "a Drunkard," "a Swearer," "a Sabbath-Breaker," and "a Street-Walker." Among the more powerful of these pieces is "A Word to a Condemned Malefactor," spelling out the gospel message to those awaiting the hangman's noose. Although this tract is not a sermon in the usual sense, Alexander Knox's comment about Wesley's published sermons is no doubt applicable here as well: "they bear the impress and breathe the spirit of John Wesley."

[1.] What a condition are you in! The sentence is passed; you are condemned to die; and this sentence is to be executed shortly! You have no way to escape; these fetters, these walls, these gates and bars, these keepers, cut off all hope. Therefore, die you must. But must you die like a beast, without thinking what it is to die? You need not; you will not; you will think a little first; you will consider, "What is death?" It is leaving this world, these houses, lands, and all things under the sun; leaving all these things, never to return; your place will know you no more. It is leaving these pleasures; for there is no eating, drinking, gaming, no merriment in the grave. It is leaving your acquaintance, companions, friends; your father, mother, wife, children. You cannot stay with them, nor can they go with you; you must part; perhaps for ever. It is leaving a part of yourself; leaving this body which has accompanied you so long. Your soul must now drop its old companion, to rot and moulder into dust. It must enter upon a new, strange, unbodied state. It must stand naked before God!

2. But, O, how will you stand before God; the great, the holy, the just, the terrible God? Is it not his own word, "Without holiness no man shall see the Lord?" No man shall see him with joy; rather, he will call for the mountains to fall upon him, and the rocks to cover him. And what do you think holiness is? It is purity both of heart and life. It is the mind that was in Christ, enabling us to walk as he also walked. It is the loving God with all our heart; the loving our neighbour, every man, as ourselves; and the doing to all men, in every point, as we would they should do unto us. The least part of holiness is to do good to all men, and to do no evil either in word or work. This is only the outside of it. But this is more than you have. You are far from it; far as darkness from light. You have not the mind that was in Christ: There was no pride, no malice in him; no hatred, no revenge, no furious anger, no foolish or worldly desire. You have not walked as Christ walked; no rather as the devil would have walked, had he been in a body; the works of the devil you have done, not the works of God. You have not loved God with all your heart. You have not loved him at all. You have not thought about him. You hardly knew or cared whether there was any God in the world. You have not done to others as you would they should do to you; far, very far from it. Have you done all the good you could do to all men? If so, you had never come to this place. You have done evil exceedingly; your sins against God and man are more than the hairs of your head. Insomuch that even the world cannot bear you; the world itself spews you out. Even the men that know not God declare you are not fit to live upon the earth.

3. O repent, repent! Know yourself; see and feel what a sinner you are. Think of the innumerable sins you have committed, even from your youth up. How many wicked words have you spoken? How many wicked actions have you done? Think of your inward sins; your pride, malice, hatred, anger, revenge, lust! Think of your sinful nature, totally alienated from the life of God. How is your whole soul prone to evil, void of good, corrupt, full of all abominations! Feel that your carnal mind is enmity against God. Well may the wrath of God abide upon you. He is of purer eyes than to behold iniquity: He

hath said, "The soul that sinneth, it shall die." It shall die eternally, shall be "punished with everlasting destruction, from the presence of the Lord and from the glory of his power."

4. How then can you escape the damnation of hell—the lake of fire burning with brimstone; "where the worm dieth not, and the fire is not quenched?" You can never redeem your own soul. You cannot atone for the sins that are past. If you could leave off sin now, and live unblamable for the time to come, that would be no atonement for what is past. Nay, if you could live like an angel for a thousand years, that would not atone for one sin. But neither can you do this; you cannot leave off sin; it has the dominion over you. If all your past sins were now to be forgiven, you would immediately sin again; that is, unless your heart were cleansed; unless it were created anew. And who can do this? Who can bring a clean thing out of an unclean? Surely none but God. So you are utterly sinful, guilty, helpless! What can you do to be saved?

5. One thing is needful: "Believe in the Lord Jesus Christ, and thou shalt be saved!" Believe (not as the devils only, but) with that faith which is the gift of God, which is wrought in a poor, guilty, helpless sinner by the power of the Holy Ghost. See all thy sins on Jesus laid. God laid on him the iniquities of us all. He suffered once the just for the unjust. He bore our sins in his own body on the tree. He was wounded for thy sins; he was bruised for thy iniquities. "Behold the Lamb of God taking away the sin of the world!" taking away thy sins, even thine, and reconciling thee unto God the Father! "Look unto him and be thou saved!" If thou look unto Him by faith, if thou cleave to Him with thy whole heart, if thou receive Him both to atone, to teach, and to govern thee in all things, thou shalt be saved, thou art saved, both from the guilt, the punishment, and all the power of sin. Thou shalt have peace with God, and a peace in thy own soul, that passeth all understanding. Thy soul shall magnify the Lord, and thy spirit rejoice in God thy Saviour. The love of God shall be shed abroad in thy heart, enabling thee to trample sin under thy feet. And thou wilt then have an hope full of immortality. Thou wilt no longer be afraid to die, but rather long for the hour, having a desire to depart, and to be with Christ.

6. This is the faith that worketh by love, the way that leadeth to the kingdom. Do you earnestly desire to walk therein? Then put away all hindrances. Beware of company: At the peril of your soul, keep from

those who neither know nor seek God. Your old acquaintance are no acquaintance for you, unless they too acquaint themselves with God. Let them laugh at you, or say you are running mad. It is enough, if you have praise of God. Beware of strong drink. Touch it not, lest you should not know when to stop. You have no need of this to cheer your spirits; but of the peace and the love of God. Beware of men that pretend to show you the way to heaven, and know it not themselves. There is no other name whereby you can be saved, but the name of our Lord Jesus Christ. And there is no other way whereby you can find the virtue of his name but by faith. Beware of Satan transformed into an angel of light, and telling you it is presumption to believe in Christ, as your Lord and your God, your wisdom and righteousness, sanctification and redemption. Believe in him with your whole heart. Cast your whole soul upon his love. Trust him alone; love him alone; fear him alone; and cleave to him alone; till he shall say to you (as to the dying malefactor of old), "This day shalt thou be with me in paradise."

Practicing Poet

Poetic imagination seems to have been bred into the Wesley consciousness. Charles, of course, came to be known as the Poet of Methodism because of his prolific production of popular hymns. Both his father and brother Samuel wrote and published poetry, and sister Hetty's poems appeared in the Gentleman's Magazine. *John was no exception to this family inclination toward poetic expression. From an early age, his interests and talents turned often toward poetry. When John was but twenty-one, his father wrote to him at Oxford, "I like your verses on the 65th Psalm and would not have you bury your talent." His mother, however, was a bit more circumspect: "I would not have you leave making verses; rather make poetry sometimes your diversion, though never your business."*

In keeping with these sentiments, Wesley never thought of himself primarily as a poet; but poetry was quite often for him a creative outlet. He came to see it as a useful tool for teaching and promoting Christian truth and virtue. The fascination was lifelong, the writing and reading of "pious and elegant poetry" being one of the few diversions he continued to consider appropriate to "the more excellent way." His involvement with the poetic arts took several forms: he was a reader, a collector, a writer, a translator, an editor, and a publisher of poetry.

His affinity for poetry was part of his larger fascination with language—the meaning of words, the rhythm and beauty of phrases, the direct and clear expression of ideas. Throughout his works, his carefully developed writing style weaves together classical, scriptural, and colloquial strands. This particular linguistic interest is also evident in his production of such specialized works as dictionaries of both the English and German languages and grammar textbooks for five languages.

Collector of Poetry

Poetic lines of all sorts, from epitaphs to German hymns, caught Wesley's eye. He often filled blank pages in his diaries with lines plucked from hither and yon, occasionally bawdy in the early years, usually more religious in later years. One of his early commonplace books he dedicated entirely to a collection of poetry, ranging from masterpieces of Milton and Pope to some trite, even crude, anonymous ditties. One page in his first Oxford diary became a repository for a list of fascinating colloquial expressions, probably gathered during his travels in the north country in the late 1720s. Another page lists titles of songs, mostly from stage plays current at the time, which may in fact represent his repertoire for flute playing as much as his interest in the lyrics. Wesley's penchant for collecting poetry was soon subsumed by his broader religious designs and reached a somewhat sanctified fruition in his publication of three volumes of Moral and Sacred Poems *in 1744, carefully selected from many sources. Ironically, he seems to have cared more for the content of the poems than the copyright laws that protected some of them, and his literary piracy cost him £20 in legal settlements.*

[From Oxford Diary I]

Belinda has such wondrous charms,
'Tis heaven to lie within her arms;
And she's so charitably given
She wishes all mankind in heaven.

....

'Tis hard, 'tis very hard, I swear,
　To rhyme upon a theme so bare:
Within no brains; without no hair!

....

A blooming youth lies buried here,
　　Euphemius to his country dear;
Nature adorned his mind and face,
　　With every muse and every grace,
About the marriage state to prove
　　But death had quicker wings than love!

....

Part of the Provost of Aberdeen College's translation of the Bible:

Absalom was hanging in a tree
　　Crying, the Lord have Marcy;
Joab came by and full angry was he,
　　And run his spear up his arsy.

....

[List of colloquialisms from the area around Epworth in Lincolnshire; for the meanings of many of these terms, see John Wright, English Dialect Dictionary *(1906), and Joan Sims-Kimbery,* Wodds and Doggerybaw: A Lincolnshire Dialect Dictionary *(1995).]*

You muckspout, you clartikettle, I'll tan your bone-cart; ously fummart, silly kedgel; a twichel, a smooting, a blossom; rough robins, forking robins, through your ribs; as good do it soon as sins; I'm neither daunch nor divorous; in a stickle, stranny, sliving, flecked and spunged, halloking, heppen; I'll uppod ye, to fridge, smoored, bare whittle and whang; the hogglecroggles, a hurrendurren, a dagbite, 'tis no raggle, rigwelted, swizzoned, to kink, bug, abboon, nawther, rattenly, to clam, to clawny, to hover, to set a gate, to remble, to threpe, perseverance; murl, emse, orned, my stomach upbraids me, tull, gif, teethy, cummered, as rough as a heckle, behint, owry, obstakle, snacking, nazzarly, a bunch-clod, a nidgcock, to glog, to gausfer, to splawder, to raum, to stocken, to spray, to quail, a gatch, thepes, grissons, hoven, kedge, to whetter, marrow, never to braid of one, to paragaud, a mike, a gime, to addle, sulky, a doubler, craply, nothing but, to fugle, to fadge, to notch, a trail-tongs, a farrand.

155

[*From his commonplace book* "Collection of Poetry," *1730*]

Upon John Dryden

At all religions, present and the past
    Thou still hast railed, yet chose the worst at last.
True to thyself; 'tis what thou didst before:
    Rail at all women, and then wed a whore.

....

The Spider
By Mr. Pope

Artist, who underneath my table
    Thy curious texture has displaid,
Who, if we may believe the Fable
    Wast once a lovely, blooming maid:

Insidious, watchful, restless spider,
    Fear no officious damsel's broom,
Extend thy artful cobweb wider,
    And spread thy banner round my room.

While I thy wondrous fabric stare at
    And think on poets' haply fate,
Like thee, condemned to lonely garret
    And rudely banished rooms of state.

And as from out thy tortured body
    Thou drawst thy slender threads with pain,
So does he labour, like a noddy,
    To spin materials from his brain.

He for some tawdry, fluttering creature
    That makes a glittering in his eye;
And that's a conquest little better
    Than thine o'er captive butterfly.

Thus far, 'tis plain, we both agree:
    And (time perhaps may quickly show it)
'Tis ten to one, but poverty
    End both the spider and the poet.

....

A Collection of Moral and Sacred Poems
from the most celebrated English Authors

To the Right Honourable the Countess of Huntingdon.

Madam,

It has been a common remark, for many years, that poetry, which might answer the noblest purposes, has been prostituted to the vilest, even to confound the distinctions between virtue and vice, good and evil; and that to such a degree, that among the numerous poems now extant in our language there is an exceeding small proportion which does not, more or less, fall under this heavy censure. So that a great difficulty lies on those who are not willing, on the one hand, to be deprived of an elegant amusement, nor, on the other, to purchase it at the heard of innocence or virtue.

Hence it is, that many have placed a chaste collection of English poems among the chief desiderata of this age. Your mentioning this a year or two ago, and expressing a desire to see such a collection, determined me not to delay the design I have long had of attempting something in this kind. I therefore revised all the English poems I knew and selected what appeared most valuable in them. Only Spenser's works I was constrained to omit, because scarce intelligible to the generality of modern readers.

I shall rejoice if the want of which you complained be in some measure supplied by the following collection, of which this, at least, may be affirmed: there is nothing therein contrary to virtue, nothing that can any way offend the chastest ear, or give pain to the tenderest heart. And perhaps whatever is really essential to the most sublime divinity, as well as the purest and most refined morality, will be found therein. Nor is it a small circumstance, that the most just and important sentiments are here represented with the utmost advantage, with all the ornaments both of wit and language, and in the clearest, fullest, strongest light.

Writer of Poetry

John Wesley's first published original works were poems, included in David Lewis's Miscellaneous Poems by Several Hands *(1726). Wesley soon began to exercise this talent to produce hymns for the use of the Methodists; some of his own work appeared in the first* Collection of Psalms and Hymns *(1737) published in Charleston. Although brother Charles soon became the major source of original writing for the many collections of hymns, the brothers decided not to distinguish authorship. These publications were nearly always a joint venture, with John exercising his editorial prerogatives in almost every case, even over his brother's work. His reflections on poetry in general are expressed most concisely in the preface to the definitive collection of hymns in 1780, which he referred to as "a little body of experimental and practical divinity" (see* Works, *7:74-75).*

The seven former verses of the 46th Psalm

[This work was published in Lewis's Miscellaneous Poems, *and all but three stanzas were included in the Charleston* Collection of Psalms and Hymns, *as they are produced here.]*

> On God supreme our hope depends,
> Whose omnipresent sight
> Even to the pathless realms extends
> Of uncreated night.
>
> Plunged in th' abyss of deep distress,
> To him we raise our cry;
> His mercy bids our sorrows cease,
> And fills our tongue with joy.
>
> Though earth her ancient seat forsake,
> By pangs convulsive torn;
> Though her self-balanced fabric shake,
> And ruined nature mourn:
>
> Though hills be in the ocean lost,
> With all their shaggy load:
> No fear shall e'er molest the just,
> Or shake his trust in God.
>
> Nations remote, and realms unknown,
> In vain reject his sway;
> For lo! Jehovah's voice is shown,
> And earth shall melt away.

Lest war's devouring surges rise,
   And rage on every side;
The Lord of Hosts our refuge is,
   And Jacob's God our guide.

....

[Written about the same time as the above, and sent to brother Samuel:]

By a cool fountain's flow'ry side
   The fair Celinda lay;
Her looks increased the summer's pride,
   Her eyes the blaze of day.

Quick through the air to this retreat
   A bee industrious flew,
Prepared to rifle every sweet
   Under the balmy dew.

Drawn by the fragrance of her breath
   Her rosy lips he found;
There in full transport sucked in death,
   And dropped upon the ground.

Enjoy, blest bee, enjoy thy fate,
   Nor at thy fall repine;
Each God would quit his blissful state
   To share a death like thine.

....

[The following hymn by John Wesley first appeared in the Collection of
Psalms and Hymns *of 1741]*

"A Morning Hymn"

We lift our hearts to Thee,
   O Day-Star from on high!
The sun itself is but Thy shade,
   Yet cheers both earth and sky.

O let Thy orient beams
The night of sin disperse!
The mists of error and of vice
Which shade the universe!

How beauteous nature now!
How dark and sad before!
With joy we view the pleasing change,
And nature's God adore.

O may no gloomy crime
Pollute the rising day:
Or Jesu's blood, like evening dew,
Wash all the stains away.

May we this life improve,
To mourn for errors past,
And live this short revolving day
As if it were our last.

To God the Father, Son,
And Spirit, One and Three,
Be glory, as it was, is now,
And shall forever be.

....

*A Collection of Hymns
for the Use of the People Called Methodists*
(1780)

Preface

...May I be permitted to add a few words with regard to the poetry? Then I will speak to those who are judges thereof with all freedom and unreserve. To these I may say, without offence: (1) In these hymns there is no doggerel, no botches, nothing put in to patch up the rhyme, no feeble expletives. (2) Here is nothing turgid or bombast on the one hand, or low and creeping on the other. (3) Here are no *cant* expressions, no words without meaning. Those who impute this to us know not what they say. We talk common sense (whether they understand it or not) both in verse and prose, and use no word but in a fixed and determinate sense. (4) Here are, allow me to say, both the purity, the strength, and the elegance of the English language—and, at the same time, the utmost simplicity and plainness, suited to every capacity. Lastly, I desire men of taste to judge—these are the only competent judges—whether there be not in some of the following hymns the true spirit of poetry, such as cannot be acquired by art and labour, but must be the gift of nature. By labour a man may become a tolerable imitator of Spenser, Shakespeare, or Milton, and may heap together pretty compound epithets, as "pale-eyed," "meek-eyed," and the like; but unless he be born a poet, he will never attain the genuine *spirit of poetry*. . . .

Translator of Poetry

John's poetical abilities also helped him translate many hymns from foreign languages, especially German. He was introduced to the Moravian hymns en route to Georgia, and his appreciation for this German poetry led him "to English" nearly three dozen of the choicest items from the Moravian hymnal, Das Gesangbuch de Gemeinde in Herrnhuth *(1735). The hymns he chose were those he "judged to be most scriptural and most suitable to sound experience." The translation is rather free at points, so that, in spite of his stated intent to be faithful to the original text, Wesley's inclination to "improve" these lines often led to such liberties as the inclusion (in the first hymn below, stanza 1, line 6) of a phrase from St. Augustine for which there is no basis either in the Tersteegen or any scriptural text.*

The following selections are from among those that still remain in the current United Methodist Hymnal. *The number of stanzas, however, has often been greatly reduced from the original.*

"Thou Hidden Love of God" by Gerhardt Tersteegen
(1697–1769)
tr. by John Wesley

[First published in A Collection of Psalms and Hymns *(1738) with eight stanzas, of which the following are stanzas 1, 4, 6, and 8; see* Works, *7:491-94.]*

Thou hidden love of God, whose height,
  Whose depth unfathomed, no man knows;
I see from far thy beauteous light,
  Inly I sigh for Thy repose;
My heart is pained, nor can it be
At rest, till it finds rest in Thee.

Is there a thing beneath the sun,
  That strives with thee my heart to share?
Ah! tear it thence, and reign alone,
  The Lord of every motion there!
Then shall my heart from earth be free,
When it has found repose in Thee.

O Love, thy sovereign aid impart
  To save me from low-thoughted care!
Chase this self-will through all my heart,
  Through all its latent mazes there;
Make me thy duteous child, that I
Ceaseless may, "Abba, Father," cry.

Each moment draw from earth away
  My heart, that lowly waits thy call;
Speak to my inmost soul, and say,
  "I am thy Love, thy God, thy All!"
To feel thy power, to hear thy voice,
To taste thy love, is all my choice.

....

"Living by Christ" by Paul Gerhardt (1607–1676)
tr. by John Wesley

[First published in Hymns and Sacred Poems *(1739) with sixteen stanzas; see* Works, *7:530-31.]*

Jesu, thy boundless love to me
  No thought can reach, no tongue declare;
O knit my thankful heart to thee,
  And reign without a rival there!

Thine wholly, thine alone I am;
Be thou alone my constant flame!

O grant that nothing in my soul
   May dwell, but Thy pure love alone!
O may thy love possess me whole,
   My joy, my treasure, and my crown;
Strange flames far from my soul heart remove—
My every act, word, thought, be love.

O Love, how cheering is thy ray!
   All pain before thy presence flies!
Care, anguish, sorrow, melt away
   Where'er thy healing beams arise;
O Jesu, nothing may I see,
Nothing desire or seek but thee!

In suffering be thy love my peace,
   In weakness be thy love my power;
And when the storms of life shall cease,
   Jesu, in that important hour,
In death as life be thou my guide,
And save me, who for me hast died.

Editor of Poetry

Although Wesley never made poetry "his business" as such, he did get into the business of publishing poetry, as we have seen. In addition to the collections already mentioned, Wesley produced editions of some of his favorite English poets, edited in such a fashion as to be more understandable and useful to the common, unlettered people of his day. His edition of Milton's Paradise Lost *for instance, omitted many lines which he "despaired of explaining to the unlearned." In truth, he may also have disagreed with some of the theology in the excised portions. His tutorial instincts (presumptuousness?) combined with his pragmatic religiosity led him to alter the text in such a way as to "correct" its form. He was aiming for more simplicity and clarity while trying to do away with "mere ornamentation," intending thereby to improve the poem's practical effect—to admonish and instruct the reader.*

Wesley was not the only one to try to "improve" Milton; perhaps no one succeeded. That he tried says something about his view of the arts and his role in the culture of his day. The following selections from his prefaces to extracts of Milton and Young indicate his purpose and rationale in such endeavors. The sample from Paradise Lost *illustrates his method and technique of abridging.*

An Extract from Milton's Paradise Lost

TO THE READER

Of all the poems which have hitherto appeared in the world, in whatever age or nation, the preference has generally been given, by impartial judges, to Milton's "Paradise Lost." But this inimitable work, amidst all its beauties, is unintelligible to abundance of readers: The immense learning which he has everywhere crowded together, making it quite obscure to persons of a common education.

This difficulty, almost insuperable as it appears, I have endeavoured to remove in the following extract: first, by omitting those lines which I despaired of explaining to the unlearned; and secondly, by adding short and easy notes, such as, I trust, will make the main of this excellent poem clear and intelligible to any uneducated person of a tolerable good understanding.

To those passages which I apprehend to be peculiarly excellent, either with regard to sentiment or expression, I have prefixed a star; and these, I believe, it would be worthwhile to read over and over, or even to commit to memory.

....

[Milton:]
> ...our better part remains
> To work in close design, by fraud or guile
> What force effected not: that he no less
> At length from us may find, who overcomes
> By force, hath overcome but half his foe.

[Wesley's extract:]
> ...our better part remains
> To work by guile what force effected not:

164

That he at length may find, who overcomes
By force, hath overcome but half his foe.

....

An Extract from Dr. Young's Night Thoughts on Life, Death, and Immortality

TO THE READER

My design in the following extract is, (1) To leave out all the lines which seem to me, either to contain childish conceits, to sink into prosaic flatness, to rise into the turgid, the false sublime, or to be incurably obscure to common readers; (2) To explain the words which are obscure, not in themselves, but only to unlearned readers; (3) To point out, especially to these, by a single or double mark, what appear to me to be the sublimest strokes of poetry, and the most pathetic strokes of nature and passion.

It may be objected by some that I have left out too much; by others that I have left out too little. I answer, (1) I have left out no more than I apprehended to be either childish, or flat, or turgid, or obscure: So obscure as not to be explained without more words than suited with my design; (2) I have left in no more of what I conceived liable to any of these objections than was necessary to preserve some tolerable connection between the preceding and following lines.

Perhaps a more plausible objection will be that the explanations are too short. But be pleased to observe, it was no part of my design to explain anything at large; but barely to put, as often as I could, a plain word for a hard one: And where one did not occur, to use two or three, or as few as possible.

But I am sensible it may be objected farther, the word added to explain the other does not always express the meaning of it; at least, not so exactly and fully as might be. I answer, (1) I allow this; but it was the best I could find without spending more time upon it than I could afford; (2) Where the word added does not express the common meaning of the word, it often expresses the Doctor's peculiar meaning, who frequently takes words in a very uncommon, not to say improper, sense; (3) I have made a little attempt; such as I could consistently with abundance of other employment. Let one that has more leisure and more abilities supply what is here wanting.

CHAPTER 12

The Would-Be Husband

Wesley's long-standing ideal of celibacy (for himself) withstood several challenges during the first two decades of his ministry. Sophy Hopkey (see page 77) was not the first woman to steal his heart, nor was she the last. A decade later, in his mid-forties, Wesley became convinced that "a believer might marry, without suffering loss in his soul." He was to discover, however, that tying a successful matrimonial knot was more easily rationalized than carried out. He soon became engaged to a young woman who, after a drawn-out and confusing series of events, finally married one of his preachers. Within fifteen months, John's affections had been captured by another woman, whom he rather quickly married (over the objections of his brother), only to find himself estranged from her before the decade was out. Wesley's perception of his changing "circumstances" can be seen in several documents from his own pen during this period.

The Jilted Fiancé

Shortly before his brother Charles married Sarah Gwynne in April 1749, John Wesley fell in love with Grace Murray. She was a young widow thirteen

166

years his junior whom he had employed in the Orphan House, Newcastle, to take care of the "sick and worn-out preachers." Grace had nursed Wesley back to health in August 1748, and for the next year or so directed her attentions alternately to Wesley and one of his preachers, John Bennett (who had also benefitted from her healing touch). On more than one occasion during that period, Wesley had entered into an espousal de praesenti with Grace, a recognized form of civil marriage contract under the current common law of England. Before Wesley could work out all the necessary conditions preliminary to the final nuptials in a church, his brother Charles had successfully and secretly intervened, seeing that Grace was married to John Bennett.

Wesley's own narrative of these events, in some ways nearly as confusing as the events themselves, gives a step-by-step description of the shifting tides of romance in this affair. It also includes an illuminating document that outlines "the grounds on which [he] had proceeded," surveying his attitudes toward the married state from the time he was a child. The holograph of this narrative is presently in the British Library, London ("An Account of an Amour of John Wesley," Add. MSS. 7119). It was published in its entirety in 1910 by J. Augustin Léger in Wesley's Last Love.

1. In June 1748, we had a Conference in London. Several of our brethren then objected to the *Thoughts upon Marriage,* and in a full and friendly debate convinced me that a believer might marry, without suffering loss in his soul.

2. In August following, I was taken ill at Newcastle. Grace Murray attended me continually. I observed her more narrowly than ever before, both as to her temper, sense and behaviour. I esteemed and loved her more and more. And, when I was a little recovered, I told her, sliding into it I know not how, "If ever I marry, I think you will be the person." After some time I spoke to her more directly. She seemed utterly amazed, and said, "This is too great a blessing for me: I can't tell how to believe it. This is all I could have wished for under Heaven, if I had dared to wish for it."

3. From that time I conversed with her as my own. The night before I left Newcastle, I told her, "I am convinced God has called you to be my fellow-labourer in the Gospel. I will take you with me to Ireland in spring. Now we must part for a time. But, if we meet again, I trust we shall part no more." She begged we might not part so soon, saying, "It was more than she could bear." Upon which I took her with me through Yorkshire and Derbyshire, where she was

unspeakably useful both to me and to the societies. I left her in Cheshire with John Bennett, and went on my way rejoicing.

4. Not long after I received a letter from John Bennett and another from her. He desired my consent to marry her. She said, "She believed it was the will of God." Hence I date her fall: here was the first false step, which God permitted indeed, but not approved. I was utterly amazed, but wrote a mild answer to both, supposing they were married already. She replied in so affectionate a manner, that I thought the whole design was at an end....

8. We passed several months together in Ireland. I saw the work of God prosper in her hands. She lightened my burthen more than can be expressed. She examined all the women in the smaller societies and the believers in every place. She settled all the women-bands; visited the sick; prayed with the mourners, more and more of whom received remission of sins during her conversation or prayer. Meantime she was to me both a servant and friend, as well as a fellow-labourer in the Gospel. She provided everything I wanted. She told me with all faithfulness and freedom, if she thought anything amiss in my behaviour. And (what I never saw in any other to this day) she knew to reconcile the utmost plainness of speech, with such deep esteem and respect, as I often trembled at, not thinking it was due to any creature: And to join with the most exquisite modesty, a tenderness not to be expressed.

9. The more we conversed together, the more I loved her; and, before I returned from Ireland, we contracted by a contract *de prae-senti:* All this while she neither wrote to J. B. nor he to her: So that the affair between *them* was as if it had never been.

10. We returned together to Bristol. It was there, or at Kingswood, that she heard some idle tales concerning me and Molly Francis. They were so plausibly related that she believed them: And in a sudden vehement fit of jealousy writ a loving letter to J. B. Of this she told me the next day in great agony of mind: but it was too late. His passion revived: And he wrote her word, "He would meet her when she came into the North."...

15. The next morning, she told me what had past. I was more perplext than ever. As I now knew she loved me, and as she was contracted to me before, I knew not whether I ought to let her go? For several days I was utterly unresolved: Till on Wednesday, September 6, I put it home to herself, "Which will you choose?" and she declared

again and again, "I am determined by conscience, as well as inclination, to live and die with you."

16. We came to Newcastle the same evening. The next day I wrote to John Bennett....

Newcastle upon Tyne
September 7, 1749

My Dear Brother

1. The friendship between you and me has continued long. I pray God it may continue to our live's [*sic*] end.

But if I love you, I must deal plainly with you. And surely you desire I should. Oh that you would consider what I say! with meekness and love, and with earnest continual prayer to God!

2. You expressed a willingness some years ago, to be one of my helpers in the work of the Gospel. I gladly received you into the number, and you objected to none of the rules whereby they act. If you had, you might have continued at your own place; in friendship, though not in union, with me.

3. As one of my helpers, I desired you, three years ago, to assist me at Newcastle. In my house there I had placed a servant whom I had tried several years, and found faithful in all things. Therefore I trusted her in the highest degree, and put her in the highest office, that any woman can bear amongst us.

4. Both by the nature and rules of your office you was engaged to do nothing of importance without consulting me. She was likewise engaged by the very nature of hers, as well as by the confidence I reposed in her, to consult me in all things: to take no step of any moment, without my knowledge and consent: over and above which she was peculiarly engaged hereto, by her own voluntary and express promise.

5. Notwithstanding this, you were scarce out of my house, when without ever consulting me, you solicited her to take a step of the last importance without my consent or knowledge. You, whom I had trusted in all things, thus betrayed your trust, and moved her to do so too. You, to whom I had done no wrong, wronged me, and that in an uncommon manner. You endeavoured at the time when I expected nothing else, to rob me of a most faithful and most useful servant; the fellow to whom, for the work committed to her care, I knew not where to find in the three kingdoms.

6. Last autumn I observed her more narrowly, and perceived she was such a person, as I had sought in vain for many years, and then determined never to part with. I told her this, but told her withal,

"I could not as yet proceed any farther, because I could do nothing without consulting my brother, as he had done nothing without consulting me." She answered, "It was so great a blessing that she knew not how to believe it. It seemed all as a dream." I repeated it again, and there was no shadow of objection made.

7. I told her farther, "I am convinced it is not the will of God that you should be shut up in a corner. I am convinced you ought to labour with me in the Gospel. I therefore design to take you to Ireland in the spring. Now we must part for a season; but if we meet again, I trust we shall part no more."

And from this time, I looked upon her as my own, and resolved that nothing but death should part us.

8. Three days after I left her, without ever consulting me, you solicited her again. And in a few days more, prevailed upon her to comply, and promise marriage to you.

9. That very night God warned you in a vision or dream, of one who had a prior right. But whom at your instance, she pushed away. Yet you construed it in quite another manner.

10. However, thus far you went: You asked her (instead of me), "whether there was any such engagement?" Partly out of fear, partly out of love blinding her eyes, she replied, "There was not." And 'tis true, there was no explicit an engagement as would stand good in law. But such an one there was, as ought in conscience to have prevented any other, till it should be dissolved.

11. Upon her return from Ireland, God again interposed by means of those who were near you; but you construed this likewise your own way: You rushed forward, and by vehement importunity forced her tender and compassionate mind, to promise you again.

12. Now, my brother, pray earnestly that God would show you and me, what is right in this matter. Was not your very first step wrong? Was it acting faithfully, even as a friend, to move such a thing without my consent or knowledge?

Was it not much more wrong, considering you as an helper? Who as such, ought to do nothing without my advice?

Was you not hereby tempting her likewise to do extremely wrong; who was likewise engaged even as a friend, but much more as an housekeeper, to take no step, without first consulting me?

Was not all this quite unjust and unkind? as well as treacherous and unfaithful? . . .

[14.] O that you would take Scripture and reason for your rule, instead of blind and impetuous passion! I can say no more—only this—You may tear her away by violence. But my consent I cannot, dare to give: Nor I fear can God give you his blessing.

170

This William Shent promised to deliver with his own hand. But it was not delivered at all.

17. In the afternoon, without any importunity or constraint, she wrote a letter to J. B. The purport of it was, "That she was more and more convinced, both he and she had sinned against God, in entering on any engagement at all, without Mr. W.'s knowledge and consent."

18. Friday, September 8, we set out for Berwick, visiting all the intermediate societies. Every hour gave me fresh proof of her usefulness on the one hand, and her affection on the other. Yet I could not consent to her repeated request, to marry immediately. I told her "before this could be done, it would be needful, (1) To satisfy J. B., (2) To procure my brother's consent, and, (3) To send an account of the reasons on which I proceed, to every helper, and every society in England, at the same time desiring their prayers." She said she should not be willing to stay above a year. I replied, "Perhaps less time will suffice." . . .

[21.] The more I knew her, the more I loved her. She frequently told me, "In time past I could have married another, if you would have given me away. But now it is impossible we should part: God has united us for ever." Abundance of conversation to the same effect, we had in our return to Newcastle: Where on Sunday 17, we continued conversing together till late at night, and she gave me all the assurances which words could give, of the most intense and inviolable affection. The same she renewed every day, yea, every hour when we were alone, unless when we were employed in prayer: which indeed took up a considerable part of the time we spent together. . . .

27. As soon as I had finished my letter to J. B. on the 7th instant, I had sent a copy of it to my brother at Bristol. The thought of my marrying at all, but especially of my marrying a servant, and one so low-born, appeared above measure shocking to him. Thence he inferred, that it would appear so to all mankind: and consequently, that it would break up all our societies, and put a stop to the whole work of God.

28. Full of this, instead of writing to me (who would have met him any where at the first summons) he hurried up from Bristol to Leeds. There he met with Robert Swindells, and William Shent; who informed him (which he had heard slightly mentioned before)

"That G. M. was engaged to J. B." This was adding oil to the flame: So he posted to Newcastle, taking with him William Shent, not many degrees cooler than himself.

29. Here he met with Jane Keith, a woman of strong sense and exquisite subtlety. She had long been prejudiced against G. M., which had broke out more than once. She gave him just such an account as he wished to hear, and at his request, set it down in writing. The sum of it was, "(1) That Mr. W. was in love with G. M. beyond all sense and reason; (2) that he had shown this in the most public manner, and had avowed it to all the society; and (3) that all the town was in an uproar, and all the societies ready to fly in pieces."

30. My brother, believing all this, flew on for Whitehaven, concluding G. M. and I were there together. He reached it (with W. Shent) on Monday. I was not at all surprised when I saw him. He urged, "All our preachers would leave us, all our societies disperse, if I married so mean a woman." He then objected, that she was engaged to J. B. As I knew she was pre-engaged to me, as I regarded not her birth, but her qualification, and as I believed those consequences might be prevented, I could see no valid objection yet. However I did not insist on my own judgment; but desired the whole might be preferred to Mr. Perronet which he readily consented to.

31. As soon as I was alone, I began to consider with myself, whether I was *in my senses*, or no? Whether love had *put out my eyes* (as my brother affirmed) or I had the use of them still? I weighed the steps I had taken, yet again, and the grounds on which I had proceeded. A short account of these I wrote down simply, in the following terms.

1. From the time I was six or seven years old, if any one spoke to me concerning marrying, I used to say, I thought I never should, "Because I should never find such a woman as my father had."

2. When I was about seventeen (and so till I was six or seven and twenty) I had no thought of marrying, "Because I could not keep a wife."

3. I was then persuaded, "It was unlawful for a priest to marry," grounding that persuasion on the (supposed) sense of the primitive church.

4. Not long after, by reading some of the mystic writers, I was brought to think "marriage was the less perfect state," and that

172

there was some degree (at least) of "taint upon the mind, necessarily attending the marriage-bed."

5. At the same time I viewed in a strong light St. Paul's words to the Corinthians: And judged it "Impossible for a married man to be so without carefulness, or to attend upon the Lord with so little distraction, as a single man might do."

6. Likewise, being desirous to lay out all I could, in feeding the hungry, and clothing the naked, I could not think of marrying, "because it would bring such expense, as would swallow up all I now gave away."

7. But my grand objection for these twelve years past has been, "A dispensation of the Gospel has been committed to me. And I will do nothing which directly or indirectly tends to hinder my preaching the Gospel."

8. My first objection was easily removed by my finding some, though very few women, whom I could not but allow to be equal to my mother, both in knowledge and piety.

9. My second, "that I could not keep a wife," held only till I found reason to believe, there were persons in the world, who if I were so inclined, were both able and willing to keep *me*.

10. My third vanished away when I read with my own eyes Bp. Beveridge's *Codex Conciliorum*. I then found the very Council of Nice had determined just the contrary to what I had supposed.

11. St. Paul slowly and gradually awakened me out of my mystic dream; and convinced me, "The bed is undefiled, and no necessary hindrance to the highest perfection." Though still I did not quite shake off the weight, till our last conference in London.

12. I was next, though very unwillingly convinced, that there might be such a case as Dr. Koker's: who often declared, he was never so free from care, never served God with so little distraction, as since his marriage with one, who was both able and willing, to bear that care for him.

13. The two other objections weighed with me still, increase of expense and hindering the Gospel. But with regard to the former, I now clearly perceive, that my marriage would bring little expense, if I married one I maintain now, who would afterward desire nothing more than she had before: And would cheerfully consent, that our children (if any) should be wholly brought up at Kingswood.

14. As to the latter, I have the strongest assurance, which the nature of the thing will allow, that the person proposed would not hinder, but exceedingly further me in the work of the Gospel. For, from a close observation of several years (three of which she spent

under my own roof) I am persuaded she is in every capacity an help meet for me.

15. First, as a housekeeper....

16. As a nurse....

17. As a companion....

18. As a friend....

19. Lastly, as a fellow labourer in the Gospel of Christ (the light wherein my wife is to be chiefly considered)....

26. But it is objected to this, [First.] That my marrying her would turn the greater part of our preachers out of the way: insomuch that they would despise my authority, and act no more in conjunction with me.

Secondly. That it would break up our societies, and cause them to cry out, "Every man to his tents, O Israel!"

Thirdly. That it would give such scandal to the world, as never could be removed.

27. I cannot receive any one of these propositions without proof.... The short is this, (1) "I have scriptural reason to marry. (2) I know no person so proper as this...."

42. Tuesday [Oct.] 3rd, we rode to Old-Hutton, and about 9 the next night reached Leeds. Here I found, not my brother, but Mr. Whitefield. I lay down by him on the bed. He told me, "My brother would not come, till J. B. and G. M. were married." I was troubled. He perceived it. He wept and prayed over me. But I could not shed a tear. He said all that was in his power to comfort me: But it was in vain. He told me, "It was his judgment that she was MY wife, and that he had said so to J. B.: That he would fain have persuaded them to wait, and not to marry till they had seen me: But that my brother's impetuosity prevailed and bore down all before it."...

44. Thurs. [Oct.] 5, about 8. One came in from Newcastle, and told us, "They were married on Tuesday." My brother came an hour after. I felt no anger. Yet I did not desire to see him. But Mr. Wh. constrained me. After a few words had past, he accosted me with, "...I renounce all intercourse with you, but what I would have with an heathen man or a publican." I felt little emotion. It was only adding a drop of water to a drowning man. Yet I calmly accepted his renunciation, and acquiesced therein. Poor Mr. Wh. and J. Nelson burst into tears. They prayed, cried, and intreated, till the storm past away. We could not speak, but only fell on each other's neck.

45. J. B. then came in. Neither of us could speak. But we kissed each other and wept. Soon after, I talked with my brother alone. He seemed utterly amazed. He clearly saw, I was not what he had thought, and now blamed her only: which confirmed me in believing, my presage was true, and I should see her face no more.

46. But the great mystery to me was this. By what means under heaven, could she (who I knew, whatever others thought, had for ten years loved me as her own soul) be prevailed upon to marry another? Especially after so solemn a contract with me. I could not unravel it till I read my brother's papers: what I learned from them (and some others) was this....

55. On Tues. morning, Oct. 3, they were married. They all then rode on contentedly to Leeds, to give me the meeting there, as well that I might have the pleasure of seeing the bride, as "that I might acknowledge my sin" (those were my brother's expressions) before J. B. and them all.

56. But this I was not altogether ready to do. Neither did I apprehend she desired my company any more: Till on Friday Oct. 6, I was informed, "Both J. B. and his wife desired to see me." I went, But O! what an interview! It was not soon, that words could find their way. We sat weeping at each other, till I asked her, "What did you say to my brother, to make him accost me thus?" She fell at my feet: said "She never had spoke, nor could speak against me," uttering many other words to the same effect, in the midst of numberless sighs and tears. Before she rose, he fell on his knees too, and asked my pardon for what he had spoken of me. Between them both, I knew not what to say or do. I can forgive. But who can redress the wrong?

57. After dinner I talked with her alone. She averred with the utmost emotion, being all dissolved in tears, "That she never laid the blame on me, whom she knew to be wholly innocent: That she would rather die than speak against one, to whom she had so deep obligations. That at the time I first spoke to her at Newcastle, she loved me above all persons living: that after her engagement with J. B. her heart was divided till she went to Ireland: that then it was whole with me, and from that time, till J. B. met us at Epworth: that after his speaking she was divided again, till I talked with her on the road; from which hour she loved me more and more, till we parted at Hineley-Hill: That, when my brother took her thence, she thought he was carrying her to me: that, when she knew more of his

design, she told him, "I will do nothing, till I have seen Mr. W.": But that when it was told her at Newcastle, among a thousand other things, "Mr. W. will have nothing to say to you," then she said, "Well, I will have Mr. B. if he will have me." If these things are so, hardly has such a case been from the beginning of the world!

The New Husband

John Wesley married Mary Vazeille in February 1751. There is no known record of where the ceremony occurred or who officiated. The marriage notices in the Gentleman's Magazine *include the following simple statement:*

Feb. 18—Rev. Mr. John Wesley, methodist preacher, to a merchant's widow in Threadneedle-street, with a jointure [inherited annuity] of £300 per annum.

Charles had been "thunderstruck" when he found out his brother was "resolved to marry," and had "groaned" for several days at the prospect of John's decision and the effect it would have on Methodism. But John had become clearly convinced and now "fully believed that, in my present circumstances, I might be more useful in a married state." Charles was also surprised at John's choice of a bride; if Grace Murray had been unsatisfactory in Charles' eyes because of her lowly state as a servant, this wealthy widow ranked little higher.

Charles had little opportunity to meddle in this case, however. Barely two weeks after John had announced his marital intentions to his brother, he was married. John's plans had been accelerated when, on Sunday, February 10, 1751, he accidentally slipped on the ice while crossing London Bridge and sprained his foot. He recuperated at Mrs. Vazeille's, spending his time, as he later reported, "partly in prayer, reading, and conversation, and partly in writing a Hebrew grammar and Lessons for Children." *After a week or so (the* London Magazine *gives the date as February 19), John and Mary were married.*

The newly married Wesley was back on the job before his foot was healed, preaching on the 19th and 20th from a kneeling position. A fortnight later, being "tolerably able to ride, though not to walk," he set out for Bristol for a conference of the preachers, leaving his wife in London. He returned to London for six days in March before setting out for an eight-week journey to

Scotland and the North Country. His Journal *notes at this point, "I cannot understand how a Methodist preacher can answer it to God to preach one sermon or travel one day less in a married than in a single state. In this respect surely 'it remaineth that they who have wives be as though they had none.'"*

The following letters, written during those first two tours away from home, not only express Wesley's genuine affection but also show his unequivocal view of his wife's duties and obligations in his absence. See Works, *26:451-52, 57-58.*

Bristol, March 11, 1751

And can my dear Molly spend four whole days, Friday, Saturday, Sunday, and Monday, without saying one word to me? However, you will forgive me if I am not so patient. I want to be talking to you, if not with you. I want to converse a little in the only way which is now allowed me. My body is stronger and stronger—and so is my love to you. God grant it may never go beyond his will! O that we may always continue to love one another as Christ loved us!

Do you neglect none of your temporal business? Have you wrote to Spain? And sold your jewels? And settled with Mr. Blisson? And does my dear Jenny continue to press forward? Do not you forget the poor? Have you visited the prison? My dear, be not angry that I put you upon so much work. I want you to crowd all your life with the work of faith and the labour of love. How can we ever do enough for him that has done and suffered so much for us? Are not you willing to suffer also for him? To endure the contradiction of sinners? Surely you are willing to bear whatever his wise Providence permits to fall upon you.

Let your own heart tell you what mine feels, when I bless God that I am

Ever yours.

Manchester, April 7, 1751

Last night I had the pleasure of receiving two letters from my dearest earthly friend. I can't answer them till I tell you how I love you—though you knew it before. You feel it in your own breast. For (thanks be to God) your heart is as my heart. And in token of it you have given me your hand.

If you find yourself at any time heavy for a season, you know where to go for help. You will cry without delay:

> Take this poor, flutt'ring heart to rest,
> And lodge it, Saviour, in thy breast!

In June, if it please God to continue our life and health, you shall travel with me. I want to have you always near me. And yet even that want is made easy. I was glad you was not with me last week. For it has rained every day.

I think you might have found a better husband. But Oh! where could I have found so good a wife? If I was not to bless God, surely the stones would cry out!

I suppose you mean Miss Mady Perronet. I am glad she is with you. I love her dearly. Nevertheless it will be inconvenient on some accounts. To prevent which inconveniences you will quit your house (if you live) at midsummer. We agree in desiring to cut off every needless expense. O how exactly your heart agrees with mine! Thanks be to God for this unspeakable gift.

My dear soul, adieu!

The Rejected Husband

Wesley's friend Alexander Knox once wrote, "It is certain that Mr. Wesley had a predilection for the female character, . . . partly from his generally finding in females a quicker and fuller responsiveness to his own ideas of interior piety and affectionate devotion." For Knox, such a preference explained why Wesley wrote "with peculiar effluence of thought and frankness of communication" to a wide range of female correspondents. One further observation by Knox is telling: "He so literally talks upon paper as to make it inconceivable that he should have conversed with them in any other style than that in which he wrote to them."

Molly Wesley seems to have had similar feelings about her husband John's correspondence with women. But she apparently was not quite so willing as Knox to see Wesley's literary expressions of affection as being entirely "pure and paternal." Among a growing list of marital tensions, the problems of privacy and trust were among the major issues that eventually drew the marriage asunder.

Molly took the first initiative toward separation; she left John on several occasions, beginning in 1757. John's attitude toward his wife's departure in one instance is illustrated by a comment in his journal: "Non eam reliqui, non dimisi, non revocabo *[I did not leave her; I did not send her away, I shall not call her back]."*

He did, however, send letters after her, spelling out the problems as he understood them and outlining the conditions under which harmony could be restored. If these letters are indeed an example of the way Wesley would have conversed in this situation, one can easily understand why Mrs. Wesley spent much of the last few years of her life away from her husband. Likewise, if there is any truth to his assertions, one can easily understand why he did not call her back.

Coleford, October 23, 1759

Dear Molly,

I will tell you simply and plainly the things which I dislike. If you remove them, well. If not, I am but where I was. I dislike (1) your showing any one my letters and private papers without my leave. This never did any good yet, either to you or me or any one. It only sharpens and embitters your own spirit. And the same effect it naturally has upon others. The same it would have upon me, but that (by the grace of God) I do not think of it. It can do no good. It can never bring me nearer, though it may drive me farther off.

I dislike (2) Not having the command of my own house, not being at liberty to invite even my nearest relations so much as to drink a dish of tea without disobliging *you*. I dislike (3) the being myself a prisoner in my own house; the having my chamber door watched continually so that no person can go in or out but such as have your good leave. I dislike (4) the being but a prisoner at large, even when I go abroad, inasmuch as you are highly disgusted if I do not give you an account of every place I go to and every person with whom I converse. I dislike (5) the not being safe in my own house. My house is *not* my castle. I cannot call even my study, even my bureau, my own. They are liable to be plundered every day. You say, "I plunder you of nothing but papers." I am not sure of that. How is it possible I should? I miss money too, and he that will steal a pin will steal a pound. But were it so, a scholar's papers are his treasure—my Journal in particular. "But I took only such papers as relate to Sarah Ryan and Sarah Crosby." That is not true. What are Mr. Landey's letters to them? Besides, you have taken parts of my Journal which relate to neither one nor the other. I dislike (6) your treatment of my servants (though, indeed, they are not properly mine). You do all that in you lies to make their lives a burthen to them. You browbeat, harass, rate them like dogs, make them afraid to speak to me. You treat them with such haughtiness, sternness, sourness, surliness, ill-nature, as never were known in any house of mine for near a dozen years. You forget even good breeding, and use such coarse language as befits none but a fishwife.

I dislike (7) your talking against me behind my back, and that every day and almost every hour of the day; making my faults (real or supposed) the standing topic of your conversation. I dislike (8) your slandering me, laying to my charge things which you know are false. Such are (to go but a few days back—that I beat you, which you told James Burges; that I rode to Kingswood with Sarah Ryan, which you told Sarah Crosby; and that I required you, when we were first married, never to sit in my presence without my leave, which you told Mrs. Lee, Mrs. Fry, and several others, and stood it before my face. I dislike (9) your common custom of saying things not true. To instance only in two or three particulars. You told Mr. Ireland "Mr. Vazeille learnt Spanish in a fortnight." You told Mr. Fry "Mrs. Ellison was the author as to my intrigue in Georgia." You told Mrs. Ellison "you never said any such thing; you never charged her with it." You also told her "that I had laid a plot to serve you as Susannah was served by the two elders." I dislike (10) your extreme, immeasurable bitterness to all who endeavour to defend my character (as my brother, Joseph Jones, Clayton Carthy), breaking out even into foul, unmannerly language, such as ought not to defile a gentlewoman's lips if she did not believe one word of the Bible.

And now, Molly, what would any one advise you to that has a real concern for your happiness? Certainly (1) to show, read, touch those letters no more, if you did not restore them to their proper owner; (2) to allow me the command of my own house, with free leave to invite thither whom I please; (3) to allow *me* my liberty there that any who will may come to me without let or hindrance; (4) to let me go where I please and to whom I please without giving an account to any; (5) to assure me you will take no more of my papers nor anything of mine without my consent; (6) to treat all the servants where you are, whether you like them or no, with courtesy and humanity, and to speak (if you speak at all) to them, as well as others, with good nature and good manners; (7) to speak no evil of me behind my back; (8) never to accuse me falsely; (9) to be extremely cautious of saying anything that is not strictly true, both as to the matter and manner; and (10) to avoid all bitterness of expression till you can avoid all bitterness of spirit.

These are the advices which I now give you in the fear of God and in tender love to your soul. Nor can I give you a stronger proof that I am

Your affectionate Husband

....

York, July 15, 1774

My Dear,

1. I think it needful to write one letter more in order to state the case between you and me from the beginning. I can't, indeed, do this so exactly as I would, because I have not either those letters or those parts of my Journal which give a particular account of all circumstances just as they occurred. I have therefore only my memory to depend on; and that is not very retentive of evil. So that it is probable I shall omit abundance of things which might have thrown still more light on the subject. However, I will do as well as I can, simply relating the fact to the best of my memory and judgment.

2. Before we married, I saw you was a well-bred woman of great address and a middling understanding; at the same time I believed you to be of a mild, sweet, and even temper. By conversing with you twenty days after we were married, I was confirmed in the belief. Full of this, I wrote to you soon after our first parting in the openness and simplicity of my heart. And in this belief I continued after my return till we went down to Kingswood.

3. Here, as I came one morning into your room, I saw a sight which I little expected. You was all thunder and lightning: I stared and listened; said little, and retired. You quickly followed me into the other room, fell upon your knees, and asked my pardon. I desired you to think of it no more, saying, It is with *me* as if it had never been. In two or three weeks, you relapsed again and again, and as often owned your fault, only with less and less concern. You first found we were *both* in fault, and then all the fault was on *my side*.

4. We returned to London, and your natural temper appeared more and more. In order to soften it as I could, I tried every method I could devise. Sometimes I reasoned with you at large, sometimes

in few words. At other times I declined argument, and tried what persuasion would do. And many times I heard all you said, and answered only by silence. But argument and persuasion, many words and few, speaking and silence, were all one. They made no impression at all. One might as well attempt to convince or persuade the north wind.

5. Finding there was no prevailing upon you by speaking, I tried what writing would do. And I wrote with all plainness; yet in as mild a manner as I could, and with all the softness and tenderness I was master of. But what effect did it produce? Just none at all; you construed it all into ill-nature, and was not easily prevailed upon to *forgive* so *high an affront.*

6. I think your quarrel with my brother was near this time, which continued about seven years; during two or three of which it was more or less a constant bone of contention between us, till I told you plainly, "I dare not sit and hear my brother spoken against. Therefore, whenever you begin to talk of him, I must rise and leave the room."

7. In the midst of this you drew new matter of offence from my acquaintance with Mrs. Lefevre, a dove-like woman, full of faith and humble love and harmless as a little child. I should have rejoiced to converse with her frequently and largely; but for your sake I abstained. I did not often talk with her at all, and visited her but twice or thrice in two years. Notwithstanding which, though you sometimes said you thought her a good woman, yet at other times you did not scruple to say you "questioned if I did not lie with her." And afterward you seemed to make no question of it.

8. Some time after, you took offence of my being so much with Mrs. Blackwell, and was "sure she did me no good." But this blew over, and you was often in a good humour for a week together, till October 1757. Sarah Ryan, the housekeeper at Bristol, then put a period to the quarrel between my brother and you. Meantime she asked me once and again, "Sir, should I sit and hear Mrs. Wesley talk against you by the hour together?" I said, "Hear her, if you can thereby do her any good." A while after, she came to me and said, "Indeed, sir, I can bear it no longer. It would wound my own soul." Immediately you was violently jealous of her, and required me not to speak or write to her. At the same time you insisted on the "liberty of opening and reading all letters directed to me." This you had

often done before: but I still insisted on my own liberty of speaking and writing to whom I judged proper; and of seeing my own letters first, and letting you read only those I saw fit.

9. Sunday, February 25, 1758, you went into my study, opened my bureau, and took many of my letters and papers. But on your restoring most of them two days after, I said, "Now, my dear, let all that is past be forgotten; and if either of us find any fresh ground of complaint, let us tell it to Mr. Blackwell, or Jo. Jones, or Tho. Walsh, but to no other person whatever." You agreed; and on Monday, March 6, when I took my leave of you to set out for Ireland, I thought we had as tender a parting as we had had for several years.

10. To confirm this good understanding, I wrote to you a few days after all that was in my heart. But from your answer I learned it had a quite contrary effect: you *resented* it deeply; so that for ten or twelve weeks together, though I wrote letter after letter, I received not one line. Meantime you told Mrs. Vigor and twenty more, "Mr. Wesley *never* writes to *me*. You must inquire concerning him of Sarah Ryan; he writes to her *every week*." So far from it, that I did not write to her at all for above twelve weeks before I left Ireland. Yet I really thought you would not tell a willful lie—at least, not in cold blood; till poor, dying T. Walsh asked me at Limerick, "How did you part with Mrs. W. the last time?" On my saying, "Very affectionately," he replied, "Why, what a woman is this! She told me your parting words were, 'I hope to see your wicked face no more.' " I now saw you was resolved to blacken me at all events, and would stick at no means to accomplish it. Nevertheless I laboured for peace; and at my return to Bristol, to avoid grieving *you,* did not converse with Sarah Ryan (though we were in the same house) twenty minutes in ten days' time. I returned to London. Soon after, you grew jealous of Sarah Crosby, and led me a weary life, unless I told you every place to which I went and every person I saw there.

11. Perceiving you still rose in your demands, I resolved to break through at once, and to show you I would be my own master, and go where I pleased, without asking any one's leave. Accordingly on Monday, December 18, I set out for Norwich; the first journey I had taken since we were married without telling you where I was going.

I cannot but add a few words: not by way of reproach, but of advice. God has used many means to curb your stubborn will and break the impetuosity of your temper. He has given you a dutiful but sickly daughter; He has taken away one of your sons. Another has been a grievous cross; as the third probably will be. He has suffered you to be defrauded of much money; He has chastened you with strong pain. And still He may say, "How long liftest thou up thyself against Me?" Are you more humble, more gentle, more patient, more placable than you was? I fear quite the reverse; I fear your natural tempers are rather increased than diminished. O beware lest God give you up to your own heart's lusts, and let you follow your own imaginations!

Under all these conflicts it might be an unspeakable blessing that you have an husband who knows your temper and can bear with it; who, after you have tried him numberless ways, laid to his charge things that he knew not, robbed him, betrayed his confidence, revealed his secrets, given him a thousand treacherous wounds, purposely aspersed and murdered his character, and made it your *business* so to do, under the poor pretence of vindicating your own character (whereas of what importance is *your* character to mankind, if you was buried just now? or if you had never lived, what loss would it be to the cause of God?);—who, I say, after all these provocations, is still willing to forgive you all; to overlook what is past, as if it had not been, and to receive you with open arms; not only while you have a sword in your hand, with which you are continually striking at me, though you cannot hurt me. If, notwithstanding, you continue striking at me still, what can I, what can all reasonable men think, but that either you are utterly out of your senses or your eye is not single; that you married me only for my money; that, being disappointed, you was almost always out of humour; that this laid you open to a thousand suspicions, which, once awakened, could sleep no more?

My dear Molly, let the time past suffice. If you have not (to prevent my giving it to bad women) robbed me of my substance too; if you do not blacken me, on purpose that when this breaks out, no one may believe it; stop, and consider what you do. As yet the breach may be repaired; you have wronged me much, but not beyond forgiveness. I love you still, and am as clear from all other women as the day I was born. At length know *me*, and know *yourself.* Your enemy I cannot be; but let me be your friend. Suspect me no more; asperse me no more; provoke me no more. Do not any longer contend for mastery, for power, money, or praise. Be content to be a private, insignificant person, known and loved by God and me. Attempt no more to abridge me of the liberty which I claim by the laws of God and man. Leave *me* to be governed by God and my own conscience. Then shall I govern *you* with gentle sway, and show that I do indeed love you, even as Christ the Church.

These charges and the scandalous periods of separation contributed to Mrs. Wesley's growing reputation among the Methodist people as "a troubler of their happiness and peace." She begged her husband to "put a stop to this torrent of evil that is poured out against me." At best, John's attitude was only conditionally compromising. The two strong-minded individuals never resolved their differences satisfactorily. Mrs. Wesley ended her days living apart from John. She died on October 8, 1781; John was out of town. Although he returned to London on the day of her burial, Wesley was not informed of it until a day or two later.

CHAPTER 13

The Anxious Earthen Vessel

The Modest Epitaph Writer

From a very early age, Wesley was conscious of that fragile thread called health, upon which life itself depended. Although he lived to a ripe old age, he was well aware that any serious illness might signal the approach of his last days. With that specter in mind, he quite frequently paused on his birthday to reflect upon his health, in his later years noting in particular when his vigor and vitality were as those of a man thirty years his junior. His consciousness of the fragility of life is reflected in many Journal references to sudden deaths, often followed by words like "such a vapour is life" (cf. James 4:14) or some other wistful comment. In some cases, he uses those occasions to admonish readers to be sure to make a will, if they have not done so already.

Wesley's diaries and his published Journal contain numerous references to physical problems (noted in the daily diaries under the summary of God's providential acts evident for that day, which also included the weather), from "spitting blood" and "lameness" during his Oxford days to "impetuous flux" and "seasickness" in his later years. One particularly serious bout with illness took place late in 1753, not only preventing him from preaching for four months, but also inspiring him to write his own epitaph. His friend George Whitefield wrote a letter to Wesley upon hearing of "the apparent approach of his dissolution": "If in the land of the dying [i.e., not yet dead], I hope to pay my last respects to you next week. If not, Rev. and very dear Sir, F-a-r-e-w-e-l-l. . . . My heart is too big, tears trickle down too fast."

Wesley's own account of this illness is contained in his Journal *for 1753 (see* Works, *20:482-83).*

Sat. [Nov.] 24. I rode home, and was pretty well till night, but my cough was then worse than ever. My fever returned at the same time, together with the pain in my left breast. So that I should probably have stayed at home on Sunday the 25, had it not been advertised in the public papers that I would preach a charity sermon at the chapel, both morning and afternoon. My cough did not interrupt me while I preached in the morning, but it was extremely troublesome while I administered the Sacrament. In the afternoon I consulted my friends whether I should attempt to preach again or no. They thought I should, as it had been advertised. I did so, but very few could hear. My fever increased much while I was preaching. However, I ventured to meet the society. And for near an hour my voice and strength were restored, so that I felt neither pain nor weakness.

Mon. 26. Dr. Fothergill told me plain, I must not stay in town a day longer, adding, "If anything does thee good, it must be the country air, with rest, asses' milk, and riding daily." So (not being able to sit an horse) about noon I took coach for Lewisham.

In the evening (not knowing how it might please God to dispose of me), to prevent vile panegyric, I wrote as follows:

HERE LIETH THE BODY
OF
JOHN WESLEY
A BRAND PLUCKED OUT OF THE BURNING:
WHO DIED OF A CONSUMPTION
IN THE FIFTY-FIRST YEAR OF HIS AGE
NOT LEAVING, AFTER HIS DEBTS ARE PAID,
TEN POUNDS BEHIND HIM:

PRAYING,
GOD BE MERCIFUL TO ME,
AN UNPROFITABLE SERVANT!
HE ORDERED THAT THIS, IF ANY INSCRIPTION,
SHOULD BE PLACED ON HIS TOMBSTONE.

Wed. 28. I found no change for the better, the medicines which had helped me before now taking no effect. About noon (the time that some of our brethren in London had set apart for joining in prayer) a thought came into my mind to make an experiment. So I ordered some stone brimstone to be powdered, mixed with the white of an egg, and spread on brown paper, which I applied to my side. The pain ceased in five minutes, the fever in half an hour, and from this hour I began to recover strength. The next day I was able to ride, which I continued to do every day till January 1. Nor did the weather hinder me once, it being always tolerably fair (however it was before) between twelve and one o'clock.

An Honest Heathen

Wesley's lifelong quest for self-knowledge was not a superficial exercise. In his own spiritual pilgrimage, Wesley's attempt to "press on to perfection" seems to be marked by a continuing desire for a sense of assurance. The first experience of assurance in 1738 seems not to have had an abiding satisfaction for his heart, as we saw above (page 99). The periods of despair and angst became less frequent but apparently no less intense as time went on. A comment to his brother in 1772 is telling: "I often cry out, Vitae me redde priori! [Let me return to my former life!] Let me be again an Oxford Methodist! I am often in doubt whether it would not be best for me to resume all my Oxford rules, great and small."

The following letter was written by John to his brother Charles during a period when the Methodist movement was experiencing a great deal of upheaval and tension. Sections transcribed from shorthand are shown in brackets.

Whitehaven, June 27, 1766

Dear Brother,

I think you and I have abundantly too little intercourse with each other. Are we not *old acquaintances*? Have we not known each other for half a century? and are we not jointly engaged in such a work as probably no two other men upon earth are? Why, then, do we keep at such a distance? It is a mere device of Satan. But surely we ought not at this time of day to be ignorant of his devices. Let us therefore make the full use of the little time that remains. *We* at least should *think aloud* and use to the uttermost the light and grace on each bestowed. We should help each other,

> Of little life the best to make,
> And manage wisely the last stake.

In one of my last I was saying I do not feel the wrath of God abiding on me; nor can I believe it does. And yet (this is the mystery) [I do not love God. I never did]. Therefore [I never] believed in the Christian sense of the word. Therefore [I am only an] honest heathen, a proselyte of the Temple, one of the φοβούμενοι τὸν θεόν [God-fearers]. And yet to be so employed of God! and so hedged in that I can neither get forward nor backward! Surely there never was such an instance before, from the beginning of the world! If I [ever have had] *that faith,* it would not be so strange. But [I never had any] other ἔλεγχος [evidence] of the eternal or invisible world than [I have] now; and that is [none at all], unless such as faintly shines from reasons glimmering ray. [I have no] direct witness, I do not say that [I am a child of God], but of anything invisible or eternal.

And yet I dare not preach otherwise than I do, either concerning faith, or love, or justification, or perfection. And yet I find rather an increase than a decrease of zeal for the whole work of God and every part of it. I am Φερόμενος [borne along], I know not how, that I can't stand still. I want all the world to come to ὃν οὐκ οἶδα [what I do not know]. Neither am I impelled to this by fear of any kind. I have no more fear than love. Or if I have [any fear, it is not that of falling] into hell but of falling into nothing.

I hope you are with Billy Evans. If there is an Israelite indeed, I think he is one. O insist everywhere on *full* redemption, receivable by *faith alone!* Consequently to be looked for now. You are *made,* as it were, for this very thing. Just here you are in your element. In connexion I beat you; but in strong, pointed *sentences* you beat me. Go on, in your *own way,* what God has peculiarly called you to. Press the *instantaneous* blessing: then I shall have more time for my peculiar calling, enforcing the *gradual* work.

We must have a thorough *reform of the preachers.* I wish you would *come to Leeds* with John Jones in the machine. It comes in two days; and after staying two days, you might return. I would willingly bear your expenses up and down. I believe it will help, not hurt, your health.

My love to Sally.

CHAPTER 14

The Catholic and Anti-Catholic Spirit

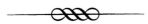

Wesley often appears to be a very opinionated person; he was not hesitant to defend his religious and political views against an opposing position. As an Englishman of the eighteenth century, he shared many of the prejudices of the contemporary English temper, including the long-standing bias against Roman Catholics. However, Wesley did not adopt the total antipathy toward papists typical of the period. As the leader of a minority religious movement that experienced persecution, Wesley might be expected to favor and promote toleration wherever and whenever possible. He was therefore quite willing to extend an olive branch to Roman Catholics in Ireland, pointing to the common ground they shared as Christians. This did not lessen either his own convictions on theological matters or his own feelings about the political threat that the papists posed in England.

The Irenic Theologian

Wesley faced many mobs. The motives of these riotous gangs were quite varied, but religious prejudice was often one springboard that helped incite them to action. In Ireland, some of the crowds that attacked Wesley and the Methodists contained large numbers of "Romanists." In 1749, during his third visit to Ireland, he wrote both his Short Address to the Inhabitants of Ireland, *an apology for Methodism in the face of previous opposition and disturbances, and his* Letter to a Roman Catholic, *an appeal for mutual respect and cooperation. In spite of the possible motive of self-preservation (that could have prompted such a letter to any religious group that joined his opposition), Wesley exhibits an ecumenical sensitivity in both the tone and the content of this* Letter *that exceeds what one might expect under those circumstances and has had far-reaching implications for more recent ventures in ecumenical cooperation.*

To a Roman Catholic

Dublin, July 18, 1749

1. You have heard ten thousand stories of us who are commonly called Protestants, of which, if you believe only one in a thousand, you must think very hardly of us. But this is quite contrary to our Lord's rule, "Judge not, that ye be not judged"; and has many ill consequences, particularly this—it inclines us to think as hardly of you. Hence we are on both sides less willing to help one another, and more ready to hurt each other. Hence brotherly love is utterly destroyed; and each side, looking on the other as monsters, gives way to anger, hatred, malice, to every unkind affection, which have frequently broke out in such inhuman barbarities as are scarce named among the heathens.

2. Now, can nothing be done, even allowing us on both sides to retain our own opinions, for the softening our hearts towards each other, the giving a check to this flood of unkindness, and restoring at least some small degree of love among our neighbours and countrymen? Do not you wish for this? Are you not fully convinced that malice, hatred, revenge, bitterness, whether in us or in you, in our hearts or yours, are an abomination to the Lord? Be our opinions right, or be they wrong, these tempers are undeniably wrong. They are the broad road that leads to destruction, to the nethermost hell.

3. I do not suppose all the bitterness is on your side. I know there is too much on our side also much, that I fear many Protestants (so called) will be angry at me too for writing to you in this manner, and will say, "It is showing you too much favour; you deserve no such treatment at our hands."

4. But I think you do. I think you deserve the tenderest regard I can show, were it only because the same God hath raised you and me from the dust of the earth, and has made us both capable of loving and enjoying Him to eternity; were it only because the Son of God has bought you and me with His own blood. How much more, if you are a person fearing God (as without question many of you are) and studying to have a conscience void of offence towards God and towards man!

5. I shall therefore endeavour, as mildly and inoffensively as I can, to remove in some measure the ground of your unkindness, by plainly declaring what our belief and what our practice is; that you may see we are not altogether such monsters as perhaps you imagined us to be.

A true Protestant may express his belief in these or the like words:—

6. As I am assured that there is an infinite and independent Being, and that it is impossible there should be more than one; so I believe that this one God is the Father of all things, especially of angels and men; that He is in a peculiar manner the Father of those whom He regenerates by His Spirit, whom He adopts in His Son as co-heirs with Him, and crowns with an eternal inheritance; but in a still higher sense the Father of His only Son, whom He hath begotten from eternity.

I believe this Father of all, not only to be able to do whatsoever pleaseth Him, but also to have an eternal right of making what and when and how He pleaseth, and of possessing and disposing of all that He has made; and that He of His own goodness created heaven and earth and all that is therein.

7. I believe that Jesus of Nazareth was the Saviour of the world, the Messiah so long foretold; that, being anointed with the Holy Ghost, He was a Prophet, revealing to us the whole will of God; that He was a Priest, who gave Himself a sacrifice for sin, and still makes intercession for transgressors; that He is a King, who has all power in heaven and in earth, and will reign till He has subdued all things to Himself.

I believe He is the proper, natural Son of God, God of God, very God of very God; and that He is the Lord of all, having absolute, supreme, universal dominion over all things; but more peculiarly our Lord, who believe in Him, both by conquest, purchase, and voluntary obligation.

I believe that He was made man, joining the human nature with the divine in one person; being conceived by the singular operation of the Holy Ghost, and born of the blessed Virgin Mary, who, as well after as before she brought Him forth, continued a pure and unspotted virgin.

I believe He suffered inexpressible pains both of body and soul, and at last death, even the death of the cross, at the time that Pontius Pilate governed Judaea under the Roman Emperor; that His body was then laid in the grave, and His soul went to the place of separate spirits; that the third day He rose again from the dead; that He ascended into heaven; where He remains in the midst of the throne of God, in the highest power and glory, as Mediator till the end of the world, as God to all eternity; that in the end He will come down from heaven to judge every man according to his works, both those who shall be then alive and all who have died before that day.

8. I believe the infinite and eternal Spirit of God, equal with the Father and the Son, to be not only perfectly holy in Himself, but the immediate cause of all holiness in us; enlightening our understandings, rectifying our wills and affections, renewing our natures, uniting our persons to Christ, assuring us of the adoption of sons, leading us in our actions, purifying and sanctifying our souls and bodies, to a full and eternal enjoyment of God.

9. I believe that Christ by His Apostles gathered unto Himself a Church, to which He has continually added such as shall be saved; that this catholic (that is, universal) Church, extending to all nations and all ages, is holy in all its members, who have fellowship with God the Father, Son, and Holy Ghost; that they have fellowship with the holy angels, who constantly minister to these heirs of salvation; and with all the living members of Christ on earth, as well as all who are departed in His faith and fear.

10. I believe God forgives all the sins of them that truly repent and unfeignedly believe His holy gospel; and that at the last day all men shall rise again, every one with his own body.

I believe that, as the unjust shall after their resurrection be tormented in hell for ever, so the just shall enjoy inconceivable happiness in the presence of God to all eternity.

11. Now, is there anything wrong with this? Is there any one point which you do not believe as well as we?

But you think we ought to believe more. We will not now enter into the dispute. Only let me ask, If a man sincerely believes thus much, and practices accordingly, can any one possibly persuade you to think that such a man shall perish everlastingly?

12. "But does he practice accordingly?" If he does not, we grant all his faith will not save him. And this leads me to show you in a few and plain words what the practice of a true Protestant is.

I say, a true Protestant: for I disclaim all common swearers, Sabbath-breakers, drunkards; all whoremongers, liars, cheats, extortioners; in a word, all that live in open sin. These are no Protestants; they are no Christians at all. Give them their own name: they are open heathens. They are the curse of the nation, the bane of society, the shame of mankind, the scum of the earth.

13. A true Protestant believes in God, has a full confidence in His mercy, fears Him with a filial fear, and loves Him with all his soul. He worships God in spirit and in truth, in everything gives Him thanks; calls upon Him with his heart as well as his lips at all times and in all places; honours His holy name and His Word, and serves Him truly all the days of his life.

Now, do not you yourself approve of this? Is there any one point you can condemn? Do not you practice as well as approve it? Can you ever be happy, if you do not? Can you ever expect true peace in this or glory in the world to come, if you do not believe in God through Christ? if you do not thus fear and love God? My dear friend, consider, I am not persuading you to leave or change your religion, but to follow after that fear and love of God without which all religion is vain. I say not a word to you about your opinions or outward manner of worship. But I say, all worship is an abomination to the Lord, unless you worship Him in spirit and in truth, with your heart as well as your lips, with your spirit and with your understanding also. Be your form of worship what it will, but in everything give Him thanks, else it is all but lost labour. Use whatever outward observances you please; but put your whole trust in Him, but honour His holy name and His Word, and serve Him truly all the days of your life.

14. Again: a true Protestant loves his neighbour—that is, every man, friend or enemy, good or bad—as himself, as he loves his own soul, as Christ loved us. And as Christ laid down His life for us, so is he ready to lay down his life for his brethren. He shows this love by doing to all men in all points as he would they should do unto him. He loves, honours, and obeys his father and mother, and helps them to the uttermost of his power. He honours and obeys the King, and all that are put in authority under him. He cheerfully submits to all his governors, teachers, spiritual pastors, and masters. He behaves lowly and reverently to all his betters. He hurts nobody by word or deed. He is true and just in all his dealings. He bears no malice or hatred in his heart. He abstains from all evil-speaking, lying, and slandering; neither is guile found in his mouth. Knowing his body to be the temple of the Holy Ghost, he keeps it in sobriety, temperance, and chastity. He does not desire other men's goods; but is content with that he hath, labours to get his own living, and to do the whole will of God in that state of life unto which it has pleased God to call him.

15. Have you anything to reprove in this? Are you not herein even as he? If not (tell the truth), are you not condemned both by God and your own conscience? Can you fall short of any one point hereof without falling short of being a Christian?

Come, my brother, and let us reason together. Are you right, if you only love your friend and hate your enemy? Do not even the heathens and publicans so? You are called to love your enemies, to bless them that curse you, and to pray for them that despitefully use you and persecute you. But are you not disobedient to the heavenly calling? Does your tender love to all men—not only the good, but also the evil and unthankful—approve you the child of your Father which is in heaven? Otherwise, whatever you believe and whatever you practice, you are of your father the devil. Are you ready to lay down your life for your brethren? and do you do unto all as you would they should do unto you? If not, do not deceive your own soul: you are but a heathen still. Do you love, honour, and obey your father and mother, and help them to the utmost of your power? Do you honour and obey all in authority? all your governors, spiritual pastors, and masters? Do you behave lowly and reverently to all your betters? Do you hurt nobody by word or deed? Are you true and just in all your dealings? Do you take care to pay whatever you owe? Do you feel no malice, or envy, or revenge, no hatred or bitterness to any man? If you do, it is plain you are not of God; for all these are the tempers of the devil. Do you speak the truth from your heart to all men, and that in tenderness and love? Are you an "Israelite indeed, in whom is no guile"? Do you keep your body in sobriety, temperance, and chastity, as knowing it is the temple of the Holy Ghost, and that, if any man defile the temple of God, him will God destroy? Have you learned, in every state wherein you are, therewith to be content? Do you labour to get your own living, abhorring idleness as you abhor hell-fire? The devil tempts other men; but an idle man tempts the devil: an idle man's brain is the devil's shop, where he is continually working mischief. Are you not slothful in business? Whatever your hand finds to do, do you do it with your might? And do you do all as unto the Lord, as a sacrifice unto God, acceptable in Christ Jesus?

This, and this alone, is the old religion. This is true, primitive Christianity. Oh, when shall it spread over all the earth? when shall it be found both in us and you? Without waiting for others, let each of us by the grace of God amend one.

16. Are we not thus far agreed? Let us thank God for this, and receive it as a fresh token of his love. But if God still loveth us, we ought also to love one another. We ought, without this endless jangling about opinions, to provoke one another to love and to good works. Let the points wherein we differ stand aside: here are enough wherein we agree, enough to be the ground of every Christian temper and of every Christian action.

O brethren, let us not still fall out by the way! I hope to see you in heaven. And if I practice the religion above described, you dare not say I shall go to hell. You cannot think so. None can persuade you to it. Your own conscience tells you the contrary. Then, if we cannot as yet think alike in all things, at least we may love alike. Herein we cannot possibly do amiss. For of one point none can doubt a moment—"God is love; and he that dwelleth in love, dwelleth in God, and God in him."

17. In the name, then, and in the strength of God, let us resolve, first, not to hurt one another; to do nothing unkind or unfriendly to each other, nothing which we would not have done to ourselves. Rather let us endeavour after every instance of a kind, friendly and Christian behaviour towards each other.

Let us resolve, secondly, God being our helper, to speak nothing harsh or unkind of each other. The sure way to avoid this is to say all the good we can both of and to one another; in all our conversation, either with or concerning each other, to use only the language of love, to speak with all softness and tenderness, with the most endearing expression which is consistent with truth and sincerity.

Let us, thirdly, resolve to harbour no unkind thought, no unfriendly temper, towards each other. Let us lay the axe to the root of the tree; let us examine all that rises in our heart, and suffer no disposition there which is contrary to tender affection. Then shall we easily refrain from unkind actions and words, when the very root of bitterness is cut up.

Let us, fourthly, endeavour to help each other on in whatever we are agreed leads to the kingdom. So far as we can, let us always rejoice to strengthen each other's hands in God. Above all, let us each take heed to himself (since each must give an account of himself to God) that he fall not short of the religion of love, that he be not condemned in that he himself approveth. O let you and I (whatever others do) press on to the prize of our high calling! that, being justified by faith, we may have peace with God through our Lord Jesus Christ; that we may rejoice in God through Jesus Christ, by whom we have received the atonement; that the love of God may be shed abroad in our hearts by the Holy Ghost which is given unto us. Let us count all things but loss for the excellency of the knowledge of Jesus Christ our Lord; being ready for Him to suffer the loss of all things, and counting them but dung, that we may win Christ. I am
Your affectionate servant for Christ's sake.

Protestant Patriot

Wesley was a man of his times. Nowhere is this more obvious than in his reaction to the Relief Act of 1778 that relaxed the laws against Roman Catholics. Wesley had a typically English fear of "popery" and its potential threat to the well-being of the English state.

This deep-seated bias did not necessarily negate the "Catholic spirit" exhibited in the letter in the previous section and in the sermon of that title. Wesley was convinced that no contradiction existed between his openness to religious dialogue with the Roman Catholics and his argument against their "intoler-

ant, persecuting principles." His support of Lord George Gordon's controversial Protestant Association, however, disappointed many, whose fears were realized when the Gordon riots erupted less than six months later.

This letter, published in the Public Advertiser *(1780), was reprinted as a broadsheet. Wesley noted in his* Journal, *"Many were grievously offended, but I cannot help it; I must follow my own conscience."*

To the Printer of the PUBLIC ADVERTISER.

Sir,

Some time ago a pamphlet was sent me entitled, "An Appeal from the Protestant Association, to the People of Great Britain." A day or two since a kind of answer to this was put into my hand, which pronounces "its style contemptible, its reasoning futile, and its object malicious." On the contrary, I think the style of it is clear, easy and natural; the reasoning (in general) strong and conclusive; the object, or design, kind and benevolent. And in pursuance of the same kind and benevolent design, namely, to preserve our happy constitution, I shall endeavour to confirm the substance of that tract, by a few plain arguments.

With persecution I have nothing to do. I persecute no man for his religious principles. Let there be as "boundless a freedom in religion," as any man can conceive. But this does not touch the point: I will set religion, true or false, utterly out of the question. Suppose the Bible, if you please, to be a fable, and the Koran to be the word of God. I consider not, whether the Romish religion to be true or false; I build nothing on one or the other suppositions. Therefore away with all your commonplace declamation about intolerance and persecution for religion! Suppose every word of Pope *Pius's* creed to be true; suppose the Council of *Trent* to have been infallible: yet, I insist upon it, that no government not Roman Catholic ought to tolerate men of the Roman Catholic persuasion.

I prove this by a plain argument; (let him answer it that can)—That no Roman Catholic does or can give security for his allegiance or peaceable behaviour, I prove thus. It is a Roman Catholic maxim established not by private men, but by a public council, that "no faith is to be kept with heretics." This has been openly avowed by the Council of *Constance:* but it never was openly disclaimed (whether private persons avow or disavow it). It is a fixed maxim of the Church of *Rome.* But as long as it is so, nothing can be more plain, than that the members of that Church can give no reasonable security to any government of their allegiance or peaceable behaviour. Therefore, they ought not to be tolerated by any government, Protestant, Mahometan, or pagan.

You may say, "Nay, but they will take an *Oath* of Allegiance." True, five hundred oaths; but the maxim, "No faith is to be kept with heretics," sweeps them all away as a spider's web. So that still, no governors that are not Roman Catholics can have any security of their allegiance.

Again, those who acknowledge the *spiritual power* of the pope can give no security of their allegiance to any government; but all Roman Catholics acknowledge this: therefore, they can give no security for their allegiance.

The power of granting *pardons* for all sins, past, present, and to come, is and has been for many centuries one branch of his *spiritual power.*

But those who acknowledge him to have this spiritual power, can give no security for their allegiance: since they believe the pope can pardon rebellions, high treason, and all other sins whatsoever.

The power *of dispensing* with any promise, oath or vow, is another branch of the *spiritual power* of the pope. And all who acknowledge his spiritual power, must acknowledge this. But whoever acknowledges the *dispensing power* of the pope, can give no security of his allegiance to any government.

Oaths and promises are none: they are light as air, a dispensation makes them all null and void.

Nay, not only the pope, but even a priest, has *power to pardon sins!* This is an essential doctrine of the Church of Rome. But they that acknowledge this, cannot possibly give any security for their allegiance to any government. Oaths are no security at all; for the priest can pardon both perjury and high treason.

Setting then religion aside, it is plain, that upon principles of reason, no government ought to tolerate men, who cannot give any security to that government, for their allegiance and peaceable behaviour. But this no Romanist can do, not only while he holds that "No faith is to be kept with heretics," but so long as he acknowledges either priestly absolution, or the *spiritual power* of the pope.

"But the late act, you say, does not either *tolerate* or *encourage* Roman Catholics." I appeal to matter of fact. Do not the Romanists themselves understand it as a toleration? You know they do. And does it not already (let alone what it *may* do by and by) *encourage* them to preach openly, to build chapels (at Bath and elsewhere), to raise seminaries, and to make numerous converts day by day to their intolerant, persecuting principles? I can point out, if need be, several of the persons. And they are increasing daily.

But "nothing dangerous to English liberty is to be apprehended from them." I am not certain of that. Some time since a Romish priest came to one I knew: and after talking with her largely, broke out, "You are no heretic! You have the experience of a real Christian!" "And would you," she asked, "burn me alive?" He said, "God forbid!—Unless it were for the good of the Church!"

Now what security could she have had for her life, if it had depended on that man? The *good of the Church* would have burst all the ties of truth, justice, and mercy. Especially when seconded by the absolution of a priest, or (if need were) a papal pardon.

If any one please to answer this, and to set his name, I shall probably reply.—But the productions of anonymous writers, I do not promise to take any notice of.

I am, sir, your humble servant,

JOHN WESLEY

City Road, Jan. 21, 1780.

CHAPTER 15

The Careful Planner

John Wesley was the all-important link in the Methodist "connexion." He, more than anyone else, knew the possibly disastrous implications this held for the future of the movement. By the 1760s, the chances of maintaining a vital and continuing alliance with the evangelical wing of the Church of England were becoming increasingly dim. Many tensions seemed to be pulling the connexion apart into a congregational system. Wesley saw the preachers themselves as the key to any perpetuation of their "union." His outlook toward the future settled into two types of proposals: the establishment of some form of council, or the designation of a single successor to his position.

The Center of Union

As early as 1760, Wesley had suggested the possibility of establishing a council to guide Methodism. The council would, of course, only come into power after his death. Wesley again spelled out the idea in 1769 in a letter "To the Traveling Preachers," later reprinted in the "Large" Minutes (1770). This letter exhibits the particular concerns that Wesley had in mind *as he looked to the future of Methodism as a continuing order of lay preachers within the Church of England.*

Leeds, August 4, 1769

My dear brethren,

1. It has long been my desire that all those ministers of our Church who believe and preach salvation by faith might cordially agree between themselves, and not hinder but help one another. After occasionally pressing this in private conversation wherever I had opportunity, I wrote down my thoughts upon the head and sent them to each in a letter. Out of fifty or sixty to whom I wrote, only three vouchsafed me an answer. So I give this up; I can do no more. They are a rope of sand, and such they will continue.

2. But it is otherwise with the travelling preachers in our Connexion. You are at present one body. You act in concert with each other and by united counsels. And now is the time to consider what can be done in order to continue this union. Indeed, as long as I live there will be no great difficulty. I am under God a center of union to all our travelling as well as local preachers.

They all know me and my communication. They all love me for my work's sake; and therefore, were it only out of regard to me, they will continue connected with each other. But by what means may this Connexion be preserved when God removes me from you?

3. I take it for granted it cannot be preserved by any means between those who have not a single eye. Those who aim at anything but the glory of God and the salvation of men, who desire or seek any earthly thing, whether honour, profit, or ease, will not, cannot continue in the Connexion; it will not answer their design. Some of them, perhaps a fourth of the whole number, will secure preferment in the Church. Others will turn Independents, and get separate congregations, like John Edwards and Charles Skelton. Lay your accounts with this, and be not surprised if some you do not suspect be of this number.

4. But what method can be taken to preserve a firm union between those who choose to remain together? Perhaps you might take some such steps as these:

On notice of my death, let all the preachers in England and Ireland repair to London within six weeks.

Let them seek God by solemn fasting and prayer.

Let them draw up articles of agreement to be signed by those who choose to act in concert.

Let those be dismissed who do not choose it in the most friendly manner possible.

Let them choose by votes a committee of three, five, or seven, each of whom is to be Moderator in his turn.

Let the Committee do what I do now; propose preachers to be tried, admitted, or excluded; fix the place of each preacher for the ensuing year and the time of the next Conference.

5. Can anything be done now in order to lay a foundation for this future union? Would it not be well, for any that are willing, to sign some articles of agreement before God calls me hence? Suppose something like these:

"We whose names are under-written, being thoroughly convinced of the necessity of a close union between those whom God is pleased to use as instruments in this glorious work, in order to preserve this union between ourselves, are resolved, God being our Helper,

I. *To devote ourselves entirely to God,* denying ourselves, taking up our cross daily, steadily aiming at one thing—to save our own souls and them that hear us.

II. *To preach the old Methodist doctrines,* and no other, contained in the *Minutes* of the Conferences.

III. To observe and enforce the whole *Methodist discipline* laid down in the said *Minutes.*"

The Perpetual Image

As time went on, Wesley increasingly felt that a strong union among the preachers depended upon their having a single strong leader. As he approached his seventieth birthday, he decided to designate a successor. John William Fletcher was his choice.

Fletcher was the vicar of Madeley and one of the few Church of England clergy still connected with Methodism in 1773. Fletcher was proving himself equal to the challenges of leadership, not least of all by writing a series of Checks to Antinomianism *(1771–75) that defended Wesley's theology against the Calvinist attack. He was also considered by Wesley to be without equal in piety.*

This letter to Fletcher is a telling indicator of Wesley's expectations for the future leaders of Methodism. The description Wesley gives may, in fact, have been patterned after his perception of his own role in the movement, perhaps (though not necessarily) idealized. At that point, Fletcher was probably the best choice Wesley could have made; unfortunately Fletcher died before Wesley. The movement was entrusted in the end to the Conference by the Deed of Declaration (1784).

Shoreham, January [15], 1773

Dear Sir,

What an amazing work has God wrought in these kingdoms in less than forty years! And it not only continues but increases throughout England, Scotland, and Ireland; nay, it has lately spread into New York, Pennsylvania, Virginia, Maryland, and Carolina. But the wise men of the world say, "When Mr. Wesley drops, then all this is at an end!" And so it surely will unless, before God calls him hence, one is found to stand in his place. For οὐκ ἀγαθὸν πολυκοιρανίη εἰς κοίρανοςἔστω [the rule of many is not good; let there be one ruler]. I see more and more, unless there be one προεστώς [leader], the work can never be carried on. The body of the preachers is not united; nor will any part of them submit to the rest: so that either there must be *one* to preside over *all* or the work will indeed come to an end.

But who is sufficient for these things? qualified to preside both over the preachers and people? He must be a man of faith and love and one that has a single eye to the advancement of the kingdom of God. He must have a clear understanding; a knowledge of men and things, particularly of the Methodist doctrine and discipline; a ready utterance; diligence and activity, with a tolerable share of health. There must be added to these, favour with the people, with the Methodists in general. For unless God turn their eyes and their hearts towards him, he will be quite incapable of the work. He must likewise have some degree of learning; because there are many adversaries, learned as well as unlearned, whose mouths must be stopped. But this cannot be done unless he be able to meet them on their own ground.

But has God provided one so qualified? Who is he? *Thou art the man!* God has given you a measure of loving faith and a single eye to His glory. He has given you some knowledge of men and things, particularly of the whole plan of Methodism. You are blessed with some health, activity, and diligence, together with a degree of learning.

And to all these He has lately added, by a way none could have foreseen, favour both with the preachers and the whole people.

Come out in the name of God! Come to the help of the Lord against the mighty! Come while I am alive and capable of labour!

> *Dum superest Lachesi quod torqueat, et pedibus me*
> *Porto meis, nullo dextram subeunte bacillo.*
> > [While Lachesis has some thread of life to spin,
> > And I walk on my own feet, without the help of a staff.]

Come while I am able, God assisting, to build you up to faith, to ripen your gifts, and to introduce you to the people. *Nil tanti* [Nothing is worth so much]. What possible employment can you have which is of so *great importance?*

But you will naturally say, "I am not equal to the task; I have neither grace nor gifts for such an employment." You say true; it is certain you have not. And who has? But do you not know Him who is able to give them? perhaps not at once, but rather day by day: as each is, so shall your strength be.

"But this implies," you may say, "a thousand crosses, such as I feel I am not able to bear." You are not able to bear them now; and they are not now come. Whenever they do come, will He not send them in due number, weight, and measure? And will they not all be for your profit, that you may be a partaker of His holiness?

Without conferring, therefore, with flesh and blood, come and strengthen the hands, comfort the heart, and share the labour of
Your affectionate friend and brother.

The Philanthropic Testator

Fully aware of the transitory nature of existence, Wesley had made a will as early as 1747, following the advice he often gave to his people. Two decades later, he twice prepared updated versions that included his wife among his beneficiaries (see Tyerman, Life of Wesley, 2:15f.). His final will, drawn up in 1789, is concerned primarily with the disposition of his books, manuscripts, and personal belongings.

Wesley had often been accused of having an income greater than that of an Anglican bishop (see page 271). But his own principle with regard to money was not only to "gain all you can" and to "save all you can," but also to "give all you can." His estate consisted primarily of his books and publishing interests, the income from which was designated for the use of the Methodist connexion. He had once said, in his Earnest Appeal *(1745), that if he left more than ten pounds at his death, any one could call him a thief and a robber (cf. his proposed epitaph, page 189). In his last will, given below, the only money directly dispersed was the six pounds to be given to the six poor people who were to be his pallbearers and the money in his bureau and pockets to be divided among his wife's grandchildren and four other friends. The value of his property, however, appears to have been rather substantial.*

In the name of God, Amen.

I, John Wesley, Clerk, sometime Fellow of Lincoln College, Oxford, revoking all others, appoint this to be my last Will and Testament.

I give all my books, now on sale, and the copies of them (only subject to a rent-charge of eighty-five pounds a year to the widow and children of my brother), to my faithful friends, John Horton, merchant; George Wolff, merchant; and William Marriott, stockbroker, all of London, in trust for the general Fund of the Methodist Conference in carrying on the work of God by Itinerant Preachers; on condition that they permit the following Committee, Thomas Coke, James Creighton, Peard Dickinson, Thomas Rankin, George Whitfield, and the London Assistant for the time being, still to superintend the printing-press, and to employ Hannah Paramore and George Paramore, as heretofore, unless four of the Committee judge a change to be needful.

I give the books, furniture, and whatever belongs to me in the three houses at Kingswood, in trust to Thomas Coke, Alexander Mather, and Henry Moore, to be still employed in teaching and maintaining the children of poor Travelling Preachers.

I give to Thomas Coke, Doctor John Whitehead, and Henry Moore, all the books which are in my study and bedchamber at London, and in my studies elsewhere, in trust, for the use of the Preachers who shall labour there from time to time.

I give the coins, and whatever else is in the drawer of my bureau at London, to my dear grand-daughters, Mary and Jane Smith.

I give all my manuscripts to Thomas Coke, Doctor Whitehead, and Henry Moore, to be burned or published as they see good.

I give whatever money remains in my bureau and pockets, at my decease, to be equally divided between Thomas Briscoe, William Collins, John Easton, and Isaac Brown.

I desire my gowns, cassocks, sashes, and bands may remain at the chapels for the use of the clergymen attending there.

I desire the London Assistant for the time being to divide the rest of my wearing apparel between those four of the Travelling Preachers that want it most; only my pelisse I give to the Rev. Mr. Creighton; my watch to my friend Joseph Bradford; my gold seal to Elizabeth Ritchie.

I give my chaise and horses to James Ward and Charles Wheeler, in trust, to be sold, and the money divided, one half to Hannah Abbott, and the other to the poor members of the select society.

Out of the first money which arises from the sale of books, I bequeath to my dear sister, Martha Hall (if alive), forty pounds; to Mr. Creighton aforesaid, forty pounds; and to the Rev. Mr. Heath, sixty pounds.

And whereas I am empowered by a late Deed to name the persons who are to preach in the new chapel in London (the Clergymen for continuance), and by another Deed to name a Committee for appointing Preachers in the new chapel at Bath, I do hereby appoint John Richardson, Thomas Coke, James Creighton, Peard Dickinson, Clerks; Alexander Mather, William Thompson, Henry Moore, Andrew Blair, John Valton, Joseph Bradford, James Rogers, and William Myles, to preach in the new chapel at London, and to be the Committee for appointing Preachers in the new chapel at Bath.

I likewise appoint Henry Brooke, painter; Arthur Keene, gent.; and William Whitestone, stationer, all of Dublin, to receive the annuity of five pounds (English), left to Kingswood School by the late Roger Shiel, Esq.

I give six pounds to be divided among the six poor men, named by the Assistant, who shall carry my body to the grave; for I particularly desire there may be no hearse, no coach, no escutcheon, no pomp, except the tears of them that loved me, and are following me to Abraham's bosom. I solemnly adjure my Executors, in the name of God, punctually to observe this.

Lastly, I give to each of those Travelling Preachers who shall remain in the Connexion six months after my decease, a little token of my love, the eight volumes of sermons.

The Rev.ᵈ JOHN WESLEY, M.A.

Bodlidge sculp, King Street, Upper Moor-Fields.

1. John Wesley, engraved by Bodlidge in *The Arminian Magazine*, 1778

Wesley published this portrait of himself during the first year of his monthly *Arminian Magazine* (1778) as an initial response to a reader's request for "pictures or other decorations or embellishments." In spite of receiving Wesley's own stamp of approval at the time, the likeness apparently was ill received by the readers (see fig. 2).

2. John Wesley in
The Arminian Magazine, 1779

Wesley published this portrait of himself (artist unknown) in 1779 to replace the earlier portrait in *The Arminian Magazine.* About the engravings in the *Magazine,* he told the readers in 1781, "I'll have better or none at all" (see fig. 7).

3. John Wesley, engraved by Vertue, 1742, with vignette of Epworth rectory fire

The embellishments on the 1742 engraving of the young Mr. Wesley by George Vertue (1684–1756) include a vignette depicting Wesley's escape from the Epworth rectory fire as "a brand plucked out of the fire," an image that became fixed in Wesley's self-consciousness (see pages 42, 44, 81, 93, 187).

4. Page from Wesley's Oxford Diary, March 17, 1734

Entry for March 17, 1734, in Wesley's Oxford Diary (see pages 60-61).

5. John Wesley, painted by Hone, engraved by Bland in *Explanatory Notes*, 1755

Wesley chose this engraving by Bland of a painting by Nathaniel Hone, R.A. (1719–1784) to be the frontispiece of his *Explanatory Notes Upon the Old Testament* (1755). The engraver smoothed out many wrinkles evident in the painting and made Wesley appear much younger than the 63 years of age indicated by the caption.

6. John Wesley, painted by Hamilton in National Portrait Gallery, London

This painting by William Hamilton, R.A. (1751–1801), represents Wesley in his 85th year. An entry in his Journal for December 22, 1787, purportedly refers to this work: "I yielded to the importunity of a painter and sat an hour and a half in all for my picture. I think it was the best that ever was taken."

7. John Wesley in
The Arminian Magazine, 1783

Wesley published this portrait of himself (artist unknown) in *The Arminian Magazine* (1783), an odd choice in the light of his expressed desire in 1780 for "striking likenesses in the *Magazine*" (see fig. 1 and fig. 2).

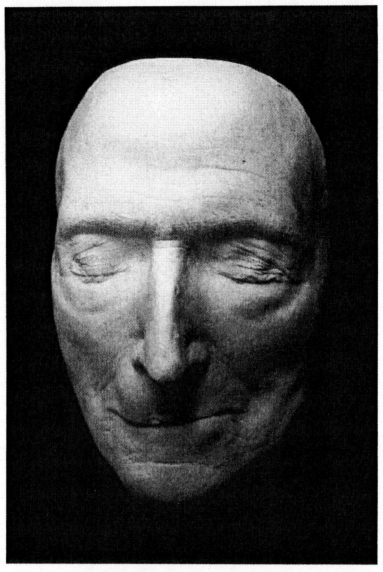

8. Wesley's death mask,
replica at Duke University

Replica of Wesley's death mask, a plaster facial cast taken shortly after his death in 1791. Although visual representations of Wesley vary greatly, the prominent nose is one of the common features in nearly every portrayal.

Wm Bromley sculpt

9. John Wesley, engraved by Wm. Bromley in *The European Magazine*, 1791

This portrait of John Wesley appeared in *The European Magazine* almost immediately after Wesley's death in March 1791. This familiar profile was engraved by William Bromley (1769–1842), who gained his reputation engraving the Elgin Marbles for the Trustees of the British Museum.

10. John Wesley, engraved by W. Greatback in Isaac Taylor, *Wesley and Methodism*, 1851

This portrait of Wesley has traditionally been attributed to Thomas Worlidge (1700–1766). It was used as the frontispiece for *Wesley and Methodism* (1851) by Isaac Taylor, who was told that the portrait was done at the Foundery while Wesley was preaching. The visage portrayed seems but a caricature of the "venerable" image described by John Hampson (see page 277).

11. Wesley as Reynard the Fox, frontispiece to *Fanatical Conversion*, 1779

This bawdy illustration, published as the frontispiece to *Fanatical Conversion* (1779), shows Wesley as Reynard the Fox, standing on a table, "haranguing in a barn" to a congregation of animals and characters mentioned at various places in Wesley's *Journal* (see footnotes, pages 296-303).

12. John Wesley, bust by Enoch Wood

This Staffordshire bust of Wesley was modeled from life in 1781 or 1784 by Enoch Wood (1759–1840). Nearly fifty years later, the artist told Adam Clarke that Wesley had thought this likeness "much the best" that anyone had attempted. Adam Clarke considered this bust "the only proper likeness of that illustrious man." *(See page 375 and fig. 15.)*

13. The Apotheosis of John Wesley
"Carried by Angels into Abraham's Bosom"

This print, published shortly after Wesley's death in 1791, carries the caption, "John Wesley, that Excellent Minister of the Gospel, carried by Angels into Abraham's Bosom," followed by a quotation from Matthew 25:21.

14. John Wesley, engraved by T. A. Dean, painted by John Jackson, 1827

John Jackson, R. A. (177?–1831), attempted to synthesize the various eighteenth-century portrayals into a "standard" portrait of Wesley (see page 362). This engraving by T. A. Dean was used as the frontispiece to the *Collection of Hymns* (1830) and became a familiar sight to generations of British Methodists.

15. John Wesley, painted
by Frank O. Salisbury, 1927

Frank O. Salisbury used the Enoch Wood bust of Wesley as the model
for this portrait, which has become familiar to recent generations of
Methodists (see page 374 and fig. 12).

I appoint John Horton, George Wolff, and William Marriott, aforesaid, to be Executors of this my last Will and Testament; for which trouble they will receive no recompense till the resurrection of the just.

Witness my hand and seal, the 20th day of February, 1789.

JOHN WESLEY (Seal)

Signed, sealed, and delivered, by the said Testator, as and for his last Will and Testament, in the presence of us,

WILLIAM CLULOW,
ELIZABETH CLULOW.

Should there be any part of my personal estate undisposed of by this my Will, I give the same unto my two nieces, Elizabeth Ellison and Susanna Collett, equally.

JOHN WESLEY

WILLIAM CLULOW,
ELIZABETH CLULOW,

Feb. 25, 1789

I give my types, printing-presses, types [*sic*], and everything pertaining thereto, to Mr. Thomas Rankin and Mr. George Whitfield, in trust, for the use of the Conference.

JOHN WESLEY

Part II

Wesley as Seen by His Contemporaries

The Family Perspective

John Wesley was born into a large household of children, most of whom were female. His older brother, Samuel, had gone to London to attend school the year after John was born, and his younger brother, Charles, was four and one-half years his junior. Thus during much of John's childhood, he was at home in the rectory of Epworth with his parents and six sisters (eventually numbering seven). He admired his parents and loved his siblings. There was a good bit of candor among family members, even at the expense of harmony and personal feelings. When tensions developed in the family, John often sided with his sisters, even against his father. This resulted in a close bond between John and his sisters which lasted well beyond his years in the Epworth rectory.

None of the Wesley family ever wrote an explicit description of John. But we can get a good idea of his background and his relationship to the family from just a few selections from the family correspondence.

Son to Susanna

John Wesley is often portrayed as the special object of his mother's concern. Susanna undoubtedly had a close relationship with John, but that should not cloud the fact that she was close to her other children as well. One of the clear-est pictures of her relationship with John, as well as the other children, can be found in a letter written in response to John's request in 1732 for a descrip-tion of "her way of education." She was at first averse to writing out such a description. claiming that "it can't (I think) be of service to anyone to know how I used to employ my time and care in bringing up my children." She added that "no one can, without renouncing the world in the most literal sense, observe my method." She soon relented, however, and sent to John the following letter. Susanna was sixty-three years old when she wrote this letter, her youngest child being at that time twenty-two.

After his mother's death ten years later, John published this letter in his Journal *"for the benefit of those who are entrusted, as she was, with the care of a numerous family." Susanna's outline describes in some detail the cir-cumstances under which John was raised; John presumably felt he had bene-fited from this "method." See* Works, *19:286-91; 25:330-31.*

July 24, 1732

Dear Son,

According to your desire, I have collected the principal rules I observed in educating my family; which I now send you as they occurred to my mind, and you may (if you think they can be of use to any) dispose of them in what order you please.

The children were always put into a regular method of living, in such things as they were capable of, from their birth as in dressing, undressing, changing their linen, etc. The first quarter commonly passes in sleep. After that they were, if possible, laid into their cra-dles awake, and rocked to sleep; and so they were kept rocking till it was time for them to awake. This was done to bring them to a regu-lar course of sleeping; which at first was three hours in the morning and three in the afternoon; afterwards two hours, till they needed none at all.

When turned a year old (and some before), they were taught to fear the rod and to cry softly; by which means they escaped abun-dance of correction they might otherwise have had, and that most odious noise of the crying of children was rarely heard in the house, but the family usually lived in as much quietness as if there had not been a child among them.

As soon as they were grown pretty strong, they were confined to three meals a day. At dinner their little table and chairs were set by ours, where they could be overlooked; and they were suffered to eat and drink (small [*i.e.*, weak] beer) as much as they would; but not to call for anything. If they wanted aught they used to whisper to the maid which attended them, who came and spake to me; and as soon as they could handle a knife and fork, they were set to our table. They were never suffered to choose their meat, but always made eat such things as were provided for the family.

Mornings they had always spoon-meat; sometimes on nights. But whatever they had, they were never permitted to eat at those meals of more than one thing, and of that sparingly enough. Drinking or eating between meals was never allowed unless in case of sickness, which seldom happened. Nor were they suffered to go into the kitchen to ask anything of the servants when they were at meat; if it was known they did, they were certainly beat and the servants severely reprimanded.

At six, as soon as family prayers were over, they had their supper; at seven the maid washed them and, beginning at the youngest, she undressed and got them all to bed by eight; at which time she left them in their several rooms awake, for there was no such thing allowed of in our house as sitting by a child till it fell asleep.

They were so constantly used to eat and drink what was given them that, when any of them was ill, there was no difficulty in making them take the most unpleasant medicine; for they durst not refuse it, though some of them would presently throw it up....

In order to form the minds of children, the first thing to be done is to conquer their will and bring them to an obedient temper. To inform the understanding is a work of time and must with children proceed by slow degrees as they are able to bear it; but the subjecting the will is a thing that must be done at once—and the sooner the better. For by neglecting timely correction, they will contract a stubbornness and obstinacy which is hardly ever after conquered, and never without using such severity as would be as painful to me as to the child. In the esteem of the world they pass for kind and indulgent whom I call cruel parents, who permit their children to get habits which they know must be afterwards broken. Nay, some are so stupidly fond as in sport to teach their children to do things which in a while after they have severely beaten them for doing.

Whenever a child is corrected, it must be conquered; and this will be no hard matter to do if it be not grown headstrong by too much indulgence. And when the will of a child is totally subdued, and it is brought to revere and stand in awe of the parents, then a great many childish follies and inadvertences may be passed by.…

I insist upon conquering the will of children betimes, because this is the only strong and rational foundation of a religious education, without which both precept and example will be ineffectual. But when this is thoroughly done, then a child is capable of being governed by the reason and piety of its parents, till its own understanding comes to maturity and the principles of religion have taken root in the mind.

I cannot yet dismiss this subject. As self-will is the root of all sin and misery, so whatever cherishes this in children ensures their after-wretchedness and irreligion; whatever checks and mortifies it promotes their future happiness and piety. This is still more evident if we farther consider that religion is nothing else than the doing the will of God, and not our own; that the one grand impediment to our temporal and eternal happiness being this self-will, no indulgences of it can be trivial, no denial unprofitable. Heaven or hell depends on this alone. So that the parent who studies to subdue it in his child works together with God in the renewing and saving a soul. The parent who indulges it does the devil's work, makes religion impracticable, salvation unattainable, and does all that in him lies to damn his child, soul and body, for ever.

The children of this family were taught, as soon as they could speak, the Lord's Prayer, which they were made to say at rising and bedtime constantly; to which, as they grew bigger, were added a short prayer for their parents and some collects, a short catechism, and some portions of Scripture, as their memories could bear.

They were very early made to distinguish the Sabbath from other days, before they could well speak or go. They were as soon taught to be still at family prayers and to ask a blessing immediately after, which they used to do by signs, before they could kneel or speak.

They were quickly made to understand they might have nothing they cried for, and instructed to speak handsomely for what they wanted. They were not suffered to ask even the lowest servant for aught without saying, "Pray give me such a thing"; and the servant was chid if she ever let them omit that word. Taking God's name in vain, cursing and swearing, profaneness, obscenity, rude, ill-bred names, were never heard among them. Nor were they ever permitted to call each other by their proper names without the addition of brother or sister.

None of them were taught to read till five years old, except Kezzy in whose case I was overruled; and she was more years learning than any of the rest had been months. The way of teaching was this: the day before a child began to learn, the house was set in order, everyone's work appointed them, and a charge given that none should come into the room from nine till twelve, or from two till five; which, you know, were our school hours. One day was allowed the child wherein to learn its letters; and each of them did in that time know all its letters, great and small, except Molly and Nancy, who were a day and a half before they knew them perfectly; for which I then thought them very dull; but since I have observed how long many children are learning the horn-book, I have changed my opinion. But the reason why I thought them so then was because the rest learned so readily; and your brother Samuel, who was the first child I ever taught, learned the alphabet in a few hours. He was five years old on the 10th of February; the next day he began to learn; and, as soon as he knew the letters, began at the first chapter of Genesis. He was taught to spell the first verse, then to read it over and over, till he could read it off-hand without any hesitation; so on to the second, etc., till he took ten verses for a lesson, which he quickly did. . . .

The same method was observed with them all. As soon as they knew the letters, they were put first to spell, and read one line, then a verse; never leaving till perfect in their lesson, were it shorter or longer. So one or other continued reading at school-time, without any intermission, and before we left school each child read what he had learned that morning; and, ere we parted in the after-noon, what they had learned that day.

There was no such thing as loud talking or playing allowed of, but every one was kept close to their business for the six hours of school. And it is almost incredible what a child may be taught in a quarter of a year by a vigorous application, if it have but a tolerable capacity and good health. Every one of these, Kezzy excepted, could read better in that time than the most of women can do as long as they live.

Rising out of their places, or going out of the room, was not permitted unless for good cause; and running into the yard, garden, or street, without leave, was always esteemed a capital offence.

For some years we went on very well. Never were children in better order. Never were children better disposed to piety or in more subjection to their parents, till that fatal dispersion of them, after the fire, into several families. In these they were left at full liberty to converse with servants, which before they had always been restrained from; and to run abroad and play with any children, good or bad. They soon learned to neglect a strict observation of the Sabbath, and got knowledge of several songs and bad things which before they had no notion of. That civil behaviour which made them admired when at home by all which saw them was in great measure lost, and a clownish accent and many rude ways were learned which were not reformed without some difficulty.

When the house was rebuilt and the children all brought home, we entered upon a strict reform; and then was begun the custom of singing Psalms at beginning and leaving school, morning and evening. Then also that of a general retirement at five o'clock was entered upon, when the oldest took the youngest that could speak, and the second the next, to whom they read the Psalms for the day and a chapter in the New Testament; as in the morning they were directed to read the Psalms and a chapter in the Old, after which they went to their private prayers, before they got their breakfast or came into the family. And, I thank God, this custom is still preserved among us.

There were several by-laws observed among us, which slipped my memory, or else they had been inserted in their proper place; but I mention them here, because I think them useful.

1. It had been observed that cowardice and fear of punishment often led children into lying, till they get a custom of it, which they cannot leave. To prevent this, a law was made that whoever was charged with a fault, of which they were guilty, if they would ingenuously confess it and promise to amend, should not be beaten. This rule prevented a great deal of lying, and would have done more if one in the family would have observed it. But he could not be prevailed on, and therefore was often imposed on by false colours and equivocations, which none would have used (except one) had they been kindly dealt with. And some, in spite of all, would always speak truth plainly.

2. That no sinful action, as lying, pilfering, playing at church, or on the Lord's day, disobedience, quarrelling, etc., should ever pass unpunished.

3. That no child should ever be chid or beat twice for the same fault, and that, if they amended, they should never be upbraided with it afterwards.

4. That every signal act of obedience, especially when it crossed upon their own inclinations, should be always commended and frequently rewarded, according to the merits of the cause.

5. That if ever any child performed an act of obedience, or did anything with an intention to please, though the performance was not well, yet the obedience and intention should be kindly accepted, and the child with sweetness directed how to do better for the future.

6. That propriety be inviolably preserved, and none suffered to invade the property of another in the smallest matter, though it were but of the value of a farthing or a pin, which they might not take from the owner without, much less against, his consent. This rule can never be too much inculcated on the minds of children, and from the want of parents or governors doing it as they ought proceeds that shameful neglect of justice which we may observe in the world.

7. That promises be strictly observed; and a gift once bestowed, and so the right passed away from the donor, be not resumed, but left to the disposal of him to whom it was given; unless it were conditional, and the condition of the obligation not performed.

8. That no girl be taught to work till she can read very well; and then that she be kept to her work with the same application, and the same time, that she was held to in reading. This rule also is much to be observed; for the putting children to learn sewing before they can read perfectly is the very reason why so few women can read fit to be heard, and never to be well understood.

Son to Samuel

John Wesley's correspondence with both of his parents reflects a close relationship. Susanna's letters of advice to John were numerous and personal. Samuel's letters to John also present a rather clear picture of a loving relationship built upon shared interests and mutual respect. John unhesitatingly sought his parents' advice; they responded willingly.

The following letter from Samuel was written at a critical time in John's vocational deliberations. He had received his baccalaureate degree at Oxford and was contemplating taking Holy Orders, hoping to become a Fellow at the University (perhaps with the aid of Dr. Morley, rector of Lincoln College). Many of the father's assumptions about John's character, abilities, and inclinations come through rather clearly in his carefully stated words of advice. See Works, *25:157-59.*

Wroot, January 26, 1724/25

Dear Son,

I'm so well pleased with your present behaviour, or at least with your letters, that I hope I shall have no occasion to remember any more some things that are past. And since you have now for some time bit upon the bridle, I'll take care hereafter to put a little honey upon it as oft as I'm able. But then it shall be of my own *mero motu* [mere motion], as the last 5 pounds was, for I will bear no rivals in my kindness.

I did not forget you with Dr. Morley, but have moved that way as much as possible, though I must confess hitherto with no great prospect or hope of success.

As for what you mention of entering into Holy Orders, 'tis indeed a great work, and I am pleased to find you think it so, as well as that you don't admire a callow clergyman any more than I do. As for the motives you take notice of, my thoughts are: (1) It's no *harm* to desire getting into that office, even as Eli's sons, "to eat a piece of bread"; "for the labourer is worthy of his hire." Though, (2) a desire and intention to lead a stricter life and a belief one should do so, is a better reason; though this should by all means be begun before, or else, ten to one, 'twill deceive us afterward. (3) If a man be *unwilling* and *undesirous* to enter into Orders, 'tis easy to guess whether he can say, so much as with common honesty, that he believes he's "moved by the Holy Spirit" to do it. But, (4) the principal spring and motive, to which all the former should be only secondary, must certainly be the glory of God and the service of his church in the edification and salvation of our neighbour. And woe to him who with any meaner leading view attempts so sacred a work. For which, (5) he should take all the care he possibly can, with the advice of wiser and elder men—especially imploring with all humility, sincerity, and intention of mind, and with fasting and prayer, the direction and assistance of Almighty God and his Holy Spirit, to qualify and prepare him for it.

The knowledge of the languages is a very considerable help in this matter, which, I thank God, all my three sons have to a very laudable degree, though God knows I had ne'er more than a smattering of any of 'em. But then this must be prosecuted to the thorough understanding the original text of the Scriptures, by constant and long conversing with them. You ask me which is the best commentary on the Bible. I answer, The Bible. For the several paraphrases and translations of it in the Polyglot, compared with the original and with one another, are in my opinion, to an honest, devout, industrious, and humble mind, infinitely preferable to any commentary I ever saw writ upon it, though Grotius is the best (for the most part), especially on the Old Testament.

And now, the providence of God (I hope it was) has engaged me in such a work wherein you may be very assistant to me, I trust promote his glory, and at the same time notably forward your own studies in the method I have just now proposed. For I've some time since designed an edition of the Holy Bible in octavo, in the Hebrew, Chaldee, Septuagint, and Vulgar Latin, and have made some progress in it; the whole scheme whereof I haven't time at present to give you, of which scarce any soul yet knows unless your brother Sam. What I desire of you on this article is, that you would immediately fall to work: read diligently the Hebrew text in the Polyglot and collate it exactly with the Vulgar Latin, which is in the second column, writing down all (even the least) variations or differences between 'em. To these I'd have you add the Samaritan text, in the last column but one (don't mind the Latin translation in the very last column), which is the very same with the Hebrew except in some very few places, only differing in the Samaritan character (I think the true Old Hebrew), the alphabet whereof you may learn in a day's time, either from the prolegomena in Walton's Polyglot or from his grammar. In a twelvemonth's time, sticking close to it in the forenoons, you will get twice through the Pentateuch. . . . In the afternoon read what you will, and be sure to walk an hour, if fair, in the fields. Get Thirlby's Chrysostom *De Sacerdotio.* Master it; digest it. I took some pains, a year or two since, in drawing up some advices to Mr. Hoole's brother, then to be my curate at Epworth, before his ordination, which mayn't be unuseful to you, wherefore I'll send 'em shortly to your brother Sam for you; but you must return 'em me again, I having no copy—and pray let none but yourself see 'em.

By all this you see I'm not for your going over hastily into Orders. When I'm for your taking 'em, you shall know it, and 'tis not impossible but I may then be with you, if God so long spare the life and health of your affectionate father,

Sam. Wesley

I like your verses on the 65th Psalm and would not have you bury your talent.

All are well and send buss [kisses].

Work and write while you can. You see time has shaken me by the hand, and death's but a little behind him. My eyes and heart are now almost all I have left, and bless God for them.

Brother John

The Wesley children had a very honest and open relationship among themselves. Their correspondence is marked by clear criticisms, words of kindness and praise, and at times a touch of humor, all of which bespeaks a closeness of spirit. When John went up to Oxford, the younger children in particular began to look upon him as a model of learning and piety. They were careful not to present him with any obvious display of esteem or respect, but at the same time, they did appeal rather persistently to him for counsel on a wide range of personal and intellectual matters. The sisters often interlaced their appeals with sarcastic or jibing comments, typical of siblings who enjoy keeping their brother's supposed dignity in its proper perspective.

The following letter was written by his sister Emilia (Emily) in response to John's advice regarding her position as assistant at Mrs. Taylor's school in Gainsborough. His offers of advice and support raise several questions in Emily's mind and provide her an opportunity for a bit of friendly sarcasm.

June 26 [1731]

Dear brother,

Your last letter surprised me exceedingly, and I'll spare you, you had need of all your interest in my heart, I will not say, to induce me to comply with your desires, but even to write to you anymore. I always measured your love by my own, and as I am very sure, your interest would be ever preferred by me, not only to that of all my relations and acquaintance except my dear mother, but even to my own, so it concerned me to the last degree to find that your affection should be so much greater for Mrs. Taylor than for her who you hitherto flattered with the title of your best loved sister and dearest friend. You are a little mistaken in your judgment of our affairs. Had I pursued my own designs it would not have proved such a disadvantage to Mrs. Taylor as you suppose. Her school flourished before I came, and would probably be the same were I gone. . . . For my part I begin to grow superstitious and fancy 'tis not the will of Providence that I should ever do more than just live, that I never must know the satisfaction of a bed of my own to lie in till my last bed of clay, or sure before this I should have been settled for myself and have known what I had to trust to. But be it as it may, life flies fast away and will soon be over. Let the prudential part of the matter be forgot. I have given that to your love. I could not yield to your arguments, and have once more laid aside all thoughts of leaving Lincoln, and be it better or worse for me. Your will shall be obeyed for I love you too well to contradict your inclinations, but give me leave to ask you these questions:

1. Whether it is prudent for you to enter into such engagements to a sister when 'tis probable you will marry and have occasion to all you have yourself.

2. Whether should Mrs. Taylor die before me, I having neglected the opportunity of providing for old age purely to oblige you, you are not obliged by conscience and honour to make amends for the effects of your counsel.

3. Whether should the loss happen above mentioned, of her death, and I old and poor stand in need of an annual support from you, you would cheerfully grant it or rather curse your own management for bringing such inconveniences on yourself when they might have been so easily avoided. And so farewell Gainsborough, etc.

I am glad you met with so much good company at Stanton but wish you would lay aside that foolish ridiculous custom of walking. Were your slim corps able to sustain such hardships, which it is not, yet the mean scurvy appearance is reason sufficient against it. I take the precept of St. Paul to Timothy, Let no man despise thee, as a positive precept binding all clergy, for which reason all actions, dresses, etc., which naturally cause contempt, ought to be avoided (by them) out of strict duty. Now I leave it to your own judgment, whether a clergyman and Fellow of a college, walking one hundred miles does not look more like a foot post than a pillar of the Church of England?

I don't doubt but you have heard of Patty being gone to live with [Uncle] Matt. What work he will make with her principles, I know not. She seems pretty much already in his way of thinking. My mother has writ to me, to know whether I think I could be convinced again to live at home. But as the proverb says, two words to a bargain. However I hope to spend part of the winter with her to content her.

I am, dear brother,
Your most affectionate sister,
Emilia Wesley

Mrs. Taylor gives her service to you
and Miss Kitty to you and her man.

CHAPTER 17

The Methodist Fellow

Wesley was the acknowledged leader of a small group of friends at Oxford that had begun meeting together in order to encourage and assist each other to fulfill the expectations of the University statutes. Oxford had been founded in part to combat heresy; the statutes expected scholarly diligence and religious orthodoxy of the students. But the early eighteenth century was the heyday of neither, and Oxford was no exception to the prevailing apathy. In spite of some efforts by the top officials at the University to change the prevalent tenor of intellectual and spiritual lethargy, the presence of a small group of diligent and pious students was, in the 1730s, a somewhat rare phenomenon on the Oxford scene.

The group began to bring notice upon itself when its activities went beyond the private bounds of scholarly study and extended into the public realm of social action. Regular attendance at Holy Communion had brought upon them the title "Sacramentarians," but only when they began visiting the prisoners, the poor, the widows, and the orphans in town did the real weight of ridicule come down upon their heads. Coincident with these developments, they were given the name "Holy Club." Within six months it changed to "Godly Club." Other epithets followed and prevailed in turn: "Reformed Club," "Enthusiasts," "Supererogation Men," and finally, "Methodists."

The first contemporary use of the term "Methodist" in relation to this group came in a letter from John Clayton to John Wesley in August 1732, where it was reported as a term of derision closely associated with Wesley's own personal presence. He seems to have personified "the Methodist." Wesley first mentioned the term in his diary two months later, in the midst of the public criticisms surrounding the death of one of their group, William Morgan. Two published attacks on Wesley and his friends during that period in late 1732 and early 1733 gave the term "Methodist" wide exposure and fixed it in the minds of the public as the title for Wesley's movement.

Attack on the Sons of Sorrow

In the fall of 1732, rumors began to spread around Oxford that Wesley had contributed to William Morgan's death by encouraging his rigorous ascetic practices. Within a short time, an anonymous letter-writer sent a scurrilous caricature of Wesley and his friends to a London newspaper, Fog's Weekly Journal. *The letter appeared in the December 9 issue. Almost immediately, the Methodists attracted more public attention. Wesley began to note frequently in his diary "talk of the Methodists"—in the conversations of the Common Room, in talks with friends, and in his interviews with various University officials.*

This letter brought no direct public response from Wesley, even though he was at this time writing a sermon to be preached before the University on January 1 ("Circumcision of the Heart"). The particular charges in this newspaper account did, however, cause a gentleman near London to request a friend to make inquiries about these "sons of sorrow," resulting in the report contained in the section "The Oxford Methodists Defended," below.

To the Author of Fog's Journal

Sir,

Our countrymen are observed to be naturally of a gloomy and melancholy temper, and it is owing to this (as is generally thought) that a great many different and wrong notions of religion sprout up among us. Whilst persons of uncheerful imaginations represent religion in so formal and unamiable a dress, men of the contrary complexion are usually frighted at her appearance, judging a life conformable to her precepts to be an unsocial state that excludes and denies us the enjoyment and relish of the most innocent pleasures. An age or two ago we find it was a fashion in several parts of England, but especially at Oxford, for every one that would be thought to live up to the principles of Christianity, to doom themselves to this absurd and perpetual melancholy; and I am afraid it will take place again very soon, for the University at present is not a little pestered with those sons of sorrow, whose number daily receives addition and carry things to as great a height, if not higher than was formerly, designing (as may well be supposed) to make the whole place nothing else but a monastery.

As this may prove of very fatal consequence, and even religion itself may suffer, it was thought proper to address you and desire that in one of your papers may be represented the errors of their mistaken devotion which, 'tis hoped, will put a stop to this sect called Methodists, as the several edicts did to the pietists in the Duchy of Saxony.

To relate every particular concerning them, as it would be exposing their characters too much, so it could not but be very tedious: I shall therefore only send you some general observations on the rules they think themselves obliged in duty to observe.

They pretend to great refinements as well as to what regards the speculative as the practical part of religion, and have a very near affinity to the Essenes among the Jews, as the pietists among the Christians in Switzerland. This proposition, that no action whatever is indifferent, is the chief hinge on which their whole scheme of religion turns. Hence they condemn several actions as bad which are not only allowed as innocent but laudable by the rest of mankind. They avoid as much as is possible every object that may affect them with any pleasant and grateful sensation. All social entertainments and diversions are disapproved of, and in endeavouring to avoid luxury, they not only exclude what is convenient, but what is absolutely necessary for the support of life, fancying (as it is thought) that religion was designed to contradict nature. They neglect and voluntarily afflict their bodies and practice several rigorous and superstitious customs which God never required of them: all Wednesdays and Fridays are strictly to be kept as fasts, and blood let once a fortnight to keep down the carnal man; at dinner they sigh for the time they are obliged to spend in eating; every morning to rise at four o'clock is supposed a duty, and to employ two hours a day in singing of psalms and hymns is judged as an indispensable duty requisite to the being of a Christian. In short, they practice every thing contrary to the judgment of other persons and allow none to have any but those of their own sect, which is the farthest from it.

Origen is proposed as a pattern, who by performing a particular operation on himself, diverted his senses from the love of earthly objects to fix them on those that were spiritual; and no doubt if they knew how to make a proper incision, they would quickly follow him as to this and perhaps, if they prevail and continue a little longer, Dr. Ch[esel]den [a well-known surgeon] may be sent for to put in practice and try that art on them which at present they are unskilled in.

As these Methodists have occasioned no small stir in Oxford, so there has not been wanting variety of conjectures about them; and as several would be desirous to know our opinions of their rise, it may not be improper to acquaint you with them, which are summed up in these few lines of Ennius,

Non sunt hi aut scientia aut arte Divini.
Sed superstitiosi Vates, impudentes Hariole;
Aut Insani, aut quibus Egestas imperat.
   [It is not by knowledge or skill that they are prophetic.
   But they are soothsaying prophets, shameless gut-gazers;
   Crazy or obedient to the behests of want.]

For some are apt to ascribe their gloomy and disconsolate way of life to want of money, thus being denied the enjoyment of those pleasures they chiefly desire; they are weighed down by an habitual sorrow and 'tis certain that their founder took formerly no small liberty in indulging his appetites. Besides Pliny seems to favour this notion, who speaking of the Essenes says, that many flocked to them, whom the surges of ill fortune having made weary of the world, have driven to take shelter in their institution and manner of life.

Others, though perhaps it may be too presumptuous, tax their characters with hypocrisy, and suppose them to use religion only as a veil to vice, and indeed if we should give credit to the several stories related of them, their greatest friends would be ashamed to stand in their defense and the sect of the neighbouring nation, which agreed in several particulars with them, being accused of the same immoralities, seem to confirm it the more.

But others again judge it owing to enthusiastic madness and

superstitious scruples, who, with the author of the *Tale of a Tub,* suppose the innovators in religion to be persons whose natural reason hath suffered great revolutions. And indeed, though among their own party they pass for religious persons and men of extraordinary parts, yet they have the misfortune to be taken by all who have ever been in their company for madmen and those whom the world is pleased to distinguish by the title of fools. If this last opinion be true, which certainly would if the question was to be decided by numbers, we must recommend them to your advice which 'tis expected will be sent the first opportunity, and desire them to follow the late ingenious Dr. Thomas Willis's prescription and provide themselves with his wonderful cap, and this we hope will very much conduce towards the clearing of their heads and expelling this gloomy stupidity.

Yours, etc.

Oxon, Nov. 5, 1732.

The Oxford Methodists Defended

Two months after the letter to Fog's Weekly *was published, Wesley admitted in a letter to his father that he was doubtful whether he could "stem the torrent" of criticism that was "rolling down from all sides." Less than two weeks later, Wesley received some unexpected help in the form of a small pamphlet, entitled* The Oxford Methodists, *published at the end of February 1733.*

The anonymous author of this tract sets forth the "rise, views, and designs" of the Methodists, using Wesley's letter to Richard Morgan, Sr. (see page 64) as the main source of information. The tone of the work is generally, though not totally, favorable toward Wesley and his friends. Wesley's own reaction, as noted in his diary, was positive at first, but the question of authorship seems to have bothered him. He immediately suspected the elder Morgan of providing the author with the letter, but the Irishman denied having read or showed Wesley's letter to anyone, adding that he could not ascertain from Wesley's inquiry whether the pamphlet was "intended as satire or vindication." This uncertainty no doubt reflected the mild sense of consternation in Wesley's own mind. In the days following the appearance of this pamphlet, Wesley visited nearly everyone to whom he had read or showed the Morgan letter, but seems not to have discovered its authorship. Current attributions of authorship to William Law are unsubstantiated.

The following selection is taken from the first edition, which is not unequivocally favorable toward the Methodists; editions after 1737 were altered so as to be less ambiguous in defending the Methodists. The portions here reproduced are from the sections of the pamphlet that respond primarily to the Fog's Weekly *notice.*

Sir,

I hope you will not think me to blame that I have not sooner answered yours wherein you inclosed *Fog's Journal* of the 9th of December last and desired me to inform myself and you of the motives, pretensions, and actions of the society of young gentlemen there styled Methodists. As I was entirely unacquainted with any of them when you made me this request, it must needs, you'll allow, take up time so thoroughly to make one's self master of this affair as to be able to answer the desire of so good a friend....

After I had heard all that could be said *against* them by their enemies, I thought I was but fair to enquire of their friends what could be said *for* them. But, alas! so strong were the prejudices against them and so general that I found it no easy matter to meet with any one that would own the name. Whereupon, depending upon the character which their enemies gave them of probity and sincerity, I made myself acquainted with one of the gentlemen and frankly opened my mind to him and desired him to inform me of their motives and views and their particular inducements to a singularity of behaviour and life which had subjected them to the censures of so many persons of learning and capacity. And from the gentleman's answer and the account he gave me of the original and design of the society, I own I was greatly edified, and I doubt not but you will likewise be much pleased. In short the account which he gave me was to the following effect: [thereupon follows about fifteen pages quoting and enlarging upon John Wesley's letter to Richard Morgan, Sr., with occasional editorial comments, such as the following:]

Observing the gentleman I talked with, and got these lights from, to be a modest and ingenuous man, I threw in his way two or three objections to the method they were in, in respect to the *singularity* of the thing, and wished their zeal were not too warm and active, etc. But I found he was very well prepared to give solid answers to what I said, and such as showed that their notions and principles were better considered and digested than their ill-willers generally imagine them to be....

Being thus abundantly satisfied in whatever I desired to know relating to this society, after having made sincere acknowledgments for his frankness and candour, I left the gentleman and the city, not without assuring him of my hearty prayers for the success of their pious designs and for their perseverance therein, and prudent conduct amidst so many opponents and gainsayers, not forgetting to drop a small largess towards promoting their pious and charitable design.

Give me leave, sir, now to make a few observations on the premises, and on the letter in *Fog's Journal* which gave occasion to this enquiry, which has ended so much to my (as I doubt not, it will to your) satisfaction....

As to the character into which he resolves the matter at last, to wit, of "enthusiastic madness," of "superstitious scrupulousness," of "folly," etc., that has been taken notice of already in the course of the narration and I shall say nothing to it here. They must be content to tarry for a better character from such persons as this writer till time, and their own continued good conduct and perseverance in the same laudable duties, have worn off the imputation and given the world a better and juster opinion of them.

But after all, sir, between friends, I cannot help saying, that I wish these young gentlemen have not, at their first setting out, fallen upon too great a refinement in some small points which their friends might have wished, that proper regard to the censure of the world (which is so necessary to augment their numbers and to prevent ridicule) had made them avoid. I am entirely satisfied with their scheme in general and think it worthy of a more primitive age; but if the dispensing with such points, if there are any such, as they in conscience think might be dispensed with, would have taken away the occasion of any part of that obloquy which a misjudging world is so ready to fix upon all good designs, I wish they had done it, that they might have had less difficulties to encounter and more hopes of success in propagating so worthy a scheme.... But if the imperfection of human nature be such, that we *must* do *too little* or *too much*, that to abate of the fervour of that zeal which excites to actions thus laudable would be to damp their ardent flame and make them relax too much, let them proceed, and keep high-tuned and unabated that divine energy of mind which shall, in God's good time, transport them to a blessed eternity where all is harmony, peace, and concord....

I have heard that a celebrated Head of one of their colleges was wont to deliver it as his opinion that no lad ever made a bright and ingenious man who had not run into some extravagant and vicious excesses in youth. Why may not the same rule hold in spirituals? *Zeal* in itself is doubtless a laudable disposition of mind, especially if it be a good thing. If in religion (than which, nothing can be more excellent) it answers to that generous ardour and lively pregnancy in youth, which puts them on enterprising great and magnanimous actions. For want of experience, indeed, it may run into some extravagance and erroneous excesses and too often miscarries either in those *depths* it unwarily adventures to rush into, or on those shelves and rocks it wants skill to discern and avoid.

This shows how necessary it is that *zeal* should ever be attended with *knowledge*.... What I have related will show that these young gentlemen have proceeded with great prudence and caution in observing the above advice as far as it concerns themselves. I wish I could say the same of their opponents, or of those rather whose more immediate part is to pilot them aright, and that they would not countenance the insults cast upon so hopeful a scheme and thereby "break the bruised reed and quench the smoking flax."

'Tis not to be questioned but most of the clamours raised against this society are owing to misapprehension and misrepresentation. . . . Let all the serious part of mankind, who alone are appealed to in this case, be judges between them and this lewd detractor, who has so ludicrously and, in some cases, so wilfully misrepresented them. To "live by rule," especially a *good* rule, was ever esteemed a sure sign of *wisdom*; to "live by none," much more to be "against all rule and method," must be a flagrant mark of *folly*. . . . And I will venture to add, that if these young gentlemen persevere to the end in this *good method*, instead of the *cap* of shame and reproach, they shall receive a *crown* of glory.

I hope, sir, you will excuse my prolixity. You say, you love to receive long letters from me; and I think I have tried your patience sufficiently, and that indulgence with which you have always favoured

Your most humble servant, etc.

CHAPTER 18

The Unassuming Spiritual Tutor: John Gambold's Description

Wesley's emergence into the public eye was slower than one might suppose, in spite of his leadership among the controversial group at Oxford. His two-year sojourn in Georgia, for instance, removed him from the English scene and the prying curiosity of cynics and critics. During that period, Wesley did, however, maintain contact with his friends in England, who continued the work he had promoted.

John Gambold of Christ Church became an Oxford Methodist about the time he received his A.M. degree. He was ordained a priest of the Church of England in 1733 and became the vicar of Stanton Harcourt, which was close to Oxford and allowed for continued contact. Gambold later fell under the influence of Peter Böhler and the Moravians, who, in Charles Wesley's words, "stole away his heart." Estranged from the Wesleys after 1741, Gambold became a Moravian minister and eventually was named the first bishop among the English Moravians.

While Wesley was in Georgia, Gambold, still an enthusiastic Methodist, wrote the following description of Wesley to a friend. This account, though obviously biased, is one of the best contemporary descriptions of the Oxford Wesley, as corroborated by his own diaries. This letter was published under the title "The Character of Mr. John Wesley" in the Methodist Magazine *(1798).*

Sir,

Mr. Wesley, late of Lincoln College, has been the instrument of so much good to me, that I shall never forget him. Could I remember him as I ought, it would have very near the same effect as if he was still present, for a conversation so unreserved as his was, so zealous in engaging his friends to every instance of Christian piety, has left nothing new to be said, nothing but that occurs to us as often as we are disposed to remember him impartially. As it is my duty to look back upon the good offices done me by the friend of my youth, and upon the grace of God which was powerful in this his servant, so I believe it might be a help to me in doing this, if I should set myself to give some account of him to you. I do not hope to retrieve many particular passages, but only to enliven my general idea of him.

About the middle of March, 1730, I became acquainted with Mr. Charles Wesley of Christ Church. I was just then come from the country, and had made a resolution to find out some persons of religion to keep company with, or else to instill something of it into those I knew already. . . . One day an old acquaintance entertained me with some reflections on the whimsical Mr. Wesley, his preciseness and pious extravagancies. Though I had lived with him four years in the same College, yet so unable was I to take notice of anything that passed, that I knew nothing of his character; but upon hearing this, I suspected he might be a good Christian. I therefore went to his room, and without any ceremony desired the benefit of his conversation. I had so large a share of it thenceforth that hardly a day passed, while I was at College, but we were together once, if not oftener.

After some time he introduced me to his brother John, of Lincoln College. "For," said he, "he is somewhat older than I and can resolve your doubts better." This, as I found afterwards, was a thing which he was deeply sensible of; for I never observed any person have a more real deference for another, than he constantly had for his brother.... Indeed he followed his brother entirely; could I describe one of them, I should describe both. And therefore I shall say no more of Charles....

The Wesleys were already talked of for some religious practices which were first occasioned by Mr. Morgan of Christ Church. He being a young man of an excellent disposition, took all opportunities to make his companions in love with a good life, to create in them a reverence for the public worship, to tell them of their faults with a sweetness and simplicity that disarmed the worst tempers. He delighted much in works of charity; he kept several children at school, and when he found beggars in the street, he would bring them into his chambers and talk to them. Many such things he did; and being acquainted with these two brothers, he invited them to join with him, and proposed that they should meet frequently to encourage one another and have some scheme to proceed by in their daily employments. About half a year after I got among them, Mr. Morgan died....

From these combined friends began a little Society (though all such names they also declined), for several others from time to time fell in, most of them only to be improved by their serious and useful discourse, and some few espousing all their resolutions and their whole way of life. Mr. John Wesley was always the chief manager, for which he was very fit. For he had not only more learning and experience than the rest, but he was blest with such activity as to be always gaining ground, and such steadiness that he lost none. What proposals he made to any were sure to charm them because he was so much in earnest; nor could they afterwards slight them because they saw him always the same. What supported this uniform vigour was the care he took to consider well of every affair before he engaged in it, making all his decisions in the fear of God, without passion, humour, or self-confidence; for though he had naturally a very clear apprehension, yet his exact prudence depended more on humility and singleness of heart. To this I may add that he had, I think, something of authority in his countenance; though as he did not want address, he could soften his manner and point it as occasion required. Yet he never assumed anything to himself above his companions; any of them might speak their mind, and their words were as strictly regarded by him as his were by them.

It was their custom to meet most evenings either at his chamber or one of the others, where after some prayers (the chief subject of which was charity), they eat their supper together and he read some book. But the chief business was to review what each had done that day, in pursuance of their common design, and to consult what steps were to be taken next.

Their undertaking included these several particulars: to converse with young students, to visit the prisons, to instruct some poor families, to take care of a school and a parish work-house. They took great pains with the younger members of the University, to rescue them from bad company and encourage them in a sober studious life....Some or other of them went to the Castle every day and another most commonly to Bocardo.... In order to release those who were confined for small debts and were bettered by their affliction (and likewise to purchase books, physic, and other necessaries), they raised a little fund to which many of their acquaintance contributed quarterly. They had prayers at the Castle most Wednesdays and Fridays, a sermon on Sunday, and the Sacrament once a month.

When they undertook any poor family, they saw them at least once a week, sometimes gave them money, admonished them of their vices, read to them, and examined their children. The school was, I think, of Mr. Wesley's own setting up; however he paid the Mistress and clothed some, if not all, of the children. When they went thither, they enquired how each child behaved, saw their work (for some could knit or spin), heard them read, heard them their prayers or their catechism, and explained part of it. In the same manner they taught the children in the Work-house, and read to the old people as they did to the prisoners.

Though some other practices of Mr. Wesley and his friends were much blamed, as their fasting on Wednesday and Friday, after the custom of the Primitive Church, their coming on those Sundays, when there was no Sacrament at their own Colleges, to receive it at Christ Church (which they thought, being the Cathedral, might properly be resorted to by any within the Diocese), yet nothing was so much disliked as these charitable employments. They seldom took any notice of the accusations brought against them; but if they made any reply, it was commonly such a plain and simple one as if there was nothing more in the case but that they had heard such doctrines of the Saviour and believed and done accordingly....

But some would have it that Mr. Wesley was a designing man. I know very well that he was so. He had the good of the University very much at heart, though it was not proper for one in his narrow sphere to make profession of it. Most of the students there are designed for Holy Orders; could some of these be induced to mix more devotion with their study, their knowledge would be more experimental, and their future preaching more effectual....

Mr. Wesley is now gone to Georgia as a missionary, where there is ignorance that aspires after divine wisdom, but no false learning that is got above it; where politeness does not superficially cure the mean and odious nature of man, nor luxury protect the sinner from the sorrows which his Maker said should be his lot; where the necessities of a fallen world stand naked and confessed before the eyes of God, and where it is most likely his arm should be made bare before men and sensibly interpose for their relief.

He is, I confess, still living, and I know that an advantageous character is more decently bestowed on the deceased....I am not making any attempt on the opinion of the public, but only studying a private edification. And though a man may not be of that importance that memorials of his person can modestly be obtruded on the world, yet a family picture of him, his relations are allowed to keep by them.

This is that idea of Mr. Wesley which I cherish for the service of my soul, and take the liberty likewise to deposit with you.

But I must not leave my friend so. I could say a great deal of his private piety, how it was nourished by a continual recourse to God, preserved by a strict watchfulness in beating down praise and reducing the craftiness and impetuosity of nature to a child-like simplicity and indifference, and in a good degree crowned with divine love, and victory over the whole set of earthly passions. He thought prayer to be more his business than anything else, and I have seen him come out of his closet with a serenity of countenance that was next to shining; it discovered what he had been at, and gave me double hope of receiving wise directions in the matter about which I came to consult him. In all his motions he attended the will of God, though he wrote several things and acquainted himself with several parts of knowledge, and took several journeys. He had neither the presumption nor the leisure to anticipate things whose season was not now, and would show some uneasiness whenever any of us, by impertinent speculations, were shifting off the appointed improvement of the present minute. By being always cheerful but never triumphing, he so husbanded the secret consolations which God gave him, that they seldom left him, and never, but in a posture of strong and long-suffering faith. Thus the repose and satisfaction of the mind being secured, there were in him no idle cravings, no chagrin or sickliness of spirit, nothing but the genuine needs of the body to be relieved by outward accommodations and refreshments. I have heard his brother say (to comfort me, who was not so happy) that he thought he had never exceeded in eating or drinking for some years. When he was just come home from a long journey and had been in different companies, he resumed his usual employments as if he had never left them; no dissipation of thought appeared, no alteration of taste. Much less was he discomposed by any slanders or affronts; he was only afraid lest he should grow proud of this conformity to his Master. In short, he used many arts to be religious, but none to seem so; with a zeal always upon the stretch, and a most transparent sincerity, he addicted himself to every good word and work.

But what I would chiefly make some remarks upon is the manner in which he directed his friends.

Because he required such a regulation of our studies as might devote them all to God, he has been cried out upon as one that discouraged learning. Far from that—the first thing he struck at in young men was that indolence, which would not submit to close thinking. Nor was he against reading much, especially at first, because then the mind ought to fill itself with materials and try everything that looks bright and perfect, though afterwards, in the coolness of a mortified heart and the simplicity of one that knows God, many of them will be forgot and superseded.

He earnestly recommended to them a method and order in all their actions. After their morning devotions (which were at a fixed and early hour, from 5 to 6 being the time, morning as well as at evening; and upon the point of early rising, he told them the well-spending of the day would very much depend), he advised them to determine with themselves what they were to do all parts of the day. By such foresight they should at every hour's end not be in doubt how to dispose of themselves; and by bringing themselves under the necessity of such a plan, they might correct the impotence of a mind that had been used to live by humour and chance, and prepare it by degrees to bear the other restraints of a holy life.

The next thing was to put them upon keeping the Fasts, visiting poor people, and coming to the weekly Sacrament, not only to subdue the body, increase charity, and obtain divine grace, but (as he expressed it) to cut off their retreat to the world. He judged that if they did these things, men would cast out their names as evil and by the impossibility of keeping fair any longer with the world, oblige them to take their whole refuge in Christianity. But those whose resolutions he thought would not bear this test, he left to gather strength by their secret exercises.

It was his earnest care to introduce them to the treasures of wisdom and hope in the Holy Scriptures; to teach them not only to endure that book (for which, I fear, all before their conversion, especially scholars, have not a particular relish but a particular loathing), but to form themselves by it and to fly to it as the great antidote against the darkness of this world. For some years past he and his friends read the New Testament together at evening. After every portion of it, having heard the conjectures the rest had to offer, he made his observations on the phrase, design, and difficult places; one or two wrote these down from his mouth.

Because the more thoroughly we know the diseases of our souls, the more we will undergo to purchase their health and attend more seriously on the great Physician, he laid much stress upon self-examination. He taught them (besides what occurs in his *Collection of Prayers*) to take account of their actions in a very exact manner by writing a constant diary; in this they noted down in ciphers, once if not oftener in the day, what chiefly their employments had been in several parts of it and how they had performed each. Mr. Wesley had these records of his life by him for many years back. And some I have known who, to seal their conviction and make their repentance more solemn, would write down such reflections upon themselves as the anguish of their soul at that time suggest, adding any spiritual maxim which some experience of their own had confirmed to them.

Then to keep in their minds an awful sense of God's presence, with a constant dependence on his help, he advised them to ejaculatory prayers. The use of this naturally accompanies self-examination, for the soul distressed at her own deformity, treachery, and darkness, will have continually something to beg, to complain of, or at least to spread and expose before the eyes of God. They had a book of ejaculations relating to the chief virtues, which, lying by them as they stood at their studies, they at intervals snatched a short petition out of it....

The last means he recommended was meditation. It is a great benefit to a man to detain himself, not for a moment, but for a considerable while, in a deep attention to divine things. It composes the tumultuous breast and makes all the passions forget their own gratification, for a rest and tranquility in which they are pleasingly destroyed. It dulls the eye to the world and disposes all the powers of the body to wait for higher orders in exerting their common functions. Some acquaintance with God is certainly attained by it, if not in the way of reasoning and distinct conceptions, yet at least by the slight which is put upon all that man can think or do, and by boldly lifting up a naked helpless heart to receive the stamp of eternal Truth. Their usual time of meditating was the hour next before dinner.

After this, he committed them to God. What remained for him to do was to encourage them in the discomforts and temptations they might feel (for which his word was, "Be strong") and to guard against all spiritual delusions. The business now was, not to bid them run for the prize, but to lend a helping hand to support the load they carried with them, and to hinder them from dropping into strange paths. He was very judicious in prescribing to those states whose causes lie the deepest, for some such he met with in his friends. One way whereby God cleanses the soul and prepares it for himself is by throwing a cloud over a man's natural wit and sagacity, denying all visible success to his religious endeavours, infusing a general weariness and deep compunction. Of this he had trial in his brother. Another way is to draw a man with the cords of love, to feast him for some moments with so much of the *substance* of things hoped for as shall captivate him for his whole life after, and in one taste of the sweetness of God, do the work of a thousand arguments. Thus was his pupil Mr. Hervey dealt with, of whom I must say thus much, though he is in England, that he is a man of surprising greatness of soul; and if you look for his virtues, you will not be able to discover them one by one, but you will see that he walks before God with a reverence and alacrity which includes them all.

In this spiritual care of his acquaintance, Mr. Wesley persisted amidst all discouragements; he overlooked not only one's absurd or disagreeable qualities, but even his coldness and neglect of him, if he thought it might be conquered. He helped one in things out of religion, that he might be more welcome to help him in that. His knowledge of the world and his insight into physic were often of use to us.

If any one could have provoked him, I should, for I was very slow in coming into their measures and very remiss in doing my part. I frequently contradicted his assertions, or, which is much the same, distinguished upon them: I hardly ever submitted to his advice at the time he gave it, though I relented afterwards. One time he was in fear that I had taken up notions that were not safe and pursued my spiritual improvement in an erroneous, because inactive way. So he came over and stayed with me near a week. He accosted me with the utmost softness, condoled with me the incumbrances of my constitution, heard all I had to say, and endeavoured to pick out my meaning, and yielded to me as far as he could. I never saw more humility in him than at this time; it was enough to cool the warmest imaginations that swell an overseeing heart. It was indeed his custom to humble himself most before the proud, not to reproach them; but in a way of secret intercession to procure their pardon. His pupil Mr. Morgan (brother to him of Christ Church) put that unwearied hope, for which he was remarkable, to the trial....

Mr. Wesley had not only friends in Oxford to assist, but a great many correspondents. He set apart one day at least in the week (and he was no slow composer) for writing letters, in which, without levity or affectation, but with plainness and fervour beyond his own common rate (for he was not writing to the world) he gave his advice in particular cases and vindicated the strict original sense of the Gospel precepts.

John Gambold

CHAPTER 19

Wesley in Georgia

Wesley had set out for Georgia in 1735 with high aspirations (see page 74). The distractions and disappointments of the following two years, however, precipitated his hasty departure from the colony at the end of 1737. The shadow of these events followed him back to England and continued to haunt him throughout his lifetime.

The following selections illustrate the perceptions of four persons who were in Georgia with Wesley. Their attitudes toward Wesley range from very friendly (Ingham) to very antagonistic (Williams). Stephens tries to be somewhat mediating in his view, while Thicknesse makes no effort to conceal a prejudice nurtured by subsequent misfortune. The first two reports were written at the time of the events they describe; the second two are later recollections.

The Christian Exemplar

When John Wesley decided to go to Georgia in 1735, he tried to recruit some friends to accompany him. Benjamin Ingham accepted at the last minute. He was an Oxford Methodist who, though not a member of John's core group of Methodists, had been instrumental in spreading the Wesleyan design at Oxford through his association with Charles Wesley, James Hervey, and others.

Shortly after arriving in Georgia, Ingham wrote to his family and friends at Ossett in Yorkshire. The following selection from that letter exhibits the motives and methods that moved Wesley and his friends and reflects the high hopes and expectations that sustained them in their mission to Georgia. Ingham admired Wesley as an example of Christian living, and although Ingham later became closely associated with the Moravians, he maintained contact with the Wesleys throughout his life.

A contemporary copy of this letter, never published during Ingham's lifetime, is in the Lincolnshire Archives.

Savannah, May 1st, 1736

To my much-honoured Mother, my dearly beloved Brethren and Sisters, and all my Christian Friends:

Grace, mercy and peace be multiplied from Almighty God, the Father, and from our Lord Jesus Christ, with the Holy Ghost; to whom be glory, honour, and praise for ever and ever. Amen....

I can now inform you that we are all arrived in safety in Georgia. But, because I believe that a relation of our voyage will not be unacceptable to you, I shall, with God's assistance, set down both the chief occurrences thereof, and also the reasons which moved me to undertake it....

About six weeks before we took shipping for Georgia, I received a letter from the Rev. Mr. John Wesley, Fellow of Lincoln College, Oxford, the substance whereof was as follows: "Fast and pray; and then send me word whether you dare go with me to the Indians." Having observed his directions, about three days after the receipt of this, I answered him to this effect: "I am satisfied that God's providence has placed me in my present station. Whether He would have me go to the Indians or not, I am not as yet informed. I dare not go without being called." I kept his letter secret for some days. I was utterly averse from going; I did not in the least intend it. I thought we had heathens enew [enough] at home. However, I continued to pray that God would be pleased to direct me, whether He would have me go, or not.

About a fortnight after this, Mr. John Wesley came to London, as also his brother Charles, and Mr. Salmon, a gentleman of Brazen-Nose [Brasenose] College, Oxford. The first time I was with them, I desired to know the reasons which moved them to leave England. They answered, they thought they could be better Christians, alleging particular advantages which they might reasonably expect would further their spiritual progress by going amongst the Indians. Some of their reasons I approved of; to others I objected, alleging that a man might be a Christian in any place, but chiefly insisting upon this, that no one ought to go without being called of God. They told me, if I required a voice or sign from heaven, that was not now to be expected; and that a man had no other way of knowing God's will, but by consulting his own reason, and his friends, and by observing the order of God's providence. They, therefore, thought it a sufficient call to choose that way of life which they had reason to believe would most promote their Christian welfare....

A few days after this, Mr. Wesley began to be more importunate with me, urging me with my promise, telling me he had now little hope of Mr. Salmon; and, as for Mr. Hall, he could not properly be said to go with him, for his design was to go amongst the Indians, whereas Mr. Hall was only to go to Savannah, and be minister there; and as for his brother Charles, he went over only as secretary to the trustees for the colony of Georgia.

I still refused, telling him, "If Mr. Hall went, I would not go." Nevertheless, I prayed very earnestly almost night and day, revolving upon it. My heart began to be now more and more affected. It pleased God to let me see I might be a better Christian by going with Mr. Wesley. I thought, by living with him and having his example always before mine eyes, I should be enabled to rise regularly and early, and to spend all my time carefully, which are great and necessary points in Christianity, and wherein I grew very deficient by being in London. Besides these there were three other reasons which moved me. I thought, I should not meet with so many temptations to sensuality and indulgence among the Indians as in England. Hereby, likewise, I saw I should be freed from the slavery of worldly interests and the danger and drudgery of hunting for preferment, which hinders so many from being Christians, making them to betray the Church to serve the State, and to deny Jesus Christ to please worldly-minded men. The last and chief reason was the goodness of the work, and the great and glorious promises that are made to those who forsake all for the sake of the gospel....

Having now no further doubt, but, that I was intended by Providence to accompany Mr. Wesley, on Tuesday, October 14, he, his brother, Mr. Charles, myself, and Mr. Delamotte, son of a merchant in London, who had a mind to give himself up entirely to God and leave the world, being accompanied by Mr. Morgan, Mr. Burton (one of the trustees), and Mr. James Hutton, took boat at Westminster, for Gravesend. We arrived there about four in the afternoon, and immediately went on board the ship, called the *Symmonds.*

Tuesday, October 21. We left Gravesend, and went down the river, though very slowly, the wind not being favourable to us. We now began to be more in earnest. We resolved to rise early, and to spend our time regularly and carefully. The first hour, we allotted ourselves, was to pray for ourselves and absent friends. The next, we read the Scriptures; and, from six to breakfast, we generally read something relating to the Primitive Church. At eight, we had public prayers. The forenoon I spent either in teaching and instructing the children, or reading antiquity; *Mr. John Wesley* in learning German; *Mr. Charles* mostly in writing; *Mr. Delamotte* in learning Greek or navigation. At twelve, we all met together, to join in prayer, and to exhort one another, consulting both how to profit our neighbours and ourselves. After dinner, I taught the children, or conversed religiously with some of the passengers, as also Messrs. Wesleys constantly did. At four, we had public prayer. From five to six, we spent in private; then we supped. At seven, I read to as many of the passengers as were willing to hear, and instructed them in Christianity. Mr. John Wesley joined with the Moravians in their public devotion. At eight, we all met together again, to give an account of what we had done, whom we had conversed with, deliberating on the best method of proceeding with such and such persons; what advice, direction, exhortation, or reproof was necessary for them; and sometimes we read a little, concluding with prayer; and so we went to bed about nine, sleeping soundly upon mats and blankets, regarding neither the noise of the sea or sailors. "The angels of the Lord are round about them that fear Him."...

Sunday, January 25. About half an hour past seven, a great sea broke in upon us, which split the main-sail, carried away the companion, filled between decks, and rushed into the great cabin. This made most of the people tremble; and, I believe, they would then have been glad to have been Christians, how light soever they made of religion before. I myself was made sensible, that, nothing will enable us to smile in the face of death, but a life of extraordinary holiness. I was under some fear for a little while; but I recollected myself again, by reflecting that every thing came by the will of God; and that whatever He willed was the best for me....

On Tuesday, we found land; and, on Thursday afternoon, 5th of February, we got safe into Tybee-road, in the mouth of the river Savannah, in the province of Georgia, in America. Messrs. Wesleys, Mr. Delamotte, and I had some discourse about our manner of living in this new country. I was struck with a deep, religious awe, considering the greatness and importance of the work I came upon, but was comforted with these words in the Psalms: "O! tarry thou the Lord's leisure; be strong, and He shall comfort thy heart; and put thou thy trust in the Lord." From the whole service, I was moved to think that the Gospel would be propagated over the whole world. May God, of His great mercy, graciously be pleased to grant it....

Oh what a work have we before us! Who is sufficient for these things? I am nothing. I have nothing. I can do nothing. O! my dearest friends, pray for us. Pray earnestly for us; and more especially for me, your very weak, though most dutiful son, and affectionate brother,

Benjamin Ingham

The Partisan Priest

The controversies surrounding Wesley's actions as a parish priest and unsuccessful suitor divided the Savannah community into hostile factions. In the midst of the ensuing legal proceedings, William Stephens arrived from England. A former member of Parliament and friend of James Oglethorpe, Stephens conscientiously gathered as much information about the colony as he could. His work brought him into the favor of the Georgia Trustees; in 1743 he became president of the colony.

Stephens's observations, quite detailed and self-consciously neutral, though not actually free from party spirit, were published in London in A Journal of the Proceedings in Georgia *(3 volumes, 1742). The follow-*

ing selections shed light on Wesley's activities and attitudes during his last month in America after he had been indicted by the Savannah grand jury. Stephens seems particularly interested in Wesley's preaching and in his temperate yet unconciliatory attitude toward his enemies.

Thursday [November 3]. ...I had from different hands a long detail of the cause of discord between Mr. Causton and the Parson, ever since Mr. Williamson married Miss Hopkey (niece to Mr. Causton), which was told me variously, as the relators inclined; but it was carried now to that height as to engage great part of the town, which was so divided that Mr. Causton and Mr. Wesley drew their greatest attention and the partisans on both sides did not stick to throw plenty of scandal against their adversaries.

Friday. Great part of my time taken up this day in listening to abundance of tales which were obtruded upon me, and told very partially (I observed) by most in favour of one or the other, as they liked or disliked. Nevertheless, I would not seem averse to hearing what came in my way, believing that out of such abundance something probably might be learnt worth regarding, and I should the more readily discover their several dispositions....

Sunday [November 6]. Went to church in the forenoon, where we had (what is commonly called) the second Service only, and a sermon not to be found fault with, upon mutual forgiveness. But I was concerned to see so thin an audience, which proceeded from a grown aversion to the preacher since this public strife sprung up. Several of the *Scotch* gentlemen having hinted to me their desire of a conference, I sat with three or four of them over a cup of tea towards evening for a hour, when they told me, in the name of all the rest, of Mr. Wesley's informing them lately that Mr. Causton persuaded him to write to the Trustees and acquaint them that the Scotch here were universally a turbulent people who neither regarded divine or human laws, but lived idle and continually fomented mischief. From whence they inferred that they were never to expect common justice; but upon my asking how long since it was that Mr. Causton said this to the Parson, I was answered, more than a year. From whence it seemed to me that Mr. Wesley, who had kept it smothering in his breast so long, brought it forth now maliciously at this juncture when he and Mr. Causton were fallen out, in order to exasperate the Scotch against him, whom at this time he lived in good accord with.

Monday. Went in the morning and took my breakfast with Mr. Wesley, when I paid him the ten pounds sent by me from an unknown hand; and then we had some talk about the differences betwixt him and Mr. Causton, which he put in another light than what I had it on the other side. I desired him to be free, assuring him that my ears were equally open and I should be glad to be instrumental (if it lay in my power) to reconcile those animosities which began first between two friends and had now drawn almost the whole town into parties in the quarrel. I found it manifest the first rise of it was upon young Williamson's marrying Mr. Causton's niece, whom the Parson had a liking to for himself, and who, whilst she was unmarried, used constantly to receive the Sacrament, which is here administered weekly to some few who frequently resort to Mr. Wesley for their better edification in private; but upon Miss Hopkey's entering into the state of wedlock, she refrained from such private lectures and refused to go to him when sent for—probably by direction from her husband—for which reason (or some other unknown to me) Mr. Wesley refused her the Sacrament at the next communion and she went home from the table. So far Mr. Wesley acknowledged to me; but in his own justification said he had given her notice before not to offer herself there till she had first conferred with him in private. Mr. Wesley told me farther, he would at some other opportunity explain these things more fully and believed I would hear it impartially. So we parted, and I spent the rest of the day in settling my own little affairs at home, and beginning to provide for our future living....

Sunday [November 13]. Mr. Wesley preached on these words, "Is it lawful to give tribute unto Caesar or not?" from whence he discoursed largely on the duties of magistrates in their several subordinate ranks and degrees, and the obedience due from the people; setting forth how far it was, nevertheless, consistent with Christian liberty for people to insist on their rights when they found themselves oppressed by inferior magistrates exercising a discretionary authority which exceeded their commission; as an instance whereof he laid down St. Paul's behaviour when the chief captain had him before him, and how apprehensive the chief captain was, of his having gone too far, as it is related in the twenty-second chapter of the Acts; and on another occasion, when St. Paul had been evil entreated of the magistrates at Philippi, who the next day ordered him to be set at liberty, etc., he then put on a peculiar spirit, in the thirty-seventh verse of the sixteenth of the Acts. This seeming to be urged with an uncommon emphasis, some were of opinion that it pointed directly at Mr. Watson's case, who was one of the audience, and who had been advised by the magistrates, upon his being newly discharged, to make haste out of the province, and whom (it was said) Mr. Wesley was now very intimate with. The congregation was very thin again, which I was sorry to see; but I found that the magistrates and many of the principal inhabitants of late had wholly absented themselves from church; nevertheless, I thought it my duty not to abstain from the public worship, whatever failings the minister might have, which in time would be more fully known, whether more or less grievous, but at present represented in a bad light by too many....

Thursday [November 17]. In the evening Mr. Brownfield came and sat with me alone. He entered freely with me into discourse, which I gave the readier attention to, knowing him to be capable of informing me of most of the transactions here; but at the same time I knew it behooved me to be upon my guard, lest he should mislead me through prejudice. He professed neutrality as to all parties, condemning, without distinction, most of their proceedings and laying open the different motives which they went on, particularly the Parson, Mr. Causton, Bradley, etc., whom he equally censured for violence and passion....

Sunday [November 20]. Mr. Wesley gave us a sermon upon the several kinds of passion, from these words, "Jesus wept," setting forth how far they were consistent with Christianity, as our blessed Saviour himself was subject to all of them in his human nature, except hatred, which he showed in nothing but against vice and therein personally towards none. The well-regulating those passions, therefore, was the Christian's duty. In treating of which he showed himself a good casuist (as I thought), but such a metaphysical discourse would have been better adapted, in my apprehension, to a learned audience than such a poor, thin congregation of people, who rather stood in need of plain doctrine.

Wednesday [November 23]...Mr. Wesley having sent to Mr. Causton for a copy of some papers occasioned through their falling out, Mr. Causton sent him word that if he would come to him, or give him an opportunity of a few words, he would give him copies of anything he asked; and Mr. Wesley thereupon sending him word he would wait on him after dinner, Mr. Causton desired me to be present and hear what passed. When they met, some marks of resentment were easily discoverable from their words, as might be expected betwixt two persons at variance, recriminating on each other; wherein I really thought Mr. Causton most vehement, alleging high provocations (too long to insert here) which I presume he lays fully upon before the Trustees, as it is likewise to be presumed Mr. Wesley does on his part. What I thought most worth my observing therefore was, that though the Parson appeared more temperate in the debate, yet he showed a greater aversion to a coalition than the other. For Mr. Causton very readily told him (after the first heat was over) that to show his disposition to an accommodation, he should find him come to church again and willing to pass over a good many things that seemed to obstruct a good understanding with one another. But no such advances were made (as I could find) by Mr. Wesley, who by his replies seemed to be of opinion that a reconciliation was hardly possible. However from what happened, I hoped that this beginning might lead on farther steps the same way and end well at last. They parted with mutual civilities. . . . And meeting [Mr. Williamson] on his coming ashore, I told him what had passed this day, and the hopes I had of seeing two old friends unite again; which he was so far from being pleased at, that he made a solemn asseveration, if such an agreement came to pass, he would not stay under the same roof an hour. From whence I doubted the breach would widen again.

Thursday [November 24]. . . . At my return to town, I was a little surprised to hear that Mr. Wesley had fixed up a public advertisement signifying his intent of going soon for England. . . .

Saturday [November 26]. . . . I read a public advertisement fixed up in the common place by Mr. Williamson and signifying that, whereas Mr. Wesley had given public notice of his intention to go soon for England, he did hereby notify that there was a cause depending in this Court, where he had brought his action against the said Mr. Wesley for one thousand pounds damages, and therefore, if anyone should aid and assist Mr. Wesley in going out of the province, he would prosecute such person with the utmost rigour. So that from what each of them had advertised, I now began to lay aside all hopes of an accommodation betwixt those families; which would be a means (I feared) of keeping these party divisions alive, many being led by their passions to espouse that side which carried on an opposition to such as they were at personal enmity with; whilst several of them, I plainly saw, cared little in reality for either.

Sunday [November 27]. Mr. Wesley, in his discourse this day on Acts 20:26, 27, took occasion to explain what was meant by the counsel of God, and enforced the practice of all Christian duties very pathetically, which he was well qualified to do always. Some people imagined from the choice of his text that he meant it as a sort of farewell sermon, but it did not appear so to me from any particular expressions that could show it. . . .

Friday [December 2]. This being the day of Mr. Wesley's intended going off, the magistrates met, and he sent them a very short letter of two lines unsealed, acquainting them that some matters of moment required his waiting on the Trustees, and he desired to know if they had any design to stop him. To which they returned a verbal answer, importing that since he did not think fit to enter into a recognizance for his appearing at the Court to answer what was alleged against him, they could not give up the authority of the Court. After which they gave public notice to all constables and tithingmen, in case he attempted to go off, to apprehend him or any person who would aid and assist him therein.

Saturday [December 3]. Notwithstanding all the precaution that was taken, it was known this morning that Mr. Wesley went off last night, and with him Coates a constable, Gough a tithingman, and one Campbell a barber. This surprised most people (even many of those who wished him best) that he should take such company with him, for there scarce could be found men more obnoxious. . . . As I was always ready and willing, in conversation or otherwise, to make allowance for Mr. Wesley's failing in policy, and (out of respect to his function) careful not to run hastily into an entire belief of all I heard laid to his charge, I was now asked by diverse, in a sneering way, what my sentiments were of him, which indeed piled me. *Noscitur ex Sociis* [one is known by the company he keeps] was the common by-word, and all I had to say was, that he must stand or fall by himself when his cause came before the Trustees.

The Bail-Jumping Deserter

Among the jurymen who indicted Wesley in August 1737 was Robert Williams, a merchant from Bristol who had settled in Savannah in 1736.

Upon returning to Bristol in 1739, he discovered that this same Mr. Wesley was preaching to large crowds in the Horsefair at the edge of town. Williams drew up the following legal deposition in the spring of 1740 to warn the citizens of Bristol of Wesley's past misdemeanors. In response, Wesley published the first extract from his own journal, giving his account of what had happened in Georgia (see page 113).

Williams's broadside, entitled "The Life and Conversation of that Holy Man Mr. John Wesley, during his Abode at Georgia," was republished twice in successive years, each time to be answered again in print by Wesley (see page 115). Whitefield also responded to the note at the end of Williams's reprinted attack by stating, in the Weekly History *(no. 72), that he thought the whole prosecution to be "groundless" and Wesley's published response to be "a true account."*

In the following transcription, some of the repetitive legal terminology (such as "the said," "the aforesaid") has been omitted in order to make the document more readable.

The AFFIDAVIT of Mr. ROBERT WILLIAMS,
of the City of BRISTOL, Merchant,
in relation to Mr. WESLEY'S Conduct during his Abode
at SAVANNAH in GEORGIA.

ROBERT WILLIAMS, of the City of Bristol, merchant, maketh oath, that he well knows John Wesley, late of Savannah in the Province of Georgia, clerk, but now resident in the City [of] Bristol; and saith, that about the month of August (which was in the year of our Lord 1736), he, this Deponent, arrived at Savannah on board the ship Grenadier (William Woodward commander) in order to trade and settle plantations there (he having before obtained a grant from the trustees for five hundred acres of land); and saith, that he continued there for the space of [about three years] and then left the colony in order to proceed to England, and accordingly arrived at the Port of London the beginning of November last (to wit) 1739; and this Deponent saith, that during the time he was at Savannah he traded very largely, built very considerable buildings both at Savannah and other parts of the colony, and greatly improved large tracts of land there, and was esteemed to have one of the chief settlements in the colony; and this Deponent saith, that soon after he arrived at Savannah (Wesley then being, and for near the space of twelve months before, having been resident there), the common conversation in company there was concerning John Wesley, his method of preaching and manner of life and behaviour, and how he had seduced the common persons, there settled, to idleness, and what other mischiefs he had there done; and particularly saith, it was then common fame, and a current report and received opinion amongst most of the principal settlers there, that Wesley had been guilty of using too great familiarities with one Mrs. Sophia Christiana Hopkey (niece to Thomas Causton, Esq., Chief Magistrate of the Town of Savannah), and that he continued so to do till such time as Sophia Christiana Hopkey was married to one Mr. William Williamson, of Savannah (a gentleman of considerable note there); and this Deponent saith, that after Sophia Christiana Hopkey was married to Mr. Williamson, a report was, that some uneasiness had arisen between them, touching several letters and messages sent by Wesley to Mrs. Williamson, desiring her to meet him at diverse unseasonable hours and places in the night (many of which were at Wesley's own closet); and that thereupon Mr. Williamson had applied to Wesley to desist from such proceedings and practices for the future, and that Wesley solemnly promised to desist accordingly; but this Deponent saith, that notwithstanding such protestations he, Wesley, did not desist from such practices, but persisted therein, which this Deponent the better knows, for that he, this Deponent (being esteemed one of the chief settlers there) was, by virtue of a precept or summons from Thomas Christie, Esq. (Recorder of Savannah), summoned, with forty three others of the principal inhabitants of the Town and County of Savannah, to appear on the Grand Jury at a Court to be held before the Bailiffs and Recorder of the town on the 22nd day of August, which was in the year of our Lord 1737, in order to inquire into the behaviour and proceedings of Wesley, in the particulars before-mentioned; and this Deponent further saith, that while the Court was sitting, and this Deponent and [the] other persons were charged and sworn on the Grand Jury, two several Bills of Indictment were preferred against John Wesley on the prosecution of William Williamson, for misdemeanors, and for writing and sending the several letters and messages to Sophia Christiana, wife of William Williamson, to meet him at unseasonable times and places, and endeavouring to seduce her as aforesaid; and this Deponent saith, that after the said Bills were preferred and sent to this Deponent and the rest of the Grand Jury, there were at least ten credible witnesses produced before them in support of the charges against John Wesley, and the other charges in the Bills were also proved to be true; and thereupon this Deponent and the rest of the Grand Jury unanimously agreed to, and accordingly did find the Bills against Wesley for the offences aforesaid; and this Deponent saith, that the same day on which the Bills of Indictment were found, he, this Deponent, was in company with some of the Bailiffs (Judges of the Court) who told this Deponent, that as the Bills of Indictment were found against Wesley, they would show him (being a clergyman) all the lenity they could, especially in a new colony, and therefore would admit him to bail if he could get any proper persons who would bail him for his appearance at the then next Sessions; and this Deponent saith, that afterwards (and this Deponent believes the same day) John Wesley was bailed by two freeholders of the Town of Savannah, one of which he believes to be Henry Lloyd, for Wesley's appearance at the then next Sessions in order to take his trial for the offences aforesaid; and this Deponent further saith, that a little before the Sessions came on (at which Wesley was bailed to take his trial) he, Wesley, about the middle of the night, in a secret clandestine manner, quitted the colony, deserted his bail, and went off in a boat for Purysburg (being about twenty miles from Savannah) and from thence (as was reported) walked on foot to Charlestown in South Carolina (being about two hundred miles) and from thence embarked for England; and this Deponent saith, that the next day after Wesley so quitted the colony and deserted his bail, the Justices having notice thereof, threatened to prosecute and imprison his bail, for such his desertion and leaving the colony, who were in the utmost confusion concerning the same; but by the interposition of this Deponent and several other of the inhabitants of the colony, on behalf of the bail, and the lenity of the Justices there, and to prevent destruction to their respective families, they, the Justices, on this Deponent's leaving the colony (being the 3rd day of June 1739), had respited the recognizances of the bail during pleasure.

ROBERT WILLIAMS

Sworn at the City of BRISTOL aforesaid,
the 14th day of March 1739[–40], before
me (one of his Majesty's Justices
of the Peace of and for the said City)

STEPHEN CLUTTERBUCK, Mayor

N.B. He who desires farther satisfaction, may apply himself to the Reverend Mr. GEORGE WHITEFIELD, who is lately come from BRISTOL.

The Improper Pastor

Of the various accounts of Wesley in Georgia, the following is unique in that the author lived, as a teenager, under the same roof with Sophy Hopkey and Mr. Causton. Philip Thicknesse (1719–92) had emigrated to Georgia in 1735. Upon his return to England two years later, he was employed by the Georgia Trustees. His candor soon put him in Oglethorpe's disfavor, the first of a long line of personal misfortunes that befell Thicknesse and that seem to affect the tone of his later recollections.

Thicknesse sent the following anonymous notice to the Gentleman's Magazine *just after Wesley had died in 1791 and the first biography of the Methodist leader, by John Hampson, had appeared. This brief recollection is similar in tone and content to the longer reflections Thicknesse included in his* Memoirs, *first published in 1788. In those, he acknowledged that he was in his seventieth year and "never pretended to be an accurate writer." He does, however, among his descriptions of Wesley's improprieties in this letter, give an unflinching witness to the color of the young Wesley's hair (see a different description, page 278).*

I shall not feel quite easy till I have supplied, in some measure, the want of information which the ingenious Mr. Hampson laments the want of, relating to Mr. John Wesley's conduct during the short time he visited Georgia and chiefly resided at Savannah in that colony; for, though it is much more than half a century ago, some facts are still fresh in my memory,...for, though I was then a boy, I was not insensible to the beauty and virtues of that young lady [Sophy Hopkey], nor to the conduct of Mr. Wesley; and, beside, I was not only upon the spot when that fracas between the parties happened, but lived under the same roof and under the same protection of her uncle Mr. Causton, who was a man of too much integrity to be guilty of such proceedings as Mr. Wesley has loaded him with. Wesley had arrived at Savannah a short time before I did. Dr. Hutton had given me a letter to him, and I was permitted to be one of his *early* congregation at morning prayers in the chapel of Savannah; and I almost constantly went thither with Miss Sophia. After prayers, she, and I believe some other females, went constantly home with Mr. Wesley to his lodgings in order to be further instructed; and I well remember wondering why I was not asked also. Surely, said I, my soul is of as much importance as theirs; and if I am to be excluded a *part* of the benefit, I will withdraw myself altogether; and did so. Mr. Williamson, a young adventurer like myself, but some years older, and who went over in the same ship with me, paid his addresses to Miss Sophia, and in a short time after married her; and then, having seen the many letters which Mr. John Wesley had written to that young lady (letters which I understood then, and have been assured since, contained an *olio* of religion and love), he forbade his wife attending either his chapel or his house in future; and that was the foundation of the future quarrel between him and Mr. Williamson's family. It is not many years since I saw Mr. Williamson, his lady, and his son ...; Mr. Williamson was then old and infirm; but we talked this matter over together, and he then assured me that he thought the letters *so very improper* that he had some thoughts of publishing them.... However great and good Mr. Wesley's life or general conduct may have been, I will not suffer the names of people as virtuous as himself to be so stigmatized. Nor is what Mr. Wesley has said of the Indians true. I knew them well, lived much with, nay, could speak their language. They lived indeed in a state of nature and strangers to the gospel, but they possessed virtues (till Christians corrupted them) which would do honour to human nature. Mr. Wesley, indeed, wore the Indian shoe called *Maugazeens,* and slept rolled up in a blanket (at least he told me he did); but I can avow that he made a long and fatiguing journey with me through the woods to Frederica, but chose to return by water as the easiest way back. A bad woman, whom he had offended at Savannah, decoyed him into her house, threw him upon her bed, and with her scissors cut off one side of his fine long Adonis locks of auburn hair—hair which he took infinite pains to have in the most exact order, which, with his benign and humble countenance, gave him a very pleasing aspect. And I well remember seeing him preach afterwards at Savannah chapel, with his hair so long on one side, and so short on the other, that those who saw him on the worst side might have observed, "What a cropped head of hair the young parson has on!" When I returned to England, I found my sister among his flock, and she prevailed upon me to accompany her to hear him preach. We both sat in Lady Huntingdon's pew; and when her Ladyship asked Mr. John Wesley whether he or his brother Charles preached (for they, were both in the pew with us), he replied, "My brother Charles." "That," said she, "will be a great disappointment to the young man before you (naming my name), for he is come on purpose to hear *you*." Upon which (for he knew me) he very obligingly took his brother's task and charmed me with his persuasive eloquence. Yet when I met him a few years since in the Welsh passage-boat, I could hardly prevail upon him to be commonly civil, though I had travelled with him by land and sailed with him from Georgia to South Carolina! Yet the only censure he had bestowed on me at Georgia was, in a letter to Dr. Hutton, "that I did not give him so much of my company as I ought"; but then, he did not give me so much of his as I wished, for I wished to accompany Miss Sophia to the *after-church* lecture, but was never asked.

A Wanderer.

CHAPTER 20

Before and After Aldersgate

John Wesley's experience of assurance in May 1738 came not only in the midst of rather constant pressure from his Moravian friends to hope and pray for such an event, but also in the immediate aftermath of his brother Charles's experience of "true" belief in the Moravian pattern. Not everyone agreed that the results of his experience matched the expectations. Some of Wesley's friends at first thought him daft for thinking he was now for the first time a Christian. On the other hand, the Moravians came to have doubts about the validity of his faith because of his continuing bouts of doubt and despair.

A Brother's Faith

Charles Wesley's journal includes a rather detailed account of his own evangelical experience of faith in May 1738, just three days before John's "heart-warming" experience. Charles's account of that period provides a remarkable contrast to John's account (see pages 94-99). Not only is the setting quite different but the terminology is much less familiar (I felt "a strange palpitation of heart"). Similarities between the two accounts do appear: the

258

continuing assaults of doubt and fear, the pressing desire for confidence, even the notable reliance upon the Psalter. The reference to brother John's experience on the 24th is noticeably brief.

THE DAY OF PENTECOST

Sunday, May 21, 1738. I waked in hope and expectation of His coming. At nine my brother and some friends came, and sang an hymn to the Holy Ghost. In about half an hour they went: I betook myself to prayer; the substance as follows: "O Jesus, Thou hast said, 'I will come unto you'; Thou hast said, 'I will send the Comforter unto you'; Thou hast said, 'My Father and I will come unto you, and make our abode with you.' Thou art God who canst not lie; I wholly rely upon Thy most true promise: accomplish it in Thy time and manner." Having said this, I was composing myself to sleep, in quietness and peace when I heard one come in (Mrs. Musgrave, I thought, by the voice) and say, "In the name of Jesus of Nazareth, arise and believe, and thou shalt be healed of all thy infirmities." I wondered how it should enter into her head to speak in that manner. The words struck me to the heart. I sighed, and said within myself, "Oh that Christ would but speak thus to me!" I lay musing and trembling, then thought, "But what if it should be Him? I will send at least to see." I rang, and, Mrs. Turner coming, I desired her to send up Mrs. Musgrave. She went down, and, returning, said, "Mrs. Musgrave has not been here." My heart sunk within me at the word and I hoped it might be Christ indeed. However, I sent her down again to inquire, and felt in the meantime a strange palpitation of heart. I said, yet feared to say, "I believe, I believe!" She came up again and said, "It was I, a weak, sinful creature, spoke; but the words were Christ's. He commanded me to say them, and so constrained me that I could not forbear."

I sent for Mr. Bray and asked him whether I believed. He answered, I ought not to doubt of it: it was Christ spoke to me. He knew it, and willed us to pray together. "But first," said he, "I will read what I have casually opened upon: 'Blessed is the man whose unrighteousness is forgiven, and whose sin is covered: blessed is the man to whom the Lord imputeth no sin, and in whose spirit is no guile.'" Still I felt a violent opposition and reluctance to believe; yet still the Spirit of God strove with my own and the evil spirit, till by degrees He chased away the darkness of my unbelief. I found myself convinced, I knew not how nor when; and immediately fell into intercession.

Mr. Bray then told me, his sister had been ordered by Christ to come and say those words to me. This she afterwards confirmed and related to me more at large the manner of her believing. . . .

I now found myself at peace with God and rejoiced in hope of loving Christ. My temper for the rest of the day was, mistrust of my own great, but before unknown, weakness. I saw that by faith I stood; by the continual support of faith, which kept me from falling, though of myself I am ever sinking into sin. I went to bed still sensible of my own weakness (I humbly hope to be more and more so), yet confident of Christ's protection.

Monday, May 22. Under His protection I waked next morning, and rejoiced in reading the 107th Psalm, so nobly describing what God had done for my soul. . . .

My brother coming, we joined in intercession for him. In the midst of prayer, I almost believed the Holy Ghost was coming upon him. In the evening we sang and prayed again. I found myself very weak in body, but thought I ought to pray for my friends, being the only priest among them. I kneeled down and was immediately strengthened, both mind and body. The enemy did not lose such an opportunity of tempting me to pride, but, God be praised, my strength did I ascribe unto Him. I was often since assisted to pray readily and earnestly, without a form. Not unto me, O Lord, not unto me, but to Thy Name be the glory! . . .

Tuesday, May 23. I waked under the protection of Christ and gave myself up, soul and body, to Him. At nine I began an hymn upon my conversion, but was persuaded to break off for fear of pride. Mr. Bray coming, encouraged me to proceed in spite of Satan. I prayed Christ to stand by me, and finished the hymn.

Wednesday, May 24. Being to receive the sacrament today, I was assaulted by the fear of my old accustomed deadness, but soon recovered my confidence in Christ, that He would give me so much sense of His love now as He saw good for me. I received without any sensible devotion, much as I used to be, only that I was afterwards perfectly calm and satisfied, without doubt, fear, or scruple.

We passed the afternoon in prayer, singing, and conference. For full of dispute. I bore my testimony with plainness and confidence, declaring what God had done for my soul. Not hurt, but strengthened hereby.

At eight I prayed by myself for love; with some feeling, and assurance of feeling more. Towards ten, my brother was brought in triumph by a troop of our friends, and declared, "I believe." We sang the hymn with great joy, and parted with prayer. At midnight I gave myself up to Christ, assured I was safe, sleeping or waking. Had continual experience of His power to overrule all temptation; and confessed, with joy and surprise, that He was able to do exceeding abundantly for me, above what I can ask or think.

A Wild Enthusiast

For some time after his experience at the society meeting in Aldersgate Street, Wesley agreed with the Moravians that this event marked the actual beginning of his life as a Christian. To many who had known Wesley during the previous decade of his ministry, this assumption seemed utter nonsense. Elizabeth Hutton, with whom Wesley often stayed when he was in London, was among those who thought him "not a quite right man" as a result of his own comments during that period.

Mrs. Hutton, the mother of James Hutton, was concerned that John's wild ideas were leading her children into fanaticism. John, whom she called "my son's pope," seems in fact to have influenced the young Hutton to join the Moravians, a group that had close ties with the Wesleys at this time and that attracted many Methodists as the years passed. The Huttons lived next door to Samuel Wesley, Jr., in Westminster, before Samuel moved to Tiverton. It is not surprising, then, that she should write to Samuel to complain about "the sheer wildfire of enthusiasm" in the conduct of John Wesley, as she came to call it. The view of Wesley in the following letter by Mrs. Hutton was shared by many at the time, including the recipient, John's brother Samuel.

June 6, 1738

Dear Sir,

You will be surprised to see a letter from me, but Mr. Hutton and I are really under a very great concern and know not whom to apply to if you cannot help us. After you left London and your brothers had lost the conveniency of your house, believing them good and pious Christians, we invited them to make the same use of ours, and thought such an offer would not be unacceptable to God or to them, which they received with signs of friendship and took up with such accommodations as our house could afford, from time to time, as they had occasion. Mr. Charles, at his arrival in England, was received and treated with such tenderness and love as he could have been in your house, Mr. John the same; and as occasion has offered at different times, ten or twelve of their friends. But your brother John seems to be turned a wild enthusiast, or fanatic, and, to our very great affliction, is drawing our two children into these wild notions, by their great opinion of Mr. John's sanctity and judgment. It would be a great charity to many other honest, well-meaning, simple souls, as well as to my children, if you could either *confine* or *convert* Mr. John when he is with you. For after his behaviour on Sunday the 28th of May, when you hear it, you will think him not "a quite right man."

Without ever acquainting Mr. Hutton with any of his notions or designs, when Mr. Hutton had ended a sermon of Bishop Blackhall's which he had been reading in his study to a great number of people, Mr. John got up and told the people that five days before he was not a Christian, and this he was as well assured of as that five days before he was not in that room; and the way for them all to be Christians was to believe and own that they were not now Christians. Mr. Hutton was much surprised at this unexpected injudicious speech but only said, "Have a care, Mr. Wesley, how you despise, the benefits received by the two Sacraments." I not being in the study when this speech was made, had heard nothing of it when he came into the parlor to supper, where were my two children, two or three of his deluded followers, two or three ladies who board with me, my niece, and two or three gentlemen of Mr. John's acquaintance, though not got into his new notions. He made the same wild speech again, to which I made answer, "If you was not a Christian ever since I knew you, you was a great hypocrite, for you made us all believe you was one." He said, "When we had renounced every thing but faith and then got into Christ, then, and not till then, had we any reason to believe we were *Christians*; and when we had so got Christ, we might keep Him, and so be kept from sin."

Mr. Hutton said, "If faith only was necessary to save us, why did our Lord give us that Divine sermon?" Mr. John said, "That was the letter that killeth." "Hold," says Mr. Hutton, "you seem not to know what you say; are our Lord's words *the letter that killeth?*" Mr. John said, "If we had no faith." Mr. Hutton replied, "I did not ask you how we should receive it? but why our Lord gave it, as also the account of the judgment in the twenty-fifth of Matthew, if works are not what he expects, but faith only?"

Now it is a most melancholy thing to have not only our two children, but many others, to disregard all teaching but by such a spirit as comes to some in dreams, to others in such visions as will surprise you to hear of. If there cannot be some stop put to this, and unless he can be taught true humility, the mischief he will do wherever he goes among the ignorant but well-meaning Christians will be very great.

Mr. Charles went from my son's where he lay ill for some time; and would not come to our house, where I offered him the choice of two of my best rooms; but he would accept of neither, but chose to go to a poor brazier's in *Little Britain*, that that brazier might help him forward in his conversion, which was completed on May 22 [*sic*], as his brother John was praying. Mr. John was converted, or I know not what, or how, but made a Christian, May 25 [*sic*]. A woman had besides a previous dream: a ball of fire fell upon her and burst, and fired her soul. Another young man, when he was in St. Dunstan's Church, just as he was going to receive the Sacrament, had God the Father come to him, but did not stay with him. But God the Son did stay, who came with him holding his cross in his hands.

I cannot understand the use of these relations; but if you doubt the truth, or your brother denies them, I can produce undeniable proofs of the relation of such facts from the persons who related the facts, that they had received such appearances.

Mr. John has abridged the life of one Halyburton, a Presbyterian teacher in Scotland. My son had designed to print it, to show the experiences of that holy man, of indwelling, &c. Mr. Hutton and I have forbid our son being concerned in handing such books into the world. But if your brother John or Charles think it will tend to promote God's glory, they will soon convince my son God's glory is to be preferred to his parents' commands. Then you will see what I never expected, my son promoting *rank fanaticism.*

If you can, dear Sir, put a stop to such madness, which will be a work worthy of you, a singular charity, and very much oblige

Your sincere and affectionate servant,

E. Hutton.

To the Rev. Mr. Wesley,
    Tiverton, Devon.

An Open Enemy of Christ

John Wesley had been instrumental in the evangelical "awakening" and Moravian inclinations of James Hutton, the son whom Elizabeth mentioned in the letter above. Wesley also shared with Hutton the leadership of the Fetter Lane Society in London after Peter Böhler left England in early May 1738. Hutton continued his association with the Moravian Brethren throughout his lifetime. Wesley's ties were not so lasting.

Hutton's biographer, Daniel Benham, recorded one of the initial problems between Wesley and his spiritual mentors at that time, an event that occurred during Wesley's trip to Germany soon after his Aldersgate experience.

John Wesley and Benjamin Ingham reached Marienborn on the 4th of July [1738], where Ingham was admitted to partake of the Holy Communion. But when the congregation saw Wesley to be *homo perturbatus* [a troubled person] and that his head had gained an ascendancy over his heart, and being desirous not to interfere with his plan of effecting good as a clergyman of the English Church when he should become more settled (for he always claimed to be a zealous English Churchman), they deemed it not prudent to admit him to that sacred service.... The refusal of the Brethren to admit him to the Communion with Ingham gave Wesley offence, which unhappily he concealed and brooded over.

The theological point at issue soon became obvious: the Moravians felt that Wesley's faith was inadequate, indicated by his continued doubts and his reliance upon the means of grace as necessary to the Christian life. The Moravians would not accept the idea of "degrees" of faith. They also considered Wesley's approach to be a form of works-righteousness and a dangerous threat to the proclamation that a proper faith was fully sufficient for salvation. The psychological point of tension was more subtle: Wesley still did not seem to them to measure up to the full expectations of a Moravian conversion.

At the end of 1739, Wesley and his closest followers in London broke away from the Fetter Lane Society and started meeting at the old Foundery in Moorfields. During this period of increasing tension, Hutton wrote a letter to

Count Ludwig von Zinzendorf, leader and protector of the Moravians in Germany. The following selection illustrates the growing animosity that resulted in a complete severing of relations between Wesley and the Moravians by 1742.

14 March 1739/40

Most beloved bishop and brother, . . .

John Wesley being resolved to *do* all things himself, and having told many souls that they were justified who have since discovered themselves to be otherwise, and having mixed the works of the law with the Gospel as *means* of grace, is at enmity against the Brethren. Envy is not extinct in him; his heroes falling every day almost, into poor sinners frightens him, but at London the spirit of the Brethren prevails against him. In a conference lately, where he was speaking that souls ought to go to church as often as they could, I besought him only to be easy and not disturb himself, and I would go to church as often as he would meet me there; but he would not insist on it. He seeks occasion against the Brethren, but I hope he will find none in us. I desired him simply to keep to his office in the body of Christ, *i.e.* namely, to awaken souls in preaching but not to pretend to lead them to Christ. But he will have the glory of doing all things. I fear by and by he will be an open enemy of Christ and his Church. Charles Wesley is coming to London and determined to oppose all such as shall not use the means of grace (after his sense of them); I am determined to be still—I will let our Saviour govern this whirl-wind.

Charles [Wesley] had determined to go to Germany, but now he will not, since he has seen Nowers. John Wesley has carried Nowers wherever he could, speaking against the Brethren. I told Nowers he should smart for speaking against us—I mean the Herrndyk brethren, who are part of my herd. John Wesley and Charles Wesley, both of them, are dangerous snares to many young women; several are in love with them. I wish they were once married to some good sisters, but I would not give them one of my sisters if I had many.

CHAPTER 21

The Rabble-Rouser Reconsidered

Different people often view the same event in different lights. The follow-ing three selections illustrate different perspectives of Wesley's role in relation to the causes and effects of the disruptions that often accompanied the Methodist preacher.

A Soldier of Christ: Charles's View of the Wednesbury Riot

In his account of the rioting at Wednesbury in 1743 (see pages 120-25), John Wesley refers repeatedly to the work of divine providence in the disruptive activities of the mobs. He also exhibits what might be called a martyr complex. In his own journal account of these events, Charles makes more explicit some of the implicit perspectives in John's account. Charles had not witnessed the riot, but arrived in the area shortly afterward and recorded several reports from those who had seen the events, including his brother John. A comparison of Charles's account with John's points out some difference in the interpretation of events. Charles Wesley's journal was not published during his lifetime.

Friday, October 21st. My brother came, delivered out of the mouth of the lion. He *looked* like a soldier of Christ. His clothes were torn to tatters. The mob of Wednesbury, Darlaston, and Walsal, were permitted to take him by night out of the Society house and carry him about several hours, with a full purpose to murder him. But his work is not finished, or he had now been with the souls under the altar....

Tuesday, October 25th. [I was] much encouraged by the faith and patience of our brethren from Wednesbury, who gave me some particulars of the late persecution. My brother, they told me, had been dragged about for three hours by the mob of three towns. Those of Wednesbury and Darlaston were disarmed by a few words he spoke and thenceforward laboured to screen him from their old allies of Walsal, till they were overpowered themselves and most of them knocked down. Three of the brethren and one young woman kept near him all the time, striving to intercept the blows. Sometimes he was almost borne upon their shoulders through the violence of the multitude, who struck at him continually that he might fall. And if he had once been down, he would have rose no more. Many blows he escaped through his lowness of stature, and his enemies were struck down by them. His feet never once slipped, for in their hands the angels bore him up.

The ruffians ran about asking, "Which is the minister?" and lost, and found, and lost him again. That Hand which struck the men of Sodom and the Syrians blind withheld or turned them aside. Some cried, "Drown him! throw him into a pit!" Some, "Hang him up upon the next tree!" Others, "Away with him! away with him!" and some did him the infinite honour to cry, in express terms, "Crucify him!" One and all said, "Kill him!" but they were not agreed what death to put him to. In Walsal several said, "Carry him out of the town—don't kill him here, don't bring his blood upon us!"

To some who cried, "Strip him, tear off his clothes!" he mildly answered, "That you need not do; I will give you my clothes, if you want them." In the intervals of tumult, he spoke, the brethren assured me, with as much composure and correctness as he used to do in their societies. The Spirit of glory rested on him. As many as he spoke to, or but laid his hand on, he turned into friends. He did not wonder (as he himself told me) that the martyrs should feel no pain in the flames; for none of their blows hurt him, although one was so violent as to make his nose and mouth gush out with blood.

At the first justice's, whither they carried him, one of his poor accusers mentioned the only crime alleged against him: "Sir, it is a downright shame. He makes people rise at five in the morning to sing psalms." Another said, "To be plain, sir, if I must speak the truth, all the fault I find with him is, that he preaches better than our parsons." Mr. Justice did not care to meddle with him, or with those who were murdering an innocent man at his Worship's door. A second justice in like manner remanded him to the mob. The Mayor of Walsal refused him protection when entering his house, for fear the mob should pull it down. Just as he was within another door, one fastened his hand in his hair and drew him backward, almost to the ground. A brother, with the peril of his life, fell on the man's hand and bit it, which forced him to loose his hold.

The instrument of his deliverance at last was the ringleader of the mob, the greatest profligate in the country. He carried him through the river upon his shoulders. A sister they threw into it. Another's arm they broke. No farther hurt was done our people but many of our enemies were sadly wounded.

The minister of Darlaston sent my brother word he would join with him in any measures to punish the rioters, that the meek behaviour of our people and their constancy in suffering convinced him the counsel was of God, and he wished all his parish Methodists.

They pressed me to come and preach to them in the midst of the town. This was the sign agreed on betwixt my brother and me: if they asked me, I was to go. Accordingly, we set out in the dark and came to Francis Ward's, whence my brother had been carried last Thursday night. I found the brethren assembled, standing fast in one mind and spirit, in nothing terrified by their adversaries. The word given me for them was, "Watch ye, stand fast in the faith, quit yourselves like men, be strong." Jesus was in the midst and covered us with a covering of his Spirit. Never was I before in so primitive an assembly. We sang praises lustily and with a good courage, and could all set to our seal to the truth of our Lord's saying, "Blessed are they that are persecuted for righteousness' sake."

I took several new members into the society, and among them, the young man whose arm was broke and (upon trial) Munchin, the late captain of the mob. He has been constantly under the word since he rescued my brother. I asked him what he thought of him. "Think of him!" said he, "That he is a mon of God, and God was on his side when so mony of us could not kill one mon."

We rode through the town, unmolested, to Birmingham....

The Author of Confusion: White's Sermon Against the Methodists

The mobs and riots that centered upon Wesley were not always a direct reaction to his own religious ideas and activities; Wesley was often the victim of public anger directed toward more general grievances. In some cases, however, secular and religious complaints were combined in attacks directly aimed at the Methodists and their leader.

Such was the case at Roughlee in 1748 (see page 125). The minister at nearby Cone, George White, had used several tactics to incite mobs against the Methodists. Just before Wesley came into the area in August 1748, White had preached a strong sermon against the Methodists. The argument of the sermon was that the transient Methodist preachers, through their ignorance and enthusiasm, were disrupting the economy of the kingdom and the peace and order of the church and should therefore be suppressed. Although the sermon mainly attacked the lay preachers, it also made some specific inflammatory remarks about Wesley himself.

Within days, White's sermon was published, purportedly "at the request of the audience" (title page). It brought a published response from William Grimshaw (see "That Good Man" below), who had shared with Wesley the vehemence of the mob's actions at Roughlee.

Wesley later described White in his Journal *(1752): "He was for some years a Popish priest. Then he called himself a Protestant and had the living of Colne. It was his manner first to hire and then head the mob, when they and he were tolerably drunk. But he drank himself first into a jail and then into his grave."*

A Sermon Against the Methodists

The Epistle Dedicatory,
to The Most Reverend, his Grace,
The Lord Archbishop of Canterbury.

My Lord,

If in these remoter parts we may have the honour to style ourselves under your Grace's peculiar patronage, doubtless it is our
duty to convey to your Grace some idea of the many bold insurrec-
tions which threaten our spiritual government; the consequence of
which, my Lord, is a schismatical rebellion against the best of
churches; a farther breach into our unhappy divisions; a contempt
of the great command (six days shalt thou labour, etc.); a defiance
of all laws, civil and ecclesiastical; a professed disrespect to learning
and education; a visible ruin of our trade and manufacture; in short,
a shameful progress of enthusiasm and a confusion not to be paral-
lelled in any other Christian dominion...

A SERMON, &c.
1 Cor. 14:33, For God is not the Author of Confusion
but of Peace, as in all Churches of the Saints.

...I shall take occasion from these words, first, to point out such
practices as create a shameful confusion amongst us, and are
directly contrary to peace and the decent customs of all churches of
the faithful. Secondly, shall endeavour to mention such persuasive
inferences or observations as may possibly for the future prevent the
said confusion and many other notorious ill consequences.

If *fact* did not demonstrate to us what a system of uncommon
notions ignorance and superstition has lately introduced, we could
scarce believe any such thing possible within the limits of
Christianity, much less in these our Kingdoms, where *rationality* in
religion has ever been so much reverenced, and where it has been
the constant ambition of writers in almost every age to shew themselves men of *sense* and *understanding*. ...

Shall our reason be lost in a labyrinth of wild enthusiasm, wander
amidst gloomy fancies and imagination, to *establish* what no nation
though ever so barbarous, and in other respects injurious to the
deity, has at any time presumed to *tolerate!*

If we take a survey of the different constitutions and establishments of life, we shall find that *order* and *regularity* is necessary to their essential preservation.

According to the doctrine of the Church of *England*, in the 23rd Article, it is not lawful for any man to minister or preach in any congregation, except he be called to that office by men who have public authority.

Now these pretended preachers are not called to that office by men who have public authority, consequently it is not lawful for them to minister or preach in any congregation.

But in order to promote this scheme of confusion and irregularity, some of the leaders have found it necessary to usher in the notions of inspiration; to persuade a giddy multitude that learning is no ways requisite to the duties of the ministry; that the Apostles, though mean and illiterate, were the chosen of Christ; and that they feel in themselves a Spirit by which they are led to preach.

'Tis a demonstration therefore that these men have no *immediate commission* from heaven, as having no extraordinary inspiration. 'Tis a demonstration likewise, that they have none from men in *public authority*, consequently since they can plead no authority at all, but such as is grounded on their own pretended feelings of the Spirit, even Christianity itself obliges us to decry their proceedings, as full of *confusion* and *tumult*, not to say, *imposture* and *lucrative assurance....*[1]

Believe me, the pretence of religion has perhaps occasioned the greatest calamities in life, and served as a cloak even to the most

---

1. Poor ignorant men who never have been conversant farther than their plow, who little know the constitution of any church, may easily be led astray with visionary notions about religion. Their brain, unaccustomed to a manly application with respect to articles of this nature, seems as it were adapted to such impressions.... Yet give me leave to observe, that their teachers cozen an handsome subsistence out of these irregular expeditions.... It appears from many very probable accounts that Mr. Wesley has in reality a better income than most of our bishops, though now and then (no great wonder) it costs him some little pains to escape certain rough compliments. As to the under Lay-Praters, I have reasons to assert that, by means of a certain allowance from the *schismatic* General, a contribution from their *very wise* hearers, and the constant maintenance of themselves and horses, they may be supposed in a better way of living than the generality of our vicars and curates; and doubtless find it much more agreeable to their constitution to travel abroad at the expence of a *sanctified face* and a *good assurance*, than to sweat *ignominiously* at the *loom, anvil,* and various other mechanic employments, which nature had so manifestly designed them for.

inhuman murders and plunderings, the most insatiable avarice and lust. Let us therefore beware lest we take superstition for religion; supersitition, the degradation of human reason, the weakness of the brain, a dream of the night, terrifying where there is no danger, and promising security in the midst of ruin.

True religion, being a system of real reason, will always stand the test of a judicious enquiry. . . . Let me once more entreat this set of people, by all the ties of Christian peace, by all the endearing desires of an orthodox Church, to render obedience to the present laws, laws so evidently pointing out to us a safe and rational conduct.

But if all our reasonings and entreaties cannot remove *ignorance* or *stubbornness*; if even before our Church they are resolved to continue this lawless system of confusion, I must beg leave to assure you, that the sense of duty which I owe to my God, the obligations I am under, not only as a regular minister, but even as a rational inhabitant, to see honest industry flourish, instead of superstitious idleness, will always give me true courage to oppose, to my utmost power, attempts so unnatural and unjust; being at the same time confident, that I have the pleasure to speak to a number of rational gentlemen and tradesmen, who have an equal zeal for the preservation of our undoubted rights.

That Good Man: William Grimshaw's Defense of Wesley

William Grimshaw, perpetual curate of Haworth and one of several Anglican clerical supporters of Wesley, not only faced the mob with Wesley at Roughlee in 1748 but also collaborated (though not wholeheartedly) with Wesley in an unsuccessful lawsuit against the Rev. Mr. White in October of that year. Although the legal proceedings were eventually dropped, Grimshaw proceeded along another line of action against White by publishing a ninety-six-page rebuttal of White's inflammatory sermon in An Answer to a Sermon Lately Preached against the Methodists *(1749).*

In this lengthy treatise, an example of polemical overkill, Grimshaw provides an explanation of the Methodists' theology. His primary assumption, seen in the selection below, is that Methodism is really the true expression of the Church of England. Grimshaw does respond, however, to each of White's accusations, including the insinuation that the lay preachers were pretenders to a position above their natural station in life, lured into such pretensions by the encouragement and lucrative example of their leader. Grimshaw attempts to exonerate Wesley from the increasingly prevalent charge that he had accumulated a fortune. He portrays, instead, an image of Wesley that was to become familiar—a man who donated most of his income to others, leaving himself a bare subsistence allowance on which to live (see pages 207 and 340).

Reverend Sir,

In the first advertisement of the Sermon you have lately published against the Methodists, you would needs give the world some reason to expect a *non-pareil*, something so elaborate and accomplished as to be altogether unanswerable. But upon its appearing, how are we disappointed! How far is the performance short of the promise! For my part, I can in no wise see how it is unanswerable except it be that it deserves not any answer at all. 'Tis so full of palpable contradictions, absurdities, falsities, groundless suggestions, and malicious surmises, etc., that it in some sort vindicates the people a'was intended to asperse, and flirts back the dirt it should have cast upon *them*, [instead] upon its own *author*. Pray what have you said more than any poor, petulant wretch dares to say? The very tinkers and colliers of your parish have of late acted the parson as well as you have done, and with as much regard to truth and the honour of God....

Ah, Sir, you little know, but, I pray God make you sensible and thankful for it too before you die, how these dear servants of the Lord laboured night and day for you, without a penny from your purse, whilst you boarded at Chester Castle, and for three years together since, whilst you have been raking about in London and up and down the country. And now, at your return to your Sock, do you find that any amongst them that follow these good men, who deserve so well at our hands, behave disorderly at Church? Do they live dishonestly or unpeaceably among their neighbours? Or do they wrong or defraud you, or any man, of their dues? Surely men of their principles will do no such things, nor occasion any such confusion as your merciless spirit would brand them with.

On the contrary; your own late riotous conduct, heading a lawless rabble of irreligious, dissolute wretches, under the name and title of Commander in Chief, spiriting them up to the perpetration of many grievous outrages, and inhumanly treating and abusing numbers of poor, inoffensive people. I must say this is a far more shameful violation of order in both Church and State, done too under a zeal for religion and in defense of the Church of England!...Ah, poor, blind Pharisee, "First pull the beam out of your own eye." I wish you be not one of them of whom our Lord prophesies, "The time cometh, that whosoever killeth you, will think that he doth God service" (John 16:2)....

The disuse, I say, of the Homilies and Thirty-Nine Articles of our religion is certainly the chief occasion of all this mischief in our Church. Had they been constantly read, 'tis very probable that all these evils had not only been effectually prevented, but Methodism also, which is nothing else but the revival of the doctrines contained therein, had never appeared, those books and what the Methodists preach being all one. This, let me add, some few of our clergy are so well advised of, that they purposely evade the reading them to the people for fear of increasing *Methodism*,[2] a term very likely made use of by the art of the Devil to prevent the true end of their ministry, I mean, the making good Christians....

Your marginal reference upon lucrative assurance may next be considered. And here again what a medley of falsities, disingenuous surmizes, and groundless slanders, are trumped together.... "Poor ignorant men (say you) who never have been conversant further than the plough, who little know the constitution of any church, may be easily led astray with visionary notions about religion." ...Take the blame and shame and curse to yourself, if you find that several in your parish, for want of knowing the principles of the Church they profess to call themselves members of, are become dupes and ninny-hammers to the Methodist preachers; or rather, to speak more properly and as the truth is, being stirred up by the Holy Ghost, are, like wise men, prudently and seasonably searching for the true principles of our Church indeed, the truth as it is in Jesus or the salvation of their souls at these men's mouths, for want of proper instructions from their proper guides....

In the next words you fall upon Mr. Wesley. . . . Mr. Wesley's fellowship, I am credibly informed, is about £100 per annum, out of which £30 are deducted by the College for non-residence. The

---

2. A certain old clergyman of my acquaintance, lately deceased, being asked by his curate if he might read the Homilies in the church, answered, No; for if he should do so, all the congregation would turn Methodists.

remainder, with the profits arising from the sale of his books, are so entirely laid out in carrying on the great and good work he is engaged in, that he scarcely provides necessaries for himself. This is a true relation of that good man's estate, of whom you are pleased roundly and falsely to affirm, "That he has a better income than most of our Bishops." Prove your assertion. . . .

I shall only take notice of this one thing more in your marginal reference, and that is the offence you take at men attempting to preach, "who have never been conversant further than the plough." A plough! Sir, an edifying machine! Were you well at it, it would not only best become the name you are pleased to give yourself of *Agricola Candidus* (in English *George*, alias Husbandman, *White*), but possibly you might receive the first true call to the ministry from thence: a plough may make as good a priest as a popish academy. Try the expedient a while; and who knows but—should you think it a disgrace to follow a Lay-Prater from that instrument, remember for your credit and comfort, that Elisha was plowing with twelve yokes of oxen when he was called to succeed Elijah in the prophetic office (1 Kings 19:19f.); and St. Chrysostom, as afore observed, has spoke very honourably of a plowman. Where then can be the harm or shame in such a call? However, *Ne saevi, magne Sacerdos* [Do not rage, great Priest]. Be not offended, I only propose it.

Wesley as Preacher

Wesley was a well-known preacher in his day. His renown, however, was not based upon any remarkable speaking ability or spellbinding oratorical skills. Thomas Haweis described his mode of address as "chaste and solemn," not illumined by "those coruscations of eloquence" which marked the discourses of more effusive preachers such as George Whitefield. The tone of his voice was described variously as "clear, pleasant," and "conversational." He apparently did not put on a dramatic show. One listener, after commenting that Wesley's sermon was a "combination of terror and tenderness," noted that "but for an occasional lifting of his right hand, he might have been a speaking statue."

Wesley's ability to gather a crowd and hold their attention was grounded in what he said, rather than how he said it. In his later years, his growing reputation as the leader of the Methodists made him an attraction wherever he went. Commenting upon Wesley, Joseph Benson once remarked that "a man about eighty-seven years of age, who preached twice or thrice a day, who carried on an extensive correspondence, and who conversed with all the ease and cheerfulness of a man in the meridian of life, was a sort of phenomenon which attracted the attention of all ranks and degrees of men." The crowds were often held spellbound in part by the simple impression of his "venerable form" (see fig. 5 and fig. 6). He was frequently described as having an "apostolic" appearance, as in the following description by one of his preachers, John Hampson:

His face, for an old man, was one of the finest we have seen. A clear, smooth forehead, an aquiline nose, an eye the brightest and most piercing that can be conceived; and a freshness of complexion scarcely ever to be found at his years, and impressive of the most perfect health—conspired to render him a venerable and interesting figure. Few have seen him without being struck with his appearance; and many who had been greatly prejudiced against him have been known to change their opinion the moment they have been introduced into his presence.... In dress, he was a pattern of neatness and simplicity. A narrow, plaited stock; a coat with a small upright collar; no buckles at his knees; no silk or velvet in any part of his apparel, and a head as white as snow, gave an idea of something primitive and apostolic; while an air of neatness and cleanliness was diffused over his whole person.

Firsthand accounts of Wesley's preaching are most often very brief and general. Sir Walter Scott, who in his early years heard Wesley preach, remembered that he "told many excellent stories." A more critical commentator noted that the Methodist preachers all aped Wesley, and that although "they have a multitude of texts, they have in fact but the substance of one sermon among them all." He went on to say that "perhaps the best way to expose their rant and ribaldry would be to take their harangues down in shorthand and publish them word for word."

Although few if any of Wesley's hearers went to that extreme (there is one purported case), some did on occasion leave a rather good report. One commentator, after outlining the content of the sermon (which followed the outline of one of Wesley's published sermons rather closely), noted that soon after Wesley had begun speaking, he paused and said, "This I learned of a good man, W. Roman—to pause every now and then, especially in the winter time, that those who happen to be troubled with coughs may have an opportunity of easing themselves without interrupting the congregation." For such insights, we rely almost exclusively on the reports of firsthand observers.

A Rigid Zealot

One of the best descriptions of Wesley's early preaching is the account by the well-known Hebrew scholar, Dr. Benjamin Kennicott, who was a student at Oxford in 1744 when Wesley preached his last University sermon in St. Mary's Church ("Scriptural Christianity"). Kennicott sent the following description to a friend in a letter.

On Friday last, being St. Bartholomew's Day, the famous Methodist, Mr. John Wesley, Fellow of Lincoln College, preached before the university; which being a matter of great curiosity at present, and may possibly be greater in its consequences, I shall be particular in the account of it. All that are Masters of Arts, and on the foundation of any college, are set down in a roll, as they take their degree, and in that order preach before the university, or pay three guineas for a preacher in their stead; and as no clergyman can avoid his turn, so the university can refuse none; otherwise Mr. Wesley would not have preached. He came to Oxford some time before, and preached frequently in courts, public-houses, and elsewhere. On Friday morning, having held forth twice in private, at five and at eight, he came to St. Mary's at ten o'clock. There were present the vice-chancellor, the proctors, most of the heads of houses, a vast number of gownsmen, and a multitude of private people, with many of his followers, both brethren and sisters, who, with general faces and plain attire, came from around to attend their master and teacher.

When he mounted the pulpit, I fixed my eyes on him and his behaviour. He is neither tall nor fat; for the latter would ill become a Methodist. His black hair quite smooth, and parted very exactly, added to a peculiar composure in his countenance, showed him to be an uncommon man. His prayer was soft, short, and conformable to the rules of the university. His text, Acts 5:31: "And they were all filled with the Holy Ghost." And now he began to exalt his voice. He spoke the text very slowly and with an agreeable emphasis. His introduction was to prove that the word all in the text was meant, not only of the apostles and those who received the extraordinary, but of others who received the ordinary influences (only) of the Holy Spirit; and that of such there were many in the infancy of the Gospel, persons who had no business to perform besides the reformation of their own lives, and therefore wanted the ordinary Divine influences only to refresh them in their conversion and complete their Christianity. And this he chose to do, because if the Holy Ghost was necessary for men as private persons at first, it must be so in all ages.

His division of the text was, first, to show the influence of Christianity in its infancy on individuals; secondly, in its progress from one period to another; thirdly, in its final completion in the universal conversion of the world to the Christian faith. Under these three heads he expressed himself like a very good scholar, but a rigid zealot; and then he came to what he called his plain, practical conclusion. Here was what he had been preparing for all along; and he fired his address with so much zeal and unbounded satire as quite spoiled what otherwise might have been turned to great advantage; for as I liked some, so I disliked other parts of his discourse extremely. Having, under his third head, displayed the happiness of the world under it—complete final reformation—"Now," says he, "where is this Christianity to be found. Is this a Christian nation? Is this a Christian city?"—asserting the contrary to both. I liked some of his freedom; such as calling the generality of young gownsmen "a generation of triflers," and many other just invectives. But considering how many shining lights are here that are the glory of the Christian cause, his sacred censure was much too flaming and strong, and his charity much too weak in not making large allowances. But so far from allowances, that, after having summed up the measure of our iniquities, he concluded with a lifted up eye in this most solemn form, "It is time for Thee, Lord, to lay to Thine hand,"—words full of such presumption and seeming imprecation, that they gave an universal shock. This, and the assertion that Oxford was not a Christian city, and this country not a Christian nation, were the most offensive parts of the sermon, except when he accused the whole body (and confessed himself to be one of the number) of the sin of perjury; and for this reason, because, upon becoming members of the college, every person takes an oath to observe the statutes of the university, and no one observes them in all things. But this gave me no uneasiness; for in every oath the intention of the legislator is the only thing you swear to observe; and the legislators here mean that you shall observe all their laws, or upon the violation of them submit to the punishment if required;

and this being explained in the statute-book given to every member, does, I think, solve the whole difficulty. Had these things been omitted, and his censures moderated, I think his discourse, as to style and delivery, would have been uncommonly pleasing to others as well as to myself. He is allowed to be a man of great parts, and that by the excellent Dean of Christ Church (Dr. Conybeare); for the day he preached, the dean generously said of him, "John Wesley will always be thought a man of sound sense, though an enthusiast." However, the Vice-Chancellor sent for the sermon, and I hear the heads of colleges intend to show their resentment.

The Personification of Piety

Nothing is quite so frank as the candid comments of a foreign observer. Professor Johan Henrik Liden, a visiting scholar from the University of Uppsala, Sweden, met Wesley in London during the year 1769. His comments, made in a personal journal, give a picture of Wesley that is somewhat unique in its expression and quite personal in its tone. This selection, translated by Dr. K. A. Jansson appears in WHS, *1929, pages 2-3.*

Sunday, October 15th [1769]

Today I learned for the first time to know Mr. John Wesley, so well known here in England, and called the spiritual Father of the so-called Methodists. He arrived home yesterday from his summer journey to Ireland, where he has visited his people. He preached today at the forenoon service in the Methodist Chapel in Spitalfield for an audience of more than 4,000 people. His text was Luke 1:68. The sermon was short but eminently evangelical. He has not great oratorical gifts, no outward appearance, but he speaks clear and pleasant. After the Holy Communion, which in all English Churches is held with closed doors at the end of the preaching service, when none but the Communicants usually are present, and which here was celebrated very orderly and pathetic. I went forward to shake hands with Mr. Wesley, who already through Mr. Ley knew my name, and was received by him in his usual amiable and friendly way. He is a small, thin old man, with his own long and strait hair, and looks as the worst country curate in Sweden, but has learning as a Bishop and zeal for the glory of God which is quite extraordinary. His talk is very agreeable, and his mild face and pious manner secure him the love of all right-minded men. He is the personification of piety, and he seems to me as a living representation of the loving Apostle John. The old man Wesley is already 66 years, but very lively and exceedingly industrious. I also spoke with his younger brother, Mr. Charles Wesley, also he a Methodist minister and a pious man, but neither in learning or activity can he be compared with the older brother. Both promised to visit me soon.

I took dinner today with my good friend, Mr. Ley, a pious minister. In the afternoon I went in his company once more to hear Mr. Wesley preach. It was in his chapel in the Foundery near Moorfield. His subject was now The Love of Jesus, of which he spoke in a splendid way. The audience was here just as great as in the forenoon, but as the Chapel here is smaller the throng was past bearing. At the request of Mr. Wesley I remained to attend their so-called Private Society, when only Methodists were present, furnished with tickets, to prevent strangers to attend. First a psalm was sung, and then Mr. Wesley to their edification spoke about practical Christianity, and encouraged them to diligent prayer and celebrating the Lord's Supper as the best means to grow in grace, exhorted them to peace, unity, and love as the distinct character of a Christian. Afterwards some finance matters were attended to, and the whole was ended with prayer and song about 8 P.M.

The song of the Methodists is the most beautiful I ever heard. Their fine psalms have exceedingly beautiful melodies composed by great masters. They sing in a proper way, with devotion, serene mind and charm. It added not a little to the harmonious charm of the song that some lines were sung by only the women, and afterwards the whole congregation joined in the chorus.

Nov. 2nd. It is unpardonable that during the blessed Passion Week it never is preached a word about the Suffering of Jesus, but about entirely other subjects. What is this but to be ashamed of the Cross of Jesus, which however for ever is the foundation of our salvation. This is the real reason why Mr. Wesley created so great attention by his sermons, because he spoke of a crucified Saviour and faith in his merit—such the people never had heard. Educated people pronounced this doctrine enthusiastic and heretic—just as if not the greatest heresy is to forget Christ.

CHAPTER 23

Radical Protestant or Pernicious Papist?

Wesley's theological writings were subject to misinterpretation for several reasons. His own theology shifted in some areas down through the years; he changed his mind on some topics as a result of continued study and reflection, and he often sharpened his ideas and emphases in the midst of controversies. His theological work, mediating in intention, but often polemic in tone, was marked by expressions that often overstated one side of his usually balanced position in order to redress the imbalance in his opponent's position. As a result, critics frequently accused him of being either inconsistent, self-contradictory, or hypocritical, especially if they compared writings from different periods. Or they accused him of being on one or another extreme side of an issue, if they considered only one work without regard to the controversial context or the larger body of his thought.

The question of the role of "faith" and "works" in the process of salvation was an issue upon which Wesley confused many people. He was always inclined to hold these two elements together as both theologically and practi-

cally necessary to a full understanding and appropriation of salvation and the Christian life. However, his emphasis did occasionally shift from one side of the balance to the other.

Under the influence of the Moravians in 1737 and 1738, he began to lean very heavily in the direction of a sole emphasis on faith (sola fide). *But the dangers of that position, which could easily lead to a disregard for the disciplines of the Christian life, led Wesley within a short time to swing back to his earlier concern for a faith that necessarily "works in love" and results in holy living. His continuing conflict with the Calvinists, whose views of predestination he also saw as promoting antinomianism (a disregard for works, or matters of the "law"), led him finally to stress the "necessity" of good works in the process of salvation (see* The Scripture Way of Salvation, *1767) in order to counteract the imbalance of their solifidianism.*

Many criticisms of Wesley thus point either to seeming contradictions or to extremist views of one sort or another in his writings. An example of the former appears in a letter to the editor of the Gentleman's Magazine *in 1739. Wesley is accused of a "gross contradiction" on the issue of faith and works, having reversed his opinions on the matter without having disclaimed his former position:*

It is well known, that one of the principal things the Rev. Mr. Wesley insists upon as a fundamental point of the Christian religion is that faith justifies alone, i.e, without works. In the preface to the *Hymns and Sacred Poems* lately published at London by Mr. John Wesley and his brother (page v) we are told, that "even the condition of our acceptance with God, is not our holiness either of heart or life, but faith alone; faith CONTRA-DISTINGUISHED from holiness, as well as from good works." And then immediately follow these words. "Other foundation therefore can no man lay, without being an adversary to CHRIST and his gospel than faith alone, faith, tho' necessarily producing both, yet NOT INCLUDING EITHER GOOD WORKS, OR HOLINESS."

But in a sermon on this text, "By grace ye are saved thro' faith" (Ephes. 2:8), written and published in 1738, by the same Mr. John Wesley (page 14) is the following expression: "But we speak of a faith which is necessarily INCLUSIVE OF ALL GOOD WORKS AND ALL HOLINESS."

It is presumed that Mr. J. Wesley wrote the said preface as well as the sermon; and that the said sermon, tho' published last year, is still approved of by him, because he very lately distributed several stitched pamphlets of it with his own hands.

Several serious persons are of opinion, that Mr. Wesley and his adherents would behave with greater modesty, if they left off to rail at the clergy [of the Church of England] and charge them with omitting to preach the fundamental doctrines of the Christian religion, till they reconcile both sides this contradiction....

Besides being accused of holding irreconcilable positions together in his own writings, Wesley was also accused of taking the extreme opposite positions. The following selections show Wesley in the first instance to be a radical solifidian, emphasizing faith to the exclusion of works, and in the second instance to be a Papist at heart, promoting good works in Roman Catholic fashion while disregarding the doctrine of justification by faith.

A Moravian Sympathizer

Thomas Church was a clergyman of the Church of England. In his Remarks on the Rev. Mr. John Wesley's Last Journal *(1744), he takes a traditional English view of the necessity of both faith and works. Although Wesley generally held this same view, his association with the Moravians during the period covered in his early journals led him to emphasize the role of faith to such an extent as to overshadow the place of good works. The most pointed barbs in Church's criticism come through in those places where he accuses Wesley of falling into the very dangers that Wesley himself was trying to help others avoid—antinomianism, Calvinism, and enthusiasm.*

Rev. Sir,

You must not expect any apology for my giving you the present trouble. The great importance of the points which I shall have occasion to consider in this letter renders all such quite unnecessary. If ever there was a subject wherein the honour and life of virtue, piety, and pure religion are concerned, it is now the subject before me....

You will easily understand that I chiefly mean the denying the necessity of good works as the conditions of our justification. This is a subject which has more than once perplexed and disturbed the minds of men and in the last century particularly occasioned great confusions in this nation....I am sorry to say that you with some others have of late unhappily revived the dispute....And it appears from what you have lately published, that since you have preached the doctrine, it has had its old consequences. or rather worse ones; it has been more misunderstood, more perverted and abused, than ever.

Suffer me then, sir, to apply to you on this occasion with all Christian freedom. The joint necessity of faith and good works in order to our pardon, acceptance and salvation is the true doctrine, and proper at all times to be inculcated. The terms of the gospel, expressly insisted on and required therein, are "repentance toward God, and faith toward our Lord Jesus Christ" [Acts 20:21]. The great advantage of this doctrine is not only its usefulness, but its clearness. It is not liable to be mistaken, at least not easily. But when we run into extremes and undervalue either of these terms, or so teach one of them as to appear to exclude the other, we cannot but fall into infinite absurdities; we involve the consciences of the weak in the most fatal perplexities; we give an handle to others to justify their impieties; we confirm the enemies of religion in their prejudices against it....

It is time to come to particulars. I have read over the extract of your journal, from November 1, 1739 to September 3, 1741, wherein you give an account of the tenets and proceedings of the Moravians, particularly those in *England*....But I cannot express my astonishment and concern when I read the account you have given of them; I hope for your own sake that you have not injured them.

The substance of what you say of them is as follows. They have a cant word among them, into which they resolve almost every thing. This is *stillness.* Their notion of this is, that it is *ceasing from all outward works* and leaving off the works of the Christian law; that this is the way to attain faith, not to pray, fast, receive the sacrament, read the gospel, go to church, do temporal good, or attempt to do spiritual good; accordingly they undervalue good works, especially works of outward mercy; and not barely neglect what are usually called the means of grace, but justify their neglect, pleading and arguing against them, denying them to be really such,...saying, that it is impossible for a man to use these means without trusting in them;...nay that the using them is to such, deadly poison, and destroying them;...that as many go to hell by praying as by thieving....You pray; that is the Devil. You read the Bible; that is the Devil. You communicate; that is the Devil.

In short, sir, according to the doctrine of these blasphemous wretches (for as you have described them 'tis impossible to speak more favourably of them), there is but one commandment, one duty, in the New Testament, which is *to believe*, and that when a man does believe, he is not obliged to do any thing which is commanded there. One of them told you that no one has any degree of faith till he is as perfect as God is perfect; there are no degrees of faith, no justifying faith where there is any doubt....

One end of my making these extracts from the several parts of your journals, I own, is to give the most public warning I could to all sober serious persons, to all who have not totally cast off their regard for religion and virtue, that they be not deceived by any professions or pretences to think well of or mix with these *Moravians*....

But, sir, this is not my only design. I have a further view in writing this letter to you, which I have already intimated. I intend to apply to you in the most serious manner and consider how far you may be concerned in these unhappy, these grievous doctrines. If through your means they have been either raised or spread; much more, if you still continue to give occasion to them; if they are no other than the consequences of what you have of late done and taught, and even in this very journal still teach; if some of their errors you have actually espoused, and in some cases proceed to worse lengths than even they have run; it will be clear, that you are in a great degree partaker of their guilt, that your disowning and protesting against some of their opinions is not sufficient to discharge you, and that you may and ought to do much more, to recant the errors which have given such scandal and offence, and thus to make your church and nation what amends you can. . . .

Do not mistake me. I by no means charge you with believing or teaching such pernicious tenets. But have you not prepared the way for them? By unsettling the minds of weak people, and perplexing them with intricate points, very liable and easy to be mistaken—By countenancing and commending these *Moravians*, and being the occasion of so many of them coming over among us—By still speaking of them, and treating them, as if they were in the main the best Christians in the world, and only deluded or mistaken in a few points. . . .

[But now as to particulars...] To proceed to another passage, "the new path of salvation by faith and work—the old way of salvation by faith only." This you give us as your doctrine. With regard to the antiquity of it I may have occasion to speak hereafter. It is the dangerous tendency of it which I am now to view. And here I am sorry to say, you go the utmost lengths of antinomianism, and deny the necessity of good works in order to salvation, which is what very few of those of your own side of the question would agree with you in. Most, when this consequence has been objected to them, have disowned and loudly exclaimed against it, pleasing themselves with some vain distinctions between the conditions of justification, and those of salvation, and excluding good works only from being the former of these. . . .

But you have ventured farther to exclude them also from being terms of our salvation and thus have denied their necessity entirely; unless, which I charitably hope, the sentence before me be only a slip of your pen, and do not contain your real sentiments. In which case however you are obliged to obviate the danger of so mischievous a tenet by openly recanting it, confessing your want of judgment and accuracy, and warning your followers especially against being subverted by it.

For indeed, if they have frequently heard you teach and inculcate this doctrine, that faith in opposition to good works, and in exclusion of them, is the only way of salvation; the consequence of their thinking it the only commandment and duty is clear and evident. Or rather, these are only two different expressions for one and the same thing. And can it then be any way surprising, that so many of your disciples have turned Moravians, when in this very journal, wrote and published to guard against the errors of these men, you have been hasty and careless enough to avow the most fatal of them all, and that from which all the rest necessarily spring? And this only not in the very same terms? I defy you here to justify yourself so, as to shew any thing more than a verbal difference between you. . . .

You have now, sir, my sentiments, indeed more largely than I first intended, upon the chief points of your *Journal.* I have endeavoured to set before you the many errors and irregularities both with regard to faith and practice, which have followed your setting up this new sect of *Methodists.* I have studied to convince you, how far you have occasioned the many gross enormities of the *Moravians,* which you complain of, and how far you are accountable for them. Consider now, for it is greatly your concern to do so, whether you have yet sufficiently cleared your self. You have indeed openly disowned some of the chief of them. But it is impossible for you to put an entire stop to them, or to prevent more of your followers from falling into them, while you still too much commend these men, hold other principles in common with them equally pernicious, nay from which all these naturally follow, maintain other errors still more than theirs; and are guilty of presumption and enthusiasm to the highest degree.

The consequences of *Methodism*, which have hitherto appeared, are bad enough to induce you to leave it. It has in fact introduced many disorders, *Enthusiasm, Antinomianism, Calvinism*, a neglect and contempt of God's ordinances, and almost all other duties, a great increase of our sects and divisions, and in fine, presumption and despair, at least in greater abundance than they were known before. Nor are these accidental consequences, but what follow too closely from your principles and proceedings. Many of them you now see and lament. And therefore the plea that you do not intend them, will no longer serve you. . . .

I intended here to consider also your sentiments concerning church communion, and how far you can justly style your self a minister of the Church of *England*. . . .But this letter has swelled to a length beyond my expectation. And therefore these particulars may very properly be deferred to another. In the meantime, I remain,

Reverend Sir,

Your Servant, &c.

Thomas Church

A Jesuit in Disguise

The anonymous author of The Jesuit Detected *(1773), no doubt a Calvinist, takes Wesley to task for his stress on the necessity of good works in the order of salvation. The Calvinist would see the imputation of Christ's righteousness (by which a person is counted as righteous), received by faith in justification, as fully satisfying the shortcomings of human sinfulness in the process of salvation. Wesley's views of sanctification, the impartation of Christ's righteousness (whereby a person actually becomes righteous) as well as the necessity of works as "fruits meet for repentance," seemed to the Calvinist to be a throwback to the Roman Catholic view of stressing obedience to the Law of the Old Covenant. The writer thus claims to be uncovering a*

Papist in the form of Wesley; or to use the words of the subtitle, "The Church of Rome discovered in the disguise of a Protestant."

ADVERTISEMENT:

If the doctrine advanced by Mr. Wesley in his writings, and the evasive manner he answers those that either speak or write of salvation by Jesus Christ alone, without works, doth not entitle him to the character of a Jesuit, I shall ask him pardon for calling him the "Jesuit detected."

THE JESUIT DETECTED

...The first thing Mr. Wesley is charged with is giving his great "I say," or "I say so," or "unquestionably it is right," c. as a sufficient proof. However, Mr. Wesley owns the truth for once, [that] he did not bring proof, but that he could have brought proof.

Mr. Wesley can certainly bring proof from the council of Trent against the doctrine of the imputation of the righteousness of Jesus Christ to guilty man, as such; and Mr. Wesley will have the greatest part of those that are called Christians to join issue with him and the council of Trent to oppose the doctrine of imputation.

Therefore [for] Mr. Wesley now to say he could bring proof, looks as if he had no more to do but, as before, to say "I know it is so," or "unquestionably it is true." . . .

However, it appears very plain from Mr. Wesley's doctrine, that infallibility, or at least the doctrine of Trent, is what he maintains, only a little mellowed or softened by his manner of enforcing it.

It is true, men think antichrist is only to be found in Rome; but were they seriously to consult God in the revelation he has given of himself, they would know, Satan is too arch an enemy not to set up the same doctrine in the heart of every man; and that this doctrine of the Church of Rome is, in all its branches, calculated to suit the pride of man.

Man, therefore, naturally falls in with it. And it is no marvel that it branches itself out into many orders and sects.

That this is true in Mr. Wesley is very evident; for the doctrine he has advanced in all his writings is firmly held and maintained by every order of the Church of Rome.

That Mr. Wesley's doctrine is not scriptural, is manifestly proved by several; and, in particular, by Mr. Hervey and Mr. Cudworth.

That Mr. Wesley's doctrine is the same as the doctrine of the Church of Rome, will appear to be a demonstration by comparing what Mr. Wesley's doctrine is, or he himself advances, with the doctrine of the Church of Rome.

ROME	MR. WESLEY
I	**I**
(P. 379) Justification cometh of the free grace of God, thro' his infinite mercies and the merits of our Saviour's passion; and when acknowledging themselves to be sinners, thro' the fear of God's judgments, they turn themselves to consider the merit of God, are lifted up into hope, trusting that God will be merciful unto them for Christ's sake.	(P. 5, 6) . . . Mr. Wesley says, for Christ's sake why will you use that hurtful and unscriptural phrases, the imputed righteousness of Christ? Men who scruple to use, men who never heard the expression may yet be humbled as repenting criminals, at his feet, and rely as devoted pensioners on his merits; but this imputed righteousness hath done immense hurt.
After this disposition, or preparation, followeth justification.	I have abundent proof, that, the frequent use of this unnecessary phrase, instead of furthering men's progress in vital holiness, has made them satisfied without any holiness at all; yea and encouraged them to work all uncleanness with greediness. (This discovers the cause of Mr. Wesley's malice against the imputed righteousness of the blessed Jesus.)
The Council of Trent saith, the point of difference is this; that the Protestants hold, that Christ's passion and obedience, imputed to us, becometh our righteousness; and not any righteousness which is in ourselves, is our justification.	
VIII	**VIII**
According to the measure of our charity, greater or less, so is the measure of our righteousness; not by imputation of Christ's righteousness through	(P. 11) The one thing we lack, saith Mr. Wesley, is not the imputed righteousness of Christ, it is the love of God we want, or charity.

faith, but charity, or the love of
God, is the thing we lack.

XII

Christ's satisfaction will not
avail, except we ourselves
make recompense, and satisfy
the justice of God. For God
hath, by covenant and promise,
bound himself to reward our
works with life everlasting.
Therefore man doth in justice
deserve it; for the New
Testament expresseth the
covenant to be for working and
works. The old law saith, do
these things and thou shalt live;
so is it said in the new, if thou
wilt enter into life keep the
commandment; and life eternal is the hire and wages for
labouring, and not the imputed
justice or merits of Christ.

XII

Mr. Wesley says, neither our
Lord's being baptized, nor his
keeping of the law, or his fulfilling the moral law, was requisite in order to his purchasing
redemption for us; for Man,
Wesley says, is bound under
the covenant of grace, as well
as covenant of works, to obey
in his own person, that is, keep
the law; for Christ hath not fulfilled the condition of the new
covenant. (P. 14, 15)

XIII

The Church of Rome saith,
that idle invention that works
are mentioned, not because
they are rewarded, but,
because they are tokens that
the doer is in Christ, for
whose, that is Christ's obedience, God promiseth the
crown of life, the Church saith
is not worth confuting; it is so
flatly contrary to holy
Scripture; which ascribeth distinctly that reward is unto the
workman for his works, and

XIII

. . . This is the grand palpable
objection to that whole
scheme; for says Mr. Wesley, it
makes void the law, and consequently makes thousands content to live and die transgressors
of the law, namely, because
Christ died for them. *(Well done
Mr. Wesley for thy Anti-Christ)*

not for Christ's obedience
imputed unto him. (P. 699.)

XVI

The Church of Rome declares,
it is impious and ungodly to say
the commandments or law cannot be kept; or that it is impossible for us to fulfill the law.
For says the Church of Rome,
God hath by covenant, and
promise, bound himself to
reward our works with life everlasting. Therefore good works
do in justice deserve it; faithful
promise maketh due debt. And
life eternal is the hire and
wages for labouring in God's
vineyard, and not the imputed
righteousness of Christ. Holy
Scripture ascribeth distinctly
that reward is unto the workman for his works, and not for
Christ's obedience him.

XVI

Mr. Wesley would sooner turn
Turk, Deist, yea an Atheist,
than believe that the righteousness our Lord Jesus Christ
wrought out in his life, death,
and resurrection, is the cause
of our justification, or the purchase of our salvation; much
less that Christ hath satisfied
the demand of the law, for him
or any man; and says, if so, he
is not obliged to love his neighbour because Christ hath satisfied the demands of the law for
him. (P. 30) . . . That man cannot fulfill the whole law, or that
the fulfilling of the law is not
in the power of sinful man Mr.
Wesley denies; saying, God
made imputed to or entered
into a covenant with rebel
man, and not with Christ; nor
did Christ perform the condition of the covenant; but man
must, otherwise it would be
Calvinism or Antinomianism.

Note: The foregoing sentiments of the Church of Rome
are taken from a Book intitled,
*A Defense of the Reformed
Catholick of Mr. William Perkins,
by Robert Abbott, a Doctor of
Divinity*, printed 1606.

Note: The foregoing sentiments of the Rev. Mr. Wesley
are taken from his *Answer to
all that is material in the Rev.
Mr. Hervey's Eleven Letters to the
Rev. Mr. John Wesley*, printed
1765.

. . . As the title page says, the Jesuit is detected; not by fire and faggot, but by the precious word of God, in which the truth is made manifest, concerning eternal life in Christ Jesus.

This may suffice, and let Mr. Wesley know, there are some who fear God. Peradventure also it may fall into the hands of some one or other, who may, from what is here said, inquire into the matter, and search the Scriptures, to see for themselves, if Mr. Wesley should not, that eternal life is given to guilty man, and that life is in the Son of God; and that he that hath not the Son hath not life, and he that hath the Son of God hath life; in contradistinction to all popish doctrine whether maintained by Mr. Wesley or any other. And may that truth, which God hath made manifest in the Scripture, concerning eternal life in Christ Jesus, open, and prevail in our mind, that we may be delivered from every lie of Satan, and from every false and corrupt doctrine of man. . . .

It is true, the Church of Rome and Mr. Wesley agree in their doctrine of being saved by what they do, consequently they find no use for the death of Christ to take away sin. . . .

Mr. Wesley had, indeed, found the weight of the Scripture arguments, by Mr. Cudworth, in favour of the imputation of God's righteousness, in opposition to his, Mr. Wesley's, inherent righteousness, &c. . . .

If Mr. Wesley and his followers have no other righteousness to rely on, or trust to, than what he, Mr. Wesley, maintains and avows in his writings to be his and their righteousness, he may well say his race of glory is run; unless mercifully prevented by that very imputed righteousness they reject; which righteousness is, by the precious testimony of the Holy Ghost, declared to be imputed to the most guilty, without works, unto and upon all them that believe; for there is no difference. Otherwise Mr. Wesley and his followers must, after all their parade of their own righteousness and holiness, lie down in shame and sorrow.

May God's truth therefore convert him and his followers, and all mankind, from the error of his and their ways, without which the consequences will be dreadful indeed!

The Fanatic Saint Displayed: Profane Polemical Poetry

*Wesley was not a favorite target of the satirists in his day—he had no espe-
cially obnoxious personal trait, no eccentric political or social program, no
strange physical quirk to exploit, such as Whitefield's squint. But his occasional forays into public controversy usually stirred up the latent fears and
suspicions many people had of his religious "excesses." The resulting flood of
sharp attacks included poems, plays, or popular ditties that used the whet-
stone of humor to sharpen their bite.*

*The decade of the 1770s saw Wesley under just such an attack. His strong
criticism of the Calvinists (Methodist and otherwise) brought a flurry of
sharply worded, emotional retorts. And as the American cauldron threatened
to boil over in 1775, Wesley's Calm Address to our American Colonies
managed to fan the flame of controversy on both sides of the Atlantic. In the
midst of this turmoil, an anonymous author produced a series of six satirical
poems intended to mock the enthusiastic mob of fanatics known as
Methodists. These poems magnified and projected every imaginable peculiar-*

ity of this movement upon the image of its leader. No contemptuous bit of roguery was off-limits as the author drew his obscene caricature of Wesley. Abuse was heaped upon abuse. And just in case the reader failed to catch the point of the barbs, a frontispiece in each pamphlet depicted the twisted images that the words or imagination might have left hazy.

The satirist's method, typical for this period, is similar in each of these works: expanding upon popular rumors, playing on fears and suspicions, referring to dark classical allusions, and twisting words out of their original meaning or context. The author often oversteps the boundaries of humor into the realm of vulgarity and invective. The scurrilous tone of these works is set by the titles, such as The Fanatic Saints; or Bedlamites Inspired *and* Perfection; a Poetical Epistle Calmly Addressed to the Greatest Hypocrite in England. *The content varies only slightly from one piece to another, with a great deal of internal repetition as well. The line of attack against the Methodists and their leader is perhaps predictable: their piety is really pretense, their "feelings" are based in madness, their supposed pastoral concern is an excuse for sexual exploitation, their conversions and healings are really chicanery or diabolical deception, their preaching and publishing are the means of feeding ambition, their money intended "for the poor" is diverted to Wesley's pockets, and their confusing doctrines are camouflages for stupidity and irrationality.*

Most of these themes occur in the last of this series to be published, Fanatical Conversion; or Methodism Displayed: a Satire. *The rest of the subtitle indicates the author's method and approach:* Illustrated and verified by notes from J. Wesley's fanatical journals, and by the author unravelling the delusive craft of that well-invented system of pious sorcery which turns lions into lambs, called, in derision, Methodism *(1779). The portrait of Wesley (as Reynard the fox, see fig. 11) has just a hint of reality, a necessary ingredient in the author's design to unmask the hypocritical Wesley and reveal him as a lustful, ambitious, demonic, papistical old lecher. The prolific references to Wesley's* Journal *in the footnotes give the impression of verifying the caustic comments in the endless stream of heroic couplets in the text. I have changed the original page citations in the notes to refer to dates so that the present reader may locate these entries in any edition of Wesley's* Journal *and discover the way the satirist has used (or misused) the journal entry. Some entries thus cited are illustrated in the frontispiece by number, as noted in brackets.*

Luke Tyerman, Victorian biographer of Wesley, claimed that among the hundreds of pamphlets attacking Wesley, he had seen "nothing which for profanity, pollution, and violent abuse equals these." The following selections illustrate the manner in which the abuse, generally aimed at the fanatical

*fringe of the Methodist movement, was heaped upon Wesley himself as the
leader of this band of self-proclaimed saints. The anonymous author explains
his design and method in the Preface.*

FANATICAL CONVERSION

Preface

The writer's design in this satire is to account for "fanatical conversion" among Methodists in a *natural* way, though it has hitherto been
represented by Brother Whitefield, Brother Wesley, and others in
their pious Journals and pastoral writings, as *supernatural* and *miraculous*, to serve their holy purposes. The author, however, with all the
impious assurance of an infidel, presumes to treat it here as the auda-
cious offspring of infamous imposture. The groundwork of this poem
is raised upon those authentic and important records of Methodism,
the Journals and other sacred tracts of that venerable, hierophantic
mystagogue of the sinless Foundery. All the facts, or cases of conversion, at which the poet takes the wicked liberty of laughing will be
found in those hallowed Journals, as referred to in the notes.[1]

If any misrepresentation should appear, it is not willful, but
merely owing to the author's want of capacity for comprehending
relations of facts so deeply involved in witchcraft, necromancy, mystery, miracle, and physic; he owns he has no mystic genius....

Of visionary gifts, and fancied grace,[2]
Pour'd forth on saints who run conversion's race,[3]
Where John, Diocesan[4] of all Moorfields,[5]

---

1. N.B. Only Wesley's and not Whitefield's journals are here used, because Brother
Wesley disclaims working by Brother Whitefield's last. In short, he handsomely
gives Brother Whitefield up as a *fanatic*, to save himself from that importation (see
letter to Henry Stebbing, quoted in *Journal* on July 31, 1739).
2. They may be from God, or they may not, says J. Wesley (June 22, 1739). So again
(September 6, 1742), where some of these converts fancied that they felt the blood
of Christ running upon their arms, down their throats, on their breasts and hearts.
See a wild hymn (June 1, 1752).
3. They must run all the *Heats* before Perfection comes (July 23, 1739). *Satan* hinders their running sometimes (August 3, 1739).
4. See *The Love-Feast, a Poem,* by the same author, where Reynard is consecrated.
5. But a scanty district for an itinerant Apostle, who boasts *that the whole world is his
parish* (June 11, 1739). [Both Bedlam and Wesley's chapel, the Foundery, were in
the area of Moorfields in London, a circumstance to which the author frequently

Perfection's[6] milk to gaping suckling[7] yields,
Whilst my unhallow'd Muse attempts to sing,
Aid her, ye Pow'rs of Bedlam! aid her song,
To you these myst'ries and their priest belong.[8]
Ye parents of enthusiastic whim,
Who make the heads of *John's elected*[9] swim,
Hecate,[10] Trophonius,[11] and Pandora,[12] join
Your spirits, and assist the bard's design
To trace the craft of Founderies and Locks!—
Pandora, hither bring thy mystic box;

---

alludes.] This instance of apostolical usurpation reminds the author of the following anecdote, related to him by an eminent Divine of The Church of England who was well acquainted with the late Mr. Bate, Rector of Deptford Parish. Pope John thought it fit frequently to exhort, preach, and even baptize there, without leave from the Rector, who one Sunday evening paid a visit unexpectedly to a certain lady in that parish in whose house John then was. . . . [The Rector] addressed himself thus to John: "My visit, Brother Wesley is, in truth, to you—you exhort, you preach, you pray, you visit the sick, nay, sir, you even *baptize* in my parish, and without my leave. I have hitherto been silent, Brother Wesley, but it is now high time to ask you, Whether you have ever had my permission for this kind of pious usurpation in my parish?" John, with some hesitation and confusion, at last squeezed out the reluctant monosyllable, "No." "Why then, Brother Wesley," says the Rector, "the least I can expect (and that I pre-emptorily insist upon) is, that you acknowledge yourself in an *error.*" John stammered out, "Sir, I do." "Well, Brother," replies the rector, "then what is become of your boasted *Perfection?* But one word more, and I take my leave: If you continue to carry on these pious works of supererogation in my parish, I shall most certainly cite you to answer for your presumption in Doctors-Commons."
6. So Madam Bourignon calls it in her "Light Risen in Darkness," Part 4, Letter 22.
7. Such as Brother Russen, lately hanged for rapes on children of ten years old. Such as some others, who shall he named in my intended *Fanatic Anecdotes,* which will be shortly published [not known to have been published]. The author could have added the name of another celebrated Disciple of Perfection [Westley Hall], nearly related, by affinity, to the great Teacher of this doctrine; but he is said to be now no more. . . . Another *Suckling of Perfection,* the pious Major Webb, preached lately in his regimentals at the Foundery, having escaped with the loss of one eye only from America.
8. That these Methodistic Societies are really *mad,* Brother Wesley himself declares (November 13, 1742), where he says, "I met the wild, staring, loving Society."
9. So these Saints call themselves.
10. The Deity of Wizards and Witches.
11. Trophonius and his brother, celebrated impostors of antiquity.
12. The story of her and her Box of Mischiefs is well known.

To Reynard's[13] Tabernacle lent at last,[14]
Infecting converts with its pois'nous blast;[15]
Whose strong effluviae[16] young and old confound,
And stretch the passive virgin on the ground;[17]
Chiefly on Watch-Nights, or Love's annual Feast,[18]
When victims fall before lewd Murcia's priest,
Celestial impregnation to receive,
And share those gifts which all who feel[19] believe:
....

These mad-folks[20] foam, rant, caper, and curvet,
Flame, shiver, tremble, dance, chant, rave, and fret;
Not as the moon, that mistress of the seas,
Exerts her sway, but as their leaders please.
....

Genius of Wesley! prompt me while I sing,
And to my mind thy wond'rous legends bring:
Open that chaos, rude and wild, to me,
Where *lies*, like jumbled atoms, disagree;
To ev'ry striking case[21] my eye direct,
Whilst Truth, and Evans,[22] teach me to detect
Egregious *sophistry*, beneath the veil
Of *piety* conceal'd.—Each specious tale,
O! that my pen, like Caleb's, could defeat,

---

13. Of this pious character see more in the author's "Sketches for Tabernacle-Frames," "Love-Feast," "Perfection," and his other *fanatic satires.*
14. Having first served the purposes of Paganism, Montanism, Mahometanism, Popery, and fanaticism in general.
15. Seven or eight dropped down *dead* (November 23, 1742).
16. Read *Journal*, September 26, 1770.
17. For females in such delicate attitudes, see J. Wesley's journals throughout.
18. These Feasts are held much oftener; but there is one grand *annual Carnival,* as celebrated in the author's poem called *The Love-Feast.*
19. These inward Fruits of the Spirit must be *felt*, says J. Wesley (July 31, 1739). These, says he, are *very sensible operations* (ibid).
20. Such insane persons have more of the real power of God in them, says J. Wesley, than persons who are in their senses (September 19, 1764).
21. In fanatic Journals, whether miraculous or invented, natural or supernatural, diabolical or divine, magical or visionary, physical or fanciful, true or false.
22. The Reverend Mr. Caleb Evans, who some little time ago published a well-known tract called *Sophistry Detected,* never yet answered. A *lie*, once proved and fixed, must descend with the *liar* to the grave. "*Haeret Lateri lethalis Arundo* [The deadly arrow still sticks in his side]."

And stage to public scorn a public Cheat![23]
O'erthrow that wooden God whom made folks trust,
Compos'd of mean Ambition,[24] Craft, and Lust:[25]
From mask'd Imposture's visage tear the crape,[26]
And shew a Wizard[27] in his proper shape!
Till then, ye Bedlamites, let converts roar
In concert with yourselves—rejoice, deplore,
Toss, tumble, caper, when their flesh rebels,
And play more tricks than fools at Sadlers-Wells;[28]
Wild, stupid, staring, not convinc'd of sin,[29]
Charm'd, stunn'd, and cut, with Nonsense, Noise, and—Gin.[30]
Shall frisky Terentilla first appear,
A *Saint* when distant, and a Strumpet near,
With all *Perfection's* virtues amply curst,
Replete with *Grace*, with *Lewdness* almost burst?[31]
Shall she, an angry Saviour to appease,
Merry implore with coats above her knees?[32]
Stripp'd into buff, incur no heathen's scoff,
But seize on Christ with all her fig-leaves off[33]
Disgusting Penitence!—The Muse must turn
Her eyes from sights that make old Reynard burn—

---

23. Who, like his Brother Edmonds, puts darkness for light, and light for darkness (July 16, 1740).
24. Else why were forty guineas offered to Erasmus, a mock Bishop of Acadia, to make a certain Foundery Apostle a Bishop? Yet see May 12, 1765.
25. See November 15, 1767.
26. *Scit te Proserpina canum;*
Personam Capiti detrahet illa tuo (see December 23, 1755).
[Proserpine knows you to be white-haired;
She will strip off the mask from your head]
27. Some fanatic leaders have a very favourable opinion of witchcraft, See J. Wesley's *Journal* (September 2, 1751 [see fig. 21 in frontispiece]), commending Glanvill on Witchcraft, and pay believing his absurd stories.
28. Though a Playhouse is the Devil's Hot-Bed, yet Saints will sometimes submit to preach there (see April 29, 1754—then, says John, God took possession of Satan's ground.
29. See December 28, 1742 [see fig. 15 in frontispiece].
30. See frontispiece to *The Fanatic Saints, a Satire*. Gin is a great Inspirer.
31. J. Wesley declares his Lambs are *hot* (see January 21, 1761).
32. See May 20, and July 1, 1739 [see fig. 7 in frontispiece].
33. See this sweetly pious picture, May 4, 1757, in a letter from Miss Berresford.

In vain;—for now, plung'd in the Vale of Years,
Lusty Assistants wipe off pious tears;
And wanton Magdalens, in deep despair,
For absolution to young Limbs repair.[34]
Thus 'tis the husband once of ev'ry wife
Still sins by *proxy* in the eve of life.[35]
....
Do heathens ask, Whence come these agitations,
These frantic spasms in Heav'n's choice[36] congregations?
Why such is ev'ry convert's sad condition?
I answer—John's Priest, Wizard, and Physician:[37]
Starv'd *bodied*[38] with apt nostrums he controls,
And with worse physic stupefies their *souls*
Hence such stupendous case—some devis'd,
Few real, most false, yet duly journaliz'd;
In methodistic order printed fair,
And sold near Bedlam to make Madmen stare.
His *ipse dixit* credit must ensure,
Who causes the disease,[39] and sells the cure;[40]
His Master Loyola's old game, "who knew,"
Like Wesley, "those with whom he had to do."[41]

---

34. Like the Landlady of the Inn at Alnwick between *two* of these Saints (April 22, 1765).
35. Some foolish fanatic leaders brag of their great influence over married women (July 19, 1764).
36. The Chosen, Elect, etc., are names which these presumptuous fanatics give themselves.
37. As a Wizard and Exorcist, see October 28, 1739 [see fig. 7 in frontispiece]; as Physician, see September 21, 1739; March 10, 1742; June 17, 1742.
38. See fasting and prayer prescribed (March 10, 1742). Again, fasting and universal self-denial (July 27, 1755). To a poor woman and her two children, half starved, John gives a handful of his pills (October 11, 1756).
39. *Ignem, cuius Scintillas ipse dedisti,*
    Flagrantem late et rapientem cuncta videbis. Juvenal.
    [You will see the fire, whose sparks you yourself have kindled,
    Blazing far and wide and carrying all before them.]
40. Our author's Reynard actually travels about the country with his *quackery* of pots and bottles in his *carriage.*
41. So says J. Wesley (August 16, 1742)—"I wonder any man should judge him to be an Enthusiast—No—He knew the people with whom he had to do"—speaking of Ignatius Loyola.

Thus, Ambo-dexter-like, John raises wealth,
A *Quack*[42] in sickness, and a *Pest* in health.

··

From *Pagan* lips no answer will suffice:—
Against John's self, *John's self* oppos'd shall rise.
When blows once shook the teeth in Wesley's head,
Against perception's sense what madman said
Such batt'ries (though the very blood they drew)
Were yet *unfelt?*—say, Reynard, was it *you?*[43]
Thus *feelings* are by Saints sometimes *deny'd*[44]
And then (for weighty reasons) magnify'd.

··

For this, deluded wives tithe husbands' bills,[45]
And preaching taylors live on plunder's tills.[46]
Apt texts encouragement to theft afford;
"A cheerful giver's pleasing to the Lord."[47]
The Bedlam Prophet hence collects his tolls,
And fed by rapine,[48] in his chariot rolls.[49]

··

When lewdness ceases to excite desire,
These Men of God absolve their flock for *hire;*
And frisky converts must be born again,[50]

---

42. December 4, 1746 [see fig. 19 in frontispiece]; November 22, 1747; January 16, 1748.
43. October 12, 1742; October 20, 1743.
44. *Infallible* (January 8, 1738); *Fallible* (June 22, 1739).
45. Remember the case of the City-Marshall's wife and the case of the thirty-pound note and the pistols, alluded to already. J. Wesley brags of his influence over *married* women (July 19, 1764).
46. Masters' tills, plundered by pious shopmen and apprentices, for building chapels and feeding vagrant preachers—a fact too well known in the City of London, and too often felt.
47. This text is forever quoted by rooking Methodist preachers to excite *liberality* among their flock. As they cite it for their own purposes, the author retorts it *ironically* upon them for his—the honest purpose of satirizing Knaves. Let no Christian truly pious be offended. See the case of Mary Cheesebrook, a woman of pleasure, much praised for this kind of liberality to vagrant preachers (November 22, 1747).
48. Collected from pious wives, pilfering servants, etc., as already hinted.
49. December 2, 1768—"My *Servant* and my *Carriage*" Field-preachers at first were too meek and humble to ride even on *horseback.*
50. Hear Mrs. Cole, in Foote's *Farce of the Minor, upon Regeneration.*

When leaders feel their overtures are vain;
Till then, the sexes shou'd together rove,
And, unrestrain'd, indulge promiscuous love.[51]
In procreation lies much Christian merit:
This Hall[52] supports with true Wesleyan spirit.
Sinless Bourignon[53] this sound doctrine preach'd:
At length its comforts to Old Bedlam reach'd.
Numberless vouchers Reynard's chances[54] bring:
He never dips but demonstrations spring
In ev'ry *lot*, to shew that Heav'n design'd
All males and females shou'd produce *their kind.*[55]
From this sweet doctrine flies that am'rous spark
Which lights the Found'ry tinder in the dark;
At midnight[56] raising Bacchanalian screams,[57]
Whilst Virgins are debauch'd in *sainted* dreams.[58]
In such lewd *orgies* what sound brain can trace
The slightest shades of *new-found Light,* or *Grace?*

....

No more then chant, but with a cat-like purr,
Petition Wesley to extract the burr;
For when *less* Devils pious victims seize,
A *greater* Devil drives 'em out with ease.[59]

---

51. J. Wesley applauds Jane Muncy for opposing the order that *unmarried* men and women should have no intercourse (July 31, 1741).
52. For this curious Saint [Westley Hall], see J. Wesley's *Journal,* December 1 and 22, 1747—alluded to in this Poem, [page 297, note 7].
53. Antoinette Bourignon of Lisle; an enthusiastic preacher of Perfection and of the promiscuous use of women.
54. On dipping into the Bible, by way of lottery, . . . see May 25; June 1, 4, and 6; October 29, 1738; April 20, 1741; and a thousand other places.
55. Satan, well knowing that some Saints pique themselves upon putting every point of their pious theory in practice, at one time, in a most unfriendly manner, personated the apostle of the Foundery, and made dreadful ravages among the female converts; as shall be related in my *Fanatic Anecdotes* [never published].
56. At this witching time of night, Wesley says his tribes find peculiar blessings (April 9, 1742).
57. August 11, 1740, April 18, 1742.
58. Nay, sometimes Satan leaps upon a devoted convert in broad daylight, whilst she is wide awake (April 27, 1752).
59. October 23 and 28, 1739 [see fig. 7 and 12 in frontispiece], January 13, 1743.

In witchcraft's science this one rule is sure;
The strongest Wizard works the greatest cure.[60]
....
Thou Prophet! more than Prophet![61]—Moses, Paul,
Not all th' apostles, nor the Head of all,[62]
(If thou say'st *true*), thy miracles excel.[63]
May this fond notion with thy converts dwell!
Those sinless tribes in strong delusion stup'd,
By pious fraud impov'rished, gull'd, and dup'd.
But, if thine own salvation's worth a thought,
'Midst all the miracles thy hand has wrought,
Let *one*, still greater, thy vast Fame ensure;
On your own head, and heart, effect a cure:[64]
Purge that from frenzy; *this* from censure save;
And dread to die a Madman,[65] or a Knave.[66]

---

60. The Devil could not stand at all against J. Wesley. See October 17, 1739; May 13, September 18, October 26, 1740; February 4, May 3, 1741; January 13, 1743.

61. "Now I know thou art a Prophet of the Lord," said the incredulous Quaker to Brother Wesley (May 1, 1739). Thou "blessed of the Lord!" says another to J. Wesley (July 31, 1741). "Such honour," says J. Wesley, "have all the Saints." He says, that the wisdom of God employed the *fittest instruments*, i.e., his Brother and himself (see *Farther Appeal*, pp. 114ff.); that Wesley has a *prophetic Spirit* (March 29, 1740); proclaims his Mission as equal to that of Christ and the Apostles (April 2, 1739)....

62. Christ himself.

63. See a certain fanatic Bedlamite's Journals throughout. Hear what a Brother of our Reynard says upon his own *miracles* (April 17 and 29, 1739, May 10, 1741, *Last Appeal* p. 123, . . . June 30, 1739, where a comparison is made between the miracles of Christ and his Apostles and J. Wesley's; the blind cured, October 23, 1742; one just dead cured, December 25, 1742; the very sight of Wesley cures, April 8, 1750).

64. See December 1742, January 13, 1743, where Christ, the great Physician, comes through J. Wesley. But, Physician! heal thyself. See a consultation of physicians upon John's brain (May 18, 1772).

65. Our Reynard was always *crack-brained*. So was poor J. Wesley (see May 7, July 17, 1739); hear him of himself (February 1, 1738; October 14, 1739; March 7, 1738). *Idem agit simile* [Things that are alike, act alike]—our Reynard is an *Alter idem* [second self], as like as if he were spit out of his mouth.

66. Half-Christians (from whom Mr. Wesley desires God to deliver him; par. 8 in a letter to his father, quoted in *Journal*, March 28, 1739) may think that the author is here guilty of the grossest abuse. J. Wesley shall set him right; for he avers that no Methodist preacher can be saved unless he is despised (ibid., par. 20). God forbid, says he to his Brother Whitefield, that you should ever be other than *generally scandalous* (at end of letter quoted in *Journal*, June 11, 1739). The author will always be ready to contribute as much as possible to the salvation of these itinerant Apostles....

CHAPTER 25

The Old Fox Unmasked

In his later years, Wesley was attacked most vehemently on two fronts: on the political front for his views on the American revolt and on the theological front for his anti-Calvinist statements. The accusations ranged from plagiarism to ambition, from his being a Papist to his being a weathercock. In both areas, his friend and lieutenant, John Fletcher, stood by his side and defended Wesley against attack. The following selections illustrate the attacks and the defense.

The Plagiarist Politician

No publication by Wesley created as great a storm as his Calm Address to our American Colonies *(1775). The tract was in large part an extract and paraphrase of Samuel Johnson's* Taxation no Tyranny. *In addition to the inherently debatable nature of the material, two circumstances inflamed the controversy surrounding Wesley's publication: (1) he had not acknowledged his debt to Johnson's publication, and (2) he had, by adopting Johnson's position, reverted his own position as stated in an earlier tract,* Free Thoughts on the Present State of Public Affairs *(1770). Consequently, Wesley was charged with plagiarism and inconsistency, to which was added a string of other criticisms. Opponents were quick to question Wesley's motives and purposes in dabbling in politics, since he had stated in the earlier pamphlet, "I am no politician: Politics lie quite out of my Province."*

One of the sharpest attacks on Wesley came from Augustus Toplady, an evangelical Church of England priest whose satiric comments in An Old Fox Tarr'd and Feather'd *(1775) were aimed particularly at the questions of plagiarism and inconsistency. About half of Toplady's twenty-four page tract displays parallel passages from Johnson and Wesley, demonstrating Wesley's plagiarism. The rest is a fanciful and satiric account of Wesley's motives and tactics as a "tadpole in Divinity" turned politician.*

ADVERTISEMENT

The following sheet does not enter seriously and *argumentatively* into the merits of either side of the dispute now depending between England and America. This has already been done by others, and probably will be by more. The intention of these pages is, (1) To shew Mr. Wesley's *honesty*, as a PLAGIARIST; and, (2) To raise a little skin by giving the Fox a gentle flogging as a TURN-COAT.

AN OLD FOX, &c.
SECTION I.
"Another face of things was seen,
And I became a Tory"

Whereunto shall I liken Mr. *John Wesley*? and with what shall I compare him?

I will liken him unto *a low and puny* TADPOLE *in Divinity*, which proudly seeks to dis-embowel *an high and mighty* WHALE *in Politics*.

For it came to pass, some months since, that *Doctor Samuel Johnson* set forth an eighteen-penny pamphlet, entitled *Taxation no Tyranny*.

And, some days ago, a methodist weather-cock saluted the public with a two-penny paper (extracted by whole paragraphs together from the aforesaid Doctor), ycleped [called], *A Calm Address to our American Colonies*. The occasion whereof was this:

There dwelleth, about 99 Miles, one furlong, and thirteen inches, from a place called the Foundery, in Moorfields (next door to a noted Mad-house), a priest, named, *Vulposo*.

This priest is *a PERFECT man,* and an upright: hating forgery, adultery, and covetousness.

Now, he happen'd to buy Dr. Johnson's pamphlet abovemention'd: and, upon reading thereof, he thus mused within himself.

"This tract, called, *Taxation no Tyranny,* cost me one shilling and six-pence.

"What a man *buys* and *pays* for, is certainly his *own.*

"Therefore, this tract is no longer its *author's* but *mine.*

"Consequently, I shall do no evil, if I gut the substance of it, and republish it under my own name.

"There is an old Greek proverb, which saith, . . . *know thy opportunity,* and seize it. There is also a Latin poet, who saith, *Male dum recitas, incipit esse TUUM.* [When you read badly, it begins to be yours].

"No tense like the present. Doctor *Johnson* has been, for several weeks, absent from the kingdom, on a tour to *Paris.* Therefore, 'tis now or never. Like a mouse that has robbed a pantry, I'll venture forth, with my stolen morsel, while the cat's out of the way.

"Now, it is not that I care for government, any more than Judas cared for the poor: But I have long wished to be taken notice of, at Court; and this pilfering may procure me some preferment in the Church.

"I once begg'd and pray'd a foreign vagrant (who styled himself *Erasmus,* Bishop of *Arcadia*) to give ME episcopal consecration, that I might be a bishop at large, and have it in my power to ordain my ragged regiment of lay-preachers.

"Notwithstanding, tho' I gave the man many fair speeches, he would not hearken to my voice.

"But who knows, whether, in the borrow'd plumes of Dr. *Johnson,* I may not, per chance, obtain a pension, if not slip into an English cathedral; or (at least) be appointed to the first American bishoprick?

"Alas, Alas! a sudden thrill goes through me, and my cogitations are perplex'd within me! For, before I can be made a Bishop, my infamous plagiarism may be found out.

"However, worst come to worst, what if it be? 'Tis not the first time that my old foxship has been started, and my impositions have been detected.

"Many writers have lustily plunder'd the works of other men: but I am resolved to out-plunder, and to out-blunder, them all."

SECTION II.

And it came to pass, while the priest thus communed with his own heart, that a very aged man, in black clothing, rendered himself visible, and said:

"Fear not, my son, to do the thing which thy soul lusteth after:

"For much riches, and renown, and comfort, shall it add unto thee.

"Nothing venture, nothing have. Snatch the precious moment. Distill the Doctor's pamphlet. And when thou hast extracted the substance thereof, cork it up, for sale, in two-penny phials.

"Yet a little while, and revolving winds will waft the Doctor back to his native shore.

"Imitate, therefore, certain worthy sons of mine (vulgarly called, housebreakers); who are never better pleased, than with committing an unmolested burglary, when a family is from home."

And therewith the black veteran gave the priest a tweak by the elbow: who, shaking his Locks, and taking his quill in hand, enter'd immediately on the business of distillation.

How faithfully, how dextrously, how judiciously, and how plentifully, he executed the task; will appear from the following synopsis; where the *very words* of Dr. Johnson are given, on one side; and the *very words* of the Foundery Priest, on the other.

Doctor Johnson	Wesley
1. "An English colony is a number of persons, to whom the King grants a charter, permitting them to settle in some *distant* country." (Tax. no Tyr. P. 25.)	1. "An English colony is a number of persons, to whom the King grants a charter, permitting them to settle in some *far* country." (Ad. to the Amer. Col. P. 3.)
2. "And enabling them to constitute a corporation, enjoying such powers as the charter grants, to be administer'd in such *forms* as the charter prescribes." *Ibid.*	2. "As a corporation enjoying such powers as the charter grants, to be administered in such *a manner* as the charter prescribes." P. 4

3. "As a corporation, they make laws for themselves: but, as a corporation subsisting by a grant from an higher authority, to the control of that authority they continue subject."

Ibid.

4. "The *Parliament of* England has a right to bind them [the Americans] by statutes,—and has therefore a legal and constitutional power of laying upon them any tax or impost,—for the defense of America, for the purpose of raising a revenue, or for any other end beneficial to the Empire."

P. 30

5. "It is, say the American advocates, the natural distinction of a freeman, and the legal distinction of an Englishman,—that nothing can be taken from him, but by his own consent. This consent is given, for every man, by his representative in Parliament."

P. 31

6. "Whatever is true of taxation is true of every other law."

P. 32

3. "As a corporation, they make laws for themselves: but, as a corporation subsisting by a grant from an higher authority, to the control of that authority they *still* continue subject."

Ibid.

4. "The *Supreme Power in* England has a legal right of laying any tax upon them, for any end beneficial to the whole Empire."

Ibid.

5. "But you object, It is the privilege of a freeman and an Englishman, to be taxed, only by his own consent. And his consent is given for every man by his representative in Parliament."

Ibid.

6. "Whatever holds with regard to taxation, holds with regard to all other laws."

P. 5

29. "They may have a right to all which the King has given them: but it is a conceit of the other hemisphere, that men have a right to all which they have given to themselves."

Ibid.

29. "They have a right to all which the King has given them: but not to all which they have given themselves."

Ibid.

....

THUS, gentle reader, it appears that the Foundery Wasp has made very free with the Johnsonian hive. No fewer than *thirty-one* borrowed paragraphs in the course of only *ten pages*! In fact, there are more of these pilfer'd goods stowed in the narrow compass of those five leaves. But the adduced specimens may suffice to convince thee, with what an *unsparing* hand the Master of Arts has fleeced the Doctor of Laws.

But are Dr. Johnson's arguments and phraseology *therefore* the legitimate property of John Wesley, *because* the latter puffs them off as his own? By no means. We might as well affirm that Mr. Wesley's body natural is *therefore* the lawfull property of a leech, *because* the latter may have thought fit to pay its compliments to the veins of the former.

SECTION III.

It is not the intention of this tract, to canvass the merits of Dr. Johnson's reasonings: but, merely, to shew, that the best part of what Mr. Wesley, *most impudently*, and *most untruly*, calls, his own Address to the Americans; is, both as to matter and expression, a bundle of Lilliputian shafts picked and stolen out of Dr. *Johnson's* pin-cushion.

If Mr. *Wesley* had the least spark of shame remaining, the simple detection of such enormous literary Theft would be more terrible to his feelings, than an English *pumping*, or an American *tarring and feathering*.

I can say, *in earnest;* what this unblushing priest lately declared concerning himself; viz. "I am no Politician: Politics lye quite out of my Province."

The Arminian Fox

From a very early point in the Methodist revival, Wesley had spoken out against the dangers of Calvinism. He and Whitefield had parted ways in the late 1730s over the question of predestination, the "decrees" of election. The real threat of trusting in election to salvation, as Wesley saw it, was antinomianism ("against legalism"), which usually manifested itself as a lack of concern for living a Christian life.

The flames of controversy were fanned again at Whitefield's death in 1770. Wesley preached a funeral sermon that downplayed his old friend's Calvinism. But the Minutes *of his Conference with the Methodist preachers that year contained as strongly worded a statement against the dangers of Calvinism as he had ever made. The resulting torrent of criticism from across the country was predictable and lasted well into the following decade. One of Wesley's channels of response, beginning in 1778, was a monthly magazine, named* The Arminian Magazine *(after Jacob Arminius, a seventeenth-century critic of rigid Calvinism) to highlight his anti-Calvinist position. By that time, his critics often attacked his theology and his politics together (see last section), since his Tory/Arminianism was prone to bring an attack from the Whig/Puritans.*

The following anonymous attack appeared in The Gospel Magazine *in 1777, one of the publications to which Wesley responded with his own monthly magazine. The reference to the "Whitefields and Hills" is to Rowland Hill, whose* Imposture Detected *(1777) had asked whether "the lying apostle of the Foundery be a Jew, a papist, a pagan, or a Turk." Wesley's view of Hill was that "compared to him, Mr. Toplady himself [see last section] is a very civil, fair spoken gentleman!"*

The Serpent and the Fox;
or, An Interview between Old Nick and Old John.

There's a fox who resideth hard by,
The most perfect, and holy, and sly,
That e'er turn'd a coat, or could pilfer and lie.
As this reverend Reynard one day,
Sat thinking what game next to play,
Old Nick came a seas'nable visit to pay.

O, your servant, my friend, quoth the priest,
Tho' you carry the mark of the beast,
I never shook paws with a welcomer guest.

Many thanks, holy man, cry'd the fiend,
  'Twas because you're my very good friend
That I dropt in, with you a few moments to spend.

JOHN

Your kindness requited shall be;
  There's the Calvinist-Methodists, see,
Who're eternally troublous to you and to me.
  Now I'll stir up the hounds of the *whore*
  That's call'd *scarlet*, to worry them sore,
And then roast 'em in Smithfield, like Bonner of yore.

NICK

O, a meal of the Calvinist brood
  Will do my old stomach more good,
Than a sheep to a wolf that is starving for food.

JOHN

When America's conquer'd, you know,
  ('Till then we must leave them to crow),
I'll work up our rulers to strike an home-blow.

NICK

An excellent plan, could you do it;
  But if all the infernals too knew it,
They'd be puzzled, like me, to tell how you'll go through it.

JOHN

When they speak against vice in the Great,
  I'll cry out, that they aim at the *State*,
And the Ministry, King, and the Parliament hate.
  Thus I'll still act the part of a liar,
  Persecution's blest spirit inspire,
And then *"Calmly Address"* 'em with faggot and fire.

NICK

Ay, that's the right way, I know well:
  But how lies with *perfection* can dwell,
Is a riddle, dear John, that would puzzle all hell.

311

JOHN

Pish! you talk like a doating old elf;
Can't you see how it brings in the pelf;
And all things are lawful that serve a man's self.
As serpents, we ought to be wise,
Is not self-preservation a prize?
For this did not *Abram* the righteous tell lies?

NICK

I perceive you are subtle, tho' small:
You have reason, and Scripture, and all:
So stilted, you never can finally fall.

JOHN

From the drift of your latter reflection,
I fear you maintain some connexion
With the crocodile crew that believe in Election.

NICK

By my troth, I abhor the whole troop;
With those heroes I never could cope:
I should chuckle to see 'em all swing in a rope.

JOHN

Ah, could we but set the land free
From those bawlers about the *Decree*,
Who are such torments to you, to my brother, and me!
As for *Whitefield*, I know it right well,
He has sent down his thousands to hell;
And, for aught that I know, he's gone with 'em to dwell.

NICK

I grant, my friend John, for 'tis true,
That he was not so *perfect* as you;
Yet (confound him!) I lost him for all I could do.

JOHN

Take comfort! he's not gone to glory;
Or, at most, not above the *first* story:

For none but the *perfect* escape purgatory.
　　At best, he's in *limbo*, I'm sure,
　　And must still a long purging endure,
Ere, like me, he's made sinless, quite holy, and pure.

NICK

　　Such purging my Johnny needs none;
　　By your own mighty works it is done,
And the kingdom of glory your *merit* has won.
　　Thus wrapt in your self-righteous plod,
　　And self-raised when you throw off this clod,
You shall mount, and demand your own seat, like a god.
　　You shall not in paradise wait,
　　But climb the *third* story with state;
While your *Whitefields* and *Hills* are turn'd back from the gate.

　　Old John never dreamt that he jeer'd;
　　So Nick turn'd himself round, and he sneer'd,
And then shrugg'd up his shoulders, and strait disappeared.
　　The priest, with a simpering face,
　　Shook his hair-locks, and paus'd for a space;
Then sat down to forge lies with his usual grimace.
AUSCULTATOR.

The Patriotic Politician Vindicated

John Fletcher, the vicar of Madeley, was one of the few Anglican clergy who strongly supported the Methodist movement and participated in its activities. Wesley had designated Fletcher as his successor (see page 203). In the controversies of the 1770s, Fletcher's pen was hard at work defending Wesley. In his Checks to Antinomianism *Fletcher inveighs particularly against the Calvinists and their charge that Wesley did not understand the reformed doctrine of justification by faith alone but rather depended upon good works for salvation. Fletcher admitted that perhaps Wesley did occasionally swing too far in the direction of emphasizing the importance of good works, even perhaps having "unhappily wounded the truth in attempting to give a wolf in sheep's clothing a killing strike." But Fletcher pointed out that this emphasis was often necessary in order to prevent the dangers of antinomianism and moral lethargy.*

Fletcher also came to Wesley's defense in the flurry of criticism that followed the Calm Address. *The following selection from his* Vindication of the Calm Address, *written against Caleb Evans's* Letter to the Rev. Mr. John Wesley *(1775), illustrates Fletcher's method of defending Wesley as a conscientious, patriotic person of integrity.*

You try another method to overthrow Mr. Wesley's arguments. You object that five years ago he did not defend the measures taken with regard to America because he "doubted" whether they were at all defensible; and you have been informed that he has since represented the Americans as "an oppressed, injured people" and has warmly expressed his fears with respect to the danger of our liberties. But who could blame Mr. Wesley then, and who can blame him now? Is not a good man bound by his conscience to judge without partiality, according to the best information he has? When Mr. Wesley heard the clamours of the patriots, so called, who inveighed against the sovereign for breach of charter, he really thought that they had truth, and the charters of the colonists on their side, and therefore he considered the claims of the government upon the colonists as subversive of charter and consequently as faithless, injurious, and oppressive. Nor is it surprising that, upon such wrong information, he should have thought our liberties in danger; for if the sovereign had really violated the charters of the colonies, he might next have attempted to violate the great charter of England. But when Mr. Wesley was better informed, when he found that the charters of the colonies were as much for the sovereign as the patriots had insinuated they were against him, Mr. Wesley would not have acted as a conscientious man if he had not altered his mind according to this important and decisive information.

But supposing I mistake the reason which has determined Mr. Wesley to defend the claims of Great Britain, and supposing you have been rightly informed concerning the change of his political sentiments; what can you infer from thence, but that he once leaned too much toward your overdoing patriotism? He once "doubted" the equity of the sovereign's claims. His strong patriotism gave a hasty preponderance to his doubts, but his candour having proceeded to a close examination of the question, light has sprung up; conviction has followed, and he has laid before the public the result of his second thoughts and the arguments which have scattered his doubts. For my part, far from thinking the worse of a rational conviction because it follows a doubt and has met with some opposition in a good man's mind, I am inclined to pay it a greater regard. And if my friend's warm patriotism has been forced to yield to the strength of the arguments contained in his *Calm Address*, I am thereby encouraged to hope that your warm patriotism, sir, will not be less candid than his, and that you will yield to the arguments contained in this calm Vindication. Should this be the case, the public will see in you both, that reason and conscience can, at last, perfectly balance patriotism and loyalty in the breast of a good man.

CHAPTER 26

The Pretending Physician: William Hawes's Critique

Wesley's dabbling in medicine was viewed by many physicians of his day with a knee-jerk reaction of disdain and defensiveness. They perceived that, contrary to his own professed resolve, Wesley had in fact "gone out of his depth." And they certainly did not appreciate his suggestion that physicians and apothecaries conspired to take advantage of sick persons for their own selfish gain (see page 133).

Wesley's Primitive Physick *was the brunt of many passing sarcastic comments by critics of all sorts. But in 1776, William Hawes, a London physician, attacked the popular book and its author in an eighty-three-page pamphlet that specifically challenged many of Wesley's prescribed remedies. The young doctor, not yet forty, took on the venerable Wesley with a combination of sarcasm and critical disdain, tossing in an occasional positive medical suggestion or two of his own. Hawes was just beginning to make a name for himself through his well-publicized efforts to develop successful methods of treating asphyxia. He was elected physician to the Surrey Dispensary in 1781 and physician to the London, Bury Street, and Spital Square Dispensaries within a decade as well.*

Hawes's comments in the preface indicate that he was reacting in part to Wesley's attack on the intentions (and character) of many practicing physicians. As a result, the author's attempts at humor throughout tend to be heavy-handed and acerbic, portraying Wesley as a quack who should be seen not only as ineffectual but also as a definite menace to society. Hawes's main criticisms are that Wesley's remedies are either absurd (see nos. 11, 73, 221, 515, 943), inadequate (250, 297), incredible (129, 130, 136, 300), or downright dangerous (51, 460, 683). His sarcasm becomes particularly heavy at times (83, 402, 629), settling finally on the point that Wesley's venture into medicine is both futile and pernicious.

While Hawes's work gives the impression of being a blanket condemnation of Wesley and his book of remedies, even a cursory analysis reveals some notable omissions in Hawes's criticisms. Wesley's frequent prescription, "to be electrified," is never challenged by Hawes except in its use as a remedy for "old age" (no. 631). Hawes, incidentally, later became vice president of the London Electrical Dispensary. Hawes also made no comment on Wesley's suggestion of mouth-to-mouth resuscitation for drowning victims, a perhaps understandable omission since Hawes had founded only two years previously the "Society for the Recovery of Persons Apparently Dead by Drowning" (later The Royal Humane Society), which offered monetary rewards for workable methods of resuscitation.

The relatively primitive state of the good doctor's own theories also becomes evident in several places, such as his reliance on "bleeding" for fevers (see no. 125) and his critique of Wesley's tendency to treat only the symptoms of the disease (pain, etc.) rather than the disease itself—the fever!

Preface

The writer of the following pages was induced to communicate them to the world, from a desire to prevent the public from being longer imposed on, by an injudicious collection of pretended remedies for almost every disorder that can affect the human frame, and which has been published by Mr. John Wesley, under the title of *Primitive Physic.* This writer, or rather compiler, has laboured to give mankind the most unfavourable ideas of the practitioners in physic and pharmacy. . . . If Mr. Wesley's character and conduct, as a divine, a politician, and a practitioner in physic, were to be examined with the same degree of candour that he hath exercised towards others, he would certainly not appear in the most advantageous light. At least it would be manifest, that he was far enough from perfection, though that is a doctrine for which he is well known to be a very zealous advocate. But, perhaps, those who are not thorough-initiated in Mr. Wesley's peculiar tenets, may not have a proper idea of what those qualities are which are necessary to constitute a perfect man. . . .

Mr. Wesley's performance would, indeed, have been a very valuable acquisition to the public, if it could really have qualified every man of common sense "to prescribe to his family as well as himself." But the truth is, that those who rely on Mr. Wesley's pamphlet, will often be led to trifle with the most dangerous diseases, and while they are forming vain expectations of obtaining relief from his insignificant prescriptions, may be led to neglect timely application for real and effectual assistance, and thereby suffer irreparable mischief.

Mr. Wesley's pretended remedies are of various kinds. . . . But if the public are led to form a just estimate of the merit of Mr. Wesley's *Primitive Physic*, they will place little confidence in any remedies which have no better authority than his recommendation, whether they are marked *tried, infallible*, or distinguished by an *asterisk*. . . .

An Examination, etc.

The recipes contained in Mr. Wesley's *Primitive Physic* are one thousand and twelve; they are therefore too numerous to be particularly animadverted on: but, from the remarks which will here be made on many of them, it will, it is presumed, be sufficiently apparent, that no person can, with any degree of safety, rely on a compilation so extremely injudicious; the pretended remedies contained therein, being often of no use, and those which might be of utility, generally unattended with such directions or regard to times and circumstances as would be necessary to render them efficacious; and indeed, often calculated only to produce the most dangerous and fatal effects.

Those recipes, contained in Mr. Wesley's book, on which I shall make remarks, will be taken in the order in which they lie in his pamphlet, and referred to by the numbers or figures which he has affixed to them. When I give his recipes, or make quotations from him, which I shall frequently do, his words will be distinguished by the italic character. . . .

For an Ague

[Remedy] No. 11. *Make six middling pills of cobwebs. Take one a little before the cold fit; two a little before the next fit (suppose the next day); the other three, if need be, a little before the third fit.—This seldom fails.*

Here Mr. W[esley] appears to have excelled himself; he orders his cobwebs to be made into pills, but he does not reflect that there must be some viscid substance added to form a dry, light matter into pills; so that it is to be presumed Mr. W. is at the trouble of making the cobwebs into pills himself. But as the mind has a wonder effect on the body, and in no disease more than the present, I would recommend to Mr. W. to have his patient, *a little before the cold fit,* carried into a room where this wonder-working remedy hangs in clusters from the ceiling; here the imagination would have its full force, and astonishing cures perhaps be performed.

No. 25. *Apply to each wrist a plaister of treacle and soot.—Tried.*

As the word *tried* is affixed to this sooty application, it may be presumed that Mr. W. or his chimney-sweeper, have experienced its efficacy.

Apoplexy

No. 51. *Fill the mouth with salt.*

Mr. W. here recommends filling the mouth with salt; but the most likely consequence of this would be, *killing the patient,* by the stoppage of all respiration.

But send for a good physician immediately.

. . . The writer hopes that this is the only part of Mr. W's advice to which any regard will be paid in so dangerous a disease; where the omission of the application of the proper and judicious remedies, *only* for a few minutes, may be the cause of the death of the patient.

A Dry or Convulsive Asthma

No. 73. *Dry and powder a toad, make it into pills, and take one every hour, till the convulsions cease.*

Of all Mr. W's remedies for the convulsive asthma, *powder of toad* is the most curious; but it is suited to the credulity of the frequenters of the Foundery.

Bleeding at the Nose (to prevent)

No. 83. *Hold a red-hot poker under the nose.*

The *red-hot poker* prescription is undoubtedly new; and I am confident no one will dispute the honour of its invention with Mr. Wesley. I shall, however, beg leave to recommend this caution in the use of it, that no one should attempt the application who has not a very steady hand, lest the patient should bear the marks of his effectual cure. . . .

But, to be serious; an haemorrhage from the nose is, in general, a very salutary effort of nature to empty the loaded vessels of the head; so that such discharges of blood should by no means be hastily suppressed . . . ; such stoppage of the flux of the blood may often be productive of inflammation of the neighbouring parts, and sometimes even apoplexy and palsy may be the consequence of such injudicious prescriptions. . . .

A Cancer in the Breast

No. 129. *Of thirteen years standing, was cured by frequently applying red poppy water, plantane and rose water, mixt with honey of roses. Afterwards the waters used alone perfected the cure.*

Of this extraordinary cure we have no evidence but Mr. Wesley's *ipse dixit.*

No. 130. *Use the cold bath daily (this has cured many). This cured Mrs. Bates of Leicestershire, of a cancer in her breast, a consumption, a sciarica, and rheumatism, which she had near twenty years. She bathed daily for a month, and drank only water.*

We should be glad to be informed, in what part of Leicestershire Mrs. Bates lives; it is a county of some extent, and if the lady really exists anywhere, it would have been proper to have given a more particular direction. We are induced to say this, because the relation is too improbable to be credited by any persons of common understanding.

No. 136. *Apply goose dung and celadine beat well together, and spread on a fine rag. It will both cleanse and heal the sore.*

Mr. W. advises *horse spurs* as an internal medicine and *goose dung* as an outward application; together with many other remedies for the cure of cancers, equally unaccountable. It is a melancholy truth, that ignorant men have always curatives in abundance for incurable complaints: as for the medical virtues of the many prescriptions advised by Mr. W. for cancers, there can be little more objection to them than to his powder of toad in the convulsive asthma.

A Consumption

No. 221. *Every morning cut up a little turf of fresh earth; and lying down, breath into the hole for a quarter of an hour.—I have known a deep consumption cured thus.*

Here is another of Mr. W's remedies for a consumption, which needs only be mentioned to excite the readers risibility. It is a recipe indeed truly worthy of the acute genius of the author of *Primitive Physic.*

A Cough

No. 250. *Every cough is a dry cough at first. As long as it continues so, it may be cured by chewing immediately after you cough, the quantity of a pepper corn of Peruvian bark. Swallow your spittle as long as it is bitter, and then spit out the wood: if you cough again, do this again. It very seldom fails to cure any dry cough. I earnestly desire every one who has any regard for his health to try this within 24 hours after he first perceives a cough.*

The bark is one of those Herculean remedies against the use of which Mr. W. dissuades his readers . . . and yet he recommends this formidable remedy to every person affected with a cough. Is there any consistency in this? But he has long been distinguished for his variableness and inconsistency. . . .

A Diabetes

No. 297. *Drink wine boiled with ginger, as much and as often as your strength will bear.*

Here is a very strange remedy prescribed for the diabetes, and no regard whatever paid to the quantity of wine to be used, or the doses of ginger to be taken; surely, in prescribing wine and ginger as a medicine, the dose, and times of exhibition, were circumstances worthy of some little attention.

The Dropsy

No. 300 to 323. Mr. Wesley gives 23 prescriptions for the cure of dropsies, and says such extraordinary things of some of them, that it were to be wished the facts had been better authenticated. The Rev. Mr. Granger, in his ingenious biographical work, says of the *Primitive Physic,* that "this book, by the help of the title, hath had a good run among the Methodists, whose faith, cooperating with nature, frequently made them whole, when Mr. W. had the credit of the cure."

On Fevers

No. 402. Toasted bread and water can do no hurt in a fever; and it may, therefore, very safely be given, either in a *dry heat*, or a *moist heat*, to adopt the curious language of our profound practitioner.

It is not easy to meet with any quack, even the most assuming, who professes to cure diseases with more facility than Mr. W. If his directions are followed, disorders, of the most dangerous kind, disappear, as at the touch of the magician's wand. He cures a burning fever in an hour. What were *Hippocrates* or *Galen*, compared to John Wesley! . . .

A Slow Fever

No 425. *Use the cold bath for two or three weeks, daily.*

. . . Among all Mr. Wesley's remedies for fevers, *bleeding* is never once advised to lower the action of the vessels, which is exceedingly necessary when the pulse is hard, full, or strong, and there are other symptoms of inflammation in the habit; nor does he once advise an *emetic* or a *purgative* at the beginning of fevers, although there may be symptoms indicating their use in the strongest manner, and caused by obnoxious matters in the first passages; the removal of which, early in the disease, will often cause the fever to terminate in two or three days, when it would otherwise have run on for many weeks.

. . . Mr. Wesley, like many others who have not paid a due attention to the history and progress of diseases, often prescribes only for *symptoms*. . . . I have been thoroughly convinced from seventeen years experience, that prescribing to particular symptoms, is a most dangerous mode of practice. There are some who will prescribe for the head-ache, others for pains in the limbs, etc., not reflecting that these are only symptoms of the disease called a fever. . . .

The Gout in the Foot or Hand

No. 460. *Apply a raw lean beef-steak. Change it once in twelve hours till cured.*

Instead of making any remarks of my own upon this curious remedy, I shall only here take the liberty of transcribing what hath been said in relation to it by the Rev. Mr. Toplady. "In Mr. Wesley's book of receipts, entitled *Primitive Physic*, he advises persons who have the gout in their feet or hands, to apply raw lean beef steaks to the part affected, fresh and fresh every twelve hours. Somebody recommended this dangerous repellent to Dr. T. in the year 1764 or early in 1765. He tried the experiment; the gout was, in consequence, driven up to his stomach and head, and he died a few days after *at Bath*. . . .

I am far from meaning to insinuate, because I do not know, that the person who persuaded Dr. T. to this fatal recourse derived the recipe immediately from Mr. Wesley's medical compilation. All I ever said is, that the recipe itself is to be found there, which demonstrates the unskilful temerity wherewith the compiler sets himself up as a physician of the body.

Hoarseness

No. 515. *Rub the soles of the feet before the fire, with garlick and lard, well beaten together, over night. The hoarseness will be gone the next day.*

. . . Mr. Wesley has given such a farrago of absurd remedies for the various diseases for which he pretends to prescribe, as are enough to exhaust the patience of any ordinary reader; but my duty to the public obliges me to proceed, notwithstanding the irksomeness of the task. . . . The egregious quackery of all this is too manifest to need any further remarks.

The Itch

No. 540 to 549. If there be any disorder which Mr. Wesley understands, it appears to be the *Itch*; whether this be the result of his own feeling or experience, or of any other cause, I pretend not to determine; but his remedies for this cutaneous disease are more judicious than almost any other in his book.

The Lethargy

No. 584 to 600. As Mr. W. is a universal practitioner, he prescribes for *lunacy, raging madness,* and the *bite of a mad dog,* as well as for other diseases; but unless the friends and relations of the unhappy persons so afflicted, are as mad as the patients, they will apply for proper advice and assistance, instead of relying on the modes of cure recommended by the author of *Primitive Physic.*

Old Age

No. 629. *Take tar-water morning and evening. Tried.*

No. 630. *Or, decoction of nettles; either of these will probably renew the strength for some years.*

No. 631. *Or, be electrified daily.*

Mr. Wesley, who is a most incomparable practitioner, has remedies for a disease, of all others the most inveterate, viz. *old age. . . .* He recommends being *electrified daily.* This hint is worthy the attention of the ingenious Dr. Priestly; as when the arcana of electricity are completely laid open, an electrical shock judiciously administered, and repeated with sufficient frequency, might peradventure extend a man's life to a thousand years.

To one poisoned

No. 683. *Give one or two drachms of distilled verdigris, it vomits in an instant.*

Two drams of verdigris are indeed sufficient to poison forty or fifty people, and that such a direction should have been given in a book intended for general use, and which has passed through many editions, is a most alarming consideration and ought to have given Mr. W. the greatest concern. Indeed, it is somewhat extraordinary that when the unexpected success of the *Primitive Physic* had caused Mr. Wesley, as he says, *carefully to revise the whole, and to publish it again, with alterations,* so enormous a blunder should have passed through all the editions; for this appears to have been in fact the case. But the truth probably was, that Mr. W.'s ignorance first occasioned this dangerous prescription, and the same ignorance continuing, prevented it from being corrected in any of the editions. This however shows how little Mr. W.'s judgment is to be depended on, and the little concern he expresses for leading his readers into an error, which to some may have proved so fatal, is a strong evidence of his insensibility.

To stop Vomiting

No. 943. *Apply a large onion slit* [later editions read "across the grain"] *to the pit of the stomach. Tried.*

That a slit onion applied externally should be a good and a *tried* remedy for an internal disease, is somewhat extraordinary: but extraordinary remedies can excite no surprise to any man who is well read in Mr. W's *Primitive Physic,* and who gives any degree of credit to the marvelous assertions which are contained therein.

Mr. Wesley concludes his *Primitive Physic* with the wonderful cures performed by *cold-bathing, washing the head, water-drinking, electrifying,* and lastly *fasting-spittle*, which, *outwardly applied*, he informs us, *sometimes cures blindness and deafness*, besides various other disorders; and, *taken inwardly, it relieves or cures cancers, the gout, the king's evil, the leprosy, the palsy, the rheumatism, the stone, etc. etc.* He seems indeed to have been rather profuse of his remedies, which is hardly consonant to his own sentiments. For in his preface he says, "Experience shows that one thing will cure most disorders, at least as well as twenty put together. Then why do you add the other nineteen?" Indeed, it seemed hardly necessary that Mr. W. should publish a book containing 1012 recipes when, according to his account, the above *five* remedies will cure almost every acute and chronic disease incident to the human body. . . . But to enter into a particular examination of every absurdity advanced by Mr. Wesley would be equally tedious to me and my readers. What has been advanced, it is presumed, may be sufficient to show the futility of many of his prescriptions, the pernicious tendency of others, and his total incapacity to produce any medical treatise calculated to be of the least service to mankind. . . .

I have no personal animosity against Mr. Wesley, to whom I am totally unknown; nor have I been induced to engage in this performance by any consideration respecting the part Mr. W. has taken in the political world. . . . But I have ever wished to understand the principles of the medical art, to be useful in my profession, and serviceable to my fellow-creatures; and if this little piece be found by the candid and judicious to be of that tendency, I shall not regret the pains I have taken. I am conscious of the uprightness of my intentions, and therefore hope to meet with indulgence from the public.

The Pitiable Despot: Forged Letter on Methodist Divisions

Wesley's concern for the future of Methodism was constantly on his mind during the last two decades of his life (see page 202). The differences of opinion that occasionally surfaced among his followers during those years erupted into convulsive divisions after his death. In the midst of that turmoil, a year after Wesley's death, an anonymous writer submitted the following letter to the Gentleman's Magazine *(Feb. 1792), claiming that it was an original letter by Wesley and that it could be authenticated "by calling on the publisher."*

To anyone who knew Wesley very well, this letter was an obvious forgery, as Thomas Coke pointed out in the March issue of the magazine. But such thinly veiled caricature and coarse satire as appears in the letter might convince a credulous public because it also contained just enough of the Wesley aura to be plausible. In that sense, this letter is a useful gauge of at least one segment of public opinion that saw in the elderly Wesley a man whose longevity out-reached his leadership and whose arrogance outstripped his control of destiny.

Dear Sir,

For your obliging letter, which I received this morning, I return you thanks.

Our opinions, for the most part, perfectly coincide respecting the stability of the connexion after my head is laid in the dust. This, however, is a subject about which I am not so anxious as you seem to imagine; on the contrary, it is a matter of the utmost indifference to me, as I have long foreseen that a division must necessarily ensue, from causes so various, unavoidable, and certain, that I have long since given over all thoughts and hopes of settling it on a permanent foundation. You do not seem to be aware of the most effective cause that will bring about a division. You apprehend the most serious consequences from a struggle between the preachers for power and pre-eminence, and there being none among them of sufficient authority or abilities to support the dignity, or command the respect, and exact the explicit obedience, which is so necessary to uphold our constitution on its present principles. This, most undoubtedly, is one thing that will operate very powerfully against unity in the connexion, and is, perhaps, what I might possibly have prevented, had not a still greater difficulty arisen in my mind. I have often wished for some person of abilities to succeed me as the head of the church I have with such indefatigable pains and astonishing success established; but, convinced that none but very superior abilities would be equal to the undertaking, was I to adopt a successor of his description, I fear he might gain so much influence among the people as to usurp a share, if not the whole of that absolute and uncontrollable power, which I have hitherto, and am determined I will maintain so long as I live: never will I bear a rival near my throne. You, no doubt, see the policy of continually changing the preachers from one circuit to another, at short periods: for should any of them become popular with their different congregations, and insinuate themselves into the favor of their hearers, they might possibly obtain such influence as to establish themselves independently of me and the general connexion. Besides, the novelty of the continual change excites curiosity, and is the more necessary, as few of our preachers have abilities to render themselves in any degree tolerable any longer than they are new.

The principal cause which will inevitably effect a diminution and division in the connexion after my death, will be the failure of subscriptions and contributions towards the support of the cause; for money is as much the sinews of religious as of military power. If it is with the greatest difficulty that even I can keep them together, for want of this very necessary article: I think no one else can. Another cause, which with others will effect the division, is the disputes and contentions that will arise between the preachers and the parties that will espouse their several causes; by which means much truth will be brought to light, which will reflect so much to their disadvantage, that the eyes of the people will be opened to see their motives and principles; nor will they any longer contribute to their support, when they find all their pretensions to sanctity and love are founded on motives of interest and ambition. The consequence of which will be, a few of the most popular will establish themselves in the respective places where they have gained sufficient influence over the minds of the people. The rest must revert to their original humble callings. But this no way concerns me: I have attained the object of my views by establishing a name that will not soon perish from the face of the earth; I have founded a sect which will boast my name long after my discipline and doctrines are forgotten.

My character and reputation for sanctity is now beyond the reach of calumny; nor will any thing that may hereafter come to light, or be said concerning me, to my prejudice, however true, gain credit.

> My unsoiled name, th' austereness of my life,
> Will vouch against it,
> And so the accusation overweigh,
> That it will stifle in its own report,
> And smell of calumny.

Another cause that will operate more powerfully and effectually than any of the preceding is, the rays of Philosophy, which begin now to pervade all ranks, rapidly dispelling the mists of ignorance, which have been long, in a great degree, the mother of devotion, of slavish prejudice, and the enthusiastic bigotry of religious opinions. The decline of the Papal power is owing to the same irresistible cause; nor can it be supposed that Methodism can stand its ground when brought to the test of Truth, Reason, and Philosophy.

J. W.

City Road, Thursday morn.

CHAPTER 28

The Dying Patriarch

The Revered Father in God

The "holy living" tradition, of which Wesley was a part, was also concerned with "holy dying," or more specifically, the "art of dying well." The death-bed scene was the stage upon which the last act of the Christian's life was played, the field upon which the last test of faith was joined. The event had a ceremonial quality and a testimonial purpose. As Jeremy Taylor pointed out in his Rules and Exercises for Holy Dying *(one of Wesley's standard guidebooks from his early days at Oxford), "when a good man dies, then the joys break forth through the clouds of sickness and the conscience stands upright and confesses the glories of God." According to Taylor, certain "privileged" friends gathered around the departing saint to hear the last words of witness or to share an early glimpse of the supernatural during the dying person's passage from earthly existence into the eternal realms of glory.*

Elizabeth Ritchie (b. 1754) was one of the "privileged"; she was present during the last few days of Wesley's life and recorded in minute detail the events leading up to the very moment of his death. A longtime friend of Wesley, Elizabeth Ritchie is viewed by some biographers as being like a daughter to the aging Methodist patriarch. She went to London late in 1790 to visit her friends, James and Hester Ann Rogers, Wesley's assistants at City Road Chapel. She there learned of Wesley's need for assistance in housekeeping and accepted the responsibilities. For the next two months, she acted also as Wesley's "eyes," reading to him nearly every morning during his last days.

After Wesley's death, his friend, fellow preacher, and personal physician, Dr. John Whitehead, asked Miss Ritchie to write a descriptive narrative of Wesley's last days. After preaching Wesley's funeral sermon in City Road Chapel, Whitehead read an abridged version of her account to the gathered congregation. A fuller version of her narrative, dated March 8, 1791, was printed and given to each of the preachers in the Methodist connection. The account begins on February 17; the following selection describes the last full day of Wesley's life.

London, City Road, March 8, 1791

. . . Tuesday, March 1st, after a very restless night (though when asked whether he was in pain he generally answered "No," and never complained through his whole illness, except once, when he said that he felt a pain in his left breast, when he drew his breath), he began singing:

> All glory to God in the sky,
>   And peace upon earth be restored,
> O Jesus, exalted on high,
>   Appear our omnipotent Lord;
> Who meanly in Bethlehem born,
>   Didst stoop to redeem a lost race;
> Once more to Thy people return,
>   And reign in Thy kingdom of grace.

Here his strength failed, but, after lying still a while, he called on Mr. Bradford to give him a pen and ink; he brought them, but the right hand had well nigh forgot its cunning, and those active fingers which had been the blessed instruments of spiritual consolation and pleasing instruction to thousands could no longer perform their office. Some time after he said to me, "I want to write." I brought him a pen and ink, and on putting the pen into his hand, and holding the paper before him, he said, "I cannot." I replied, "Let me write for you, sir; tell me what you would say." "Nothing," returned he, "but that God is with us." In the forenoon he said, "I will get up." While his things were getting ready, he broke out in a manner which, considering his extreme weakness, astonished us all, in these blessed words:

> I'll praise my Maker while I've breath,
> And when my voice is lost in death,
>   Praise shall employ my nobler powers:
> My days of praise shall ne'er be past,
> While life, and thought, and being last,
>   Or immortality endures.
>
> Happy the man whose hopes rely
> On Israel's God; He made the sky,
>   And earth, and seas with all their train;
> His truth for ever stands secure,
> He saves th' oppressed, He feeds the poor,
>   And none shall find His promise vain.

Which were also the last words our reverend and dear Father ever gave out in the City Road Chapel, viz., on Tuesday evening before preaching from "We through the Spirit wait," &c. But to return to the chamber where this great and "good man met his fate," and which those who had the honour of attending felt was—

> Privileged beyond the common walk
> Of virtuous life, quite in the verge of heaven.

Some of our friends, fearing that matters respecting the meeting of the preachers at the awful event we now anticipated were not fully settled, Mr. Bradford asked our dying Father if he wished things to continue as determined upon when debated at the last Conference; or if he desired, in case of his removal, that any or all of them should be convened. He answered, "No, by no means; let all things remain as concluded at the Conference."

When he got into his chair we saw him change for death; but he, regardless of his dying frame, said, with a weak voice, "Lord, Thou givest strength to those that can speak, and to those that cannot: speak, Lord, to all our hearts, and let them know that Thou loosest tongues." He then sang:

> To Father, Son, and Holy Ghost,
> Who sweetly all agree.

Here his voice failed him, and, after gasping for breath, he said, "Now we have done—Let us all go." We were obliged to lay him down on the bed, from which he rose no more; but, after lying still and sleeping a little, he called me to him and said, "Betsy, you, Mr. Bradford, &c., pray and praise." We knelt down, and truly our hearts were filled with the divine presence; the room seemed to be filled with God. A little after he spoke to Mr. Bradford about the key and contents of his bureau; while he attended to the directions given him, Mr. Wesley called me and said, "I would have all things ready for my executors, Mr. Wolff, Mr. Horton, and Mr. Marriott"— here his voice again failed; but, taking breath, he added, "Let me be buried in nothing but what is woollen, and let my corpse be carried in my coffin into the Chapel." Then, as if done with all below, he again begged we would pray and praise. We called up several friends that were in the house, and all kneeled down. Mr. Broadbent prayed, at which time Mr. Wesley's fervour of spirit was visible to every one present, but in particular parts of the prayer his whole soul seemed to be engaged in a manner which evidently showed how ardently he longed for the full accomplishment of our united desires. One thing we could not but remark: that when Mr. Broadbent was praying in a very expressive manner, that if God was about to take away our Father and our head to his eternal rest, He would be pleased to continue and increase His blessing upon the doctrine and discipline which He had long made His aged servant the means of propagating and establishing in the world, such a degree of fervour accompanied his loud Amen, as was every way expressive of his soul's being engaged in the answer of our petitions. On rising from our knees he took Mr. Broadbent's hand, drew him near, and with the utmost placidness saluted him, and said, "Farewell, farewell." Mr. and Mrs. Rogers, Mr. Horton, &c., &c., drew near the bedside, and he took the same affectionate leave of them all.

The next pleasing, awful scene was the great exertion he made in order to make Mr. Broadbent [who had not left the room] understand that he fervently desired a sermon he had written on the Love of God should be scattered abroad, and given [away] to everybody. Something else he wished to say; but alas! his speech failed, and those lips which used to feed many were no longer able [except when particular strength was given] to convey their accustomed sounds. A little after, Mr. Horton coming in, we hoped that if he had anything of moment on his mind [which he wished to communicate], he would again try to tell us what it was, and that either Mr. Horton, or [some of] those who were most used to hear our dear Father's dying voice, would be able to interpret his meaning; but, though he strove to speak, we were still unsuccessful. Finding we could not understand what he said, he paused a little, and then, with all the remaining strength he had, cried out, "The best of all is, God is with us"; and then, as if to assert the faithfulness of our promise-keeping Jehovah, and comfort the hearts of his weeping friends, lifting up his dying arm in token of [victory, and raising his feeble voice with a] holy triumph not to be expressed, again repeated the heart-reviving words, "The best of all is, God is with us!" [Sometime after, giving him something to wet his parched lips, he said, "It will not do; we must take the consequence: never mind the poor carcase."] A little after this, seeing Mr. Rogers and Mr. Rankin stand by his bedside, he asked, "Who are these?" (his sight, now almost gone, preventing him [from distinctly] knowing his most intimate friends, except [in a peculiar light, or] by their voice); being informed who they were, Mr. Rogers then said, "Sir, we are come to rejoice with you; you are going to receive your crown." "It is the Lord's doing," he replied, "and marvelous in our eyes." On being told Mrs. [Charles] Wesley was come, he said, "He giveth His servants rest." [He thanked her as she pressed his hand, and affectionately endeavoured to kiss her.] On wetting Ms lips he said, "We thank Thee, O Lord, for these and all Thy mercies; bless the Church and King: grant us truth and peace, through Jesus Christ our Lord for ever and ever!" At another time he said, "He causeth His servants to lie down in peace." I replied, "They lie down in peace indeed who rest in our Redeemer's bosom. Lord, help us to rest in Him, and then rest with you in glory!" To which he replied, "Amen."

Then, pausing a little, he cried, "The clouds drop fatness!" and soon after, "The Lord is with us, the God of Jacob is our refuge!" He then called us to prayer. Mr. Broadbent was again the mouth of our full hearts; [and though Mr. Wesley was greatly exhausted by these exertions, he appeared still more fervent in spirit]. Several of his relations being present, Mr. Broadbent particularly thanked God for the honour He had conferred upon the family, and then fervently prayed that the glory might never be tarnished, nor they want a man to minister before the Lord to the latest generations; at the end of which petition our dying Father discovered such ardency of [affection and] desire that the prayer might be answered, by repeating his Amen, as deeply affected all present. These exertions were, however, too much for his feeble frame, and most of the night following, though he was often heard to attempt to repeat the psalm before-mentioned, he could only get out:

I'll praise—I'll praise—!

On Wednesday morning we found the closing scene drew near. Mr. Bradford, his faithful friend [and most affectionate son], prayed with him, and the last word he was heard to articulate was, "Farewell!" A few minutes before ten, while Miss [Sarah] Wesley, Mr. Horton, Mr. Brackenbury, Mr. and Mrs. Rogers, Dr. Whitehead, Mr. Broadbent, Mr. Whitfield, Mr. Bradford, and E. R. were kneeling around his bed, according to his often expressed desire, without a lingering groan, this man of God gathered up his feet in the presence of his brethren! We felt what is inexpressible; the ineffable sweetness that filled our hearts as our beloved Pastor, Father, and Friend entered his Master's joy, for a few moments blunted the edge of our painful feelings on this truly glorious, melancholy occasion. As our dear aged Father breathed his last, Mr. Bradford was inwardly saying, "Lift up your heads, O ye gates; be ye lift up, ye everlasting doors, and let this heir of glory enter in." Mr. Rogers gave out:

> Waiting to receive thy spirit,
>   Lo! the Saviour stands above:
> Shows the purchase of His merit,
>   Reaches out the crown of love.

I then said, "Let us pray for the mantle of [our] Elijah"; on which Mr. Rogers prayed [in the spirit] for the descent of the Holy Ghost on us, and all who mourn the general loss the Church Militant sustains by the removal of our much-loved Father to his great reward. Even so. Amen.—E. R.

A Most Extraordinary Character

Wesley's death brought forth a great outpouring of tribute and acclamation from friends and admirers across the British Isles. The eulogies that flowed from Methodist pens and pulpits during the following weeks were expectedly effusive in their approbation of Wesley's life and thought. But praise came from other sources as well, and even the more hesitant evaluations admit a degree of admiration for his many strengths.

The Gentleman's Magazine for March 1791 contained an obituary of Wesley that was in large part a compilation of anecdotal vignettes gleaned from the first sixty volumes of the magazine (with page references included for the curious reader). This notice may well have been written by John Nichols, editor of the magazine at the time and author of Literary Anecdotes. *Nichols felt his obituary section was an important feature, unrivaled among competing magazines: "The Obituary forms a Body of Biography which posterity will look back to with a satisfaction which any one may conceive who for a moment considers the defects of similar annals in preceding periods" (Preface, 1794).*

The last part of Wesley's obituary presents an appraisal of his character and significance that, although it falls short of unrestrained encomium, is more than empty panegyric. The moderately reserved tribute portrays a Wesley who, in spite of his controversial opinions and occasional excesses, was a remarkable and influential character.

[Died] at a quarter before ten o'clock in the morning, of a gradual decay, in his 88th year, the Rev. John Wesley, M.A. [sic] This extraordinary man was born in June 1703, at Epworth, a village in Lincolnshire, of which place his father, Samuel Wesley, was rector; a man much respected for piety and learning; as were his other sons, the Rev. Samuel and Charles Wesley, now deceased. The very childhood of John was marked by an extraordinary incident. When between six and seven years of age, the parsonage-house at Epworth took fire in the night, and, in the confusion of the family, he was forgotten. Finding his bed in flames, he ran to the window, and, happily, being perceived there by some of the men-servants, they formed a ladder, one on the shoulders of another, and took him out, unhurt, the moment before the roof fell in, as he himself relates in our vol. LV, p. 247; to which passage, and to vol. LIV, pp. 279, 353; vol. LV, p. 758, 875, 932, we refer for many curious particulars of him; and much more, of him and his father, may be seen in Mr. Badcock's letter, prefixed to the XXth number of the "Bibliotheca Topographica Britannica," pp. xli-xlviii.

He was entered a scholar of the Charter-house about 1713, where he continued for seven years under the instruction of the celebrated Dr. Walker, and Mr. Andrew Tooke, author of "The Pantheon," and contemporary with Dr. Kenrick Prescot, late master of Catherine Hall, Cambridge. Being elected off to Lincoln College, Oxford, he became there a fellow about 1725 [1726]; took the degree of M.A. in 1726 [1727]; and was joint tutor with the late rector, Dr. Hutchins. During his residence there, he was equally distinguished by application and abilities, and laid up those large and varied stores of knowledge which he directed, during his long life, to the best of purposes. But what chiefly characterised him, even at the early age of 26, was piety. By reading the works of the famous William Law, he, his brother Charles, and a few young friends, entered in that strict course of life which marks their sect at the present day. They received the sacrament every week; observed all the fasts of the church; visited prisons; rose at four o'clock, and partook of no amusements. From the exact method in which they disposed of each hour, they acquired the nick-name of Methodists, and are the only people who take to themselves a term first given in reproach. The ridicule and contempt which this singular conduct produced, John and Charles Wesley were well qualified to bear. They were neither to be intimidated by danger, affected by interest, nor deterred by disgrace.

But their honest zeal did not stop here. In 1735 they embarked for Georgia, in order to convert the Indians (see vol. VII, pp. 318, 575); but returned to England in 1737, when the charges of enthusiasm, bigotry, and fanaticism were urged with so much bitterness, and examined with so little candour, that they were forbidden to preach any more in the churches. This gave rise to field-preaching, in which George Whitefield was first; with whom the Wesleys had cordial friendship, though they separated their congregations on some differences in sentiments. John Wesley embraced the mild and general views of Arminius, which, it must be confessed, are more benevolent in their nature, and practical in their tendency, than Calvin's. His abhorrence of the doctrine and the man occasioned long, bitter, and useless controversy; though he never treated his opponents with the ill-breeding and abuse that he received from them. He now appeared as a zealous reformer, and the great leader of a sect no way differing in essentials from the Church of England. His peculiar opinions were, justification by faith, and Christian perfection; of which it may be remarked, the former is to be found in our own articles, and the latter, however he might enforce in possibility, he always disclaimed having attained himself.

In 1738 he visited, at Herrnhut in Germany, Count Zinzendorf, the chief of the Moravians. In the following year we find him again in England, and with his brother Charles, at the head of the Methodists. He preached his first *field sermon* at Bristol, on the 2nd of April, 1738 [1739], from which time his disciples have continued to increase (see vol. IX, pp. 240, 295, 558). In 1741 a serious altercation took place between him and Mr. Whitefield (see vol. XI, p. 321). In 1744, attempting to preach at a public inn at Taunton, he was regularly silenced by the magistrates (vol. XIV, p. 51). Though he remained the rest of his days nearer home, he travelled through every part of England, Scotland, and Ireland, establishing congregations in each kingdom. In 1750 [1751] he married a lady, from whom he afterward parted, and she died in 1781; by her he had no children. This separation, from whatever motives it originated, we have heard some of his followers say, was the only blot in his character. Others have observed on this head, that nothing could be more effectually disappointed than ambition or avarice in an union with John Wesley.

In 1771 he seems first to have commenced politician, by publishing "Thoughts on Public Affairs" (see vol. XLI, p. 132); which he followed up by "Thoughts on Slavery, 1774" (vol. XLIV, p. 533; vol. XLV, p. 137); "An Address to the Colonies, 1776" (vol. XLIV, p. 35); "Observations on Liberty, 1776" (ib. p. 517). A considerable portion of his Poems, Hymns, and Sermons, may be traced from our General Index of Books Reviewed. His controversy with Gill may be seen in our vol. XXIV, p. 581; with Thompson, vol. XXX, p. 145; with Hill, vol. XLII, p. 532; vol. XLVII, p. 540. His other writings it is not very easy to enumerate. Few men have written so voluminously; divinity, devotional and controversial, history, philosophy, medicine, politicks, poetry, &c. &c. were all, at different times, the subjects of his pen; and, whatever may be the opinions held of his divinity, it is impossible to deny him the merit of having done infinite good to the lower class of people. Abilities he unquestionably possessed, and a fluency which was highly acceptable, and well accommodated to his hearers. He had been gradually declining for about three years past; yet he still rose at four o'clock, and preached, travelled, and wrote, as usual. He preached at Leatherhead on the Wednesday (Feb. 23) before his death. On the Friday following, the first symptoms of his approaching dissolution appeared. The four succeeding days he spent in praising the God of his mercies and departed on the Wednesday morning, to receive the reward of a life spent in bringing "glory to God in the highest, and peace and good-will to men."

His remains, after lying in his tabernacle in a kind of state, dressed in the gown and cassock, band, &c. which he usually wore, and on his head the old clerical cap, a Bible in one hand, and a white handkerchief in the other, were, agreeably to his own directions, and after the manner of the interment of the late Mr. Whitefield, deposited in a piece of ground near his chapel at the Foundry, Moorfields, on the morning of the 9th instant, in the plainest manner consistent with decency, amidst the tears and sighs of an innumerable company of his friends and admirers, who all appeared in deep mourning on the occasion. A sermon, previously to the funeral, was preached by Thomas [*i.e.*, John] Whitehead, M.D. (one of the physicians to the London Hospital), accompanied with suitable hymns, &c. And on the 13th, the different chapels in his connexion in London were hung with black.

Where much good is done, we should not mark every little excess. The great point in which his name and mission will be honoured is this: he directed his labours towards those who had no instructor; to the highways and hedges; to the miners in Cornwall, and the colliers in Kingswood. These unhappy creatures married and buried amongst themselves, and often committed murders with impunity, before the Methodists sprang up. By the humane and active endeavours of him and his brother Charles, a sense of decency, morals, and religion, was introduced into the lowest classes of mankind; the ignorant were instructed; the wretched relieved; and the abandoned reclaimed. He met with great opposition from many of the clergy, and unhandsome treatment from the magistrates who frequently would refuse to check or punish a lawless mob, that often assembled to insult or abuse him. He was, however, one of the few characters who outlived enmity and prejudice, and received, in his latter years, every mark of respect from every denomination.

The political sentiments of popular men are of importance to the state. John Wesley was a strenuous advocate for monarchy; and all his followers in America were firmly loyal. Those of Mr. Whitefield declared in favor of independence. His personal influence was greater than, perhaps, that of any other private gentleman in any country. It is computed that in the three kingdoms there are 80,000 members of this society. He visited them alternately; travelled 8,000 miles every year; preached three or four times constantly in one day; rose at four, and employed all his time in reading, writing, attending the sick, and arranging the various parts of this numerous body of people.

Amongst his virtues, forgiveness to his enemies, and liberality to the poor, were most remarkable: he has been known to receive into even his confidence those who have basely injured him; they have not only subsisted again on his bounty, but shared in his affection.

All the profit of his literary labours, all that he received, or could collect (and it amounted to an immense sum, for he was his own printer and bookseller), was devoted to charitable purposes. And, with such opportunities of enriching himself, it is a doubt whether the sale of the books will pay all his debts. His travelling expenses were defrayed by the societies which he visited.

The superintendency of his various chapels and societies he committed, about seven years ago, by a deed enrolled in chancery (in trust for the support of his preachers and their poor families), to an hundred travelling preachers, now in various parts of these kingdoms; and among the number is the Rev. Dr. Coke, at present in America, whose mission is supposed to have increased the converts in the West India islands, and other parts of America, to near 50,000, since the conclusion of the war, and founder, in 1789, of a college in South Carolina, called Wesley College.

On a review of the character of this extraordinary man it appears, that though he was endowed with eminent talents, he was more distinguished by their use than even by their possession; though his taste was classic, and his manners elegant, he sacrificed that society in which he was particularly calculated to shine; gave up those preferments which his abilities must have obtained, and devoted a long life in practicing and enforcing the plainest duties. Instead of being "an ornament to literature," he was a blessing to his fellow creatures; instead of "the genius of the age," he was the servant of God!

One striking passage from Mr. Badcock's anecdotes of him we shall repeat from the former volume, with Mr. Wesley's short remarks on it. "In one of Mr. Wesley's earlier publications he, in the strongest language, disavows all pecuniary motives, and calls on posterity to vindicate his disinterestedness in one of the boldest apostrophes I ever read. '*Money* must needs pass through my hands,' says he; 'but I will take care (God being my helper) that the mammon of unrighteousness shall only pass through; it shall not rest there. None of the accursed thing shall be found in my tents when the Lord calleth me hence. And hear ye this, all you who have discovered the treasure which I am to leave behind me; if I leave behind me ten pounds (above my debts and the little arrears of my fellowship), you and all mankind bear witness against me, that I lived and died a thief and a robber.' I doubt not but his pride, and something *better* than his pride, will prevent the stigma." To this Mr. Wesley in January 1785, adds, that the only end he ever had in view was, "to save sinners." "What other end," he asks, "could I possibly have in view? or can have at this day? 'Deep projects of a subtle mind.' Nay, I am not subtle, but the veriest fool under the sun, if I have any earthly project at all now! For what do I want which this world can give? And, after the labour of fourscore years,

> No foot of land do I possess,
> No cottage in the wilderness;
> A poor, way-faring man,
> I dwell awhile in tents below,
> Or gladly wander to and fro,
> Till I my Canaan gain.

His executors have already given notice that a gentleman, to whom Mr. W. has bequeathed his MSS, will publish an authentic narrative of him, as soon as it can be prepared for the press; and that the truth of this performance is intended to be regularly attested. His history, if well written, will certainly be important, for in every respect, as the founder of the most numerous sect in the kingdom, as a man, and as a writer, he must be considered as one of the most extraordinary characters this or any age ever produced.

The Venerable John Wesley

The epitaph on Wesley's tombstone at City Road Chapel (now called Wesley's Chapel), London, follows the pattern of an inscription written "with the point of a diamond" by Adam Clarke upon a window in his study at Manchester sometime after Wesley's death. Clarke was only a young Methodist preacher at the time, but had been much admired by Wesley.

The tone of both epitaphs is in harmony with the note sounded by most of the eulogies that followed Wesley's death. Clarke's inscription, below, is followed by the tombstone epitaph.

Good men need not marble: I dare trust glass with
The Memory
of
JOHN WESLEY, A. M.,
Late Fellow of Lincoln College,
Oxford
Who, with indefatigable zeal and perseverance,
Travelled through these kingdoms,
Preaching JESUS,
For more than half a century.
By his unparalleled LABOURS and WRITINGS He revived
and spread
SCRIPTURAL CHRISTIANITY
Wherever he went,
For God was with him.
But having finished his work,
By keeping, preaching, and defending the FAITH, He
ceased to live among mortals,
March 2nd, MDCCXCI,
In the eighty-eighth year of his age.
As a small token of continued filial respect,
This inscription
Is humbly dedicated to the Memory of the above,
By his affectionate Son in the Gospel,
ADAM CLARK.

....

To the memory of
the venerable JOHN WESLEY, A. M.,
late Fellow of Lincoln College, Oxford. This great
light arose,
by the singular providence of God,
to enlighten these nations,
and to revive, enforce, and defend,
the pure apostolical doctrine and practice of
the Primitive Church,
which he continued to defend, both by his
labours and his writings,
for more than half a century;
and who, to his inexpressible joy,
not only beheld their influence extending,
and their efficacy witnessed
in the hearts and lives of many thousands,
as well in the Western world as in these kingdoms, but also, far
above all human power or expectation,
lived to see provision made, by the singular grace of God, for
their continuance and establishment,
to the joy of future generations.
Reader, if thou art constrain'd to bless the instrument, give
God the glory.
After having languished a few days,
he at length finished
his course and his life together,
gloriously triumphing over death,
March 2, anno Domini 1791,
in the 88th year of his age.

Part III

Wesley in Retrospect

Wesley's death quite naturally changed the boundaries of propriety with regard to public comment on his ideas and activities. With the primary protagonist off the scene, polemical attacks by non-Methodists on the deceased leader ground to a halt, and the controversies surrounding him diffused into more generalized dissension and debate within his movement.

The near absence of any postmortem criticism from outside the Methodist movement narrowed drastically the perimeters of published comment on Wesley's character and significance for decades. The wide variety of interpretive writings on the elusive Mr. Wesley during his lifetime may indeed have in some cases *concealed* as much as they *revealed* about the "real" John Wesley. Nevertheless, without the fairly persistent check of critical viewpoints, the overall tone of biographical comment after his death began to change rather noticeably toward a common or standard view.

The form and content for biographical reflections on Wesley's life were set by the eulogies that flooded the British landscape during the months after his death. These eulogies, in the absence of a lively polemic, helped set the framework for a consensus view of Wesley's character and significance that had not been quite so easily achieved previously. For several generations, a fairly universal portrait would persist that would not be seriously challenged until a new interest in the sources of Wesley studies emerged toward the end of the nineteenth century.

That Venerable Man of God:
The Wesley of the Eulogies

W esley died on March 2, 1791. His body lay in state at City
Road Chapel the day before his funeral a week later (see
fig. 7). The preacher on that occasion was Dr. John
Whitehead, a Methodist lay preacher and physician who had
attended Wesley during his last days. His sermon, given extem-
pore, was taken down in shorthand by a listener and quickly
edited by Whitehead himself for publication. The seventy-page
pamphlet also included a version of Elizabeth Ritchie's account of
Wesley's last days (see page 330) that Whitehead had read at the
end of his own discourse. We know that Whitehead's work, or a
separately published edition of Miss Ritchie's account, reached
Manchester within three or four days of the funeral, for Richard
Rodda included it there on March 13 in his "discourse on the
occasion of Wesley's death."

Similar scenes were repeated throughout the British Isles and America during the following weeks as Methodist chapels were draped in black and preachers eulogized their departed leader. Even a few Anglican clergy were moved to say a kind word in memory of a man they found to be remarkable. Some, of course, simply breathed a sigh of relief, and others less charitable spoke out against any display of honor or recognition. Wesley himself had hoped for a minimum of "vile panegyric" at his death, but nothing could control the stream of spoken and written tributes that flowed from his many friends and admirers.

Many of the funeral sermons, eulogies, and elegies for Wesley were published during the spring of 1791, within days or weeks of his death. There are sermons by such close associates of Wesley and veteran Methodists as Richard Rodda in Manchester, Thomas Taylor in Hull, and Joseph Benson, who preached the memorial sermon at the Conference in July. John Whitehead, who preached the funeral sermon, had recently come back into the Methodist connection as a local preacher, after being a Quaker for nearly two decades. Some of the prominent younger preachers, such as Thomas Coke, General Superintendent in North America, and Henry Moore, preacher in Bristol, also published their eulogies. Others, such as Samuel Bradburn, who had declined to preach Wesley's funeral sermon, wrote special tracts for publication. Elegies were written and published by old friends, such as Thomas Olivers, and newer associates, such as Miles Martindale and James Kenton. Published tributes also came from Anglicans, such as Elhanan Winchester of London (both a funeral sermon and an elegy) and William Hobrow of Liverpool. Character sketches, often anonymous, appeared in many magazines and newspapers.

These works are by no means uniform in style or content. But in spite of their different approaches and emphases, they do exhibit some common themes. In most cases, the writers confess an inadequacy for the task, either because they lacked sufficient firsthand contact with Wesley or because they sensed that an adequate testimony would require a greater person (such as Wesley himself) to do it justice. Thomas Coke is a notable exception to this sense of hesitation or humility. Many of the writers also point out that they intend no panegyric, no excessive flattery; they rarely kept this promise. Most of the writers also stress the objectivity and truthfulness of their work, pointing out that many parts of their account may seem incredible but are nonetheless true. Thomas Olivers's elegiac stanzas are frequently dotted with footnotes that declare, "This is strictly, literally true," or, "This is a real fact."

The analysis of Wesley's life and character in these writings usually focuses on the widespread good that Wesley was able to accomplish through his amazing energy during his long life. The statistics of his industriousness are already a matter of universal fascination—how many hundreds of books he published, how many tens of thousands of times he preached, how many hundreds of thousands of miles he traveled. His rising at 4:00 A.M. and his penchant for "redeeming the time" had become a fixed part of the story decades before. Now the results of that energy and industry could be surveyed whole; the good he had done for the souls and bodies of his fellow creatures could be praised. At that point, the judgment was unanimous: England was a better country for his having lived there. In fact, the amazing spread of his movement toward the end of the century was seen by many eulogists as a sign of divine approbation; certainly God was with this man.

Other themes also worked their way into some of these sermons and writings, though not quite so universally. Whitehead makes a special point that Wesley's mind was "richly furnished," a theme repeated by Samuel Bradburn and Thomas Coke. Some writers felt constrained to defend Wesley against the charge of having accumulated a vast fortune; Bradburn goes into great detail on this matter in particular. Several turned aside the charge of "enthusiasm" often levied against Wesley; Whitehead viewed Wesley's decisions and actions as reasonable and deliberate (even those of 1738) not the rash actions of an enthusiast. Many of the writers highlighted Wesley's evangelical awakening, often (as with Benson, Rodda, and Hobrow) quoting his journal account of May 24, 1738. Whitehead's attempt to downplay this "Aldersgate" experience is more than matched by Coke and Winchester, who omit any reference at all, and Kenton, who places Wesley's spiritual awakening before he went to Georgia. If the eulogist defended Wesley's doctrines, he most frequently focused on justification by faith and Christian perfection.

The sources for these reflections of Wesley's life, thought, and character, if not the firsthand observations of the speakers and writers, were most often Wesley's own journals and sermons.

Benson's and Rodda's quotations from the journal indicate that they were unaware of Wesley's attempts to correct some of his own earlier views by emendations in later editions of the *Journal.* Winchester notes that he had read, in addition to some of the sermons and journals, a few issues of the *Arminian Magazine,* part of Wesley's *Appeal to Men of Reason and Religion,* and a few other Wesley tracts. Nearly everyone quoted from Elizabeth Ritchie's account of Wesley's last days. Some, like Coke in America, relied also upon anecdotes reported by other individuals to fill in their own accounts. At the end of his sermon, Benson read an anonymous sketch of Wesley's character that had recently come into his hands (published previously in the *Gentleman's Magazine* and reprinted in pamphlet form at York).

As one might expect, there is very little criticism of Wesley in these publications. Only Rodda even mentions that Wesley faced the opposition of mobs and rioters. Samuel Bradburn, whose *Farther Account* is one of the most commendatory descriptions, comes closest to a critical comment when he mentions that Wesley "was different from himself at different times." Bradburn notes that occasionally, when Wesley was overextended, his third or fourth sermon in a day "would be far beneath what he could have made them, had he preached but twice." Winchester, a Church of England priest, mentions that some "uncharitable, censorious revilers of the pious dead" in his parish had tried to prevent him from giving his eulogy of Wesley. But few persons of this antagonistic mind went to print with their ideas. William Huntingdon of Providence Chapel, London, was a notable exception, publishing the sermon he had preached the week after Wesley's death, "The Funeral of Arminianism." Another unfavorable account was by John Annesley Colet, nephew of Wesley; he later retracted this *Impartial Review.*

Another concern rested heavy on many Methodist hearts—the seemingly inevitable divisions and strife that would come in the months and years ahead with Wesley gone. Olivers and Hobrow plead for unity; Bradburn argues for a "right spirit" among the preachers. Rodda confidently proclaims that the connection will thrive, while Coke sees the need for much prayer to overcome the unfaithfulness that made the Methodists deserve to lose their leader.

The anticipated divisions had already begun to surface when Benson's eulogy at the Conference in July 1791 called for the preachers to abide by Wesley's doctrines and discipline and to pursue the plan that Wesley "in his wisdom saw fit to adopt." Not least of the problems facing the connection and its new center of authority, the Conference, was the matter of designating an author for the official biography of Wesley. The controversy that this question engendered eventually touched all the earliest biographies of Wesley.

CHAPTER 30

Images of Power: The Controversial Early Biographies

A few days after Wesley's death, a report circulated that John Hampson, formerly an itinerant Methodist preacher, had a biography of Wesley ready to be printed. Hampson and his father had both left the Methodist connection with a grievance: Wesley had omitted them from the "Legal Hundred," the membership of the Conference as defined by the Deed of Declaration in 1784. The executors of Wesley's estate quickly cautioned the public against "receiving any spurious or hasty accounts," noting that the three gentlemen to whom Wesley had bequeathed his manuscripts would publish an "authentic narrative" as soon as it could be prepared for the press.

The committee designated in Wesley's will to determine the disposition of these manuscripts consisted of Thomas Coke, Henry Moore, and John Whitehead. Named as General Superintendent for North America in 1784, Coke had, since 1777, been a close associate of Wesley. Moore was one of the younger men named as a member of the Conference (the "Legal Hundred") in 1784. However, Coke was in America at this time and Moore was stationed in Bristol. Dr. Whitehead (Wesley's physician and a local preacher at City Road Chapel, who had delivered the funeral sermon) was thus the only member of the committee resident in London. The other two gentlemen agreed that, under the circumstances, Whitehead, having more leisure, was the most proper person to compile the biography of Wesley, using the manuscripts. It was agreed, however, to wait until Hampson's life of Wesley should be published before proceeding.

Hampson's *Memoirs of the Late Rev. John Wesley* appeared in June 1791 and was predictably not well received by the Methodists. Hampson, after leaving the connection in 1785, had become curate of Sunderland and, although he maintained a politely civil relationship with Wesley, continued to be critical of Wesley's exercise of "arbitrary power" within the Methodist connection. Hampson tried to draw a picture of Wesley that was "not flatteringly disgusting, nor exaggerated to deformity, but as nearly as possible, a just transcript of truth and nature" (1:iii). He admits in the preface to an interest in the "foibles" as well as the "excellencies" of the man (1:ix). His sources are the *journals,* sermons, and controversial tracts of Wesley, some firsthand accounts (including Elizabeth Ritchie's), and a few early Wesley manuscripts then in the possession of Joseph Priestley.

Hampson marshaled his sources to support his contention that Wesley's judgment was not always sound. He also criticized some of Wesley's doctrines. He felt that where Wesley's opinions were scriptural and just, they did not differ from the doctrines of other denominations; where the opinions were peculiar to Wesley himself, they were either "not true, or dubious, or indifferent" (3:121). And as might be expected, Wesley's establishment of the Deed of Declaration also came under especially intense criticism in this biography. Hampson had intended for the work to appear during Wesley's lifetime and had expected Wesley himself to respond to any "errors or misrepresentations." Appearing as it did almost immediately after Wesley's death, such a candid appraisal of Wesley's life and thought met a hostile audience among the Methodists. Although many later critics also saw Hampson's work as less than friendly, some have nevertheless acknowledged that his description of Wesley's character and appearance is one of the best firsthand accounts. It is often quoted by biographers in later generations (see page 277).

Hampson's work was closely followed by a published collection of *Original Letters by the Rev. John Wesley and his Friends,* edited by Joseph Priestley, scientist, theologian, and man of letters. These letters, mainly between John and his brother Samuel, along with the collection of family correspondence concerning the ghost of the Epworth rectory, were the manuscripts used by Hampson. Priestley received the documents from Samuel Badcock (see page 44) and decided to present these "great curiosities" verbatim to the public in order to throw further light upon Wesley's character and principles. Priestley's Unitarian inclinations prevented him from sympathizing with Wesley's theology; his scientific predelictions led him to conclude that the "supernatural phenomenon" at Epworth was simply a trick played by the servants. Nevertheless, in the preface to this collection, Priestley summarized the content of these materials by saying that

> the conclusion to be drawn from the whole is by no means to his [Wesley's] discredit, as he appears to have been unquestionably an honest man whose sole object it was to secure his own salvation and promote that of others, though he will appear to have been strongly tinctured with enthusiasm, from the effect of false notions of religion very early imbibed.

Priestley also noted with some satisfaction that John Wesley probably would have suppressed these documents if he had been able to get possession of them.

By this time, the question of possession was becoming an issue in the matter of the "authentic narrative" to be produced by Whitehead. Coke and Moore had agreed in July 1791 to give Whitehead the Wesley manuscripts, believing (as they later claimed) that Whitehead would produce the work for a fee of one hundred guineas. The profits from the book were to be applied to the preachers' charity, as was the custom for all works published by the Methodist connection. Once Whitehead had possession of the manuscripts, however, he began negotiating for a higher fee, ownership of the copyright, and other emoluments (such as 50 percent of the profits for the first two years) that the preachers considered inappropriate. When Coke and Moore tried to prevent Whitehead from using the manuscripts without first abiding by the stipulations of Wesley's will (that the three of them should first examine the material), Whitehead began to prove the force of the saying that "possession is nine-tenths of the law." He made examining the manuscripts difficult for the others and refused to allow Coke or Moore to review his own use of the manuscripts in the biography, saying he would not have his work "mutilated."

In the ensuing dispute, Whitehead was supported by a committee of men "of respectable and independent situations," about thirty laymen including the three executors of Wesley's will. Coke and Moore were supported by the London preachers and the Book Committee, who viewed Whitehead's maneuvering as the work of a selfish man using the situation for his own personal gain. This tension was part of a larger power struggle within Methodism between the preachers who saw themselves as inheritors of Wesley's authority and some of the laity who wanted more control over the societies. The Book Committee decided in October 1791 to appoint Coke and Moore to compile a life of Wesley "for the sole benefit of the charity to which he had bequeathed all his literary property." At about the same time, the quarterly meeting of the London preachers resolved to exclude Whitehead from the pulpit until such a time as he would fulfill the requirements of Wesley's will concerning the manuscripts.

The Book Room published Coke and Moore's *Life of the Rev. John Wesley* in April 1792 and had produced a second printing by the time of the Conference in July. The one-volume work was dedicated to the preachers, and the authors stated that their aim was to provide a "concise yet full view of the man and of the work," adding that "there is nothing material respecting him that is not given in this volume." Although they had benefitted from previous access to Wesley's papers during Wesley's lifetime, the authors were not able to quote from them in this work because Whitehead held the documents in his house. Therefore, except for the last few chapters, where personal reminiscences of the authors become quite obvious in the narrative, the work relies largely upon published sources, primarily Wesley's *Journal.*

This biography is, for all its protestations to the contrary, a prolonged eulogy of Wesley. It bears the marks of a hastily produced work and suffers from lack of substantive quotation from the manuscripts. Moore, nevertheless, later remarked that this work met "with a success which was beyond their most sanguine expectations." He no doubt was referring to the successful sale of more than ten thousand copies in the first three months and to the donation of all the profits to the preachers' fund.

Whitehead, cut off from the Book Room and the Methodist pulpits, proceeded on his own to publish his *Life of Rev. John Wesley,* the first volume appearing in 1793, the second in 1796. This biography, much more extensive than either Hampson's or Coke and Moore's, benefits greatly from access to the manuscripts. Though it has often been accused of being tinged with party feeling (as one might expect, given the circumstances), the work is remarkably free of polemic. In some ways, it is a more balanced work than Coke and Moore's, though the author is not hesitant to criticize such things as Wesley's Deed of Declaration as the cause of Methodism's "corruption and final dissolution" at the hands of a powerful party of preachers ("black-robed boys"). He also attacks Wesley's ordinations of 1784 as, in fact, Coke's "stalking-horse to gain influence and dominion." Whitehead, a Quaker for some years, was very sensitive to the charges of enthusiasm often levied against Methodism and its leader. He is therefore careful not to accentuate some of the events that emphasize the emotional side of Wesley. For instance, he treats "Aldersgate" as part of a crucial period of transition that extends over the whole of 1738 during which Wesley calmly and rationally considers the evidence (scriptural and otherwise) as to his own state of salvation. Whitehead notes in particular Wesley's own later comments on these events of 1738 in the corrections (*errata* sheets) added to the 1774 edition of his *Journal.* In these corrections, Wesley had reinterpreted his earlier views on the question of whether he had a proper faith or was a true Christian before his Aldersgate experience.

The completion of Whitehead's work in 1796 ended the first flurry of Wesley biographies. Whitehead returned the Wesley manuscripts to the preacher's house next to City Road Chapel as soon as he finished using them. John Pawson, then resident in the house and superintendent of the London circuit, restored Whitehead's membership and reinstated him as a local preacher, appointing him to preach at the Chapel. Pawson also, without anyone's knowledge or permission, proceeded to burn some of Wesley's books and manuscripts that were then at City Road. This capricious and irresponsible act, ironic in the light of the long controversy over the manuscripts, removed forever many valuable primary resources on Wesley's life, including, it seems, many of his private diaries from the middle period of his life. One other note of irony, in the light of the controversy over the "authentic" biography, appears in the revised (second) edition of Whitehead's work, published in Dublin in 1806 just after the author's death. An editor (perhaps John Jones, the publisher) removed some of Whitehead's criticisms, thus protecting the good image of the founder and the power of the preachers, but resulting in just the sort of "mutilation" of his work that Whitehead had feared. Nevertheless, Whitehead's biography was the standard "Life" for a generation and became the model of Wesleyan biography, in both form and content, for over half a century.

Testing the Memory: Early Nineteenth-Century Biographies

W hen Joseph Benson was requested by the Conference of 1808 to prepare a new edition of Wesley's works, he put the journals at the beginning of the set and prefixed the first few chapters of Whitehead's biography of Wesley (up through 1735, the beginning of the *Journal*), with no acknowledgment of authorship. Benson was, at the time, editor and corrector of the press for the Methodist connection, and his edition of Wesley's works in sixteen volumes (1809–13) provided a "uniform and elegant" publication not previously available. Wesley's own collection of his *Works* (1771–74) had not included the later sermons, the last few installments of the *Journal,* and many tracts. It had been, to use Benson's term, "but indifferently executed," with poor printing and a preponderance of nonoriginal writings (extracts, translations, and so on). Benson's new edition was by no means without error (he even neglected Wesley's own *errata* sheets), but it did provide a more complete and fairly reliable source of information for those interested in the life and thought of Wesley.

The first biographer to make use of this new edition of Wesley's works was Robert Southey. Named Poet Laureate in 1813, Southey soon turned his attention to producing his *Life of Wesley* (1820, 2 volumes). An Anglican convert from Unitarianism, he had no personal admiration for Wesley's theology or the Methodists' activities. He did feel, however, that Wesley was an influential person whose effects would probably be more universally felt than those of most statesmen or conquerors of the day (1:34-35), and he set about to write a biography worthy of the man. The result of his efforts was singularly noteworthy at the time, a biography of Wesley by a truly cultivated biographer and literary light with an audience that no Methodist could have commanded.

Southey admits that he had no "private sources of information." His list of published sources, however, is fairly comprehensive and includes, besides the three eighteenth century biographies of Wesley, some of the histories of Methodism that had begun to appear in the early nineteenth century. The Southey volumes exhibit literary polish and diligent research. But the author's bias against Wesley's theology, combined with his self-conscious exuberance in demonstrating Wesley's "errors," results in a series of intolerant jabs that mar the literary sheen and more than counterbalance his general platitudes about Wesley's character. He sees Wesley as "a man of great views, great energies, and great virtues," but one who spread superstition as well as piety. Southey waxes eloquent on what he calls the "extravagancies" and "eccentricities" of Wesley's "enthusiastic doctrines," especially instantaneous regeneration, assurance, and sinless perfection (2:19, 122-144). Southey's bias was reinforced on these points by some of the eighteenth century anti-Methodist sources that he used. From the outset he sees Wesley developing "that state of mind...which led the enthusiasts of early ages into the wilderness." Aldersgate represented for Southey a self-contradiction: "an assurance which had not assured him [Wesley]." Southey sees Wesley as a slave of popularity, ambition, and selfishness; he sees many of Wesley's ideas as dangerous and productive of great evil. Southey felt that Wesley's peculiar weakness was a "voracious credulity," a trait that he retained to the last. In many of Southey's remarks, he chooses words that seem calculated to antagonize Wesley's disciples: "the physic of intolerant discipline," "the paroxysms of the disease which Methodism excited," "the self-sufficiency of fancied inspiration."

The response of the Methodists was immediate and direct. The Conference in 1821 approved the request of the Book Committee to engage Richard Watson to prepare a review of Southey's biography. They were no doubt reacting in part to the comments made by John Gibson Lockhart in *The Quarterly Review* that the subject of Southey's work was unworthy of the labors of the Poet Laureate. The Conference also requested Adam Clarke to write a life of Wesley "suited to the present time and circumstances." Clarke was to be assisted by Henry Moore in this endeavor.

Watson's lengthy *Observations on Southey's "Life of Wesley"* (252 pages) appeared the same year. The recurrent theme in his critique, contrary to the judgment of Lockhart, is that Southey was totally unqualified for the task of writing a biography of Wesley, the Poet Laureate's mind being "but slenderly furnished" with the theological principles necessary to such an undertaking. Watson's assumption was a transparent reiteration of earlier attacks on Hampson, Whitehead, and Priestley: only a Methodist (and a "good" one at that) is qualified to write a proper biography of the founder. Watson recognizes Southey's literary skills, his intended impartiality, and even his occasional inclination toward praising Wesley. But the critic observes finally that "the Wesley of Mr. Southey is not, in several of the most important characteristics, Mr. Wesley himself." The "real" John Wesley, he thought, had eluded the non-appreciative mind of the poet.

Watson's caustic refutation of Southey's views, point by point, focuses on the questions of Wesley's conversion, his theology, his attitudes toward separation from the Church of England, and his "credulity." Only occasionally does Watson lighten his grave discussion with a bit of sarcasm aimed at the Lake Poets in general or Southey's personal peculiarities in particular. Watson sums up his own view of Wesley in a comment on "the spotless character of John Wesley: a man who had no such errors or mischiefs to repent of; whose life was a continuous effort to do good; and from whose pen nothing ever fell but what tended to promote peace and to exalt the character of society" (228). A decade later, Watson would expand this cameo into a full-length biography.

Southey, encouraged by his old friend and earlier acquaintance of Wesley, Alexander Knox, apparently intended to modify some of his own earlier imputations against Wesley (especially his "ambition") in a new edition of his biography. However, Southey died in 1843 and his son inherited the task of producing an edition (1846) with Knox's comments in an appendix. One of Knox's most perceptive observations was that Wesley's later sermons exhibited an ingenuous frankness with which former excesses in opinion are acknowledged and rejected," an insight lost on most Methodist observers, who had begun to distill the process of change in Wesley's life and thought into one watershed experience in 1738, after which everything appeared constant and whole. This new edition of Southey's work also included annotations by Samuel Taylor Coleridge, Southey's brother-in-law and another of the Lake Poets, who considered this *Life of Wesley* his "favorite among favorite books."

Adam Clarke was, in the meantime, collecting material for his biography of Wesley, assisted (as the Conference had requested) by the "communications and advice" of Henry Moore. Clarke, an assiduous scholar and friend of Wesley, was in the midst of producing his commentaries on the Bible. He soon gave over the biographical task to Moore and focused simply on collecting documents and anecdotes of the Wesley family from the few remaining descendants. These he published as *Memoirs of the Wesley Family* (1823), a rich source of original material and firsthand reflections by the last generation of those who knew the eighteenth-century Wesleys. John and Charles Wesley, subjects of Moore's projected work, were omitted from this volume. Nevertheless, Clarke's book is the only remaining source for many of the firsthand recollections about John Wesley, such as the comment by Samuel to Susanna, "I think our Jack would not attend to the most pressing necessities of nature unless he could give a *reason* for it" (513). Clarke eventually hoped to write a sketch of Wesley's life "with some anecdotes and a proper character," fully convinced that "no man out of heaven is capable of writing Mr. Wesley's life who had not an intimate acquaintance with him." He was preparing an enlarged revision of the *Memoirs* when he died in 1832. This task was finished for him by the editor of his collected works and published in 1836 as a second edition (2 volumes). Clarke, thrice President of the Conference, readily admitted to being "a constant advocate of Methodism, the admirer of its doctrines and discipline, and also of the means employed in its propagation."

Henry Moore was no less a Methodist, but less a scholar than Clarke. His *Life of the Rev. John Wesley* (2 volumes, 1824–25), written with a certain reverence, nevertheless displays a degree of mature judgment that was not so evident in his earlier collaboration with Coke. Though Moore intended to answer Southey, he lost no opportunity to attack the work of his old antagonist, Whitehead. Moore was the last surviving executor of Wesley's manuscripts, which were now in his possession. Ironically, Moore plagiarized a major portion of Whitehead's work, including many of his firsthand comments ("I have put this here. . . . ") and most of his footnotes (citing the old 1771–74 edition of Wesley's Works). Moore's claim to authority rested largely on his position as one of the last living acquaintances of Wesley; therefore he seldom admitted to quoting Whitehead or other earlier authors. Those few passages that are acknowledged as Whitehead's are at times less accurately transcribed than the vast portions of other material that he copies without acknowledgment. And the description of Wesley at the end of his work, which the reader would normally ascribe to Moore's memory, is in large part copied straight from Hampson's work.

To Whitehead's basic text, Moore adds some new material, including some previously unpublished documents and many anecdotal reminiscences. Moore constantly reminds the reader that he was in contact with Wesley quite regularly toward the end of Wesley's life. He also mentions frequently that he has many of Wesley's manuscripts "now before me," even though in some cases he simply copies the text from Whitehead. On the other hand, Moore chooses not to reveal that he was one of the young preachers named to the "Legal Hundred" by Wesley, or that he was one of the preachers ordained by Wesley in 1789 to carry on the work in England. On some points, Moore differs drastically from Whitehead, primarily on the matter of the ordinations and the Deed of Declaration of 1784. He is much more apologetic than the previous biographers, defending Wesley at almost every point. He marshals his sources cleverly in this regard, quoting Whitehead against Hampson, Watson against

Southey, and even using Southey against Hampson. This aging itinerant had the last say over his early opponents. With the advantage of the last word, the gift of longevity, Moore concludes that "thus all his [Wesley's] biographers, after striving to lessen his character among men, have been obliged to subscribe to its general excellence!" Moore's work, with all its problems, is probably on the whole the most useful of the early biographies; his is also the last of the firsthand accounts.

CHAPTER 32

Polishing the Image: Toward a "Standard" View of Wesley

Nearly all of the last generation of Wesley's acquaintances were gone when in the 1820s the Methodist Book Room in London commissioned John Jackson, R.A., to paint a portrait of John Wesley to be used as a frontispiece for the Methodist Hymnbook. Nearly everyone recognized that the previous portraits, literary and graphic, both before and after Wesley's death, failed to convey a uniform impression of his appearance. Jackson attempted, by comparing previous works (paintings, busts, etchings, and so forth), to produce "a likeness of Mr. Wesley, more perfect, and therefore better adapted to convey to posterity a more vivid impression of the *mind* and *heart,* as well as the features, of a man whose name will ever stand prominent in the records of the church of Christ" (*WMM,* 1828, page 700). The resulting portrait, which appeared in 1827, was from the first somewhat controversial because of its "synthetic" nature. The rather bland production was, nevertheless, reproduced in the Hymnbook for decades and became familiar to several generations of Methodists as the standard portrait of the founder (see fig. 14). It remained for a later critic to point out, "It is safe to say that it does not represent Wesley at any period of his life" (*WHS*, 1902, page 190).

At this same time, a similar development occurred in the literary portrayals of Wesley. Without intending to slight Moore's larger work, the Conference in 1831 requested that Richard Watson write a short biography of Wesley adapted to "general circulation." The following Conference was apparently pleased with Watson's production and asked him, in spite of Moore's continued presence, to enlarge his work into a "standard and authorized life of our venerable founder." Watson died, however, before that task could be accomplished. His short biography, nonetheless, designed for the "general reader," was reprinted several times over the next eighty years. The work is a brief summary of the literature then available, with the sources (mostly secondary) cited quite regularly, if somewhat imprecisely. No new biography appeared for a generation. Watson's work became a fixture for half a century in the Course of Study reading list for Methodist ministerial candidates in America (along with Watson's *Theological Institutes*, an attempt to systematize Wesley's theology). Though brief in scope, Watson's biography of Wesley stated the standard "inside" Methodist view of Wesley clearly and succinctly, though somewhat defensively, with an occasional theological comment. Wesley's image was now firmly in the grasp of the "establishment" Methodists.

Thomas Jackson, editor for the Methodist connection after Benson and Jabez Bunting, completed a new edition of Wesley's *Works* in 1831 and noted in his preface the nearly simultaneous appearance of Watson's biography: "In that instructive biography, Mr. Wesley's doctrinal views are well explained and the peculiarities of his character and conduct are defended with admirable ability and effect." Jackson himself carries the adulation of Wesley to new heights in his comment that "the entire history of human nature does not furnish a higher example of laborious diligence in the service of God and man." Jackson's main purpose in this new ("third") edition of the *Works* was to present a "pure text" and a "complete collection" of Wesley's original writings. While he was more careful than Benson in many ways, Jackson still did not provide a fully adequate edition. He often used the latest copies of various items without comparing earlier or first editions, even though he was aware of the possibility of editorial and typographical corruptions. He included no manuscript sources and provided no annotations or critical apparatus to assist the reader. Nevertheless, Jackson's edition of Wesley's Works, slightly revised in 1840 and 1856 (the "fourth" and "fifth" editions), was the last "complete" edition to be done for nearly 150 years; every appearance of the *Works* after 1831 in fourteen volumes (seven volumes in nineteenth-century America) is essentially a reissue of the Jackson edition.

The poetical works of the Wesleys, published at various intervals during their lifetimes, were collected and published by George Osborn in a thirteen-volume edition, *The Poetical Works of John and Charles Wesley* (1868–72). This work, not a definitive edition but still the only collected edition of the hymns and poems, presents the Wesley publications in chronological order, with only slight alterations to prevent needless duplication. The last volume also contains some previously unpublished poems of Charles Wesley. Osborn, a senior British Methodist preacher and longtime Secretary for Foreign Missions, had been encouraged for many years by Thomas Jackson to produce this work. Osborn had also received encouragement from many friends to write a life of Wesley. While declining the latter task, Osborn did, however, publish a work perhaps more valuable to future historians, *Outlines of Wesleyan Bibliography* (1869). This work was, as he said, an attempt "to make a beginning in our Connexional bibliography." The first sixty pages contain a chronological listing of the works of John and Charles Wesley, with occasional annotations. Though imperfect, as Osborn himself acknowledged, this work made an important contribution to Wesley studies at that time.

To many, it may have seemed that the possibilities for Wesley biographical studies had been exhausted. The generation that had known him was gone; the sources that told of him were extensively displayed. After Watson's work, no major new biographies of Wesley appeared for a generation. Attention turned to an analysis of Wesley's views in the context of current controversies in Methodist theology or polity. A few general assessments appeared, some candidly negative such as Isaac Taylor's *Wesley and Methodism* (1851), but most works were tied to specific issues. In America, as in Great Britain, the fragmentation of Methodism into several branches resulted in many different efforts to defend denominational distinctions on the basis of Wesley's ideas. Many of the new groups, such as Primitive Methodist, Bible Christian, Wesleyan Methodist Connection, or Free Methodist, argued that their doctrines and polities were essentially a reiteration of the "true Wesleyan" position. Abel Stevens, editor of *The Christian Advocate of the Methodist Episcopal Church,* considered the first two volumes of his *History of Methodism* (1859) to be "the fullest 'Life and Times of Wesley' yet published," and hoped that his broad and irenic perspective would help reduce sectarian tensions, an approach which he saw as being in the tradition of Southey and Taylor.

The interest in England turned especially to the issue of Methodist-Anglican relations, and the writings about Wesley generally spoke to that question. Many of the more traditional Methodists felt that the high-church trends within the Church of England (seen in the Oxford Movement of Pusey, Newman, et al.) were diametrically opposed to the evangelicalism that Methodism and its founder had long promoted. For a generation or more, Wesley's "churchmanship," and especially his views on relations to the Church of England, became the focus of attention among both Methodist and Anglican writers.

In the midst of this discussion, Luke Tyerman produced a monumental study of Wesley (1870) that would become a landmark in Wesleyan biography, not so much for its interpretive value as for the sheer volume of material that he gathered into these three volumes. Tyerman notes in his preface that "innumerable letters and other manuscripts" had come to light in the previous seventy-six years, but no biographer since Whitehead had used any "additional information worth naming." Besides, no one had ever taken the trouble to explore the hundreds of "magazines, newspapers, broadsheets, pamphlets, tracts, and songs published during Wesley's lifetime" that could illuminate his biography. Tyerman, like most of the previous biographers, was an itinerant Methodist preacher. He had retired in middle age, however, due to ill health, and spent nearly two decades collecting materials on Wesley. His main object was "to collect, collate, and register unvarnished facts." His intent was "to make Wesley his own biographer"; to this task he set his hand.

A thoroughgoing Methodist triumphalism emanates from every page of Tyerman's work, beginning with the first sentence: "Is it not a truth that Methodism is the greatest fact in the history of the church of Christ?" Tyerman clearly states, however, that "nothing derogatory to the subject of these memoirs has been kept back; . . . the work of the biographer is not to hide the facts but to publish them." He does, nevertheless, in typical Victorian fashion, occasionally refuse to quote a source, with a comment that the words are "so loathsomely impure" that it would be "a sin against God and man" to reproduce them. Thus, for instance, he only gives excerpts from the notice of the Oxford Methodists in *Fog's Weekly Journal* (see page 226). In some ways, Tyerman is not as protective as Moore; he is willing, as he says, to look at "the specks as well as the sunshine in John Wesley's history." But, at the same time, he is always ready to defend Wesley's "honor and honest fame."

Tyerman's main negative bias becomes evident rather quickly. "High churchism" of any sort is to be decried as an unfortunate blemish in the Wesleyan story since these "silly popish practices" too much resemble "the pernicious nonsense of the high church party of the present day" and should therefore never receive the approval of any evangelical Protestant. As a result, Aldersgate, which Tyerman sees not so much as a conversion but as a "consciousness" of having been saved (Wesley had been "safe" as a servant of God for ten years), is mainly significant as the point where Wesley gave up his "high church bigotry and intolerance." Tyerman is also quick to criticize the "foolish statements" of the Moravians and the "antinomian poison" of the Calvinists, both of which tinged Wesley for a time but from which Wesley was spared by the "great truths" that eventually pervaded his mind and heart.

Although Tyerman does admit that "Wesley was not faultless," the tireless biographer nevertheless explains away nearly every questionable action and thought. He attributes Wesley's incorrect reflections in later life to forgetfulness "at the moment." He agrees with Hampson that Wesley's Deed of Declaration (1784) was unfair to many of the preachers, but it was necessary to the preservation of the Methodist connection. Tyerman sees Wesley's ordinations as absurdly inconsistent with his views on the church, but these actions were promoted by Thomas Coke, who was "dangerously ambitious." In the end, Tyerman is able to overlook almost every fault he has set forth in the three volumes and conclude that Wesley's "physique, his genius, his wit, his penetration, his judgment, his memory, his beneficence, his religion, his diligence, his conversation, his courteousness, his manners, and his dress made him as perfect as we ever expect man to be on this side of heaven."

Tyerman's great contribution was to collect in these volumes a vast storehouse of information from a variety of sources. His pages became the repository of countless documents and notices quoted whole. Two reservations, however, must be noted with respect to his otherwise laudable efforts in this regard. In his wide gathering of materials, Tyerman occasionally relied upon spurious documents, such as "Sir Edward Seaward's *Narrative*," which the *Wesleyan Methodist Magazine* had quoted in November 1832. Seaward's supposed eighteenth-century journal was in fact a fictitious writing published in 1831 by Miss Jane Porter, an English novelist. Another deficiency in Tyerman's work is that he did not have full access to Wesley's literary remains that had passed from Whitehead to Moore and from Moore to his executor, Mr. Gandy. In his book *The Oxford Methodists* (1876), Tyerman recognizes, for instance, that Wesley had kept a diary and asks, "Where are those manuscripts, and why are they not given to the public?" In spite of these shortcomings and his almost obnoxious triumphalism, Tyerman made a notable contribution to the work of succeeding generations of Wesley biographers, who have frequently borrowed from his treasury of detailed information.

George J. Stevenson, a London bookseller and friend of Henry Moore, had assisted Tyerman in the collection of material for the biography. Shortly after Moore's death in 1844, Stevenson had made copies of many of those Wesley family manuscripts he himself "deemed suitable for publication." The original manuscripts were then deposited with Mr. Gandy, Moore's executor, who apparently refused the requests of subsequent inquirers. R. Denny Urlin, in his *John Wesley's Place in Church History* (1870), notes that these documents were inaccessible because Mr. Gandy "courteously but firmly declines to allow any inspection of them" (8). Encouraged by "many friends" and assisted by his collaboration with Tyerman, Stevenson published his transcriptions of the documents in *Memorials of the Wesley Family* (1876), which was an enlargement of Clarke's earlier work. A generally useful source of documents, Stevenson's work must, however, be used with care; he rather blithely perpetuates some of the family legend, such as the "tradition" that John Wesley had a middle name (see page 41).

Most authors of Wesley studies during the last three decades of the nineteenth century disavowed any intention of writing a full-fledged biography. Urlin, Julia Wedgewood (*John Wesley and the Evangelical Reaction* [1870]), and John H. Overton (*John Wesley* [1891]), all Anglicans, saw their work as selective in content and supplementary to the existing biographies. James H. Rigg and several others continued to argue the nature of Wesley's churchmanship. Several studies were written concerning Wesley's relationship to other movements and leaders. The first continental European biography of Wesley appeared in English translation in 1883—Matthew Lelièvre's *John Wesley*. Lelièvre re-emphasizes the contrast between the influence of Wesley and of Voltaire mentioned by Southey in 1820. He does not, however, go so far as William Lecky, who in his *History of England* (1878–90) claims that the "religious enthusiasm" of the Wesleyan revival had helped England escape the "contagion" of revolutionary fevers evident in France (2:611 ff.).

Out of this period, two names emerged that would continue to influence Wesley studies into the twentieth century: John Telford and Richard Green. Green's first work, *John Wesley* (1881), written on the eve of the first Ecumenical Methodist Conference was well received but represented no significant contribution to the field. The work gave only a hint at Green's interest in Wesley bibliography, the area in which his preeminence would soon be recognized. On the other hand, Telford's work, *The Life of John Wesley* (1886), quickly became the standard popular biography, replacing Watson's book as required reading in the Course of Study for Methodist preachers in America.

Telford's work is not a year-by-year outline of Wesley's activities, as was Tyerman's. Rather, Telford sets a new pattern for subsequent Wesley biographies. After narrating the story through the 1740s, he devotes most of the subsequent chapters to distinct topics: Wesley as traveler, journal-writer, churchman, preacher, writer, and so on. The author was a respected British Methodist preacher who later became connectional editor, and his modest biography is essentially free of the "party spirit" that seemed to characterize earlier works. Telford tells the story in a rather colorless, though respectful tone, acknowledging and harmonizing the standard sources. With this work, the concern of the earliest biographers for an "authentic" narrative has disappeared; the controversies have faded into the background; the "authorized" apologetical view of Watson has now become the "standard" matter-of-fact view of Telford. After a century of biographical work, the writers seemed to have nothing new to say; their task now seemed to focus on how best to tell the story.

Refining the Sources: Toward the "Standard" Works of Wesley

The second century of Wesley studies began with a letter by Richard Green, circulated among a score of friends he knew were interested in Methodist history. He proposed the establishment of a society "to accumulate exact knowledge" of the history and literature of Methodism, including the "lives of the Wesleys" and the "works by J. and C. Wesley." As a result, the Wesley Historical Society was formed in 1893, each member covenanting to add "two pages of information and enquiries" to a manuscript journal circulated among the members once a year. The society began publishing some of this material in its *Proceedings* in 1897 and has continued to the present to be a source of information and encouragement to researchers. For Green, the growing network of members, ministerial and lay, provided a practical base for promoting several projects he had in mind.

Green, a British Methodist preacher and Governor of Didsbury College, Manchester, had collected one of the finest personal libraries of Wesley materials in the world. His interest was to provide a "full and accurate" bibliography of Wesley's writings to assist the study of Wesley's "theological teaching [and] indefatigable labors." Building upon earlier works by Alexander Hey (1864), George Osborn (1869), Luke Tyerman (1870), and others, Green produced *The Works of John and Charles Wesley: A Bibliography* (1896). For the first time, researchers had a decent guide through the maze of Wesley's publications in their various editions. In spite of its short-comings, this work, with its descriptive and illustrative notes, became a standard and essential tool for Wesley scholars for more than half a century. To this work, Green shortly added *Anti-Methodist Publications* (1906), a very useful bibliography of materials from the eighteenth century, a work that most students of Wesley still continue to overlook.

Richard Green also studied Wesley's *Journal* throughout his life and recognized the need for an improved edition. Largely through his encouragement, Nehemiah Curnock, British preacher and long-time editor of the *Methodist Recorder* (1886–1906), continued the work of preparing a new edition of the journal begun by Green and Charles H. Kelly. Curnock attempted to provide a better text than previous editions by incorporating newly discovered material, most notably many of the Wesley diaries and manuscript journals. Some of these, having been part of the Wesley family papers, had been purchased from Mr. Gandy by Mr. J. J. Colman, whose son allowed them to be photographed. Other important materials had also sur-faced largely through the renewed "zeal of collectors and students" and the work of the Wesley Historical Society. Curnock's labors resulted in an eight-volume "Standard Edition" of Wesley's *Journal* (1909–16), heavily annotated and enlarged with new material. The last two volumes were completed by John Telford and appeared the year after Curnock's death.

Curnock was the first editor of the journal to include large por-tions of the Wesley shorthand diaries, though he had not fully mas-tered the complex system of cipher and abbreviation in the earlier Oxford diaries. Curnock does not allow the new material, however, to revise the image of Wesley; he simply uses it to illuminate many of the well-developed stereotypes of Wesley. Curnock's notes are marked by a persistent hero worship that leads him at times to test his imagination for ways to protect Wesley. For example, he explains that Wesley's inclusion of lying in his diary confessions "does not mean the deliberately spoken lie, but exaggeration, misrepresentation, the equivocal use of words out of their ordinary and strictly accurate and literal meaning." Such verbal tap-dancing is intermixed with a vast assortment of otherwise informative detail that makes these volumes an important contribution to the work of later researchers.

Two other "standard" collections appeared in the next two decades after the *Journal*. Edward Sugden, an Australian Methodist and Master of Queen's College, Melbourne, produced his two-volume edition of *Wesley's Standard Sermons* (1922–23) in the aftermath of the British Conference's decision in 1914 that only the "first four volumes" of Wesley's Sermons (1746–60, reprinted in 1787) were to be considered "standards of doctrine" for Methodist preaching. Sugden annotated those forty-four sermons. However, he also added in an appendix the nine additional sermons that Wesley had included in his *Works* (1771), noting that Wesley himself certainly "would never have dreamed of blocking by the dead hand of his personal authority all future developments in theology" (1.24). While the introductions and notes in this edition provide some useful information and interpretations, the body of the sermons is taken directly from Jackson's edition of the *Works* and thus represents no advance in textual accuracy.

Within a decade of Sugden's work, John Telford, then connectional editor of British Methodism, produced a "Standard Edition" of *The Letters of John Wesley* (1931) in eight volumes. Of all the Wesleyan sources, the body of letters was and is still most liable to improve from generation to generation as new manuscripts are discovered in family archives, library vaults, and a variety of other repositories. Richard Green had gathered together a collection of 1,600 letters, nearly doubling the largest previous collection that had been published in Jackson's edition of the *Works*. Green died in 1907 before the project could be published. By the time Telford had taken over the project and had prepared the material for the press, 2,670 letters were included. Telford annotated these materials carefully in his characteristically restrained manner. While this collection represented only a remnant of Wesley's actual correspondence, it was a significant advance at that time in providing source materials for the study of Wesley's life and thought.

While these "standard" editions of the journal, sermons, and letters were being produced, biographical studies of Wesley continued to pour forth, even though over one hundred books on Wesley had appeared in the previous century. Works in 1906 by an Australian, W. H. Fitchett (*Wesley and His Century*), and an American, C. T. Winchester (*The Life of John Wesley*), were added to the Course of Study reading lists. Fitchett's book replaced Telford's work in 1918 in the Methodist Episcopal Church, South, and Winchester's remained on the list in the northern M. E. Church from 1912 to 1937. Neither work is particularly remarkable except that the authors, now over a century removed from Wesley, are confident enough about his enduring fame that they can see some inconsistencies in Wesley's thoughts and actions without trying to explain them away. Fitchett, who starts his book by quoting plaudits about Wesley from such luminaries as Sir Leslie Stephen, Robert Southey, Thomas Macaulay, and Matthew Arnold, to support his notion of Wesley's greatness, goes on to include a chapter on "Wesley's Odd Opinions." Nevertheless, the traditional triumphalism not only prevails in the end, but also takes on a new dimension: Fitchett compares Wesley to nearly every major figure in English history (Shakespeare, Wellington, Pitt, Washington, et al.) and in the end determines that Wesley's influence is more enduring than all of them. Fitchett's whole book is an enlargement of Southey's projection that "there may come a time when the name of Wesley will be more generally known, and in remoter regions of the globe, than that of Frederick or of Catherine."

In a somewhat different approach, Winchester, a professor of English literature at Wesleyan University in Connecticut, tried to write his study of Wesley for the general reader who might not be Methodist. He seldom ventures into theological discussions; Wesley he sees as primarily "a man of religion." Terms like "unselfish devotion," "settled confidence," and "personal religion" pervade Winchester's discussion of Wesley's religious biography. While admitting that Wesley "was not a perfect man, and his followers then and since have perhaps often idealized him," Winchester goes on to ask, "Yet among religious reformers where is there a nobler figure; [among eighteenth-century figures], where among them all is the man whose motives were so pure, whose life was so unselfish, whose character was so spotless?"

The last of the Victorian biographers of Wesley in England was John S. Simon, successor to Richard Green both as President of the Wesley Historical Society and as Governor of Didsbury College. Upon his retirement from Didsbury in 1913 at age seventy, Simon turned his attention to his "hero," John Wesley. For the next twenty years, he sifted through the literature on Wesley, trying to "see Wesley as he was." In 1921, Simon published the first volume of what would become a five-volume study of Wesley's life. Simon mentions at the outset his heavy debt to the Curnock edition of Wesley's *Journal.* A note on the dust jacket also acknowledges that the work "covers ground which is more or less familiar to experts." Nevertheless, Simon brings to life an abundance of information about Wesley and the Methodist movement, pausing frequently to examine some of the interpretive issues raised by previous writers.

Simon's own interpretive stance is betrayed by comments such as his feeling that Tyerman was a "somewhat aggressive critic" of Wesley. Simon himself was conscious of the pitfalls of hero worship and tried to avoid the problems of previous writers and artists who, as he said, "have been so anxious to invest their saints with the glory of the aureole that its splendour has prevented us from seeing the form and features of the man." When Simon's son-in-law, A. W. Harrison, completed the fifth volume of the work after Simon died at age ninety, he readily acknowledged his own inability to match Dr. Simon's "reverent affection ('a little this side of idolatry') for the founder of Methodism." While much of Simon's work borders on the pedestrian, his is the most extensive biography in this century and is written with an air of authority, resulting in a reputation for being the standard work on Wesley. It is the last of the major biographical efforts at writing a "life and times" of Wesley. Its very size, however, has consigned it to the fate of many multivolume works, that of being a generally recognized, but unread, reference work.

The larger-than-life-size image of Wesley portrayed by most biographers during this period was matched in oils by distinguished British artist and Methodist, Frank O. Salisbury. In 1927, he happened to visit Wesley's House and Museum in City Road, London, and noticed that the building was quite dilapidated and did not have "a good portrait of John Wesley." Salisbury agreed to paint one if the Methodist authorities would restore the building. Using Enoch Wood's bust of Wesley (see fig. 12), as a starting point, along with relics from the museum such as Wesley's clerical bands and preaching robe, Salisbury produced a striking portrait that has become a favorite, if not a standard, twentieth century Wesley portrait (see fig. 15). The statuesque proportions of the image belie Wesley's diminutive physical stature and present a grand reflection of his romanticized reputation among his Methodist followers.

CHAPTER 3 4

Wesley and the Specialists: Broadening the Traditional Image

W hile biographers at the turn of the century were trying to surpass one another in summarizing Wesley's enduring significance, Elie Halévy took an old idea and developed a new hypothesis that would stir up debate for decades. In his article, *"La naissance du Methodisme en Angleterre"* (*Revue de Paris*, 1906), Halévy refined the idea first broached by Southey and repeated by Lecky, Lelièvre, and others: Wesley and his movement had contributed to "preventing the French Revolution from having an English counterpart." The biographers had needed little encouragement (or even evidence) to make such grandiose statements of Wesley's enduring significance. Halévy's approach, however, was on a different level; he formulated the idea in sociological terms and attempted to give it substantial support with historical evidence. He effectively drew the question into the realm of academic debate. Nonetheless, the Halévy thesis would be repeated many times over by writers who did not need to understand it fully to know that it sounded like an essential truth about Wesley's significance.

Shortly after Halévy's work appeared, Augustin Léger planted the seeds of another controversy. He published two works in 1910, *Wesley's Last Love,* which contained a transcript of Wesley's account of the Grace Murray affair (see page 167), and *La Jeunesse de Wesley,* which outlined Wesley's spiritual and intellectual development up to 1739. Léger was only mildly constrained by the traditional legends. He felt that most monograph studies of Methodism were "so much chaff, . . . nothing more than mere Sunday school reading" (xix) and that most studies of Wesley failed to disentangle the man from his work and his movement (xv). His most controversial idea, in *La Jeunesse,* was that Wesley's true conversion was in 1724, fourteen years before the "Aldersgate" heart-warming that Methodists were prone to emphasize as the watershed experience in Wesley's life (pages 77-82). Earlier writers had, to be sure, pointed out that Wesley himself, in later life, qualified his earlier statements concerning his "conversion." Even Tyerman had conceded to Wesley the title of Christian (in a qualified sense) before 1738. But Léger's proposition challenged unequivocally the prevailing traditional sentiment about "Aldersgate."

To the issues raised by Léger and Halévy (Wesley's spiritual development and his overall significance), another book in French added a third proposition that would set the basic constellation of issues in Wesley studies for at least half a century. Maximin Piette, a Belgian Franciscan, was convinced that the Wesleyan movement could be rightfully understood only within the framework of the larger Protestant Reformation. The first half of his dissertation for a degree from the University of Louvain, *La Reaction Wesleyenne dans l'Evolution Protestante* (1925; English ed., 1937), surveys Protestantism from Luther and Zwingli to the English Nonconformists. Then, after a rather brief description of Wesley's life, Piette points out that "a great mistake has sometimes been made in attributing to Wesley's work a novelty it did not possess" (page 474). He thus challenges the easy Methodist repetitions of the Halévy thesis, pointing out that the two revolutions in England during the seventeenth century had secured all the liberties that the English desired; they had no need of a revolution in the eighteenth century (pages 102ff.). However, Piette does not disparage Wesley's contribution to the life and thought of his day; rather, Piette refutes the idea that Wesley invented nothing—"such an off-hand, snap judgment is empty-headed" (page 412). Piette would not treat Wesley simply as a "ghost of a former time"; Wesley's statue could not be carved to make him look like a disciple of Calvin or Luther.

The task then, as Piette sees it, is clear: to discern carefully the true nature of Wesley's genius, not simply in his borrowings from the past, and especially not in the trappings of the movement he bequeathed to the world, but rather within the standards of his own life and thought. Piette concludes that Wesley's contribution to the evolution of Protestantism was to reinstate "religious experience" as the basis of a renewed Christianity; Wesley was thus "an incontestable influence on Protestant liberal theology from Friedrich Schleiermacher to William James." In this light, Piette tries to show Wesley's experience in 1738 as an important "conversion" in which his sense of the love of God became "more intense, and in some sense the principle, the centre, the mainspring of his apostolic activity" (page 556). Piette claims that "Aldersgate" was not actually the sort of radical transformation portrayed by Wesley himself or his successors. The Franciscan father challenges the usual portrayal of Wesley's "profligate" life prior to 1738, a seemingly necessary (even if forced) preconversion ingredient in the typical Christian biography based on the model of Augustine's *Confessions*. But this idea, in the end, was overshadowed by Piette's strong affirmation of Léger's idea that Wesley's "true" conversion was in 1724, "fourteen years before the time that Wesleyan legend, up to now, wishes, with official approval, to place it" (306).

This comment concerning Wesley's true conversion became the focus of the Methodist reaction to Piette's work. Timing had a great deal to do with the politely negative response; the bicentennial celebration in the 1930s of Wesley's Aldersgate experience brought forth a great outpouring of writing. The Methodists' affliction with "an incurable scriptomania," noted as early as 1833 by J. W. Baum (*Der Methodismus*, p. 158), reached epidemic proportions during this decade. The biographers continued apace repeating the Wesley story with only a slight reshuffling of the words (W. H. Hutton, 1927;

Umphrey Lee, 1928; Abram Lipsky, 1928; Arnold Lunn, 1929; Colwyn Vulliamy, 1931; Bonamy Dobree, 1933; James Laver, 1933; John S. Simon, 1934; Marjorie Bowen, 1937; Leslie Church, 1938; Elsie Harrison, 1938; Francis McConnell, 1939). At the same time, the theological specialists began to deal earnestly with the questions raised on the Continent. If Piette's work was not really a biography, neither was the work by George Croft Cell, *Rediscovering John Wesley* (1935). It was, however, an important theological study and the next serious attempt after Piette to explore Wesley's relationship to the history of Christian thought. As a result of these two books, theological works would dominate the field of Wesley studies after 1940.

Cell, a professor of historical theology at Boston University, was convinced that "the essentials of the Wesleyan Reformation represent the deeper and dynamic unity of Protestantism" (Luther, Calvin, and Wesley representing the three principal formations of Protestantism). Moreover, he thought that "the kinship of Wesleyanism and Calvinism greatly exceeded their common affiliation with Luther," and perhaps most important, that "John Wesley has made a contribution to theology no less important than his contribution to practical Christianity" (vi-viii). He was rightly disturbed about the "parsimony of genuine scholarship" exhibited by most writing about Wesley, writing which is generally characterized, he said, by an "enormous amount of copying."

As the title of his book indicates, Cell was a self-conscious revisionist. However, the value of his work rests not so much in his revisionist conclusions as in his bringing the issues into sharp focus. He is the first to attempt an analysis of Wesley's understanding of salvation in the light of historic Christian theologies. Not only do we see Kempis, Law, Taylor, and the other traditional Wesley sources march across the pages of this book, but also St. Francis, Abelard, Aquinas, Erasmus, Eckhardt, and a host of others. In the end, Cell dismisses Piette's view of Wesley's theology and spiritual development as being based on an inadequate understanding of Protestant theology. Cell's own conclusions might at places also be challenged (such as his seeing an essential unity between Wesleyanism and Calvinism), and his method might at points be criticized (such as his discarding of Wesley's own corrections to the *Journal* in 1775). However, Cell's argument is carefully conceived, clearly stated, and, though limited in scope, intentionally provocative; it is an important step toward seeing Wesley in a larger context. His most notable conclusion is the idea that Wesley's teaching was "a necessary synthesis of the Protestant ethic of grace with the Catholic ethic of holiness" (361). Like many other propositional statements that have the ring of truth, this sentence would be repeated many times over by well-meaning persons who were both unfamiliar with Cell's own qualifications to this idea and unaware of the many earlier expressions of this synthesis within the "holy living" traditions of both Catholicism and Protestantism.

Umphrey Lee (*John Wesley and Modern Religion*, 1936), professor of homiletics (later president) at Southern Methodist University, agreed with many of Cell's ideas but challenged the implicit neo-orthodox (Barthian) assumptions that lay behind the work. "The real Wesley," for Lee, is not a Calvinist and must not be limited to the boundaries of his message to the eighteenth century; neither is the key to Wesley's importance to be found in his influence upon the nineteenth century. His real significance is in the possible contributions he can make to a fuller understanding of "modern liberal religion." Lee was one of the few authors during the 1930s who chose not to see 1738 as a singular watershed in Wesley's life that marked the end of his spiritual crisis. Lee chose rather to note that crises continued to appear in Wesley's life after Aldersgate and that Wesley's theology continued to mature throughout his life.

William R. Cannon (*The Theology of John Wesley*, 1946), later the dean of Candler School of Theology, Emory University, also challenged Dr. Cell's conclusion that Wesley simply renewed the Luther-Calvin view of salvation; he especially disagreed with Cell's alignment of Wesley with Calvinism. Concerned about the challenge to theology from both "the extremes of Barthianism and militant Catholicism," Cannon systematically defends the more traditional Wesley of Methodist legend. His work analyzes the repercussions of "the one central truth" that possessed Wesley—that man is justified by faith and perfected in love." Cannon sees the theology that Wesley developed from this one central theme as an expression of a "middle way," a way that has ecumenical value within the theological dialogue of the twentieth century.

Franz Hildebrandt, a German Lutheran who found refuge among the Methodists in England, continued this line of theological discussion in his work, *From Luther to Wesley* (1951). In this book he tried to graft Wesley even more firmly to the Lutheran trunk than had Cell.

These works by Piette, Cell, Cannon, and Hildebrandt are typical of the theological studies on Wesley that began to appear in the second quarter of the century. Although not biographies of Wesley, they contributed to the overall attempt to understand Wesley by trying to comprehend his thought in a much more adequate fashion than the biographers had ever attempted.

At midcentury, the theological studies on Wesley began to develop along two lines. In the first category, the question of the theological relationships between Wesley and various segments of the Christian tradition were examined in several studies: Clifford W. Towlson, *Moravian and Methodist* (1957); John Brazier Green, *John Wesley and William Law* (1945); John M. Todd, *John Wesley and the Catholic Church* (1958); Robert Monk, *John Wesley, His Puritan Heritage* (1966); Frank Baker, *John Wesley and the Church of England* (1970). Jean Orcibal, in the *Revue de l'Histoire des Religions* (January 1951), and Robert Tuttle, in *John Wesley* (1978), looked at Wesley's relationship to the mystical traditions. Martin Schmidt examined Wesley in the light of the German Pietist influence upon him in *John Wesley* (vol. I, 1953; English ed., 1963). Albert C. Outler, in *John Wesley* (1964), broached new lines of enquiry into the sources of Wesley's thought, especially the early church fathers.

In a second category of theological inquiry during the middle decades of this century, many studies analyzed specific elements of Wesley's thought, especially key doctrines. However, since the primary interest in this essay is biographical studies, we can only pause to note these theological works, each of which is described quite adequately in the annotated bibliographies by Norwood (1959, 1972), Melton (1969), and Baker (1980), listed in the bibliography of this book. A sample list of the more important monographic studies would include the following: Harald Lindstrom on sanctification (1946), John Deschner on Christology (1960), Lycurgus Starkey on the Holy Spirit (1962), Albert Lawson on the ministry (1963), John Parris (1963) and Ole Borgen (1972) on the sacraments, John Rattenbury (1941) and John C. Bowmer (1951) on the Eucharist, Leo Cox (1964) and John L. Peters (1956) on Christian perfection, and A. Skevington Wood on evangelism (1967). Colin Williams dealt with most of these topics in his summary analysis, *John Wesley's*

Theology Today (1960) another attempt after Cannon to see the value of Wesley's thought for ecumenical dialogue.

Special studies have also appeared during the last few decades on the relationship of Wesley to the literature, science, music, society, medicine, and politics of his day. These are also described in the annotated bibliographies listed below. Many short studies of this sort have appeared in the periodical literature: *Proceedings of the Wesley Historical Society, London Quarterly and Holborn Review, Methodist History, Wesleyan Journal of Theology,* and a host of professional society journals. What is important, and becoming increasingly obvious, is that Wesley has in the last few years become a focus of interest for a widening circle of specialists in a variety of fields. While more than half of the studies on Wesley done during the 1940s and 1950s were published by the denominational presses in England or America, a much larger percentage has more recently been published by presses independent of the mainline Methodist tradition. In addition to these monographs and articles, nearly three dozen dissertations have been written on topics directly related to Wesley in the last twenty-five years.

What is alarming, however, is that biographers have continued to publish lives of Wesley without considering these specialist studies. Since the 1930s, at the same time as these many studies were being produced, the biographers have repeated the old tales about Wesley as though nothing had been written since Tyerman's or Simon's biography and Curnock's edition of the *Journal.* Typical of the attitude among writers is that of Francis J. McConnell, bishop of the Methodist Episcopal Church and social activist. In his biography, *John Wesley* (1939), McConnell is quick to deny the need for interpretation or "higher criticism" of Wesley's writings. It is as though all one needs to write Wesley's biography is a copy of his journal. McConnell does, however, continually give interpretations of his own. And if these ideas happen to differ from the conclusions of previous biographers, he takes them to task. For example, he comments that "Mrs. Harrison's imagination was not deep but fast," a well-deserved jab at his contemporary, Elsie Harrison. In her book, *Son to Susanna* (1938), Harrison manipulated historical facts rather loosely to fit her own psychological preconceptions in her somewhat sensationalist view of Wesley's relationship with his parents. It seems the psychohistorians have always been better psychologists than historians, even when their psychology has not been adequate. McConnell, no historical specialist himself, had been a student of Borden Parker Bowne at Boston University, and his work radiates the "personalist" philosophy that was typical of the Boston school. He emphasizes a Wesley who was "profoundly interested in human values" and the "release of higher human possibilities" (page 310). McConnell's was the most popular life of Wesley for at least two decades. Its liberal bent echoed the growing mind-set of The Methodist Church and particularly its national bureaucracy; it became required reading in the denomination's ministerial Course of Study for many years after the union of 1939.

The human side of Wesley was also the focus of another popular biography, Umphrey Lee's *The Lord's Horseman* (1954). The work had first been published over twenty-five years earlier, before he had become president of Southern Methodist University. In the preface to this revised edition, Lee points out that no one need apologize for writing yet another biography of a person who was one of the most interesting of men, a rationale reflected in the subtitle for this revision, *John Wesley, the Man.* In spite of the many studies written in the quarter century between editions of his work, Lee overlooks them all in favor of repeating the twice-told tales from the nineteenth century. The same sort of reissue with no revision can be seen in the appearance of Garth Lean's *Strangely Warmed: The Amazing Life of John Wesley* (1979), a reprinted earlier work (*John Wesley, Anglican,* 1964) unrevised except for a snappier title.

The continuing tendency to base Wesley biographies on stereotypes from the past is given explicit license in *John Wesley and His World,* by John Pudney (1979), and *John Wesley,* by Stanley Ayling (1979). Ayling pronounces in the preface that a new biography, "even using for the most part evidence which has not greatly changed, is likely to prove significantly different from a view of fifty or a hundred years ago" (page 9). In the end, however, the view looks remarkably like the many other pictures of Wesley that emphasize his "human side." Aside from a heavy reliance on V. H. H. Green's work, *The Young Mr. Wesley* (1961) for his view of the early years, Ayling's acknowledged obligations rest primarily upon the works of Tyerman, Telford, Curnock, and Simon, who he admits were "immoderately reverential" in their treatment of Wesley. Ayling's work is a good example of a very readable biography, but one that has very little perception of the workings of Wesley's mind. In the few comments attempted on Wesley's theology, the author confirms our suspicion that he did not read the one theological study listed in his bibliography, much less Wesley's theological writings. Pudney's work, though just as readable as Ayling's, is much shorter and fails in nearly all the same ways, except that the illustrations in Pudney's book are excellent, both in selection and reproduction.

Two works, by Green and Schmidt, stand out from most other biographical studies of Wesley in the mid-twentieth century. V. H. H. Green, while he was Senior Tutor of Lincoln College, Oxford, published his work, *The Young Mr. Wesley* (1961), after studying the Wesley diaries for several months with the help of the Rev. Wesley Swift, then Archivist of The Methodist Church in Great Britain. The Archives had only recently been opened to the public under new policies initiated by the book steward, Frank H. Cumbers. Though their work was not without error, Green and Swift managed to progress beyond the attempt of Curnock to decipher the early diaries, and Green's use of these materials, along with his familiarity with the history of Oxford, adds significantly to the store of information about Wesley that is now available. Unfortunately, Green did not use Wesley's fifth Oxford diary (1734–35) in his work, nor did he have the benefit of later researches that discovered a "key" to Wesley's diary method. Nevertheless, by using these primary materials, he made a major contribution to the biographical studies of the early Wesley, which he later incorporated into his modestly sized and excellently balanced biography of Wesley's whole life, *John Wesley* (1964).

Another major contribution to biographical studies of Wesley in the mid-twentieth century was the work of Martin Schmidt, a German Lutheran who, while professor of church history at the University of Mainz in Germany, wrote a two-volume study, *John Wesley* (1953–66; English ed., 1963–73). The results of Schmidt's extensive primary research in the archives at Halle and Herrnhut add greatly to our understanding of the German Pietist (Moravian and Salzburger) influence upon Wesley. Most of Schmidt's original contribution is found in the first volume of his work, the English translation of which is subtitled *A Theological Biography*.

Many works in recent years have attempted to capture some special feature of Wesley's life and thought or some particular relationship he had with the world about him. Many of these simply use the triumphalist framework evident in most of the available biographies. Even some of the attempts to apply scientific or psychological theories to the study of Wesley founder in the end because of their facile adoption of parts of the continuing Wesley legend. Nearly all of the authors try to reveal the "real" John Wesley without even realizing why he is in many ways so elusive to their grasp.

Part of the problem today is that the legend of Wesley the cult hero is a powerful part of the continuing tradition. Only slight straying from the facts can lead to some rather astounding statements that might sound good (or even true) but do not coincide with reality. Within just the last generation, I have heard or read many such comments about Wesley. These show that the legend is still growing and that even intelligent, well-trained persons can feel completely free of the constraint of historicity when speaking about Wesley. The following list is just a sample of statements collected from recent writers and speakers (many of them preachers):

—After the rescue of John from the rectory fire in 1709, Susanna knelt down *on the very spot* and dedicated him to God anew, saying he was "plucked as a brand from [*sic*] the burning."

—John was not the first Methodist; Charles Wesley founded the Holy Club before John returned to Oxford to take over the group.

—Before his Aldersgate experience, John Wesley could do nothing *right;* afterwards, he could do nothing *wrong.*

—Wesley was a genius in matters of organization though he was not much of a theologian.

—Wesley was one of the greatest preachers that ever lived.

Perhaps some of these involve only slight exaggerations and twisting of the facts. But only a slight exaggeration or twist in another direction would give a picture of Wesley similar to some of the crude attacks made upon him in the eighteenth century (see Part II). I have heard recent comments that claim Wesley controlled the mobs by demanding deference from the lower classes in return for his pious indications of love and concern. I have heard Wesley referred to as "an impertinent little jerk," a comment that could possibly be substantiated with chapter and verse if one were so inclined.

The radical distortions in either direction do not appear in the better biographies, such as Green's or Schmidt's. But they live on in the oral tradition and seem to grow with the years. The "popular" biographies seem to be the ones that feed this desire to build the legend. The works of Franklin Wilder on the Wesley family (e.g., *Immortal Mother*, 1967; *The Remarkable World of John Wesley*, 1978) are examples of well-intended, if triumphalist, hagiography, while works like Willie Snow Ethridge's *Strange Fires* (1971) and John Drakeford's *Take Her, Mr. Wesley* (1973) take the Wesley story beyond reality into the realm of the historical novel.

But the story of John Wesley needs no exaggeration to make it exciting; the image of Wesley needs no tinsel halo to indicate his spiritual genius; the stature of Wesley needs no pedestal to bring him into the purview of the centuries. Wesley's place in history is secure without the well-meaning help of his latter-day hagiographers. The real John Wesley is in many ways a heroic figure without any artificial attempts at exaggeration. Wesley's good image can survive the scrutiny that will reveal the frailties of his humanity and the limitations of his century.

Biographers from Watson to Ayling have said that a new look at the old Wesley has some value in itself, which may be true to some extent. But simply putting the old story in a new garb will never result in a really adequate portrayal of Wesley for any age. The many attempts of past biographers, however inadequate, may, if critically examined, help guide future writers from making the same mistakes. We do not need another attempt that exhibits the rhetorical or literary flair of the author better than the life and thought of John Wesley. We do not need another attempt to portray in Wesley the roots of some present-day sectarian peculiarities. We do need an attempt to see Wesley whole, considering his sources, his times, his controversies, his thought, his development, his private and public images, and his observers, friend and foe.

CHAPTER 35

Seeing Wesley Whole:
Toward a New Synthesis

Professor Frank Baker of Duke University began his survey of twenty years of Wesley studies (1980, see bibliography below) by stating that "no biography has captured the man whole, even though the first-rate biography is now becoming a possibility." Nearly fifty years earlier, Maximin Piette had noted the absence of a standard biography of Wesley. Nothing has appeared since then to alter that judgment. But the time approaches when the elements necessary for such a biography will be available and we can begin to hope for such a work.

At the Seventh Oxford Institute of Methodist Theological Studies (1982), Professor Albert C. Outler of Southern Methodist University pointed out the need for a "really solid, critical, and credible biography" as part of a new agenda for Wesley studies. He stressed the necessity of a fundamental new direction for Wesley studies if the field was to be rescued from "the cultists, the antiquarians, the monographers, and the coterie theologians." And although not all the sources are in place at the moment to allow for the definitive biography, a beginning certainly has been made toward that goal.

Toward the end of the twentieth century, several works contributed to a newer understanding of Wesley in his context. The biography by Henry Rack, *Reasonable Enthusiast* (1989, revised edition 2002), represents a major step in that direction. His work is not only comprehensive but also displays a wide range of scholarship that contributes important referents for crucial issues. Richard Heitzenrater's *Wesley and the People Called Methodists* (1995) presents the biographical material in the specific context of the rise and development of the Methodist movement—its organization, theology, and mission. Editions of this work have been, or are being, translated into Portuguese, Spanish, Korean, Japanese, Russian, and Bulgarian. These will allow current Wesley scholarship to be shared more broadly around the globe.

Specialist studies on Wesley continue to proliferate, advancing our knowledge in many areas. Of particular value in this scholarly enterprise has been the support of Abingdon Press through its Kingswood Books imprint, organized by Rex D. Matthews, Academic Editor, in 1988 to publish scholarly works in Wesley and Methodist studies. In its first dozen years, that series has produced about two dozen titles, contributing immensely to our knowledge of the Wesleyan heritage in many particular areas, from doctrine and theology to hymns and liturgy. A new generation of scholars have been able to contribute to the ongoing effort to discover and recapture the heart of the tradition. Of special importance in this effort is the work of historians and theologians such as Randy L. Maddox, Scott J. Jones, Ted A. Campbell, Kenneth J. Collins, and W. Stephen Gunter. Maddox's book *Responsible Grace* (1994) and Collins's *The Scripture Way of Salvation* (1997) are examples of such resources that have contributed significantly to a deeper understanding of Wesley's theology.

Beyond that particular series, other recent works have also made important contributions. Theodore Jennings (*Good News to the Poor,* 1990) continues to stress Wesley's economic ethics, as seen in his involvement with the poor. Paul Wesley Chilcote's work, *John Wesley and the Women Preachers of Early Methodism* (1991), is an important step toward recapturing the whole history of Methodism, including the women. Others are also beginning to contribute to this effort, begun by Zechariah Taft and Abel Stevens in the nineteenth century and furthered by Maldwyn Edwards in *My Dear Sister* (1980). Much work remains to be done in this field.

Ted Runyon has provided an update of Colin Williams's work in his study, *The New Creation* (1999), which applies Wesleyan principles to current situations, reflected by his borrowing of Williams's title for his own subtitle—*John Wesley's Theology Today*. John Cobb's work, *Grace and Responsibility: A Wesleyan Theology for Today* (1995) represents a similar attempt to bring Wesley to bear on issues in the contemporary context, howbeit with a "process theology" approach. A series of works published by Scarecrow Press as "Pietist and Wesleyan Studies" includes a growing list of works by an ever-broadening list of scholars in the Wesleyan traditions, such as J. Steven O'Malley, Henry H. Knight, Diana LeClerc, Tore Meistad, Laurence W. Wood, Gregory S. Clapper, Richard B. Steele, and Charles Yrigoyen.

The broadening of Wesley studies into other disciplines, and the interest of scholars from other fields, is in part the result of the establishment in the 1980s of a Wesleyan Studies Working Group within the structure of the American Academy of Religion. Papers at those meetings have been given by people whose academic *pied-à-terre* lies outside what would traditionally be understood as "Wesley studies"—literature, political theory, ethics, music, and gender studies. This cross-pollination has enhanced all the disciplines involved, but most particularly has given Wesley studies a much needed broader horizon. The same can be said from a denominational point of view, namely that discussions within groups that contain scholars from more than one "Methodist" denomination are often much richer in nature.

Institutionally, one group that has broadened and deepened the study of Wesley over the last generation has been the Oxford Institute for Methodist Theological Studies. Formed in the 1950s by Dow Kirkpatrick as a means of gathering Methodist theologians from around the world at the place where Wesley learned his theology, the Institute has met about every five years at one of the colleges of Oxford University. Since the 1980s, the agenda has included "working groups," one of which is in Wesley Studies and Early Methodism. During the last two decades of the century, the Institute as a whole increasingly focused its attention on Wesley as a source for understanding the Methodist heritage, with perspectives contributed from around the globe. The major lectures, edited and published by Ted Runyon and Doug Meeks over that period, have provided valuable insights from these discussions that increasingly demonstrate how voices can speak from a variety of locations and how perspectives from a diversity of backgrounds can help us understand what Wesley was trying to say and do.

On a smaller scale, programs in a number of regional societies, institutes, and seminars have begun to provide increasing opportunities for serious Wesley scholarship. Such organizations as the John Wesley Institute in Illinois and the Wesley Historical Society in Virginia exemplify groups that exist in several other parts of the country also. Centers for Wesleyan and Methodist studies, under a variety of names, exist at several academic institutions, including Southern Methodist University, Duke University, Drew University, Point Loma Nazarene University, Northwest Nazarene University, Oxford Brookes University, and Aoyama Gakuin University, Tokyo.

Tools to help scholars in the research of the Wesleyan heritage have increased significantly in the last few years. Betty M. Jarboe produced a comprehensive work entitled *John and Charles Wesley: A Bibliography* (1987), which lists a variety of materials about the Wesleys, including books, articles, dissertations, drama, fiction, and juvenile literature. She also produced a very helpful list of *Wesley Quotations* (1990), which provides the locations for a bookful of useful quotations on some two hundred topics. Samuel J. Rogal has also produced books that collect material on the Wesleys, including their travels and their writings. The Internet has become a useful tool as well, with a variety of sites providing such things as exhibits of Wesley materials (Rylands University Library of Manchester), collections of his writings (Northwest Nazarene University), links to Wesley sites on the Internet (Duke University), and a variety of related materials.

As Outler and others have realized for some time, of crucial importance to a definitive Wesley biography is a truly "critical" edition of Wesley's works, an edition that contains a reliable text of his writings, free from the accumulated errors of past editors and typographers. Professors Baker and Outler were instrumental in the initiation in the 1960s of a project to prepare such an edition and were part of the international team of scholars that began producing the new edition of Wesley's works. Undertaken in the first instance by

Oxford University Press, the project is now continuing at Abingdon Press under the title, *The Bicentennial Edition of the Works of John Wesley*. This edition provides for the first time a definitive text of Wesley's writings. It also identifies the sources of Wesley's many uncited quotations, providing a clearer panorama over the vast reservoir of literature within which his thought was nourished and out of which his actions flowed. Wide-ranging introductions and annotations to these works paint the backdrop against which Wesley was thinking and working, and sketch the broader context of historical events within which Wesley must be seen in order to be fully understood. In this edition, the publications of the Wesleys are carefully categorized for the first time: original writings of the Wesleys, writings of other authors abridged or extracted by Wesley, writings of other authors published with little or no alteration by Wesley.

The new edition of the *Works* was but half finished at the turn of the twenty-first century, but the importance of these volumes has become evident in their broad use as a definitive work. Of special importance to the biographical study of Wesley, the seven volumes of *Journal and Diaries*, edited by W. Reginald Ward (journals) and Richard P. Heitzenrater (diaries), not only provide an accurate text of the journal and scholarly annotations based on current research, but also contain transcriptions of Wesley's diaries for the correlative period. Ward's general introduction to the material breaks new ground in placing Wesley's journalistic writings in the context of eighteenth-century autobiographical work, and the footnotes to the journal evidence an incredible research journey into collateral primary sources as well as current scholarship. Wesley's diaries are of crucial importance to a study of his life and thought; previous editions of the *Journal* have included only part of the extant diaries, and these in somewhat inaccurate transcriptions. The diary material in these volumes, much more accurate than the text that Curnock published nearly a hundred years earlier, provides a virtual databank of information for the period of Wesley's life that it covers—1735–41 and 1782–91.

The Bicentennial Edition of the Works of John Wesley also includes new material previously unpublished, including many manuscript letters, sermons, diaries, and treatises. The Oxford diaries (1725–35), never before published, will open a new window into the ten-year period that saw the incubation of Methodism. Several of Wesley's early sermons appear in this edition for the first time, in the four volumes edited by Albert C. Outler. And the volumes of *Letters,* begun by Frank Baker, include not only many newly discovered letters, an increase of nearly one third over the last collected edition, but also many letters written to Wesley, which elucidate the context of his own writing. These examples of the wealth of material still coming to light typify the degree to which the new edition will add detailed information to our knowledge of Wesley.

Interest in providing Wesleyan sources for scholars has broadened to include Charles Wesley materials. The Charles Wesley Society was organized by S T Kimbrough in the later 1980s to promote the publication and dissemination of Charles's works. The result has been a number of fine facsimile publications, especially of hymn collections, with scholarly notes. Charles's work in the area of poetry and hymns was often a joint venture with John. The Society is also preparing for publication a new and complete edition of Charles's journal, as well some materials never before published—his journal-letters and the long-anticipated publication of an edition of his letters, the result of a lifetime of collecting by Frank Baker, one of the charter members of the Society.

The latter part of the twentieth century also witnessed a major expansion of interest in translating Wesleyan materials into other languages. Largely through the organizing efforts of L. Elbert Wethington, through the Wesley Heritage Foundation he and his wife Lois established, and with the editorial leadership of Justo L. González and a team of scholars, a major portion of Wesley's writings were translated into Spanish. Published as a fourteen-volume set, *Obras de Wesley* (1996–2000), this project was designed "for the promotion of Wesley thought and spirituality in Latin America." Similar projects are contemplated or underway in Korea, China, Russia, Germany, and other countries, as Methodists worldwide develop a lively interest in Wesley's life and thought as a crucial part of their own self-understanding.

The biographer's concern for sources, however, goes beyond the need for a better edition of Wesley's works. The biographer also requires a good grasp of Wesley's own sources to achieve an adequate perception of the man. Of crucial importance to the task of discerning John Wesley's contribution, then, is a knowledge of Scripture, a grasp of the history of Christian thought, and an understanding of classical education. These sources furnished the matrix within which Wesley expressed himself, and his writings and actions cannot be understood apart from the traditions within which he was nurtured and from which he derived his spiritual and intellectual sustenance. A grasp of Wesley's relationship to his sources is necessary to the development of an adequate hermeneutic for understanding Wesley's own writings.

An adequate biography of Wesley will not be limited, however, by the perimeters of his own writings, or even by the boundaries of his own movement. Expanding the horizons of analysis into the larger picture of the history of classical and Christian thought is a good start toward breaking Wesley out of the bonds of being considered simply as a church founder or a religious hero. The eighteenth century was an age of revolution in many fields that touched Wesley directly, even though he seems at times to have been oblivious to these changes. Developments in industry, politics, music, philosophy, literature, technology, science, medicine, and economics all left their mark on his life as well as his times. The transitions in English culture that these changes wrought cannot be overlooked in a careful analysis of Wesley's life.

Once the backdrop is carefully in place in the mind of the biographer, then Wesley himself must be scrutinized. The base upon which all else stands is a full outline of the events of his life. Sequential accuracy is essential to an understanding of Wesley's development. Incredible as it may sound, some of the chronological detail of Wesley's life is only now becoming clear through newly discovered letters and recently deciphered diaries. These details provide the framework within which Wesley, the person, can be placed. The human Wesley should always stand in the center of the picture, but a fascination with his personal idiosyncrasies should not predominate the scene. His main significance, then or now, rests not in his private meanderings, but in his thoughts and actions that touch upon the concerns of other persons.

The development of Wesley's thought and its relationship to his actions are an essential part of the story. Wesley's thought must be seen in the context of his day-to-day activities, a somewhat obvious but often overlooked fact. His theology must be appreciated as a living and growing body of thought and method of thinking, directly related to his continuing intellectual and spiritual pilgrimage. In this lifelong process, the early Wesley and the later Wesley are as important in the story as the middle Wesley. No one has yet done an adequate analysis of Wesley's thought that examines the sequence of development in the context of his reading and writing as well as of the various controversies and other events that affected his ideas from time to time. Within such a historical perspective, the sources for, and purposes of, Wesley's writings would come more clearly into focus and would lead to a more adequate understanding of Wesley's thought.

The complex task of analysis in all these fields may seem like more than one person could ever do. Such is the case. The biographer cannot do all the primary research that is necessary for an adequate biography. There are tasks to be done by people in many fields— theology, musicology, psychology, sociology, demography, philosophy, literary criticism, political science, history (of several topics, including science and technology) and perhaps others. But in the end, the biography of Wesley cannot be left solely to any one of these fields. The psychologists do not often have an adequate historical consciousness. The historians do not generally understand the subtleties of theology. The theologians tend to overlook the mundane statistics of the social scientists. The musicians often live in a world of rhythm and sound rather than of persons and places. The special tasks are best done by the specialists, but the specialists can make a better contribution if they understand and appreciate the wider ramifications of the enterprise as a whole.

Samuel Bradburn, in his eulogy of Wesley, implied that it would take a person very much like the man himself to do justice to Wesley's biography. Given the complexities and confusion in Wesley's own attempts at self-understanding, we might hope for more clarity from a current biographer than we get from Wesley as his own biographer. But we seek more than just a perceptive appreciation of Wesley's life and thought. The sensitivities and wide-ranging interests requisite to the task of catching the fullness of the elusive Mr. Wesley are considerable, for we expect the biographer to acknowledge Wesley's contributions to ongoing traditions in the light of his debts to the past, to appreciate his energy and perception within the limitations of his age, and to discern his significance in the larger scope of human history. In the end, we call upon the biographer to put together a credible, insightful, edifying, and accurate work that not only displays Wesley as he saw himself and as others saw him, but also brings his living presence into focus in and for our own time.

Selected Bibliography
of Bibliographies

Abbreviations   *AM—Arminian Magazine*
                   MA—Methodist Archives, the John Rylands University
                       Library of Manchester
                   WHS—Proceedings of the Wesley Historical Society
                   WMM—Wesleyan Methodist Magazine

Archibald, F. A. *Methodism and Literature.* Cincinnati: Walden and Stowe, 1883.

Baker, Frank, compiler. *A Union Catalogue of the Publications of John and Charles Wesley.* Durham, N.C.: Duke University, 1966.

———. *A Union Catalogue of the Publications of John and Charles Wesley,* 2d ed. rev., Stone Mountain, Ga.: George Zimmerman, 1991.

———. "Unfolding John Wesley: A Survey of Twenty Years' Studies in Wesley's Thought." *Quarterly Review* 1 (1980): 44-58.

Bowmer, John C. "Twenty-five Years (1943–68): Methodist Studies." *WHS* 37 (October 1969): 61-66.

Collins, Kenneth J. "Wesley Bibliography." Asbury Theological Seminary Library Web Site. http://www.ats.wilmore.ky.us/news/publications/wesley_bib/

Field, Clive D. "Bibliography," Part Two of *A History of the Methodist Church in Great Britain,* vol. 4. London: Epworth Press, 1988, 651-830.

———. "Bibliography of Methodist Historical Literature," *WHS,* annually in the June or September issue since 1976.

Fortney, Edward L. "The Literature of the History of Methodism." *Religion in Life* 24 (Summer 1955): 443-51.

Green, Richard. "A List (Chiefly) of Published Biographies and Biographical Notices of John Wesley." *WHS* 3 (1902): 217-36.

———. *Anti-Methodist Publications Issued during the Eighteenth Century.* London, 1902.

———. *Anti-Methodist Publications Issued during the Eighteenth Century.* New York: B. Franklin, 1973.

———. *The Works of John and Charles Wesley: A Bibliography.* London, 1896.

———. *The Works of John and Charles Wesley: A Bibliography,* 2d ed. London, 1906.

———. *The Works of John and Charles Wesley: A Bibliography.* New York: AMS Press, 1976.

Harrison, A. W. "Fifty Years of Studies in Methodist History." *WHS* 24 (June 1943): 17-25.

Jarboe, Betty M. *John and Charles Wesley: A Bibliography*. Metuchen, N.J.: Scarecrow Press, 1987.

Judson, Sandra. "Biographical and Descriptive Notes on the Rev. John Wesley." Dip. in Librarianship thesis, University of London, 1963.

Loring, Herbert R. "A Comparison of the Biographies of John Wesley since 1850 in the Light of Biographical and Critical Materials." Th.D. dissertation, Boston University, 1951.

McCullah, Thomas. "Biographers of Wesley." *London Quarterly Review* 97 (1902): 129-52.

Maser, Frederick E. "The Early Biographers of John Wesley." *Methodist History* 1 (1963): 29-42.

Melton, J. Gordon. "An Annotated Bibliography of Publications about the Life and Work of John Wesley." *Methodist History* 7 (1969): 29-46.

Norwood, Frederick A. "Methodist Historical Studies, 1930–1959." *Church History* 28 (December 1959): 391-417.

———. "Wesleyan and Methodist Historical Studies, 1960–1970, A Bibliographical Article." *Methodist History* 10 (January 1972): 23-44.

Rogal, Samuel J. "The Wesleys: A Checklist of Critical Commentary." *Bulletin of Bibliography and Magazine Notes* 28 (January-March 1971): 22-35.

Rowe, Kenneth E., ed. *The Place of Wesley in the Christian Tradition*, rev. ed. Metuchen, N.J.: Scarecrow Press, 1976.

———. *Methodist Union Catalog, pre-1976 Imprints*. Metuchen, N.J.: Scarecrow Press, 1975.

———. *United Methodist Studies: Basic Bibliographies*. Nashville: Abingdon Press, 1998.

See also:

"Checklist of Doctoral Dissertations on Methodist and Related Subjects." *Methodist History*, annually in the April or July issue from 1970 to 1979.

Index

Abbot, Robert, 292
Abelard, 379
Aglionby, William, 117
Aldersgate, 34, 37, 90, 99, 258-63, 347, 354, 357, 366, 377-78, 380, 385
Ambitious Stepmother, 56
American Academy of Religion, 389
Anabaptists, 119
Angels, 107, 144, 193-94, 245, 267
Anti-Methodist literature, 24-25, 29-30, 226-29, 252-54, 270-72, 283-93, 295-303, 304-13, 317-25, 327-28, 357, 371, 396
Antinomianism, 204, 283-84, 287-88, 292, 310, 313, 366
Aoyama Gakuin University, 390
Aquinas, Thomas, 379
Arabic, 54, 57
Archibald, F. A., 395
Arminian Magazine, The, 42, 45, 47, 310, 348; fig. 1, 2, 7
Arminius, Jacob, 310, 336
Arnold, Matthew, 373
Assurance, 71, 72, 90-91, 94, 96-100, 101, 188-89, 258-60, 262, 271-72, 274, 357

Augustine, 161-378
Aurora borealis, 55
Auscultator, 313
Authority, 71, 196
Ayling, Stanley, 383-84, 386

Badcock, Samuel, 44-46, 336, 340, 352
Baker, Frank, 381, 387, 390, 392, 395
Bannister, John, 125
Baptism, 94, 117-19, 297
Baptist Mills, 103-5
Barrowford, 126
Barthianism, 380
Bate, James, 297
Bath, City of, 104-5, 201, 208
Baum, J. W., 378
Benham, Daniel, 264
Bennett, John, 167-76
Benson, Joseph, 276, 346-49, 356-57, 363
Bethlehem Hospital (Bedlam), 296-97, 299-302
Beveridge, William, 92, 173
Bible. *See* Scripture(s)
Bibliographical studies, 364, 368, 371
Birmingham, 121, 269

Blackwell, Ebenezer, 183
Blackwell, Elizabeth, 182
Bocock, Richard, 126-27
Böhler, Peter, 97-98, 233, 264
Book of Common Prayer, 118
Borgen, Ole, 381
Boston University, 379, 383
Bourignon, Antoinette, 297, 302
Bowen, Marjorie, 379
Bowmer, John C., 381, 395
Bowne, Borden Parker, 383
Brackenbury, Robert Carr, 334
Bradburn, Samuel, 346-48, 394
Bradford, Joseph, 208, 330-32, 334
Bristol, 46, 102-106, 109-11, 112-13, 130, 168, 177, 183, 251-52, 337, 351
British Library, 167
Broadbent, John, 332-34
Bromley, William, fig. 9
Brown, Robert, 48-49
Brownfield, John, 249
Buckland, 55
Bunyan, John, 31
Burnside, Margaret (Mrs. James), 86
Burton, John, 45, 73, 74, 245
Butler, Joseph, 109-10

Calvin, John, 336, 378-80
Calvinisim/Calvinists, 92, 204, 283-84, 288, 292, 294, 304, 310-14, 337, 366, 379-80
Campbell, James, 251
Campbell, Ted A., 388
Cannon, William R., 380-82
Carthy, Clayton, 180
Causton, Martha (Mrs. Thomas), 81-82, 85
Causton, Thomas, 77, 80, 82, 83-87, 117, 247-50, 255
Celibacy, 77, 166
Cell, George Croft, 379-81
Chapone, Sally Kirkham (Varanese), 55-57
Charles Wesley Society, 392
Charleston, S. C., 120, 116, 254
Charterhouse (London), 52, 95, 336
Cheesebrook, Mary, 301

Cheselden, William, 228
Chilcote, Paul Wesley, 388
Christian perfection. *See* Perfection, Christian
Christie, Thomas, 253
Chrysostom, John, 221, 275
Church, Leslie, 379
Church, Thomas, 284-88
Church of England, 109-10, 117-19, 125, 202-4, 224, 233, 264, 271, 272-74, 284, 288, 337, 358, 365, 381
City Road Chapel, 330-32, 341, 345, 351, 355
Clapper, Gregory S., 389
Clarke, Adam, 341, 358-60, 367; fig. 12
Clayton, John, 68-69, 102, 226
Clement of Alexandria, 145
Clement of Rome, 60-61, 82
Clifton, 103-4, 105
Coates, John, 251
Cobb, John, 389
Coke, Thomas, 207-8, 326, 339, 346-48, 351, 352-54, 360, 366
Colbeck, Thomas, 126-27
Coleridge, Samuel Taylor, 359
Colet, John Annesley, 348
Collins, Kenneth J., 338
Colloquialisms, 155
Colman, J. J., 371
Colne, 125, 269
Comets, 57
Communion. *See* Sacrament(s)
Conference, 94, 140, 167, 173, 177, 204, 207, 260, 265, 310, 331, 346, 349, 353, 356, 358-60, 363, 372
Conscience, 114, 148, 169-70, 185, 193, 196-97, 199, 223, 231, 314-15, 329
Conybeare, John, 280
Cornwall, 338
Cotswolds, 55-57
Council of Constance, 199
Council of Trent, 199, 289-90
Course of Study, 363, 368, 373, 383
Covenant, 291-92
Cowper, William, 141
Cox, Leo, 381
Creighton, James, 207-8

Crosby, Sarah, 180-83
Crowther, Jonathan, 42
Cudworth, William, 289, 293
Cumbers, Frank, 384
Curnock, Nehemiah, 371-72, 374, 382-84, 391

Darlaston, 122, 267-68
Das Gesangbuch de Gemeinde in Herrnhuth, 161
Deed of Declaration, 205, 208, 339, 350-51, 354, 360, 366
Delamotte, Miss, 261
Delamotte, William, 80-82, 245-46
Deschner, John, 381
Devil, 50-51, 65, 143-44, 150, 152, 189, 196-97, 216, 260, 274, 285, 289, 293, 297, 299, 302, 310-13
Dickinson, Peard, 207-8
Didsbury College, 371-74
Dispensaries, medical, 129-30, 316-17
Dobree, Bonamy, 379
Doctrine, 31, 33, 37-38, 64, 92, 94, 141-42, 143-45, 200, 204-5, 249, 271, 281, 284-87, 288-93, 302, 328, 332, 349, 351, 360, 363, 365, 372
Drew University, 390
Dryden, John, 156
Dublin, 63, 192, 208
Duke University, 387, 390

Early church. *See* Primitive church
Early rising, 28, 72, 122, 238, 244-45, 268, 336, 338-39, 347
Eckhardt, Meister, 379
Ecumenical movement, 37-38, 192, 368, 380-82
Edwards, Jonathan, 90
Edwards, Maldwyn, 389
Eggington, Edward, 120
Enthusiasm/Enthusiast, 29, 31, 68, 99, 112, 114, 261-62, 269-71, 280, 281, 284, 288, 297, 300, 328, 336, 347, 352, 354, 357, 368
Epworth, 41, 71, 155, 175, 213, 221, 335
rectory fire, 42-45, 218, 335, 385
rectory noises/ghost, 46-51, 352

Erasmus, "Bishop of Arcadia," 299, 306
Erasmus of Rotterdam, 379
Essenes, 227-28
Eulogies, 335, 341-42, 344-49
European Magazine, fig. 9
Evans, Billy, 189
Evans, Caleb, 298, 314
Experience, 59, 70, 94, 97-98, 99, 133, 147, 161, 188, 201, 231, 235, 239, 261

Faith, 61, 90, 92-93, 97-99, 101, 108, 134, 143, 146, 151, 177, 182, 189, 194-95, 198, 199-200, 203, 205-6, 238, 258-61, 262, 264, 267-68, 281, 282-88, 291, 329, 347, 354, 380
Fanatic Saints, The, 295, 299
Fasting, 64-65, 69, 71-72, 85, 203, 220, 227, 236, 239, 285, 300, 336
Fetter Lane Society, 264
Field, Clive D., 395-96
Fitchett, W. H., 373
Fletcher, John William, 204-6, 304, 313-15
Fog's Weekly Journal, 226-29, 230-31, 366
Foote, Samuel, 301
Fortney, Edward L., 395
Fothergill, John, 189
Foundery, Old, 128, 264, 281, 296-99, 302, 305, 307, 310, 319, 338; fig. 10
Francis, Molly, 168
Francis of Assisi, 379
Frederica, Ga., 76, 78, 83, 107-8, 119, 256

Gainsborough, 222-23
Gambold, John, 233-41
Games
Pope Joan, 57
Ombre, 57
Gandy, William, 367, 371
Gentleman's Magazine, The, 21, 45, 153, 176, 255, 283, 326, 335-40, 348
Georgia, 23, 45, 73, 74-89, 90-91, 108, 113, 115-19, 129, 161, 180, 233-34, 237, 242-57, 336, 347. *See also* Savannah, Frederica

Gerard, Mr., 66
Gerhardt, Paul, 162
Germany, 101, 109, 264-65, 337, 384
Gill, John, 337
Glanville, Joseph, 106
Glanville, William, 128
González, Justo L., 392
Gordon, George, Lord, 199
Gospel Magazine, The, 310
Gough, William, 177, 251
Grace, 73, 76, 97-99, 102, 103, 106, 141, 179, 189, 197, 206, 234, 239, 281, 283, 290-91, 296, 299, 302, 342, 380. *See also* Means of grace
Granger, James, 321
Granville, Ann (Selima), 57
Green, John Brazier, 381
Green, Richard, 368, 379, 396
Green, Vivian H. H., 383-84, 386
Grimshaw, William, 126-27, 269, 272-75
Grotius, Hugo, 221
Gunter, W. Stephen, 388

Halévy, Elie, 376-77
Hall, Martha (Patty) Wesley (Mrs. Westley), 208, 224
Hall, Westley, 61, 244, 297, 302
Hamilton, William, fig. 6
Hampson, John, 255, 277, 350-52, 354, 358, 360-61, 366; fig. 10
Hanham (Hannam) Mount, 104-5
Hargrave, James, 125
Hargreaves, Kitty, 224
Harrison, A. W., 374, 396
Harrison, Elsie, 379, 382-83
Haweis, Thomas, 276
Hawes, William, 132, 316-25
Heaven, 142-43, 147, 152, 154, 193-94, 196-97, 216, 244, 271, 278
Hebrew, 54, 176, 216, 285, 311-12
Heitzenrater, Richard, 388, 391
Hell, 93, 144, 151, 189, 192, 195, 197, 216, 285, 311-12
Henry IV, 57
Hervey, James, 240, 243, 289, 292
Heylin, Alexander, 371
Hildebrandt, Franz, 380-81

Hill, Rowland, 310, 313, 337
Hobrow, William, 346-48
Hogarth, William, 149
Holiness, 37, 71-72, 74, 78, 95, 102, 140, 146, 150-51, 194, 206, 246, 283, 290, 293, 380-81
Holy Ghost. *See* Holy Spirit
Holy living, 52-53, 58-59, 63, 113, 145, 283, 329, 380
Holy Spirit, 70, 90-91, 94, 100, 103, 106, 110, 147, 151, 193-98, 220, 259-60, 268, 274, 278-79, 293, 334, 381
Homilies, 90, 101, 118, 274
Hone, Nathaniel, fig. 5
Hoole, Joseph, 42, 49, 221
Horn, Thomas, 61
Horne, Melville, 94
Horton, John, 207, 209, 332-34
Huntingdon, Selina, Countess of, 157, 257
Huntingdon, William, 348
Hutchins, Richard, 56, 336
Hutton, Elizabeth, 99, 261-64
Hutton, James, 245, 261, 264-65
Hutton, John, 256-57, 261-64
Hutton, W. H., 378
Hymns, 153-54, 158-63, 227, 260, 281, 330-31, 334, 337-38, 364

Ignatius of Loyola, 300
Indians (American). *See* Native Americans
Ingham, Benjamin, 60, 242-46, 264
Ireland, 46, 132, 167, 170, 175, 183, 191-92, 203, 205, 280, 337
Islington, 109

Jackson, John, 362-63; fig. 14
Jackson, Thomas, 363-64, 372
James, William, 378
Janson, K. A., 280
Jarboe, Betty, 390
Jennings, Theodore, 388
Jesuit Detected, The, 288-93
John Wesley Institute, 390
Johnson, Samuel, 16, 304-9
Jones, John, 183, 190

Jones, John (Dublin), 355
Jones, Joseph, 180
Jones, Scott J., 388
Judson, Sandra, 396
Justification, 98, 189, 284-85, 287, 288-92, 313, 337, 347

Keith, Jane, 172
Kelly, Charles H., 371
Kennicott, Benjamin, 278-80
Kenton, James, 346-47
Kimbrough, ST, 392
Kingswood, 46, 105, 141, 168, 173, 180, 181, 207-8, 338
Kirkham, Betty (Athenais), 55-57
Kirkham, Robert, 65
Kirkham, William, 131
Kirkpatrick, Dow, 389
Knight, Henry H., 389
Knox, Alexander, 145, 149, 178, 359
Knox, Ronald, 31
Koker, Dr., 173
Koran, 199

Lane, J., 122
Laver, James, 399
Law
    divine, 58, 69, 70, 96-97, 99, 143, 146, 148, 265, 283, 285, 288, 291-93
    human, 111, 118, 126-27, 167, 170, 218, 308
Law, William, 95-96, 229, 336, 379, 381
Lawson, Albert, 381
Lean, Garth, 383
Lecky, William, 368, 376
Leclerc, Diana, 389
Lee, Umphrey, 379-80, 383
Leeds, 128, 172, 174-75, 190
Lefevre, Mrs., 182
Léger, Augustin, 167, 377-78
Lelièvre, Matthew, 368, 376
Lewis, David, 157
Lewisham, 187
Ley, William, 281
Liden, Johan Henrik, 280-81
Lindstrom, Harald, 381
Lipsky, Abram, 379

Lloyd, Henry, 116, 254
Lockhart, John Gibson, 358
London, 46, 51, 52, 63, 68, 97, 103, 105, 109, 112, 128, 130, 139, 167, 173, 176-77, 181, 183, 185, 188, 203, 207-8, 213, 244, 261-62, 265, 273, 280, 301, 316, 338
London Magazine, 176
London Quarterly and Holborn Review, 382
Loring, Herbert R., 396
Lots, 72, 81, 302
Love feast, 104, 296, 298
Love of God, 77, 100, 102, 144, 145, 147-48, 151-52, 161-63, 195, 197-98, 290, 332, 378
Lunn, Arnold, 379
Luther, Martin, 44, 98, 103, 377-80
Lutheran(s), 92, 380

Macaulay, Thomas, 373
McConnell, Francis, 379, 382-83
McCullah, Thomas, 396
Maddox, Randy L., 388
Manchester, 341, 346, 371
Marriage, 79-82, 84-85, 115, 118, 146, 155, 167-75, 176-85, 337
Marriott, William, 207, 209, 332
Martindale, Miles, 346
Maser, Frederick E., 396
Mather, Alexander, 208
Matthews, Jacob, 117, 119
Matthews, Rex D., 388
Means of grace, 59, 69, 92, 96, 98, 100, 103, 264, 285. *See also* Fasting, Grace, Prayer, Sacrament(s)
Medicine. *See* Physic
Meditation, 61, 240
Meditative piety, 53
Meeks, M. Douglas, 390
Meistad, Tore, 389
Mellichamp, Thomas, 85
Melton, J. Gordon, 381, 396
Method(s), 15, 27, 31-32, 53, 59, 68, 70, 75, 102, 131, 164, 181, 203, 214, 217, 221, 230, 232, 238, 245, 253, 295, 336, 384
Methodism/Methodist(s), 15, 22, 30,

(Methodism/Methodist(s) continued)
37-38, 53, 64, 69, 75, 112, 114, 121,
130, 145-49, 176, 202-7, 225-32,
261, 269-72, 272-75, 281, 287-88,
294-95, 296, 326-28, 337, 338, 389,
391
the term "Methodist," 64, 69, 226, 336
Methodist, Calvinistic, 294, 310-11
Methodist Recorder, 371
Middleton, Conyers, 131, 145
Milton, John, 154, 161, 163-64
Minutes ("Large"), 202, 204
Minutes of Conference, 310
Mob(s), 121-25, 192, 267-69, 272, 338,
348, 386. *See also* Persecution, Riots
Monk, Robert, 381
Moore, Henry, 208, 346, 351, 352-54,
358-61, 364, 366-67
Moorfields, 264, 281, 296, 305, 338
Moravians, 90-91, 94, 96, 101, 107, 161,
233-34, 243, 245, 258, 261, 264-65,
283, 284-88, 337, 366, 381, 384
Morgan, Richard, Jr., 61, 70, 241, 245
Morgan, Richard, Sr., 63-70, 113, 229-30
Morgan, William, 63, 65, 68, 226, 235
Morley, John, 220
Munchin (George Clifton), 123, 269
Muncy, Jane, 302
Murray, Grace, 167-76, 377
Myles, William, 208
Mystics, 72, 92-93, 96, 173, 381

Native Americans, 45, 74-75, 80, 84, 88,
117, 243-44, 256, 336
Nelson, John, 175
Nelson, Robert, 92
Newcastle, 46, 128, 130, 167, 169, 171-
72, 174, 176
Nichols, John, 44, 335
Nonjurors, 92-93
Northwest Nazarene University, 390
Norwich, 183
Norwood, Frederick A., 381, 396
Nottingham, 125
Nowell, Will, 61
Nowers, Edward, 265

Obedience, 93, 95, 114, 148, 215, 219,
248, 272, 288, 291-92, 327
Oglethorpe, James, 45, 74, 83, 246, 255
"Old Jeffrey," 42, 46-51, 352
Olivers, Thomas, 346-48
O'Malley, J. Steven, 389
Opinions, 144-46, 191-92, 195, 197, 283,
286, 326, 328, 336-37, 351, 373
Orcibal, Jean, 381
Ordinances, 147, 288
Ordination(s), 105, 354, 360, 366
Origen, 228
Osborn, George, 364, 371
Ossett, Yorkshire, 243
Outler, Albert C., 381, 387, 390, 392
Overton, John H., 368
Oxford, 143, 278, 384
Bocardo gaol, 236
Castle, 47, 61, 65-66, 236
St. Mary's Church, 23, 278
Oxford Brookes University, 390
Oxford Institute of Methodist
Theological Studies, 387, 389-90
Oxford Methodists, 30, 63-73, 102, 113-
14, 149, 225, 366, 385. *See also*
Wesley, John, at Oxford
Oxford Methodists, The, 64, 114, 229-32
Oxford Movement, 365
Oxford University, 389
Brasenose College, 68, 244
Christ Church, 21, 52, 67, 236
Lincoln College, 220, 234, 336, 384
Merton College, 66, 67

Papists. *See* Roman Catholics
Paramore, George, 207
Paramore, Hannah, 207
Parker, Henry, 87, 117
Parris, John, 381
Pascal, Blaise, 58
Pawson, John, 165
Pendarves, Mary Granville (Aspasia),
57-58
Pensford, 104
Perfection, Christian, 64, 95-96, 145,
188-89, 297, 299, 302, 311-13, 318,
337, 347, 357, 381

Perkins, William, 292
Perronet, Mady, 178
Perronet, Vincent, 130, 172
Persecution/attacks, 28-29, 30-31, 71, 86, 120-28, 192, 199, 266-69, 294, 312, 344
Persehouse, William, 122
Peters, John L., 381
Physic, 22, 67, 129-39, 188, 215, 241, 296, 300-1, 316-25, 337, 357, 382
Physician(s), 57, 130-33, 300, 303, 316-19
Piette, Maximin, 377-79, 381
Pius IV, Pope, 199
Plagiarism, 304-6
Poetry. *See* Verses
Pohlhill, Nathaniel, 117-19
Point Loma Nazarene University, 390
Poor/poverty, 32, 65, 66, 88, 96, 103, 107, 129-30, 132, 140-41, 149, 157, 177, 207-8, 225, 236, 239, 271, 274, 295, 300, 306, 339, 388
Pope, 200-1, 261. *See also* Pius IV
Pope, Alexander, 154, 156
Porter, Jane (Sir Edward Seaward's *Narrative*), 367
Potter, John, 66
Pray/prayer, 49, 54, 59-61, 70, 76, 79, 82, 84, 94, 97-98, 110, 123, 134, 148, 168, 171, 176, 188, 203, 215-16, 220, 236-37, 239, 245, 259-61, 278, 281, 285, 300, 331-34, 348
Preachers, 199, 202-4, 208, 269, 271-72, 275, 301, 306, 327, 339, 349, 350, 353-55
Priestley, Joseph, 324, 351-52, 358
Primitive church, 84, 140, 173, 197, 236, 245, 342, 381
Prisons/prisoners, 47, 66, 96, 149-52, 179, 225, 236, 336
Protestants, 192-93, 195-96, 198-99, 269, 290, 377-80
Providence, 28, 42, 44, 45, 71-72, 92, 95, 108, 120-21, 123-25, 177, 186-87, 221, 223, 243-45, 342
Psalms/Psalter, 54, 84, 98, 108, 122, 153, 158-59, 218, 222, 227, 246, 259-60, 269, 281, 331, 334

Public Advertiser, The, 199
Pudney, John, 383
Purrysburg, 81, 116, 254

Quaker(s), 31, 303, 346, 354
Quarterly Review, The, 358

Rack, Henry, 388
Rankin, Thomas, 207, 209, 333
Rattenbury, John, 381
Reason, 52, 56, 59, 91-92, 114, 143, 171, 174, 189, 196, 200, 216, 229, 244, 270, 272, 312, 315, 328, 347, 354, 359
Reasonable Communicant, 61
Relief Act (1778), 198
Repentance, 95, 120, 239, 285, 288, 299
Resolutions, 52-53, 59-60, 61-62, 66, 76, 95, 234, 239
Revolution, 36. *See also* Halévy, Elie
Revolution/Rebellion (American), 22, 294, 304-9, 311, 314-15
Revue de l'Histoire des Religions, 381
Revue de Paris, 376
Rigg, James H., 368
Riots, 28, 120-28, 199, 266-69, 273. *See also* Mobs, Persecution
Ritchie, Elizabeth, 208, 329-34, 345, 348, 351
Rivington, Charles, 68
Robson, John, 60
Rodda, Richard, 345-48
Rogal, Samuel J., 390, 396
Rogers, Hester Ann, 330, 332-34
Rogers, James, 330, 332-34
Romaine, William, 277
Roman Catholics, 92, 191-201, 269, 284, 288-93, 381
Rose Green, 104-5
Roughlee, Yorkshire, 125-28, 269, 272
Rowe, Kenneth E., 396
Royal Humane Society, 317
Rule(s), 52-53, 57-58, 70-71, 87, 92-93, 100, 108, 113, 130, 146, 148, 169, 170, 188, 192, 214, 218-19, 227, 232, 303
Runyon, Theodore, 389-90

Ryan, Sarah, 180, 182-83
Ryder, Dudley, 128
Rylands University Library of
    Manchester, 390

Sacrament(s), 61, 66-69, 82, 85-87, 101,
    109, 110, 117-19, 187, 225, 236,
    239, 248, 260, 262-64, 280, 285,
    288, 336, 381
St. Dunstan's Church, 263
St. Paul's Cathedral, 98
Salisbury, Frank O., 374-75; fig. 15
Salmon, Matthew, 61, 244
Salvation, 52-53, 63, 72, 90-91, 94-100,
    101, 103, 106, 108, 111, 145, 146,
    148, 194, 203, 216, 220, 264, 274,
    281, 282-83, 285-86, 288, 292, 303,
    310, 313, 352, 354, 379-80
Salzburgers, 91, 195
Sanctification, 38, 98, 104, 145, 152,
    288, 381. *See also* Perfection,
    Christian
Satan. *See* Devil
Savannah, Ga., 75, 77-78, 83, 88, 96, 107-
    8, 113, 115-18, 243-44, 246-56
Schleiermacher, Friedrich, 378
Schmidt, Martin, 381, 384, 386
Scotland/Scots, 177, 205, 247, 337
Scott, Walter, Sir, 277
Scripture(s), 29, 44, 61, 91-93, 95, 97-98,
    103, 105, 108, 141, 142-44, 145-46,
    170, 174, 180, 199, 216, 218, 221,
    239, 245, 285-86, 289, 291-93, 312,
    359, 392
Self-examination, 52, 55, 59-62, 72
Shakespeare, William, 161, 373. *See also*
    Henry IV
Shent, William, 171-72
Simon, John S., 374, 379, 382-83
Sims-Kimbery, Joan, 155
Sin(s), 249, 277, 279
Solifidianism, 103, 283-84
South Leigh, 25
Southern Methodist University, 380,
    383, 387, 390
Southey, Robert, 94, 357, 361, 365, 368
Spenser, Edmund, 157, 161

Spitalfield, 280
Stanton, 55-57, 223
Stanton Harcourt, 233
Starkey, Lycurgus, 381
Steele, Richard B., 389
Stephen, Leslie, Sir, 373
Stephens, William, 242, 246-51
Stevens, Abel, 365, 389
Stevenson, George, 367
Stillness, 285
Sugden, Edward, 372
Superstition, 270, 272, 357
Sweden, 280-81
Swift, Wesley, 384
Swindells, Robert, 172

Taft, Zechariah, 389
Taylor, Mrs., 223-24
Taylor, Isaac, 364; fig. 10
Taylor, Jeremy, 92, 113, 329, 379
Taylor, Thomas, 346
Telford, John, 368-69, 371-73, 383
Tersteegan, Gerhardt, 161-62
Thicknesse, Philip, 242, 255-57
Thomas à Kempis, 82, 91, 95, 379
Thompson (Tompson), Richard, 337
Todd, John M., 381
Tooke, Andrew, 336
Tooker, Nancy, 55-56
Toplady, Augustus, 305-9, 310, 322-23
Towlson, Clifford W., 381
Tuttle, Robert, 381
Tyerman, Luke, 206, 295, 365-68, 371,
    374, 377, 382

Unitarian, 352, 357
Urlin, R. Denny, 367

Vazeille, Anthony, 180
Verses, 54, 153-65, 222, 294-303, 310-13,
    337
Vertue, George, fig. 3
Virtue(s), 28, 55-56, 58, 62-63, 147, 152,
    153, 240, 255-56, 285, 299, 339, 357
Vulliamy, Colwyn, 379

Walker, Thomas, 61

Walpole, Robert, 141
Walsall, 122, 267-68
Walsh, Thomas, 183
Ward, Francis, 121, 125, 268
Ward, W. Reginald, 391
Watson, Mr., 249
Watson, Richard, 358-59, 360, 363-64,
    369, 386
Way of the World, 57
Webb, Thomas, 297
Wedgewood, Julia, 368
Wednesbury, 28, 120-25, 266-69
Weekly History, 252
Welch, Ann (Mrs. John), 76
Wesleyan Journal of Theology, 382
Wesleyan Methodist Magazine, 362, 367
Wesley, Charles, 28, 30, 32, 47, 57, 60,
    64, 75, 94, 121, 143, 153, 158, 166-
    67, 172, 174-76, 180, 182, 188-90,
    213, 234-35, 240, 243-46, 257, 258-
    65, 281, 336, 338, 359, 364, 370-71,
    385
    Journal, 28, 258-61, 266-69, 392
Wesley, Emilia, 49, 222-24
Wesley family, 41-44, 47-51, 213-23, 367,
    371
Wesley, Hetty, 42, 50, 153
Wesley Heritage Foundation, 392
Wesley Historical Society, 370-71, 374
    Proceedings, 280, 363, 370, 382, 395-96
    Virginia, 390
Wesley, John, *passim*
    as bishop, 296, 299, 306-7
    as "a brand plucked . . .", 42, 44-45,
        81, 93, 187, 385
    Calm Address, 294, 304, 305-9, 311,
        314-15, 337
    Character of a Methodist, 145-49
    churchmanship, 365, 368
    "Circumcision of the Heart," 64, 226
    Collection of Forms of Prayer, 84, 239
    Collection of Hymns (1780), 160-61
    Collection of Psalms and Hymns (1737),
        158; (1738), 168-69; (1741), 159-60
    death, 186-87, 203-5, 329-35, 341-42,
        345-46; fig. 8

diaries, 15, 29, 52-57, 59-62, 75, 113,
    154-55, 186-87, 229, 234, 239, 355,
    371-72, 384, 391-93
Earnest Appeal, 348
engagement, 168, 170, 172, 175
epitaph, 44, 187-88, 341-42
Farther Appeal, 303
Free Grace, 283
Free Thoughts on the Present State, 304-5,
    337
as *homo perturbatus*, 101, 264
as *homo uniuslibri*, 143
Hymns and Sacred Poems (1739), 162-
    63, 283
illness, 187
income, 206-7, 271, 273, 274-75, 340
Journal, 21, 25, 28-29, 35, 44, 64, 75-
    89, 90, 94, 99, 102, 112-14, 120, 125,
    129, 177, 179, 181, 186-87, 199,
    214, 252, 269, 284-88, 295-303, 347-
    48, 353, 356, 371, 374, 379, 382, 391
legends, 25, 27-28, 29, 41-42, 44, 298,
    368, 385
letters, 29, 42, 54-55, 57-59, 63-72, 94,
    106-9, 115-17, 125-29, 177-85, 219,
    241, 253, 256, 372-73, 392
Letter to a Roman Catholic, 192-98
letter "To the Traveling Preachers,"
    202-4
martyr image, 29, 121, 266-68
Moral and Sacred Poems (1744), 154,
    157
obituary, 21, 335-40
at Oxford, 28, 32, 35, 46, 47, 52-73,
    91, 95, 102, 129, 140, 149, 153, 187,
    188, 220, 222, 225-41, 242-43, 278-
    80, 329, 336, 367, 385, 391
as papist/Jesuit, 31, 86, 284, 288-93,
    295, 304, 310, 366
physical appearance, 23-24, 27, 124,
    255-56, 276-78, 280, 352
portraits, 23-24, 44, 362-63, 374-75;
    fig. 1-15
preaching/sermons, 25, 27-29, 34-35,
    54, 61, 63-64, 94, 102-15, 116, 120-
    21, 126, 140-44, 149, 173, 177, 187,
    189, 208, 247, 249-51, 259-60, 261-

(Wesley, John, passim continued)
65, 268, 276-81, 283-84, 295, 331, 332, 337-38, 348, 356, 372, 385, 391
Primitive Physick, 131-39, 316-25
as Reynard the Fox, 295, 297-303, 305-9, 310-13; fig. 11
school for children, 235-36
"Scriptural Christianity," 278
"Scripture Way of Salvation," 283
Short Address to the Inhabitants of Ireland, 192
as theologian, 31, 140-52, 282-93, 357-58, 380-81, 385
Thoughts upon Marriage, 167
will, 206-9
Word to a Condemned Malefactor, 149-52
Works, 16, 31, 33, 154, 356-57, 360, 363-64, 372, 387-92; Spanish ed., 392
Wesley, Kezia, 217
Wesley, Mary (Molly), 48, 217
Wesley, Mary Vazeille (Mrs. John), 176-85, 337
Wesley, Matthew, 224
Wesley, Nancy (Anne), 41, 50, 217
Wesley, Samuel, Jr., 50, 94, 99, 153, 159, 213, 217, 221, 261-63, 335, 352
Wesley, Samuel, Sr., 41-44, 45-48, 49-51, 52, 65-66, 71-72, 102, 153, 172, 219-22, 335, 359
Wesley, Sarah (daughter of Charles and Sarah), 334
Wesley, Sarah Gwynne (Mrs. Charles), 166, 190, 333
Wesley, Susanna (mother), 41-44, 48-51, 52, 58, 70-71, 94, 109, 153, 172-73, 213-19, 222, 224, 359, 385
Wesley, Susanna (daughter), 41, 48-49
Westminster, 245, 261
Wethington, Elbert, 392

Wethington, Lois, 392
White, George, 125, 269-72
Whitefield, George, 73, 102, 103, 105, 110, 112, 174-75, 187, 252, 255, 276, 294, 303, 310, 312, 337-39
Whitehead, John, 207, 330, 334, 338, 345-47, 351-55, 356, 358, 360, 365, 367
Whitfield, George, 207, 209, 334
William III, 49
Williams, Colin, 381, 389
Williams, John, 23
Williams, Peter, 141
Williams, Robert, 112-13, 115-17, 242, 251-55
Williamson, Sophia Christiana Hopkey (Mrs. William), 77-78, 115-18, 166, 247-48, 253-57
Williamson, William, 78, 81-82, 84-87, 115, 117, 247-48, 250, 253, 256
Willis, Thomas, 229
Winchester, C. T., 373-74
Winchester, Elhanan, 344, 346
Witchcraft, 296, 297-99, 303
Wolff, George, 207, 209, 332
Wood, A. Skevington, 381
Wood, Enoch, 375; fig. 12, 15
Wood, Laurence W., 389
Works, good, 72-73, 92-93, 194, 197, 235, 263, 264-65, 282-87, 288, 291-93, 297, 313
Worlidge, Thomas, fig. 10
Wright, John, 155

Young, Edward, 84, 165
Yrigoyen, Charles, 389

Zinzendorf, Ludwig von, 45, 265, 337
Zwingli, Ulrich, 377

Printed in the United States
57302LVS00003B/172